DOGS,
DOG FOOD,
AND DOGMA

THE SILENT EPIDEMIC KILLING AMERICA'S DOGS
AND THE NEW SCIENCE THAT COULD SAVE
YOUR BEST FRIEND'S LIFE

--

Daniel Schulof

PRESENT TENSE
P R E S S

www.dogsdogfoodanddogma.com

Present Tense Press
P.O. Box 521385
Salt Lake City, UT 84152-1385
presenttensepress@varsitypetsonline.com

Printed in the United States of America

For my parents,
who taught me that dogs are people too.

TABLE OF CONTENTS

AUTHOR'S NOTE

--

AT ITS ESSENCE, this book is a record of my attempt to answer a deceptively simple question: *how do I give my dog the best life that I can?*

Of course, I'm no saint and my search for answers has been no act of martyrdom. I just love my dog. My heart breaks a little when I have to leave him home alone while I go off chasing my human dreams. And it swells like a balloon when I watch him overflowing with wiggly, spastic enthusiasm or when he curls his body up next to mine while I write. Like the millions of other dog owners around the world who consider their dogs to be family members, I'm emotionally invested in making my dog's short time on this planet as enjoyable as possible. I can, quite literally, sleep better at night when I know I've been a good parent.

The project began as a collection of notes, a compendium of the research I'd conducted over the years, serving no other purpose than to guide me in my own personal project to understand my dog better and give him the best life that I reasonably could. But over time it evolved. And the result of that evolution is the book you are holding today.

The evolution occurred in two stages. The first was when the scope of the project narrowed from an all-around effort to improve *every* aspect of my dog's life to one focused on a single goal: ensuring that a specific health problem, one that is both deadly and shockingly widespread in dogs today, didn't ruin that life altogether. There is so much that we do not know about how our dogs experience the world (indeed, as many philosophers have argued, there is much that we *cannot* know). But one thing we can know without a shadow of a doubt is that avoiding this particular problem is likely to give our dogs much longer and better lives. So avoiding it seemed like a surefire way to do some real, meaningful good for my best friend.

This health problem, the one that has been my personal obsession for the better part of a decade, is obesity.

I knew a bit about the topic before embarking on this project. I'm a committed athlete, albeit a recreational one, and my particular athletic niche is ultra-distance endurance sports. I run 100-mile ultramarathons, I race Ironman-distance triathlons, and I climb mountains. These are all endeavors in which adiposity (a ten-dollar word for body-fatness) is highly relevant. Because an athlete's body fat has a direct impact on physical performance, I already had a working familiarity with the peer-reviewed literature concerning human adiposity before I ever thought about its implications for my dog.

But even with my background, I was stunned to discover just how horrible obesity has been proven to be for dogs. According to recent research, being just moderately overweight is worse for a dog than a lifetime of smoking is for a human being. Obesity raises the risk of some of the most common scourges of the canine world, including osteoarthritis, kidney disease, and, most importantly, cancer, the number-one killer of dogs in America today. So what began as a project to give my dog an all-around "good life," gradually became an effort to make his life *really* good in this one particular way.

The second stage of the project's evolution was its change from a personal reference to a public one. In spite of the well-documented links between obesity and disease, recent polling suggests that at least *half* of the dogs in America today are overweight. There are, in other words, more fat dogs in our country than not-fat ones. Cigarette-smoking is getting less common in the U.S., but the odds say that your dog—yes, *your* dog—is doing the equivalent of puffing away on a cigarette as you read these very words.

In this way, the canine obesity epidemic (and make no mistake about it, the problem is most definitely a full-fledged epidemic) is something of a paradox. It has arisen in an age when dog owners love our pets more than at any other point in history. And it is a problem that is both horrible for health and completely preventable. For these reasons, you'd think that no one would let their dog get fat. And yet.

I found it difficult to explain the paradox, but at least part of the problem seemed to be attributable to a lack of awareness. When you visit your neighborhood bookstore you're likely to encounter a dazzling array of doggy-lit offerings—training and behavioral treatises penned by television stars, science books revealing the inner-workings of the canine brain, exciting tales of the canine military operatives on the front lines of foreign wars. And the number of human health and weight-loss books you'll find is sure to be downright overwhelming. Everyone from Deepak Chopra to Roseanne Barr has packaged their dietary secrets into a book or two.

But books about fighting canine obesity are an altogether rarer bird. It seemed to me that a few hundred pages of clear, skeptical, evidence-based thought about the topic might go a long way toward curtailing the silent epidemic killing America's pets. The more I learned about the topic, the clearer I saw that the fruits of my personal project might be of value to other dog owners too.

I also began to see that there's more to the paradox than meets the eye. On the whole, our (mis-)understanding of the canine obesity problem has been shaped to a large degree by agents of irrationality. And not just innocent ones, either. As my project proceeded, I saw with increasing clarity how self-interested misinformation was being deliberately wielded by some of the world's most powerful entities, to the great detriment of America's pets. And the more I learned—the further I went down the research rabbit hole—the more interesting the story became. The whole thing began to feel less like a project and more like a quest.

The quest took me to some fascinating places: the wilds of Montana, where biologists study the domestic dog's closest genetic relative, the grey wolf; the colossal factories in which dog food is produced for mere pennies and the capitalist bacchanals in which those foods are marketed; the packed-house competitions in which the world's best canine athletes strut their stuff; and dozens of veterinary clinics and dog-loving homes around the country.

While this book documents my experiences, it remains, by and large, a science book. Which is not to say that its content is jargoned, high-tech, or conceptually challenging, just that the barometer of truth I've used throughout has been the best one that mankind has yet devised—the scientific method. Where I have presented concepts as true, there's good reason for my having done so: elegant, published, peer-reviewed experiments suggest as much. Frankly, that's the only standard good enough for my dog.

But there are two other reasons that science plays such a big role in this book, one about me and one about you. The one about me has to do with the fact that there aren't any letters after my last name. As you may have noticed, I am not a veterinarian. When I set out on my quest I was, alas, but a lowly attorney. And though editing law journals and researching obscure legal nuances in high-profile litigations may have helped hone my skills as a researcher, they didn't do much for my scientific *bona fides*. I'll be the first to admit that I do not by many standards qualify as an "expert" on canine obesity, nor, really, on any other subject. So rather than ask that you trust me based on my credentials, I've taken a different approach: I have, throughout the book, outlined the scientific papers and other evidence that have shaped *why* I think what I do about canine adiposity. That way, my analysis of those issues can speak for itself.

The other reason that science is so central to the book—the one about you—is that, if you *do* happen to disagree with any of my conclusions, you'll still be able to take something valuable from the reading experience. For your reference needs, a lengthy bibliography and several hundred detailed endnotes follow the main text. So even if you think that I lose the plot here or there, you ought to be able to trace back to where I lost my way and use what remains to shape how you care for your dog going forward.

We're going to be covering a lot of topics in the pages that follow. We'll look at what exactly adipose tissue does to bodies (both canine and human). We'll dive into the history of humankind's obsession with how much fat a body ought to contain. We'll dig into the research that has shaped the veterinary community's understanding of exactly how fat a dog's body should be and why. We'll also examine why so many dogs today are in fact "too fat," and what we can do to save them. There's stuff on diet (a lot of it) and stuff on exercise (somewhat less). We'll compare modern-day dogs to wolves in both cases, to see if evolutionary principles can explain why the majority of dogs in America today are overweight while precisely zero wolves are. And we'll come face-to-face with some uncomfortable truths about the outsized role that for-profit dog food manufacturers play in regulating their own products, shaping the veterinary research agenda, and disseminating information about the role their products may be playing in bringing about an epidemic of canine obesity.

As a whole, the book is my attempt to summarize all that I believe to be true and valuable about canine body condition. It began as an effort to help and protect my own dog. But it grew to become an effort to help millions of others. Dogs just like yours. I hope you enjoy it. I hope you learn something. And I hope you're able to put that something to use in helping your own fur babies live lives that are as long and happy as reasonably possible.

DGS   July 15, 2016

PS. Oh, and one more thing. This book isn't specifically about human adiposity, but you'll see that we spend a good deal of time looking at that subject too. If you emerge with a better understanding of why people get fat or the role that adiposity plays in your own health and wellbeing, then all the better. Happy reading.

Chapter One

DOGS, CHILDREN, AND LOSS

--

"He doesn't seem like a little dog,
He's just like folks to me."

Maxine Anna Buck, "Ted"
From *The Dog's Book of Verse* (1916)

———————

THE SILENT EPIDEMIC

EVEN TODAY, YEARS LATER, it's easy for me to remember the first time I thought my dog was going to die. His name was Kody. He was only two years old. And he was in rude health, or so I had always believed.

Kody was a Rottweiler, and one typical of the breed: shoulders wide with bulky musculature, an ever-wiggling docked tail, a square head roughly the size of a medicine ball. He brimmed with youthful enthusiasm, the type that blossomed into behaviors both charming—clownish, goofy flirtation with visitors—and less so—ritualized destruction of sunglasses, handheld electronics, and, curiously, rolls of toilet paper.

When we first met, in the rural town of Rome, Georgia, at what can only be described as a Rottweiler farm, he bore little resemblance to the impressive animal he would become. He was only seven weeks old, and I stood in a pen and held him aloft as his yapping littermates tugged at my shoelaces. I sized him up as he slouched in a lazy Buddha's pose and regarded me with wary skepticism. He weighed about as much as a cantaloupe.

A friend who had come with me suggested the dog's name on our way home from the Rottweiler farm. It came from the fact that he looked, as all dock-tailed Rottie pups do, like a bear cub. The Kodiak is the largest bear in the world, so Kody's name reflected my hope that he would grow up to be big and strong. And, at two years old, he was well on his way.

Kody had come along at an opportune moment in my life. As a lonely, overworked city dweller, I was in the market for a life companion. And the dog quickly became my best friend. In its duller moments, the living arrangement we crafted for ourselves in a ground-level inner-city loft resembled one enjoyed by a couple of bachelor roommates: down time on the couch, "Hey, don't forget to grab some stuff for the fridge while you're out."

But it was often something more than that too. His overexcited whirling and wiggling every time I returned home from work. My swelling of pride when he retrieved tennis balls from impossibly faraway locations and dropped them, without fail, at my feet. The way you could always coax his stump into wagging if you used your baby voice. Falling asleep together on the couch, his head in my lap.

There is a theory in psychological circles which says that the loving emotions dog owners feel for their canine companions is a repurposing of the emotions that humans originally evolved in order to bind us to our biological children. It's a reasonable enough idea and it dovetails well with the fact that 85% of Americans today say that we consider our dogs—our "fur babies"— to be members of our families. For more than eight out of ten of us, having a dog isn't just *like* having a child, it *is* having a child.

Which is to say that the whole "your dog is going to die" thing had gotten my attention.

The man who delivered the bad news was a veterinarian named Dr. Ernie Ward. A photograph on his website portrayed Dr. Ward as a youthful-looking guy with floppy, blond-streaked hair and a goatee. According to his bio, he had published dozens of academic papers as well as a book, and had even achieved minor celebrity status as the "resident veterinarian for the *Rachael Ray Show*." He was a fitness buff too. Like me, he competed in ultra-distance triathlons, and his bio highlighted his respectable personal-best time in an Ironman.

I had come to his website looking for advice on how to exercise Kody more effectively. Specifically, how to pack more behavior-managing exhaustion into our pre-work trips to the park, adventures that were necessarily-short and, well, necessary. As Rottweiler people are fond of saying, theirs is a "breed for experts." At two years old, Kody stood two-and-a-half feet at the shoulder and weighed about 100 pounds. I had long been told that many of his human acquaintances—especially those who hadn't spent much time around large dogs—regarded him as intimidating. And who could blame them? He wasn't huge, but he certainly was a presence. And he was strong-willed, bristling (sometimes literally) with energy and "drive," and tagged with his breed's less-than-sterling reputation, to boot. In order to keep him on his best behavior, a daily bout of energy-sapping exercise was critical.

I came to Dr. Ward's website looking for help channeling Kody's energy into socially-acceptable forms, but I took away something else altogether. The website was mostly devoted to raising awareness about a health problem that, according to Dr. Ward, was quietly plaguing more than *half* of the more than 70 million dogs in America today. According to him, there were good reasons to believe that 40 million or so dogs had already fallen into the clutches of the silent epidemic and that a sizable group of them were going to develop chronic diseases, most notably cancer, as a result.

More to the point, there was good evidence that most of those dogs were going to die young.

Dr. Ward was the founder and chairman of an organization called the Association for Pet Obesity Prevention (APOP). And the deadly health epidemic against which he was crusading was canine obesity. APOP's website highlighted some startling facts about the problem, all coming from the most recent results of an annual survey the organization had conducted in partnership with veterinary hospitals around the country. 52.7% of dogs in America today (43.8 million animals) are overweight. More than 17% (13.9 million) are clinically obese. Even worse, almost all of their owners—more than 95% of them—have no idea whatsoever that there's anything wrong with their pets. It's not that they don't understand the health consequences of obesity, it's that they don't even think their dogs *are* fat. They're blind to the problem.

And, for loving dog owners, the consequences of the problem could hardly be more significant. As APOP's website flatly put it, "Obesity shortens lives."

My first reaction was to treat all of this as a "them" problem, not a "me" problem. Of course there are millions of fat dogs in America. There are, after all, millions of fat dog owners. But I'm not one of them. I'm an athlete. A marathoner. An *ultra*-marathoner, no less. I run *a lot*. I read diet books and scientific journals. I'm someone who "gets it." And I had applied all that to my relationship with Kody—hadn't I? I gave him regular exercise. I fed him "premium" kibble. I kept the table scraps to a minimum. He seemed to look about the same as most of the other dogs in the neighborhood. If anything, he probably looked fitter. He was muscular. An athlete, like his dad. The thought that he could be overweight had never even crossed my mind.

Still, I couldn't quite let it go. It frightened me to think that millions of dog owners were innocently, but mistakenly, assuming that their fat dogs were perfectly healthy, when in reality they were already seriously ill. I didn't want to be one of those people. I thought that my dog—my fur baby—deserved more. So I decided to take a closer look at him, just to make sure.

I called him over and went to work using one of Dr. Ward's diagnostic tools, a step-by-step process designed to produce a measure of doggy fatness called a Body Condition Score, or "BCS." According to Dr. Ward, measuring Kody's BCS was the standard way that veterinarians would judge whether or not he was, by scientific standards, too fat. It was a simple process that took only a few minutes. I pinched where Dr. Ward told me to pinch, felt for the bones he instructed me to feel for, and looked at indicators like the steepness of Kody's "abdominal tuck." The dog, for his part, looked suitably bewildered throughout the episode.

When the examination was through I took my handful of findings and matched them to the body condition conclusions listed on one of Dr. Ward's charts. When it was all said and done, just as I had expected, according to the great and powerful Dr. Ernie Ward, Kody was . . . "Overweight."

Overweight?

I regained a modicum of composure and then immediately did what any parent is tempted to do when confronted with bad news about his child: I rejected it. I must have done something wrong. I probably screwed up the examination. So I did the analysis again, this time consciously avoiding the urge to skew borderline BCS issues—is the amount of fat covering the dog's ribs "slightly excessive" or not?—against a finding of "Overweight." But I got the same result as before. I did it a third time. Same result. It was becoming hard to deny that, according to folks who supposedly knew what they were talking about, I had allowed Kody to become one of America's 40 million fat dogs. He thrust his big head into my lap and wagged his stump, blissfully unaware of the morbid revelation.

I stayed up late that night doing my own research about the canine obesity epidemic. I wanted to find a flaw in the logic, some kind of defense that would absolve me, the negligent dog owner. But the deeper down the rabbit hole I went, the more it looked like Dr. Ward was right on the money. Every peer-reviewed study I could find put the rate of canine obesity in America at 30% or higher. Academic researchers and veterinary nutritionists were writing that the canine obesity epidemic was "a major concern" and "the most common nutritional problem with links to morbidity in dogs" and "the number one chronic health concern in our canine companions." But most troubling of all was a recently published study which showed that even moderately overweight dogs tend to die some 16% earlier than their leaner peers, a percentage somewhat greater than the average life expectancy difference between lifelong human smokers and lifelong non-smokers. And the dogs in the study weren't clinically obese; they were just moderately overweight. Like Kody was. But their lives were being cut short as if they were *lifelong smokers*.

I had allowed my fur baby to become a smoker.

It was all starting to look like a colossal problem, no matter how you sliced it. As an economic issue, the costs of the silent epidemic must have been massive, with millions of dollars in completely avoidable medical expenses being incurred by dog owners every year. From an animal welfare perspective, it was hard to think of many more serious issues impacting pets in America today—tens of millions of dogs were, after all, doing the equivalent of smoking cigarettes.

But perhaps the most resonant angle of all from which to view the epidemic was the purely human one. Because behind every one of the silent epidemic's canine casualties there was at least one other victim: a human being whose time with her beloved companion was cut unnecessarily short, someone whose fur baby was gone for good.

What was worse was that, in many cases, it seemed like dog owners were losing their pets to obesity with absolutely no awareness of it whatsoever. Their dogs were dying young and they were chalking it all up to bad genetics or the unavoidable consequences of aging, when really it was the silent epidemic at work. So they were making the same mistakes over and over again, dog after dog, generation after generation. And it was that notion that struck an especially resounding chord with me, because it called to mind someone very specific.

THREE GENERATIONS OF LOSS

MY MOTHER does not suffer fools.

"Why do I love my dogs so much? Oh, I don't know." She sighs, as if I've asked her to explain why rainbows are nice to look at. She is an intelligent and articulate woman, and she speaks openly and enthusiastically about her life with dogs. As someone who has shared her home with canine companions for nearly 60 years, she has more than a few tales to tell.

"I guess it's a maternal instinct-type thing," she finally says. "They're my babies too, you know."

Her name is Patricia. She lives in Denver, where she is a social worker in a large university hospital. A widow whose grown children have moved away, she is ferociously independent, mild-mannered and non-confrontational, but possessing a quiet resolve and pride in her self-sufficiency and discipline. She wakes before dawn to exercise at the university fitness center or, after snowstorms, to shovel the driveway. Her home is neat and well-organized. My father died more than two decades ago and my mother has not remarried. She has, from time to time, rented out a room in her home. But, for the most part, she has lived alone for the past 20 years.

Alone, that is, except for her dogs. Her friends, only half-jokingly, describe her as their "crazy dog lady," and a quick look around her home gives you a pretty good idea what they mean. A collection of ceramic Golden Retrievers stand proudly on the fireplace mantel. Dog-shaped magnets pin dog-themed cartoon clippings and photos of "grand puppies" to the refrigerator door. Leashes and collars of varying lengths and styles occupy a coatrack, and a large, foldable kennel blocks the hallway between the kitchen and the dining room. The pockets of a down jacket overflow with poop bags and the crumbs of food rewards that my mother has used to help control her dogs when they're out for walks together on the icy winter sidewalks.

At the moment, she has just two of them, a mother-and-son pair of Black

Labs named Emma and Pete. But she has shared her home with more than a dozen different adult dogs over the years. She's sampled all sorts of breeds, from Beagles to Irish Setters. She claims that each animal has possessed a unique and uniquely charming personality and insists that she doesn't prefer any one breed over the others. But even she acknowledges that she holds a special place in her heart for one breed in particular, the Golden Retriever.

"Goldens were my first love," she admits. "I've really had some truly wonderful Goldens over the years."

According to the American Kennel Club, the Golden Retriever is the third-most popular breed in the United States. They are renowned for being gentle and affectionate, particularly with children. "Ours certainly lived up to their 'family dog' reputation," my mother says today. She brought the first one home only three months before giving birth to me and raised the two of us up alongside one another. Throughout my childhood, the sweet, shaggy dogs served both as playmates and nannies to my sister and me. In fact, my mother was so fond of the breed that she formed a licensed breeding kennel and raised a new litter of pups every year. Betsy, the rambunctious, copper-colored matriarch of Heavenly Days Kennels, birthed her first litter when I was only a grade-schooler. And with each brood that she produced, my mother faced emotional pressure from my sister and me to keep one of the pups for our family.

"If you've ever seen a troop of little Golden Retriever puppies running around a yard, and I know you have, then you how hard they are to resist," she tells me. "The pups really are adorable. And you kids could be pretty relentless."

She gave in twice. First was one of Betsy's daughters, a charming female we named Virginia. And then, just a few years later, a member of the third generation, a sweet and docile female, lighter in color than either her mother or grandmother. We named the new pup Sierra.

"Sierra was the epitome of the devoted family dog," my mother remembers. "Totally focused on her people, obsessed with love and affection, hanging on your every word."

By the time she was born I was a young teenager, and I remember her more clearly than any of our family's other Goldens. I remember her sweet temperament. I remember her willingness, even eagerness, to conform her behavior to our human expectations. And I remember the close relationship that she shared with my mother, the support she provided in the years after my father's death.

"You couldn't ask for a better companion," my mother sighs. "Honestly, more than any of the others, Sierra was my buddy. We were so close."

But with Sierra, the pattern of adding a new Golden Retriever to our household every few years came to an end. All told, in just a few years, our busy family had grown to include three generations of the sweet and loving dogs. They must have made for quite a spectacle—dragging my little mother along the icy Denver sidewalks or hanging their heads out the rear window of her Toyota as she shuttled her human kids from after-school activities to social engagements. At the end of each day, the shaggy trio would crowd into the bed that they shared with my mother and serenade her with a chorus of snores.

Today, recalling these memories is something of a bittersweet experience for my mother. They come from a vibrant, exciting time in her life. But over the years they have also come to be tinged with sadness.

***

If the bonds that tie us to our pets really are grounded in the emotions that bind us to our children, then there is a tragic element inherent to dog ownership, the magnitude of which is perhaps underappreciated. The loss of a child is rightly regarded as one of the most painful experiences that can be endured by a human being, the kind of tragedy that leaves the bereaved altered, both constitutionally and irrevocably. A 2008 study published in the *Journal of Family Psychology* showed that bereaved parents experienced greater incidences of depression, marital strife, and health problems, even as long as 18 years after the death of a child. Mortality rates among bereaved mothers in the 15 years after a child's death may be as much as four times as high as in the non-bereaved.

Fortunately, relatively few children die before their parents, at least in the developed world. Most of us wait at least 20 years before we decide to bring children into our lives. Indeed, in many countries, the average age of first-time mothers is over 30. This head start means that, as long as both parent and child live reasonably close to their average life expectancies, the odds are stacked against the tragedy.

But with our canine children the odds are flipped. A human being in the developed world is expected to live some 70 years or so longer than a dog. This vast difference in lifespan means that almost every dog will die before its master. If we love our dogs as we love our children, then almost every dog owner will one day experience the emotional trauma that is losing a child.

Sierra, the last of the Heavenly Days Goldens, died on a warm spring day in 2002. She was only seven years old. "Sierra's death was hard." My mother sighs, again, now taking a photograph of the three dogs into her hands. "It was really hard. Your dad had died some years before and you kids had gone away to college. So it was just me and the dogs. And," she pauses, "you know, Sierra was my baby. She was just such a good dog. So devoted. It was just really hard."

According to her veterinarian, Sierra died from complications stemming from a cancerous tumor that had formed in her breast and then metastasized throughout her body. Only a few years earlier, her mother, Virginia, had died of cancer too. Like her daughter, she was only seven years old. And, only a few years before that, Betsy, the matriarch of the Heavenly Days Goldens, had died of cancer at the age of eight. According to recent research, the expected lifespan of a Golden Retriever in America today is at least 11 years. Which means that none of the Heavenly Days Goldens survived even three-quarters of their expected lifespans. They all died young.

"Unfortunately, that's just how it goes with Goldens," says my mother today. "They get cancer."

She's right, Golden Retrievers do tend to get cancer. In fact, about half of all Goldens in North America will die from one form of the disease or another. And it's not just Goldens—across all breeds, cancer is the single most common cause of canine death in America. One in three dogs will encounter the disease in its lifetime. Of those, half of them will die from it.

It's tempting to interpret these daunting figures as evidence that some dogs are simply hard-wired to develop cancer at some point in their lives. Recent research has indisputably shown that one's genetic makeup can increase (sometimes dramatically) the likelihood of developing one or more cancers. And it's not hard to imagine that, after hundreds of years of selective breeding and purposeful genetic tinkering, we've inadvertently bred a propensity for cancer into many of our favorite modern-day breeds.

But that's not necessarily the whole story. After all, genes are just one of many factors that have been shown to influence cancer risk. And, at least according to Dr. Ward and APOP, one of the other relevant factors—indeed, the one *most* responsible for America's massive canine cancer epidemic—is obesity. Studies have shown that dogs with a lot of fat in their bodies are more likely to develop a host of specific cancers, including breast cancer, the single most common variant in dogs and the one responsible for killing Sierra. In fact, the statistical overlap between cancer and obesity is so significant as to make some kind of causal relationship between the two phenomena all but self-evident; both are so common among dogs in America today that, when you stop to think about it for a moment, it seems almost impossible that one couldn't be related to the other.

But cancer is an official pathophysiological "cause of death," and obesity is not. Dogs don't die "of" obesity, they die of cancer. So cancer tends to get most of our attention. The National Canine Cancer Foundation, one of several 501(c)(3) non-profit corporations devoted to funding canine cancer research and treatment, has more than a dozen local chapters and has raised millions of dollars in its efforts to find a cure for the disease. There are, by way of comparison, precisely zero organizations specifically devoted to raising money to research and treat canine obesity. Unlike cancer, obesity often goes unnoticed, both during a dog's lifetime and, too often, thereafter.

As she tells me her story, my mother shows me a photograph of the three generations of Heavenly Days Goldens in all their glory. The dogs are posing alongside preteen versions of my sister and me on a hiking trail high in the Colorado mountains. It is a happy and colorful scene, with a bold blue sky and tall evergreen trees towering above the three handsome dogs. My sister and I are smiling broadly, and the dogs, tongues lolling out the sides of their mouths, appear to be doing the same. But I suspect that, were you to ask Dr. Ernie Ward, he'd tell you that the dogs' bodies all bear the clear signature of obesity: no abdominal tuck, no narrowing at the waist, lack of definition in the ribs and hipbones, fat deposits at the base of the tail and across the chest. Though not morbidly obese, the dogs would clearly be characterized by Dr. Ward and his BCS charts as overweight.

Not that my mother ever thought that way during their lifetimes. "I've seen plenty of really fat dogs," she says today. "Where you just look at them and you're like 'oh my God, how could you let your dog get to be *that big*?' My dogs were never like that. Were they a little on the heavy side? Maybe. But I don't think most people would have thought of them as overweight."

I tend to agree. *Most people* would not have thought of the Heavenly Days Goldens as overweight. After all, they weren't morbidly obese. Their bellies weren't dragging in the dirt. As my mother's photograph shows, they were physically active, energetic, and happy. They went out for hikes with their adoring family. *Most people* would have assumed that the dogs were perfectly healthy—right up until they got cancer.

It wasn't until almost a decade after Sierra's death that my mother could even begin to entertain the idea that obesity played a role in the deaths of her beloved dogs. But she's in the minority. For most pet parents, it's just too difficult for us to imagine that we've done anything to harm our fur babies, particularly once they're gone forever. And while I commend my mother for her willingness to own up to her mistakes, the truth is that I don't think she's done anything particularly blame-worthy. She is a smart, serious, disciplined, loving woman, and one who was heavily invested in keeping her dogs as happy and healthy as possible. And yet obesity still found a way to sneak under the door and cut her beloved companions down in their prime. Maybe I'm biased, but when telling the story of canine obesity in America, it seems to me that folks like my mother aren't the ones to blame. They're not villains, they're just the collateral victims of a silent epidemic.

DOUBTING THE DOGMA

IF YOU WANT TO understand why our dogs are so fat and what we can do about it, the bookstore is a reasonable place to start. Even in the Internet Age, recent research shows that books remain one of the most important sources of health and nutrition information for laypeople. And in a world where at least 1.9 billion people are overweight or obese, it's no surprise that diet books for humans make up one of the publishing industry's most popular sectors.

Unfortunately, despite the stunning scale of the canine obesity epidemic, weight-loss books for humans are far more popular than their doggy-lit equivalents. In fact, as I write these words, there seems to be only a single title in print that focuses exclusively on the topic of canine obesity. Published in 2010 and written by APOP's Dr. Ernie Ward, it was given the wonderful title *Chow Hounds: Why Our Dogs Are Getting Fatter – A Vet's Plan to Save Their Lives*. Unfortunately, the book was published by a tiny specialty press and has only ever managed to sell a few copies. I have not once seen it on a bookstore shelf.

For an in-print examination of the canine obesity epidemic, most concerned pet owners will have to settle for the next-best thing: an all-purpose "health and nutrition" book for dogs. Such titles are common enough, and they usually devote at least some space to the topic of obesity. But despite the fact that most veterinarians consider obesity to be the most pressing health problem facing pets in America today, the discussion is likely to be both woefully short and buried beneath a mountain of other health matters. In *Dog Health and Nutrition for Dummies*, for example, only four of the book's more than 300 pages concern obesity. And in that short space, both the pathophysiology of the disease (how it works within a dog's body) as well as its sociological causes (why the disease has become so common) are covered. Longer and more rigorous books also give the topic short shrift; in the fourth edition of the *Dog Owner's Home Veterinary Handbook*, only a handful of the book's more than 600 pages relate in any way to either the pathophysiology or sociological causes of obesity.

Moreover, regardless of the doggy health book you choose, the specific views presented on those two related subjects are likely to be more or less the same. In fact, they receive such consistently similar treatment in the popular press as to suggest that there is well-established, even dogmatic, agreement about them among the experts. Here, *Dog Health and Nutrition for Dummies* again serves as a good example. According to Dr. M. Christine Zink, the book's eminently qualified veterinarian author, the pathophysiology of obesity is simple: in dogs, as in humans, the disease is merely the inevitable consequence of consuming more calories than one expends. As Dr. Zink puts it, "[t]o peel the pounds off your pooch, you need to decrease her caloric intake and increase her exercise." Simple enough.

This "calories-in, calories-out" explanation of obesity has become so central to the mainstream thinking about weight management as to have mostly become an article of faith, as have the handful of implications to which it necessarily gives rise: dietary fats, for instance, are "bad" because they contain more calories than carbohydrates or proteins (about nine calories of digestible energy per gram, with carbohydrates and proteins each containing only about four calories per gram). So, the mainstream thinking goes, if you want to help your dog lose weight, you should minimize the role that fat plays in the animal's diet.

This party line is echoed in the textbooks used to train our veterinarians. In *Canine and Feline Nutrition: A Resource for Companion Animal Professionals*, for example, one will be told that "[t]he fundamental underlying cause of obesity is an imbalance between energy intake and energy expenditure that results in a persistent energy surplus." And, in *Applied Veterinary Clinical Nutrition*, that "[a]nimals become overweight as a consequence of maintaining a state of positive energy balance; that is to say, they consume calories in excess of their caloric expenditure."

As for the social causes of the epidemic, the limited amount of in-print information again seems to suggest full agreement among the experts. The standard dogma would have us believe that canine obesity is caused by negligent dog owners. Unscrupulous pet food manufacturers warrant some blame, of course, for less-than-forthcoming nutritional labeling and wishy-washy marketing claims. But it's mostly about us. We dog owners are either unwilling to give our companions the exercise they need, unable to understand how much food they really require, or incapable of stopping ourselves from rewarding their begging with fattening food rewards.

These various explanations often crystalize around a single catchphrase: dog owners are simply "loving our pets to death." Perform a quick Google search and you will find countless instances in which the saying has been used by veterinarians, journalists, and bloggers to explain the canine obesity problem. It aptly summarizes the role that most experts assign to dog owners in bringing about the epidemic: we all want the best for our dogs, but many of us are either negligent or woefully misguided in how we are pursuing it.

In-print information about canine obesity may be hard to come by, but these two concepts—"calories-in, calories-out" and "loving them to death"—are the fundamental pillars of what mainstream discourse there is about the matter. But if you're out to protect your own dog against the dangers of obesity (or simply interested in understanding the causes of this truly bizarre epidemic), then there are a few reasons you may not want to accept these explanations at face value.

For one, it seems more than a little harsh to blame dog owners for loving our dogs to death when canine obesity hasn't received enough attention in the popular press to warrant placing even a single book about the topic on the shelves of most bookstores. And the notion that more than half of the dog owners in the country are either too stupid, too lazy, or too weak-willed to provide proper care for our fur babies strikes me as both fanciful and, frankly, insulting.

More importantly, there are good reasons to doubt the factual validity of just about everything written about nutrition in the popular press. Research has continually shown that there is little or no evidentiary basis for many of the core tenets of popular diet books. For instance, according to a 2006 paper published in the *Journal of General Internal Medicine*, "over 67% of nutrition facts in a best-seller diet book [*The South Beach Diet* by Dr. Arthur Agatson (2003)] may not be supported in the peer-reviewed literature." And, according to a 2003 study published in the *Journal of the American College of Nutrition*, "a review of the literature suggests that there are scientific contradictions in the Zone Diet [the subject of another bestselling diet book] hypothesis that cast unquestionable doubt on its potential efficacy." If books about managing canine obesity are anything like their human equivalents, it's far from certain that they are grounded in valid scientific evidence.

Even more worryingly, recent studies have exposed a similar lack of scientific rigor in the very peer-reviewed studies that are so often used to back up the advice proffered in popular diet books. In a particularly infamous recent paper, math-prodigy-turned-Stanford-medical-researcher Dr. John Ioannidis showed that, of the 49 most widely-cited studies published in the world's three most prestigious medical journals (*The New England Journal of Medicine*, *Lancet*, and *The Journal of the American Medical Association*) between 1990 and 2003, more than 40% of their findings were shown upon subsequent investigation either to be significantly exaggerated or flat-out wrong.

And, over the past few decades, the ubiquitous calories-in, calories-out model of obesity has been on the receiving end of a particularly significant amount of sophisticated criticism. The last 15 years have yielded a litany of books and peer-reviewed studies raising systematic doubts about the validity of calories-in, calories-out as the core explanation for why anyone gets fat. Research teams from institutions like Harvard, Stanford, and Duke have all published papers showing that diets featuring the same *number* of calories can lead to wildly different fat-loss outcomes, depending on the *type* of calories consumed. In an immensely popular YouTube video, endocrinologist Robert Lustig recently explained why, calorie-for-calorie, sugar plays an outsized role in making people fat. And writers like Gary Taubes (*Good Calories, Bad Calories*, 2007), Jonathan Bailor (*The Calorie Myth*, 2013), and David Ludwig (*Always Hungry?*, 2016) have written popular books that level persuasive, evidence-based attacks on the calories-in, calories out paradigm. From a scientific standpoint, calories-in, calories-out seems to be on the proverbial ropes.

At least when it comes to human nutrition. In the realm of canine obesity, it's still considered dogma.

***

Of course, none of this should suggest that what has been written about canine obesity over the years is definitively wrong. But if it's enough to give you pause for concern, then there is at least one other reason you may want to approach the mainstream canine obesity dogma with a measure of healthy skepticism: there is a very real possibility that institutional bias has come to taint the scientific waters.

This problem is hardly unique to the science of canine obesity. Whether they like to admit it or not, clinicians, research scientists, and (alas) even writers are merely human beings. Though we are all duty-bound to strive for objectivity, we remain as susceptible to cognitive limitations, undue influences, and persuasive pressures as the rest of the world. And this remains the case whether we realize it or not.

Sometimes our biases arise innocently. The pressure to publish new and provocative findings (the so-called "publication bias") has been repeatedly shown to impact the type of experiments performed by scientific researchers. The tendency to unwittingly choose study participants from one's unrepresentative local population ("selection bias") and to simply misremember data points ("recall bias") have been documented too.

These are all harmful enough to the systematic pursuit of truth. But other forms of bias are not just disruptive, but intentionally so. Most notably, financial conflicts of interest are considered so prejudicial to research findings that most academic journals and research institutions require their researchers to disclose to readers any financial relationships that they share with for-profit interests. Nevertheless, numerous cases have recently been reported in which the results of major industry-sponsored drug trials have been withheld from publication due to their commercially unhelpful findings, as well as other cases in which undisclosed financial relationships between researchers and pharmaceutical companies have otherwise influenced the research agenda. Debate over the role of corporate interests in the world of research science has recently found its way onto the vaunted pages of *The New England Journal of Medicine* as well as into the halls of Congress.

And when it comes to the research science surrounding canine obesity, you don't have to look too hard to find evidence of major financial conflicts of interest. The U.S. market for pet food exceeds $20 billion a year, and the industry's leading firms are true corporate behemoths. Many of them have, over just the past few years, used their massive financial clout to publicly sponsor the most influential veterinary medical organizations on the planet, including the American Veterinary Medical Association (AVMA), the American Animal Hospital Association (AAHA), and the World Small Animal Veterinary Association (WSAVA). Moreover, when it comes to veterinary nutrition, many of the field's leading researchers also happen to be full-time employees of one pet food company or another. In fact, a great deal of published veterinary nutritional research is conducted at private research institutions *owned and operated* by companies like Purina PetCare and Mars, Inc.

As such, the world's leading dog food manufacturers have the power to shape the veterinary nutritional research agenda itself.

Of course, none of this is proof of malfeasance. But if blindly trusting nutritional advice sponsored, funded, or produced by one of the largest human food producers in the country (say, McDonald's) strikes you as more than a little naïve, then it might just be another reason to approach the existing canine obesity dogma with a little healthy skepticism.

OVERVIEW OF THE INVESTIGATION

AT LEAST that's how it seemed to me.

I felt compelled to write a book about canine obesity in America for three different reasons. First, if my own dog was at risk of dying young, I wanted to know how to save his life. Second, helping other dog owners avoid the grief and regret that my mother had experienced seemed like a worthy project. But, perhaps more than anything else, I was also motivated by curiosity. I wanted to understand the reality behind what seemed like a paradox: how could dog owners in America today be closer than ever to our dogs and yet still be allowing them to die from a totally preventable health problem? Were we all really just "loving them to death"?

It was hard for me to wrap my head around that notion. It seemed that there was likely to be more to the story, particularly in light of all the reasons to regard the canine nutritional dogma with a healthy dose of skepticism. And, as I'd come to find out, there is more to the story. Much more.

As I explain in the pages that follow, corporate influence and institutional bias in veterinary nutritional research are far more pervasive than I first suspected. Much of the science upon which our understanding of canine obesity is based also seems to be flawed. And, perhaps most importantly of all, the problem of canine obesity itself—its prevalence, the nature of its deleterious effects—is quite possibly worse than even folks like Dr. Ernie Ward have ever dared to imagine.

The evidence I report in support of these claims has largely been gathered using interviews, first-hand observations, and other traditional investigative techniques. But a critical review of the scientific record has also been central to the work. Only by skeptically reviewing the studies that form the accepted evidentiary basis for the canine obesity dogma (as well as those that challenge it) can we truly gauge the validity of that information. And only by understanding the thinking of the researchers behind those studies can we ensure that our own knowledge is built upon the sound, logical application of the scientific method and the peer-review process that attends its professional practice. When it comes to a tough-to-understand phenomenon like an epidemic of obesity, only a firm commitment to scientific principles can lead us to the truth.

You might even say that a science-first strategy is particularly appropriate in a book about dogs. Since it requires a bit of skepticism and rationality to get its gears churning, the scientific method is never going to be the kind of thing that a dog can wring much value out of on his own. Alas, you can dress a Rottweiler up in glasses and a white lab coat, but you just can't teach him abstract concepts. If anyone's going to ensure that our thinking about canine obesity is shaped by valid scientific principles, it's not going to be our dogs; it's going to have to be us.

Over the pages that follow, we'll consider the scientific evidence relating to all manner of canine obesity questions: Why do dogs get fat? What should they eat, and how much? What role does exercise play in fighting obesity? How fat is really *too* fat?

And what we'll find is that all too often the canine obesity dogma doesn't really reflect the empirically verified reality. There really is more to why our dogs get fat than we have been led to believe.

With all that in mind, if we're out to understand why America's dogs are dying from obesity, there's really only one place to begin, with what the philosopher Daniel Dennett has called "the single best idea anyone ever had." It's one that a scientist (perhaps the most famous one in history) came up with about 150 years ago. And when trying to understand complex biological phenomena like chronic disease epidemics it is, conceptually-speaking, pretty much the only place to begin. For while an epidemic of canine obesity may seem like a uniquely modern problem, to truly understand its many diverse causes we have little choice but to start by getting our hands around its ancient roots.

Chapter Two

THE HOUR BETWEEN DOG AND WOLF

--

"I decided to try to find my father in the woods."

Paul Harding, *Tinkers* (2009)

THE VIRTUES OF CAVEMAN LIVING

OBESITY IS a disease. At least according to the American Medical Association, the influential professional organization, which, in 2013, published an updated policy paper officially saying so. Given the astounding degree to which being fat compromises all manner of vital bodily functions—circulation, respiration, movement—it seems an appropriate use of the word. Still, the condition is so wildly pervasive in the modern world that it's rare to hear it described that way, even in medical circles.

Except, that is, when it is being called a "disease of modernity." That term—often also used to describe depression, diabetes, cancers, atherosclerosis, and many other common chronic health problems—emphasizes less the condition's definitional status and more the well-documented reality that it is essentially unique to the modern age. Whether or not obesity fits anyone's personal definition of the word "disease," it is beyond legitimate dispute that neither people nor dogs were particularly fat until rather recently, historically speaking.

More to the point, the term "disease of modernity" implies that something about our modern environment is actually *making* dogs and people become fat—that one or more of the unprecedentedly rapid changes human beings have recently wrought to our global environment are to blame for one of the most pressing public health problems of our day.

The disease of modernity concept was being used to sling half-baked, "kids these days" societal gripes long before anyone much appreciated the workings of evolution via natural selection. And usually to limited effect. But when the concept is combined with a bit of Darwinian logic, it becomes a uniquely powerful tool for diagnosing the true causes of complex biological phenomena. To see why this is so, begin by considering just how rare and unnatural it is for organisms (human or otherwise) to experience long-term epidemics of chronic, non-communicable diseases. One needn't be a population geneticist to appreciate the basic evolutionary thinking at work here: genes that produce maladaptive traits—such as those giving rise to chronic diseases—reduce the evolutionary fitness of their hosts, thus discouraging those genes from spreading throughout the broader population. Epidemics of deadly, non-communicable diseases don't really make evolutionary sense. They shouldn't happen.

But there's an exception to the rule. If an organism's environment changes rapidly, traits that were highly adaptive under earlier environmental conditions can quickly become maladaptive under new ones. And, unlike meaningful changes to the genome, which usually occur over such a long time period that it can be hard to wrap our brains around it, modern humans have the unique ability to quickly affect positively massive changes to our environment. When we do so, diseases of modernity have the nasty habit of outrunning the slow pace of genetic evolution and spreading widely throughout populations.

For an example of this phenomenon in action, consider the sad case of beachfront lighting and its impact on the behavior of hatchling sea turtles. Over millions of years, most sea turtle species have evolved a tendency to flee their sand nests and move instinctively toward the shimmering, moonlit surface of the sea immediately upon hatching from their eggs. It's not hard to see why the behavior was once so adaptive: by causing defenseless hatchlings to emerge from their eggs under the cover of night and scurry quickly to the protection of the ocean, it helped them avoid the life-threatening dangers posed by beachcombing predators.

Then one day a human being invented the light bulb. Not even a century later, fields of artificial light many times brighter than the moon were illuminating much of the inland coastal darkness. And suddenly an innate attraction to the brightest nearby light field became a decidedly maladaptive trait for a fragile and defenseless hatchling sea turtle. Still, until their ancient genes come around to this modern environmental reality, hundreds of thousands of Loggerhead hatchlings will continue to die—crushed on roadways, scooped up by predatory birds, exhausted and dehydrated in the sand dunes—from this strange disease of modernity every year.

***

Rigorous attempts to use evolutionary principles to explain the underlying causes of obesity date to the first half of the twentieth century. But by most accounts the endeavor's first watershed moment didn't occur until 1985, when two unlikely individuals published a short paper that spelled out the analytical framework that has governed the subject's study ever since. Its authors were a couple of men from Emory University (my own proud *alma mater*). One, Melvin Konner, was an anthropology professor; the other, S. Boyd Eaton, a practicing radiologist. They gave their paper a pithy, unprepossessing title: "Paleolithic Nutrition: A Consideration of Its Nature and Current Implications."

When trying to identify the underlying causes of the human obesity epidemic, there are at least two reasons why the Paleolithic era is a uniquely important time period. One is the fact that it covers a particularly large chunk of our history as a species, from approximately 2.4 million years ago (when the *Homo* genus first appeared) to only the last 10,000 or 20,000 years. This means that, when compared to the rest of human history, the great majority of our genetic evolution is likely to have occurred during the Paleolithic.

It's easy to forget that, from an evolutionary perspective, most of the ways that modern-day human beings live are the products of very recent cultural innovations. But consider that the Paleolithic was some 300 times longer than the sum of all periods of human pre-history and history that have occurred since. If you were to add up all the years that have transpired since the Paleolithic ended (and these years will include the entire Mesolithic ("Middle Stone Age") and Neolithic ("New Stone Age") periods, along with everything that has happened since we left our Stone Age roots behind, including the entire Bronze Age, the entire Iron Age, the Middle Ages, the European Renaissance, the Enlightenment, the Victorian era, and the measly couple hundred years that have passed since the Industrial Revolution), they would, *in the aggregate*, amount to less than 1% of the time that passed during the Paleolithic era.

The second reason that the Paleolithic is particularly important for studying the evolutionary roots of human obesity is there are clear, identifiable differences between the diets consumed by Paleolithic humans and those usually eaten by their modern-day progeny. It is beyond legitimate dispute that our Stone Age ancestors lived exclusively as hunter-gatherers, meaning that their diets were composed entirely of those edible and nourishing substances that they could either track down and kill (wild animals) or search for and gather up (wild plants and fungi). It might sound like a fool's errand to try to guess what human beings ate millions of years ago, but for capable scientists the endeavor is less speculative than it might appear at first glance. This is partly because modern-day hunter-gatherers—readily observable and somewhat well-studied folks living in small, detached communities in remote corners of the world—to this day eat in largely the same way that our Paleolithic ancestors once did. But, more importantly, the invention of agriculture and the other production techniques behind the foods that dominate the modern-day culinary landscape didn't occur until after the end of the Paleolithic. As a result, most staples of the modern-day Western diet—cereal grains, processed foods, sweets—were simply unavailable to our Paleolithic ancestors. Thus, to a large degree, a little deductive reasoning is all that is required to identify ways in which the typical Western diet differs dramatically from the one consumed by our Paleolithic ancestors for more than 99% of our time on the planet.

Eaton and Konner highlighted some of those differences—Paleolithic humans, they claimed, ate more meat, less fat, more vegetables, and far fewer cereal grains than most of us do today—and they offered a few high-level ideas about how those differences might be contributing to the prevalence of modern-day health problems like obesity and atherosclerosis. The lasting significance of their paper, however, wasn't in these specific claims, but in the articulation of a novel concept: the notion that, according to Darwinian evolution, differences between one's ancestral environment and one's modern lifestyle simply *must* be at the root of diseases of modernity, particularly nutritionally influenced ones like obesity. Or, as Eaton and Konner put it:

> [I]t is ... valuable to estimate the typical diet that human beings were adapted to consume during the long course of our evolution. Points of convergence between this estimate and modern recommendations are encouraging, and points of divergence suggest new lines of research. The diet of our remote ancestors may be a reference standard for modern human nutrition and a model for defense against certain 'diseases of civilization.'

The idea was groundbreaking enough to get the punchy little article published in the best-regarded medical journal on the planet, *The New England Journal of Medicine.* And though it took a while to gain the attention of the mainstream nutritional authorities, it undoubtedly did so, having since been cited by more than a thousand other scholars.

Just a few decades on, the study of "ancestral health" principles has blossomed into a stand-alone academic discipline, if still perhaps something of a fringe one. It has its own professional society, The Ancestral Health Society, which publishes a peer-reviewed academic journal and puts on international symposia at major universities every year. Scholars and scientists have used evolutionary perspectives to reconsider the received wisdom about the healthfulness of all sorts of modern-day behaviors, from when we sleep and how we work to the ways that we clean and exercise our bodies. And in many cases their findings haven't been pretty. A 2012 paper published in the *Journal of Affective Disorders* summarized the evidence this way: "In effect, humans have dragged a body with a long hominid history into an overfed, malnourished, sedentary, sunlight-deficient, sleep-deprived, competitive, inequitable, and socially-isolating environment with dire consequences."

All this fretting about the perils of modernity has even given rise to a bona fide pop-culture sensation: the so-called "Paleo diet," an immensely popular dietary philosophy (according to Google, "Paleo diet" was the single most searched-for diet-related phrase on the Internet in 2013) that tells us to eat like our caveman ancestors did if we want to stay lean and healthy.

The Paleo diet and the broader ancestral health movement have their critics. But they inevitably take issue with specific recommendations—is dairy *really* Paleo?—and not the underlying study of ancestral health practices. It would be hard to deny that fundamental differences between our new, modern environment and the one we occupied for the great majority of our evolutionary past (Eaton and Konner's ecological "points of divergence") simply must be fueling modern-day chronic disease epidemics. After all, just as infectious diseases are spread by viruses, bacteria, and other organisms, chronic, non-communicable diseases have to come from *somewhere*. If the engine driving the spread of obesity, atherosclerosis, and diabetes isn't biological hay-wiring resulting from a sudden, pervasive environmental shift, then what conceivably could it be?

***

Which brings us back to dogs. According to ancestral health logic, our nation of overweight dogs is a bit like a doomed brood of hatchling sea turtles huddling under a neon hotel sign: something about our man-made modern world is causing their highly evolved biology to malfunction in truly spectacular fashion. To put things back in order we need to determine what's wrong with the current environment and then come up with a plan to correct it.

The first step of this process is to identify what's actually new about the environment that our dogs occupy. We need, in other words, to figure out the ways in which dogs are no longer living the way they've evolved to live. Fortunately for us, unlike anthropologists seeking to piece together the mysteries of human evolution, this exercise doesn't require much in the way of intellectual time travel. Because, even today, the domestic dog's closest genetic cousin is still living right under our snouts.

BETWEEN DOG AND WOLF

U.S. HIGHWAY 89 links the hardscrabble mountain town of Gardiner, Montana, to the near-infinite natural wonders of Yellowstone National Park. At the park's northern entrance, the road passes under the Roosevelt Arch, a rusticated triumphal archway whose stones bear the inscription, "For the Benefit and Enjoyment of the People." The epigraph is an excerpt from *The Act of Dedication*, the piece of federal legislation that, in 1872, made

Yellowstone the world's first national park, preserving for posterity its more than two million awe-inspiring acres.

The drive from Gardiner out into Yellowstone's Lamar Valley is long, but motorists are treated to an astounding array of roadside attractions. These include picturesque canyons, raging rivers, mountain ranges, and, famously, more than half of the world's geothermic features. Along the way, visitors are also likely to come face to face with all manner of diverse wildlife. Yellowstone is home to several hundred species of plants and animals. Bald eagles, grizzly bears, bighorn sheep, and colossal, sleepy-eyed bison are just a few of the more impressive "charismatic megafauna" likely to sidle up to your vehicle as you make your way across the park. But of all Yellowstone's wild inhabitants, only one is particularly relevant to understanding why an epidemic of obesity is killing America's dogs. That species is the gray wolf.

Wolves are indigenous to North America and packs once roamed the Northern Rockies in abundance. But the westward-ho expansion of settlers in the mid-nineteenth century funneled thousands of head of large, slow-moving, and valuable livestock smack into the middle of wolf territory. Wolves, impressive predators that they are, wreaked havoc on livestock populations. And they earned a reputation as the scourge of the cattleman's herd, one part pesky vermin, one part bloodthirsty killer.

A wide-ranging extermination campaign soon began in earnest. Hunters, trappers, cattlemen, and even public officials joined the cause. By any measure, they succeeded. In Montana alone, they killed as many as 100,000 wolves between the 1860s and the 1920s, and the gray wolf was thought to be completely extinct in the American West by 1926. It is often said that the last two wolves were shot and killed by Yellowstone park rangers.

That last bit has only recently become ironic, owing to a dramatic shift in public opinion about the relationship between government and wildlife that occurred amid the liberalism of the 1960s. Up until then, most Americans regarded wildlife as something that should be tolerated only to the extent that it served the needs and desires of man. If bison made for good eating, they should be eaten; if wolves threatened valuable livestock, they should be eradicated. And public officials such as park rangers should embody that ideology and effect policies aimed at furthering it. But the growth of the environmental movement allowed other philosophies to creep into the public consciousness, notably the idea that the actions of man should not jeopardize the outright survival of other species. That, although the eventual extinction of all species is inevitable—indeed, it has been estimated that more than 99.9% of all species that have ever walked the earth are already extinct—man should not *cause* other living beings to become extinct.

The idea caught on, and it reached something of a critical mass with the passage of *The Endangered Species Act of 1973*, a law that not only granted government the right to step in when it looks like a species is on the brink of being wiped out, but also to reestablish locally extinct species—to build vanished populations back up to what they once were.

Re-enter the wolf. By the beginning of the 1970s, the only wolves in the Lower Forty-Eight were a small band living in the very northern tip of Minnesota. But, thanks to the efforts of environmental organizations and a few dedicated individuals, the species was officially classified as endangered in 1974. A contentious battle to reintroduce wolves to the American West followed and, after much legal wrangling, a total of 66 wolves were finally reintroduced to two distinct Rocky Mountain locations—northern Idaho and Yellowstone National Park—in the mid-1990s. Today, less than two decades later, there are more than 1,600 wolves living in packs scattered widely across Montana, Wyoming, Idaho, Washington, Oregon, and California. The repopulation of wolves in the American West has been nothing short of a comprehensive success.

According to Abby Nelson, a biologist and wolf management specialist with Montana's Department of Fish, Wildlife, and Parks, the primary reason for the wolf's successful repopulation has been the species' "extreme fecundity." Wolves are genetically constructed to go forth and prosper in places like the greater Yellowstone area. They breed early and often, producing litters of five to ten pups every year, often for the better part of a decade. Additionally, about 10% of wolves will disperse from their packs upon reaching adulthood, leading to regular territorial expansion. And, as apex predators, they will succeed in just about any ecosystem they share with large numbers of suitable prey—something that the big herds of elk found throughout the Northern Rockies most certainly are.

Montana FWP is a state agency, and Abby's job involves much overseeing of the conflicts that have inevitably arisen as repopulated wolves have spread into areas previously dominated by Montana ranchers and their grazing livestock. But another (smaller) part of her job is to partner with the Yellowstone Association to take people like me out into the field and inside the fascinating world of wild wolves. To help the public understand what makes this thriving, prosperous species tick.

And so, on a chilly, overcast morning in early October, Abby and I found ourselves making the long drive from Gardiner to the Lamar Valley, a hotbed of Yellowstone's wolf activity. I'd come to Montana because I hoped that she and her colleagues could help me with a question, one whose answer might go a long way toward explaining why so many of America's dogs are dying from an epidemic of obesity: *how come wolves don't get fat?*

***

When it comes to obesity, dogs and wolves have managed to arrange themselves into a remarkable kind of "natural experiment," the results of which provide a conceptual framework that may well explain why so many of our dogs are obese. In one sense—in their respective *capacities* to become obese—dogs and wolves are strikingly similar. Indeed, on the whole, the two species possess genes that are so similar as to blur the line between one and the other. But in another sense—in the frequency with which members of the two species actually *become* obese—they could hardly be more different. On the one hand, according to APOP and others, the majority of modern-day domestic dogs are either overweight or obese. On the other, effectively zero wolves are. Thus, in a fundamental sense, understanding why America's dogs are dying from an epidemic of obesity can only begin by identifying the ways in which they no longer live like their wolf brethren have for thousands of generations.

So just how similar are the two species? A study published in 2014 in the journal *PLoS Genetics* reports that the genetic divergence between dogs and wolves occurred only about 14,000 years ago. That may sound like a long time, but in evolutionary terms it is only a heartbeat. By contrast, the genetic divergence between humans and our closest living genetic cousins, the chimpanzees, probably occurred some 13 *million* years ago—making it about a thousand times more distant than the dog-wolf split. To think of it another way, consider that if you were to take the 60 million years or so that have transpired since canine species first appeared on the evolutionary map, then condense that period into 180 days (about half a year), the split between wolves and dogs would occur only about an hour before midnight on the final day.

Because dogs and wolves diverged from their common ancestor so recently, there has been little time for genetic differences to arise between the two. In total, they share some 98% or more of their mitochondrial DNA. The overlap is so significant, in fact, that the two can be, and in many corners of the world are, successfully interbred.

Interbreeding between species is a truly rare biological phenomenon. Even when two animals are taxonomic first-cousins, it's not an enterprise that tends to work out very well for those involved, as the idea of a human being mating with a chimpanzee might suggest to you. In fact, the word "species" is usually defined as a group of individual organisms that can successfully breed with one another. So, by definition, members of different species shouldn't be able to breed with one another at all. Nevertheless, and despite the fact that most states affirmatively prohibit the breeding of dog-wolf hybrids, current estimates of their population in the United States range from 300,000 to more than a million.

Of course, one needn't be a geneticist to see just how physically similar dogs and wolves are. Notwithstanding the array of diverse forms that human tinkering has produced in the modern-day domestic dog, the two species sure look an awful lot alike: the same strong, muscular hindquarters, the same sharp, serrated teeth, the big, attentive ears, the long muzzles, the padded paws, the swinging tails, the forward-facing eyes. The French use the expression *l'heure entre chien et loup* ("the hour between dog and wolf") to refer to dusk, a time of day when the fading light makes it all but impossible to differentiate one species from the other. It's not hard to see why.

None of which is to say that there aren't genetic differences between dogs and wolves. The two are, after all, different species. Recently, geneticists have used genome-sequencing technology to identify and map out the few major differences that separate one from the other. And it turns out that most of the differences concern brain function. This is not an altogether unexpected finding, as these between-the-ears differences manifest as some remarkably different behavioral tendencies. Notably, as anyone reading these words surely knows, dogs form close emotional bonds with their humans. Bonds which make them do cute things like jump into bed with us in the morning, wait by the door when we leave for work, and turn wiggly, spastic circles when we come home.

Wolves, perhaps the quintessential "wild animals," are not usually so inclined. Teaching a wolf—even one raised from puppyhood as a pampered Park Avenue house pet—to do things like cuddle in bed and perform parlor tricks is not likely to be an enjoyable or rewarding experience, either for trainer or trainee.

Still, on the whole, dogs and wolves are about as genetically similar as two distinct species can be. But those nearly identical genes have managed to produce two species that are, in one particularly glaring way, near-polar opposites of one another.

***

Weight problems aren't exactly common among wolves. Rolf Peterson, a professor at Michigan Technological University who studies wild gray wolves at Isle Royale National Park, once put it to me this way: "I'd say there is no evidence of obese wolves in the wild."

No evidence.

Abby Nelson, who spends her professional life tracking wolves in the Yellowstone area, speaks in similarly unequivocal terms: "I have never observed a wild wolf even approaching obesity."

Never.

Wild wolves simply don't become fat. It just doesn't happen.

Importantly, this is not to say that they don't have any fat whatsoever in their bodies. In fact, they carry it in most of the same places as dogs do—packed between the internal organs, layered in deposits underneath the skin, interfused with bone marrow. Way down at the molecular level, their various types of fat tissues look just like the stuff we find in our dogs too.

Wild wolves just don't pack it on the way our dogs do. The most definitive scientific analysis of the body composition of wild wolves involved a study of 38 Alaskan wolves living in an environment where the food supply was so abundant as to be, according to the study's authors, "unlimited." The researchers found that the animals tended to maintain average body fat percentage (BFP) levels of around 3.5% in the summer and 7% in the fall. Not a single one of them ever maintained a BFP of more than 10%. This despite the fact that the animals lived in the chilly Alaskan wilderness, where a warm layer of subcutaneous body fat is a rather useful thing to have in one's body, and despite the fact that their feast-or-famine lifestyle meant that they usually lived off their stored body fat for several days in between meals. Another recent study shows that even captive wolves tend to maintain BFPs of only about 10% when fully fed, even with their roaming space drastically curtailed and their meals regulated.

The body compositions of other wild canine species have been studied too. During the summer months, when additional body fat isn't necessary to protect against harsh winter conditions, arctic foxes have been shown to maintain BFP levels of about 7%. Coyotes tend to stay at about 10%. And Australian red foxes at only 3% or 4%.

In fact, when it comes to modern-day canine species, there is really only one whose typical body composition stands out from the others: the domestic dog. Despite regular trips to the vet and specialized weight-loss foods and caring human guardians, about half the dogs in America today are so fat that it is as if they are smoking a pack of cigarettes a day. More specifically, extrapolating from data gathered by Dr. Ernie Ward and APOP, more than half of the dogs in the United States today have a BFP higher than 30%. By weight, about a third of the tissue in the average American dog is probably body fat. This means that the typical American dog has perhaps 800% as much fat in its body as the typical Alaskan wolf and is just about as fat as a garden-variety blue whale (average BFP of 35%). In a great many cases, our dogs are even fatter than that. They are, quite literally, fatter than whales.

To understand how this truly absurd reality has come to be, our first task must be to understand the basic features of the lives our dogs so recently left behind. To understand why our dogs are dying from an epidemic of obesity, we must first understand what it's like to live like a wolf.

THE (EXCEEDINGLY) PRIVATE LIVES OF WOLVES

YELLOWSTONE PRESENTLY IS home to about 60 adult wolves and 35 pups. They have divided themselves into ten packs, each including somewhere between two and 15 adolescents and full-fledged adults. Breeding females typically birth their pups in the spring and the Junction Butte pack had added five of them to its ranks not long before my October visit. They joined the four yearlings who survived from last year's breeding season, along with the pack's two leaders (the "alphas," in the formal language of wolf social dynamics), a six-year-old female and a large, three-year-old black male.

It was cold and blustery in the pre-dawn darkness as Abby and I ventured into the lesser darkness of the Lamar Valley, a kind of natural paradise found squarely in the middle of the Junction Butte pack's territory. A fresh elk kill had been reported on the eastern edge of the valley and Abby was hopeful that the pack would be feeding upon it sometime around dawn.

Because of their famously private nature, tracking wolves is a difficult business. Fortunately, many of the Yellowstone wolves wear radio-transmitting collars, devices that help the biologists with the Yellowstone Wolf Project keep track of the animals. It's something that they do phenomenally well—these packs are some of the most closely watched wolves on the planet and all the reams of data that have been gathered over the past two decades have been packaged into dozens of published studies, papers that have cast new light on all manner of wolf behavior and ecology. Yellowstone's wolves are particularly appropriate subjects for scientific study because their habitat is a national park, a place whose wildness is preserved by federal mandate. So, for research biologists and writers alike, Yellowstone is perhaps the best place in the country to see what the "natural" life of a wolf really looks like.

Abby and I spent the morning in the Lamar, tracing maps and peering through high-powered scopes. But we didn't have much luck. We drove around the park for the better part of two hours, until the sky had turned a pale shade of blue. But the wolves evaded us. Abby is a remarkably cheerful and patient person, but frustration looked to be creeping into her eyes.

"We should find Rick," she said.

Rick is Richard McIntyre, a man who is legendary among wolf buffs. A woman back at Yellowstone Association headquarters had referred to him gushingly as "the Pied Piper of Yellowstone Wolf-Watching." When Rick first came to Yellowstone, he wasn't affiliated with the Park Service. To hear him tell it, he just wanted to study wolves all on his own. But after learning of his superhuman dedication to the task of meticulously gathering data on wild wolves, the Park Service recruited him.

In any profession, it's rare to find an individual who achieves the level of total commitment that Rick brings to his professional life. He gets up before dawn seven days a week and allegedly hasn't taken a vacation or otherwise missed a single day of wolf-watching in over eight years. He recently notched his 3,000th consecutive day in the field. He lives primarily in his car, driving around the park eating blueberry Nutri-Grain bars and using telemetry technology to track wolves. He uses a high-powered, single-barrel scope to locate them high up in the pine forests and a Dictaphone to record observational data. At the end of each day, his data—what the wolves are eating, where they are going, what they are doing—is added to the massive database maintained and analyzed by the Yellowstone Wolf Project. He also makes time to give talks to park visitors, enriching their experiences with his encyclopedic knowledge and wealth of wolf anecdotes.

We caught up with him at the Tower Ranger Station in the mid-morning, the sun now bright overhead. He is a trim man with a precise and delicate manner. A shock of brown hair and boyish features belie the age otherwise suggested by his considerable experience. He stood in the parking lot, encircled by wolf-loving park visitors, giving them an oral history of wolves in Yellowstone. We listened as he told them about the Junction Butte pack, describing its lineage all the way back to the original wolves brought to the park from Alberta in the mid-1990s. He then told them about 21, a wolf whom he called the "undisputed heavyweight champ" of Yellowstone. 21 was a legendary alpha male whose physical attributes were so off-the-charts that he was comparable to a once-in-a-generation athletic talent like Michael Jordan. He weighed more than 130 pounds and dominated his territory like no other wolf in the park's history.

When the history lesson was finished, we made our way back out to the Lamar. Abby and I followed Rick as he drove slowly along, then pulled his car off to the shoulder, darted across the road, set his scope on a tripod, and peered out across the valley. We stayed quiet as he whispered notes into his Dictaphone. He looked at us and shook his head. Abby grimaced and we headed back to the cars. The pattern repeated itself a few more times and the day stretched on.

In the afternoon Abby and I set off on our own, exiting the park and heading for the Montana backcountry. We followed a dirt logging road up into the woods, through the remnants of a tiny, archaic town and past the ruins of abandoned mines. I thought that perhaps our luck had changed when, shortly after leaving the car, we came upon a set of frighteningly large, clawed animal tracks. We stopped and examined them, but Abby concluded that they were made by a bear, not a wolf. We went on, Abby looking intrepid with a can of bear spray in her grip. I tried to take heart from her bravery—even as I panicked at the sound of every snapping twig and my eyes nervously searched the enveloping woods for charging grizzlies.

We walked the hills of the Montana backcountry until the Gallatin Range purpled and the setting sun filled the big sky with shades of orange. Abby worked her radio antenna. I kept my fingers crossed. But it was not to be; I went to bed that night having yet to see my first wild wolf in the fur.

***

In fact, it wasn't until sometime later that I finally caught a fleeting glimpse of one of the elusive creatures. I had rendezvoused with the Pied Piper of Yellowstone Wolf Watching in the moments before dawn on a cool spring morning. He adjusted a single-barrel scope that he had placed atop a roadside knoll near the confluence of Soda Butte Creek and the Lamar River. True to his nickname, at least two dozen other wolf enthusiasts had followed their Piper to the spot and were now following his gaze out across the Lamar.

One of them was gracious enough to point me in the right direction and it wasn't long until I finally had a wolf in my binocular sights. He was a black-coated male (un-collared and without a tracking ID number, McIntyre referred to him simply as "Dark Black") and he emerged from behind a stand of yellow grasses, jaw slackened and watchful eyes full of intent. He moved lightly but with graceful power, paws hardly touching the ground as he floated from one grove of cottonwoods to another.

He was followed by three other adult males, two blacks and a gray, all members of the Prospect Peak pack. Each was lean and tall, with wiry musculature and legs that were somewhat longer in proportion to their bodies than most dogs. Their coats were rough and matted, both thick and wiry at the same time.

"Last night they were howling," another spectator whispered. "They had taken an elk and they were calling a denning female down out of the woods to share in the kill."

We watched them as they danced across the valley and disappeared behind a hill. We waited, scanning the landscape until mid-morning, but they did not reappear. Nevertheless, and even through binocular lenses in the flat dawn light, it was impossible to deny that the animals were leading precisely the lives that they ought to lead. That they were, in their natural habitat, thriving.

***

To understand the features that characterize that habitat, we need a true wolf expert. Enter Dr. Daniel Stahler, one of the lead biologists with the Yellowstone Wolf Project. He arrived at the park in 1997 and, other than for brief departures to earn masters and doctoral degrees, he has been there ever since. In that time, he has published more than two dozen peer-reviewed papers on the behavior and ecology of Yellowstone's wolves. He is a passionate and intelligent man, and when he gets going on a subject that's in his intellectual wheelhouse he speaks so quickly that it can be difficult to keep up with him. "With wolves nothing is easy," he told me once, referencing the ongoing drama over how to manage wolf populations outside the park. "Nothing except the biology."

We spent a few afternoons chatting about that biology in greater detail, teasing out the contours and edges of the unique "ecological niche" occupied by Yellowstone's wolves and contrasting them against the world occupied by modern-day domestic dogs. We focused on subjects like diet, physical activity, chronic disease risk, and longevity, all topics with direct links to obesity. And, in the end, a few high-level points emerged.

The first is one we've already covered: wolves don't get fat. It simply doesn't happen. According to published observational studies of wolves in the field, studies of captive wolves, studies of other wild canines, and the anecdotal observations of the Yellowstone Wolf Project's many capable biologists, obesity is simply not a disease that wolves have to contend with. Dr. Stahler just laughed when I asked him about the rate of obesity among wild wolves. "I'd say that obesity is a non-issue for them," he eventually replied.

The second point is closely related to the first. Not only do wolves not become fat, they don't often fall victim to the chronic diseases linked with obesity either. Importantly, this is not to say that wild wolves live longer than their domestic cousins. They don't. According to Trent Redfield, of the Grizzly and Wolf Discovery Center in West Yellowstone, Montana, wolves in captivity often live as long as 15 years. Wild wolves, on the other hand, rarely do so well. But there are myriad reasons for their relatively short lives and none of them have much to do with chronic diseases: the complete absence of veterinary care; the harsh climate in which they live; the constant competition for scarce resources; the bloody battles with large prey; the regular wolf-on-wolf violence; and, of course, the presence in their lives of humans (what with our itchy trigger fingers and carelessly driven automobiles and all). Dr. Stahler summarized the state of affairs this way: "Wolves live hard lives and they don't tend to live very long."

According to him, "by far" the most common cause of death inside Yellowstone National Park is other wolves. Second is infectious diseases like mange, rabies, and distemper. Third is vehicle strikes. And fourth is harvest by hunters in the areas immediately outside the park. For those wolves whose territories lie predominantly outside of the park's confines, human-caused mortality is by far the most common cause of death. Wolf-on-wolf violence (the leading cause of death within the park) "is tiny" in comparison.

Now consider the top killers of domestic dogs. A recent ten-year survey of more than 70,000 American dogs showed that the leading cause of death across adults in all breeds is cancer. It kills more than 30% of adult dogs and, in many breeds, even more than that. Second on the list is traumatic injury (car accidents), and third is infectious diseases. But fourth through sixth are other chronic, noninfectious diseases: metabolic dysfunctions (diabetes and insulin resistance), inflammatory dysfunctions (gastrointestinal disorders), and degenerative conditions (osteoarthritis). In other words, we know that chronic, non-communicable diseases like cancer are killing our dogs far more commonly than they are killing wild wolves.

Still, just as wild wolves do have the capacity to become fat, they have the capacity to develop chronic diseases too. Isolated cases of cancers, vital organ degeneration, and arthritis have been documented in wolves. But they are exceedingly rare. As leading wolf biologist Terry Kreeger has written, "[s]everal such reports [of miscellaneous diseases and pathologies] exist in the literature, but most concern captive animals. The majority of these pathologies affect individual animals, not wolf populations."

Unfortunately, when it comes to our dogs, the opposite is true: obesity and cancer are rampant, population-wide problems. The majority of dogs in America are overweight; the number-one killer of dogs in America is cancer.

In fact, when it comes to causes of death, perhaps the only similarity between dogs and wolves is that, in both cases, malnutrition is responsible for only a small fraction of deaths. Dogs, with the over-abundance of food at their disposal, obviously don't have to worry very much about malnutrition. But, somewhat surprisingly, neither do wolves. According to a recent study produced by biologists from the Yellowstone Wolf Project, only about 3% of Yellowstone's wolves die from starvation. Despite the fierce competition for resources in the wilds of Yellowstone, most wolves seem to be getting more than enough to eat.

***

So *what* exactly do they eat? In a wild habitat, one that hasn't been tainted by human development, wolves eat meat and basically nothing else. In Yellowstone, elk are the primary target, constituting about 90% of large ungulate mammals killed by wolves in the Park between 1995 and 2003. In the summertime, adult elk become harder for wolves to hunt—the prey can flee more effectively when there aren't deep snow banks to wade through— and elk kill rates drop by as much as 25%. Yellowstone's wolves compensate by consuming a somewhat more diverse selection of ungulates (mule deer, pronghorn), as well as other types of what biologists amusingly call "small prey packages" (rodents, birds, invertebrates). In other parts of the world they go for other large ungulates (deer in Minnesota, caribou in parts of Canada, moose in Alaska, livestock animals in densely populated parts of Eurasia). Food is always hard to come by in the wild and wolves are remarkably flexible and opportunistic animals, but when large mammalian prey is on the menu, it is always preferred.

When consuming a carcass, they tend to go for the vitamin-rich internal organs—the heart, the liver, the spleen, the kidneys—first. (Though rarely on the menu, Rick McIntyre told me that the most in-demand wolf delicacy of all, one brimming with essential vitamins and minerals, is an unborn fetus.) Only once these organs have been picked over do the wolves move on to the more plentiful skeletal musculature. They eat it all, picking meat off the ribs before gnawing on the breakable bones, tendons, ligaments, and hide, all of which they consume. At the end of the whole bloody affair, all that remains are the large, unbreakable bones of the carcass and, importantly, whatever plant matter was contained in the digestive tract of the deceased at the time it was killed.

The refusal of wolves to consume partially digested plant matter is well-documented in the peer-reviewed literature. "They won't touch the stuff," said Stahler. "It's striking, really. They'll consume basically the entire animal, even the lining of the digestive tract. But they won't touch the partially digested plant matter itself." Wolves are, on rare occasions, observed chomping on grass or berries but, in the end, it's meat and almost nothing else. "I would estimate that probably 99% of their nutrition comes from meat sources," Stahler explained.

For the captive wolves at the Grizzly and Wolf Discovery Center—the ones that regularly live to 15 years of age—the proportion is even greater than that. They get every last calorie from elk and deer meat.

In short, while it's commonplace to assume that an aesthetically appealing "balanced diet"—a colorful assortment of lean meats, whole grains, fresh fruits, and vegetables—is healthiest for everyone, man or beast, it is beyond dispute that wolves have, over millions and millions of years, evolved to thrive on a diet of meat, and meat alone.

***

For a number of reasons, estimating the *amount* of meat eaten by wild wolves is not particularly easy. First of all, both metabolic demands and consumption rates change dramatically with the seasons. Dan Stahler has reported that a group of Yellowstone wolves nearly doubled their daily consumption rates between early winter and late winter. Others have reported similar findings in other areas. Additionally, wolf-killed prey carcasses are a "food bonanza" for scavengers, so researchers cannot merely use total carcass weights to approximate the amount that is actually consumed by wolves. Other predators and scavengers will usually pick a wolf-killed prey carcass clean within 24 hours if left to their own devices. And it's nearly impossible for researchers to figure out exactly what percentage of a kill is going to wolves and what percentage is going to the ravens, foxes, bears, and beetles that are also feasting upon it.

With those qualifiers in mind, the best guesses at the moment suggest that wolves in stable populations tend to have somewhere in the neighborhood of 0.10 kilograms of wolf-killed prey available to eat per kilogram of wolf per day, at least in the wintertime. This translates into about 10 pounds of meat per day, for a 100-pound wolf. These studies also suggest that typically active wild wolves need slightly less than that—about 0.09 kilograms of prey per kilogram of wolf per day, or about 9 pounds of meat per 100-pound wolf per day—in order to maintain a stable body weight.

When you work out what this means in purely caloric terms, the numbers are so large that you might think you've forgotten to shift a decimal point. Using traditional calories-in, calories-out math, a 100-pound wolf needs to consume around 6,000 calories per day just to maintain its body weight. *Six thousand calories.* That is, by way of comparison, more than twice the FDA's recommended daily intake for a 160-pound man.

It is even more astounding when you consider that they don't eat very often. Wolves are feast-or-famine eaters. According to Dan Stahler, those in Yellowstone typically go two or three days between elk kills. Other biologists have reported that fasts commonly go on for *weeks*. Killing large, antlered ungulates isn't easy, after all, and wolves have become well-adapted to go for impressively long periods between kills.

But the feasting that compensates for all that fasting is equally impressive. In most cases, large ungulates like elk and moose are too big to be consumed in a single push, even by a large pack with every motivation to consume the thing as quickly as possible. Still, the wolves give it their voracious best (this is the origin of the expression "wolf it down").

"At a fresh kill," write biologists Rolf Peterson and Paolo Ciucci, "wolves typically eat until their sides are distended and their stomachs are packed." This translates into 15 or 20 pounds of meat, or roughly 25% of a wolf's total body weight *in a single meal*—surely more than any human being has ever consumed in a single day.

***

The primary reason that wolves consume so many calories seems to be that they tend to be rather active animals. "Basically, wolves spend their lives doing one of five things: resting, travelling, socializing, hunting, or eating," said Stahler. They are most active in the mornings and the evenings, he explained, and, like many household dogs, they often pass the majority of their daytime and nighttime hours sound asleep.

Trent Redfield of West Yellowstone's Grizzly and Wolf Discovery Center made similar remarks: "Wolves sleep a tremendous amount," he told me. "They practice conservation of energy."

My own observations at the Center supported this. I visited in the mid-afternoon and every one of the wolf residents slept throughout my stay, right up until their evening feedings commenced.

But although they aren't exactly hummingbirds, wild wolves do tend to do a great deal of walking and other low-level physical activity. They often propel their sizable bodies over tremendous distances, both in connection with daily hunting behavior and when instinctively dispersing from their packs after reaching adulthood. The travel associated with dispersal is perhaps the more impressive of the two types, simply due to the vast distances covered. Linear ("as the crow flies") distances of more than 500 miles, where more than 3,000 miles of actual travel has taken place, have been observed over periods of only six months. This translates into nearly 20 miles a day, every day, for half a year. During a meeting in Gardiner, Mike Jimenez, the chief of the U.S. Fish and Wildlife Service's efforts to reintroduce wolves to the American West over the past two decades, showed me a map of the western United States with a squiggly red line drawn on it, like a child's scribbling. He explained that it was the route taken by a two-year-old, radio-collared female wolf during a six-month dispersal journey. She had left the park and traveled widely throughout Montana, Wyoming, Idaho, and Utah (passing not far from my home in Salt Lake City), before dying after ingesting some poison in the mountains of Colorado only six months after leaving her pack.

But even when they're not dispersing, wolves still get around. The wolves of Montana roam territories averaging some 200 square miles, and many others occupy even larger zones. They spend as much as 50% of their lives on the move and have been observed traveling average distances of 25-30 miles between kills and chasing their prey for upwards of 10 miles at a time.

In addition to lots of walking and trotting, wolves also perform occasional (but regular) bouts of short-duration, all-out, life-or-death physical exertion. They locate and stalk their prey in packs (wolves are one of the few predatory species that hunt prey many times larger than themselves, something that requires social cooperation), attempting to get as close as possible to a target before confronting it. When the time is right, they rush at speeds of more than 30 miles per hour, usually approaching from behind. If the target has a chance to flee, the wolves give chase, still at top speed. At this point hunter and hunted literally race for their lives. In many cases, bloody, intense physical combat ensues, a tempest of teeth, antlers, and hooves.

The contest only comes to an end when either predator or prey is physically defeated. If the wolves win the day, they can feast and relax. If the prey escapes, the wolves must get up and do it all over again.

FROM WOLVES TO DOGS

THESE SIX SCIENTIFICALLY VERIFIED points about the lives of wild wolves form the core of the "ecological niche" occupied by the domestic dog's closest undomesticated relative: (1) they don't become fat, (2) they rarely suffer from chronic, non-infectious diseases, (3) they eat only meat, but

(4) they eat copious quantities of it, (5) they do a lot of walking and other low-level physical activity, and (6) they perform regular bouts of short, all-out physical effort.

To understand why our dogs are dying from obesity, we now must compare their typical modern-day lifestyles against this framework and try to identify what Boyd Eaton and Melvin Konner called "points of divergence" between the former and the latter. We must, in other words, figure out the ways in which our dogs are no longer living the lives that they have evolved to live.

But it's important to remember that identifying these differences can only be a starting point. Once we find them, we must then turn to the relevant scientific evidence—the experimental studies, the epidemiological papers, our accumulated knowledge of canine physiology—to see which points of ecological divergence can coherently explain *why* our dogs have become so fat and what we can do about it. After all, identifying points of divergence is only the first step in the process of using evolutionary principles to understand diseases of modernity, according to Boyd Eaton and Melvin Konner's model. It doesn't prove anything; it only "suggests new lines of research." To confirm whether an ecological point of divergence can really explain the canine obesity epidemic, we need to review the experimental evidence and see which theories hold water. And over the remainder of this book we will do precisely that.

Failure to see this process through in a skeptical and rigorous manner will expose us to a particularly pernicious intellectual pitfall: the tendency to jump to conclusions. After all, just because epidemics and diseases are very complex things doesn't mean that they don't sometimes appear to be very simple. And as we compare dogs with wolves over the chapters that follow, we will be confronted with myriad opportunities to slap our foreheads and say "well, of course!"

Actually, it may seem that a simple explanation for the vast difference in obesity rates between dogs and wolves has already revealed itself: wolves are wild animals that exist in an environment of caloric *scarcity*, while dogs are domestic ones for whom caloric *excess* is the norm. Well, of course our dogs fat. Sometimes it really is that simple, right?

Perhaps. But there are reasons to doubt whether this simple story can adequately explain why half the dogs in America today are undergoing a health crisis on par with a pack-a-day smoking habit. For one, as we've seen, the average number of calories consumed each day by a wild wolf positively dwarfs the number consumed by most human beings, let alone their dogs. It's a bit rich to call such a glut of nutritional fuel "scarcity."

Moreover, we've seen that wolves rarely die of malnutrition. But shouldn't we expect that outcome to be far more common if there simply weren't enough calories going around to meet everyone's needs? After all, if caloric scarcity is the norm for wild wolves, shouldn't the eventual outcome be widespread emaciation, not an epidemic of healthy, normal, not-so-fat bodies? And, for that matter, shouldn't we expect at least *some* wolves—the most dominant ones, like 21, the "undisputed heavyweight champ of Yellowstone"—to have regular access to excess calories? If obesity is really just about caloric scarcity and caloric excess, shouldn't at least some wolves be getting fat?

The subject of the next chapter is a robust and growing body of scientific evidence that can account for these objections and that shows that there may indeed be more than meets the eye on this matter. It strongly suggests that a simple scarcity/excess dichotomy (and the calories-in, calories-out model upon which it is built) does not fully explain how and why animals really get fat. This new scientific doctrine is revolutionizing nutritional science, calling into question much of what has been considered dogma for the past 50 years, both in the human domain and in the canine one. Unfortunately, it has some truly frightening things to say about how more than eight out of ten of us are feeding our dogs every day.

Chapter Three

RETHINKING THE SCIENCE OF OBESITY

--

"Bold ideas, unjustified anticipations, and speculative thought, are our only means for interpreting nature: our only organon, our only instrument, for grasping her. And we must hazard them to win our prize. Those among us who are unwilling to expose their ideas to the hazard of refutation do not take part in the scientific game."

Karl Popper, *The Logic of Scientific Discovery* (1935)

CALORIES-IN, CALORIES-OUT?

AS SCIENTIFICALLY MINDED public intellectuals go, Gary Taubes occupies something of a unique place in the world. His writing has appeared in the academic journal *Science*, as well as in *The New York Times*, *Esquire*, *The Atlantic Monthly*, and in multiple editions of *Best American Science Writing*. His books have sold hundreds of thousands of copies. His ideas have revolutionized the way that many people (professionals and laypeople alike) think about some of the most pressing scientific issues of our time. The Robert Wood Johnson Foundation has awarded him an Investigator Award in Health Policy Research and the National Association of Science Writers has awarded him a Science in Society Journalism Award on three separate occasions (an all-time record).

All of which is to say that Taubes plies his trade as a journalist. Unlike most leading scientific figures, he is not a scientist himself. At least not in the way the word is typically used—he doesn't perform his own experiments, he doesn't invent new technologies, and he doesn't wear a white lab coat to work.

But, in another sense, Taubes may be one of the preeminent scientists of our day. Armed with a skeptic's mentality, a deep appreciation for scientific principles, and a steadfast commitment to intellectual rigor, he has made it his life's work to improve the public's understanding of scientific issues. But he does it in an indirect way. Instead of producing his own scientific findings, he reports on experiments performed by *others*—what they've done right, what they've done wrong, what they've really proven, what they haven't. Taubes writes critical, high-minded reviews of published studies, often with the effect of calling bullshit on long-standing scientific wisdom. As Stevens Institute of Technology Professor John Horgan wrote in *Scientific American* in 2011, Taubes "researches topics to the point of obsession—actually, well beyond that point—and never dumbs things down for readers." His writings can be scathing (Horgan has also written that "calling Gary 'critical' is like calling Donald Trump 'self-confident'"). But even at his most biting, his arguments are always carefully reasoned and unassailably thorough.

Taubes has spilt a good deal of ink articulating the formal process that he uses to test the evidence behind conventional scientific wisdom. The prologue of one of his recent books includes a summary, and just reading about it is exhausting:

> It begins with the obvious question: what is the evidence to support the current beliefs? To answer this question, I find the point in time when the conventional wisdom was still widely considered controversial—the 1970s, for example, in the case of the dietary-fat/cholesterol hypothesis of heart disease, or the 1930s for the overeating hypothesis of obesity. It is during such periods of controversy that researchers will be most meticulous in documenting the evidence to support their positions. I then obtain the journal articles, books, or conference reports cited in support of the competing propositions to see if they were interpreted critically and without bias. And I obtain the references cited by these earlier authors, working ever backwards in time, and always asking the same questions: Did the investigators ignore evidence that might have refuted their preferred hypothesis? Did they pay attention to experimental details that might have thrown their preferred interpretation into doubt? I also search for other evidence in the scientific literature that wasn't included in these discussions but might have shed light on the validity of the competing hypotheses. And, finally, I follow the evidence forward in time from the point at which a consensus was reached to the present, to see whether these competing hypotheses were confirmed or refuted by further research. This process also includes interviews with clinical investigators and public-health authorities, those still active in research and those retired, who might point me to research I might have missed or provide further information and details on experimental

methods and interpretation of evidence.

Of course, Taubes doesn't just write about how to separate truth from fiction through skeptical investigation. He also writes about specific scientific topics. And, for the last couple of decades, one subject in particular: the intersection of nutrition and the science of obesity. His work over this period has been profoundly impactful. Taken as a whole, it amounts to a conceptual rebuke of the conventional wisdom on obesity that is at once comprehensive, convincing, highly explanatory, and, for many, so revolutionary as to warrant a complete re-think as to why so many of us get fat. In other words, Taubes may not be a lab-coat-wearing type of scientist, but if he were, as historian Richard Rhodes has written, "he would deserve and receive the Nobel Prize in Medicine." Such is the wide-ranging significance of his work.

***

Taubes started his nutrition research in the late 1990s, while working as a correspondent for the journal *Science*. He had studied physics at Harvard, engineering at Stanford, and journalism at Columbia before spending the first 15 years of his career writing about controversies in physics, biology, and chemistry. Most recently, he had reported on a fiasco concerning supposed breakthroughs in the energy production process known as cold fusion, which were announced to great fanfare only to be discredited and debunked upon closer investigation. In a series of articles, and later in the book *Bad Science*, Taubes had meticulously chronicled the cold fusion incident, highlighting the experimental design flaws, fraudulence, political malfeasance, and economic pressures that had combined to transform cold fusion research into a true miscarriage of science.

In the wake of *Bad Science*'s success, while hunting for a new topic to investigate, Taubes was prompted to turn his attention to another field of research entirely. One in which controversies were much more common than in physics. "Some of my physicist friends said if I was really interested in what they called 'pathological science'—the science of things that aren't so—I really should be looking at some of the research in public health," Taubes told me, some 20 years later.

Public health is a field concerned with promoting health and well-being at the population level. Groups like the World Health Organization and the Centers for Disease Control and Prevention pursue these goals by promoting specific research agendas, disseminating scientific information to the public, and influencing governmental health policies. The field's recent accomplishments include some of the most laudable and important health and safety initiatives of the past two centuries: vaccination programs; anti-smoking measures; improved road safety standards; and initiatives aimed at reducing infant mortality and improving sanitation in cities.

But public health has also seen its share of high-profile failures. And few have been more embarrassing than its inability to curtail the global spread of obesity in the twentieth century.

Leading public health officials had identified obesity as a priority by no later than 1952. That year, at a meeting of the western branch of the American Public Health Association, Lester Breslow, the future president of the APHA, warned his colleagues that "[i]t is clear that weight control is a major public health problem." Later that same year, at a national APHA meeting, obesity was identified as "America's No. 1 Health Problem."

For the next 60 years, governments and public health organizations worked relentlessly to solve the obesity problem. National clinical guidelines were announced. Nutritional labeling standards were created. Many millions of dollars were poured into media and marketing efforts and many billions into obesity-related research.

It has been, to say the least, a losing battle. As of 1960, the rate of obesity among adults in the United States was only about 13%. But over the next 50 years the rate nearly tripled. Today, more than two out of every three Americans are overweight. More than a third of us are clinically obese. In spite of the best efforts of well-funded public health organizations, the obesity problem has only gotten worse. It has blossomed into a full-blown epidemic.

How on Earth could that be?

There are many hypotheses. And one of them is that bad science is to blame. One of the most common criticisms of public health work is that the epidemiological research upon which it is based is particularly prone to producing misleading conclusions. Epidemiology, the study of the patterns that govern the distribution, prevalence, and spread of diseases at the population level, has been called a "basic science of public health." But unlike the laboratory experiments that fuel most scientific disciplines, the surveys and polling data upon which epidemiological studies are based are, at best, capable only of highlighting correlative relationships between variables, not causal ones. They can tell us, for instance, that American children are fatter today than they were in the 1950s, but they can't begin to tell us why.

Like many practitioners of the so-called "hard sciences," Gary Taubes's physicist friends saw that as a problem. So they suggested that Taubes turn his investigative spotlight from physics onto public health research. He did. And he was shocked by what he saw.

"When I started looking at influential epidemiological studies," Taubes told me, "I immediately saw that many of the things I had learned from physicists that they considered absolutely mandatory for good science—for getting an answer you can trust—the epidemiologists considered something of a luxury, not really necessary, because those checks and balances were just too hard to do in their field. And because they were too difficult, often unfeasible or impractical, the epidemiologists just decided they weren't necessary. Which, you know, struck me as kind of bad logic."

One of the first public health researchers Taubes interviewed—one of the most influential scientists in the entire history of nutrition and public health research—made a particularly bad impression. "The guy was clearly one of the worst scientists I had ever met in my life," Taubes recalls. "And, remember, I had just written a book called *Bad Science*. I had already interviewed what I had hoped were the worst scientists in the world. And this guy was clearly in that group."

Taubes hung up the phone, called his editor at *Science*, and told him he was onto something. He knew that, for all of public health's notable successes, one of its most prominent failures had been its inability to slow the global obesity epidemic. He wondered if a lack of scientific rigor could account for the problem, if somehow the conventional scientific wisdom about obesity—the very conclusions underlying most public health recommendations—were just wrong. "Bad scientists never get the right answer," Taubes explains today. "Science is just too hard. All the easy things have been discovered. You need a really meticulous, rigorous, cynical, skeptical approach to the data *or it will fool you*." If just a few scientists had fluffed their lines while researching the causes of obesity, a whole generation of people—scientists and laypeople alike—could have been misled.

Apparently Taubes found what he was looking for. Because he spent the next two decades trying to convince the world that we've all been misled about what makes us fat.

***

Taubes's contributions to humanity's understanding of the science of obesity are documented primarily in two books: *Good Calories, Bad Calories* and *Why We Get Fat*. Both are, if nothing else, painstakingly researched works of serious scientific and historical scholarship. *Good Calories, Bad Calories* is about 600 pages long, features more than 65 pages of bibliographic references, cites more than 600 interviews, and includes more than 400 footnotes—dimensions usually reserved for textbooks and other academic tomes. Taubes told me that it took him more than five years to write it. *Why We Get Fat* is shorter and more accessible, but it is no less cogent than its predecessor.

Fundamentally, the books advance two ideas. The first is that, despite what we've all been led to believe, consciously trying to balance calories-in and calories-out isn't the best way to avoid getting fat, at least not in the long-run. There's far more to obesity, Taubes argues, than simple caloric imbalance.

Importantly, the idea isn't that calories have nothing whatsoever to do with obesity. That would violate the first law of thermodynamics, the law of nature stating that energy can neither be created nor destroyed, it can only pass from one form to another. The first law of thermodynamics is the reason why your dog's body must grow larger if she consumes more calories than she expends—those extra calories (that energy) have to go *somewhere.*

Taubes's point isn't that calories are irrelevant to obesity. His point—and it is an achingly obvious one once you take more than a few seconds to think about the matter—is that the first law of thermodynamics doesn't say anything useful about *how* obesity works or *how* to avoid getting fat. On its face, the statement "we gain weight when we consume more calories than we expend" is a tautology, not a cause-and-effect proposition. It is no more explanatory than the statement "we are alcoholics because we drink too much" or "we get richer when we make more money than we spend." If we want to curtail obesity, we need to go a step further and understand *why* so many people consume more calories than they expend and *why* those calories get trapped in fat tissue.

The conventional wisdom about obesity—whether human or canine—offers surprisingly little in the way of an explanation for our ubiquitous overconsumption. About as far as it ever goes is to attribute our caloric excesses to personality defects. In the case of human beings, we're either burning too few calories (read: we're lazy), we're consuming more calories than we really need (we're gluttonous), or we're the unwitting victims of a "toxic food environment" that draws out both our laziness and our gluttony (we're stupid and weak-willed; we just can't help ourselves). In the case of canine obesity, it's a simpler version of the same story: dog owners are just loving our pets to death.

Taubes argues that such explanations should be unsatisfying for at least three reasons. The first is that they are woefully unsophisticated. As Susan Sontag once observed, "[t]heories that diseases are caused by mental states and can be cured by will power are always an index of how much is not understood about the physical terrain of a disease." The pathophysiology of many common diseases—not coincidentally, the ones we're best at treating—are understood way down to the sub-cellular level. But similar biochemical nuts and bolts are conspicuously absent from most mainstream explanations of the obesity epidemic. Like many theories grounded primarily in epidemiological data, the explanatory reasoning is couched in terms of behavioral tendencies and societal trends, not cellular biology.

A second reason for skepticism: the evidence supporting the conventional wisdom doesn't seem to add up. "In science," Taubes told me recently, "what you're looking for are what we call 'anomalous observations.' Are there data points that your hypothesis simply can't explain? If so, that's an indication that your theory might be wrong."

In the case of the calories-in, calories-out model of obesity, the scientific record seems to be plagued by conflicting evidence. For example, if obesity is really about gluttony, how come some extremely poor populations experience high levels of *both* obesity and malnutrition? If it's about laziness, how come the "exercise explosion" of the 1970s and 1980s coincided perfectly with the greatest period of fattening in recent American history? If it's about the toxicity of our luxurious modern lifestyles, how come extremely poor people tend to be at least as fat, if not fatter, than wealthy ones? And if managing calories is the key to losing weight, how come calorie-restricted diets have such a poor experimental track record when it comes to long-term weight loss?

The conventional wisdom about obesity also does a poor job of explaining how anyone (let alone a hundred million Americans) manages to stay lean. If our toxic food environment is causing us to become lazy and gluttonous, then why aren't we *all* fat? Is it really that lean people are just better than the rest of us at consciously balancing their calories-in with their calories-out? Taubes argues that this isn't realistic, using a simple example to drive the point home: if a pound of body fat contains about 3500 calories worth of energy (a little less than nine metabolizable calories per gram times about 453 grams per pound), a completely emaciated person who overestimates her daily caloric needs by merely *20 calories per day* (a single slurp of Coke or a single bite of a cheeseburger) will consistently gain several pounds of fat every single year. No matter how lean you are, if you overestimate your daily caloric needs by just 20 calories a day, you're soon going to wind up obese. Taubes argues that it's just not realistic to think that all of the many people who *do* manage to stay lean pull it off because they meticulously keep track of their true daily caloric needs and always eat precisely the right amount, to within 20 calories each day.

This is particularly unrealistic considering that calories-in and calories-out are what mathematicians call dependent variables, not independent ones. If we burn a lot of calories exercising, our appetites grow (increasing the likelihood that we'll consume more calories to make up for the shortfall). If we restrict the number of calories that we eat, we'll become lethargic (reducing the number of calories that we expend to make up for the shortfall). As Dr. Jeffrey Flier, dean of Harvard Medical School, and Dr. Terry Maratos-Flier, Harvard professor of medicine, wrote in *Scientific American* in 2007, our bodies are in this way constantly working to regulate their weight:

> An animal whose food is suddenly restricted tends to reduce its energy expenditure both by being less active and by slowing energy use in cells, thereby limiting weight loss. It also experiences increased hunger so that once the restriction ends, it will eat more than its prior norm until the earlier weight is attained.

It's hard to imagine that anyone could consciously calculate her precise caloric needs every day of her life, despite these wild fluctuations in daily energy expenditure.

This becomes an even more persuasive objection when you think about its implications for less brainy animals. As Daniel Stahler and his colleagues made clear, wolves and other wild animals don't become obese. Sure, some animals are "functionally fat," like whales and hibernators. And there will always be a range of body types in any population, some relatively large and others relatively small. But none of them, not even big, dominant alpha-males, who have access to more calories than they could ever eat, suffer from true obesity—the kind of excessive adiposity that results in compromised mobility, diabetes and other metabolic dysfunctions, and high rates of cancer and other chronic diseases.

But if obesity is really just about caloric imbalance, wouldn't some of them be screwing up the math? Wouldn't at least a few of Yellowstone's wolves—the big, dominant males like No. 21, the "undisputed heavyweight champ" of Yellowstone—be taking in the 20 extra calories that would cause them to become seriously fat? With all the "wolfing it down" that they do, wouldn't at least one of them be averaging an extra bite of food a day?

***

In an effort to reconcile these misgivings, Taubes traced the calories-in, calories-out model all the way back to its roots. And he found that, prior to World War II, the notion that obesity was caused by overconsumption was but one of several competing hypotheses that researchers had proposed to explain why we get fat. He discovered that, at the time, some scientists actually had different ideas. But, for a host of reasons, their competing hypotheses largely fell by the wayside over the second half of the twentieth century. On the other hand, the calories-in, calories-out model was zealously promoted by a series of charismatic and ambitious American scientists in the wake of World War II. As a result of their efforts, calories-in, calories-out became the conventional wisdom on obesity, so much so that any competing ideas would come to be considered scientific heresy.

Except, as Taubes realized, one of those forgotten ideas seemed to succeed in all the ways that the conventional wisdom about obesity seemed to fail. As a conceptual paradigm, it could explain obesity at a cellular and physiological level, without implicating wishy-washy notions like "personality defects." It could account for the existence of lean individuals, even in populations with rampant obesity. And, most persuasively of all, it was supported by a robust (and ever-growing) body of experimental evidence.

THE CARBOHYDRATE-INSULIN MODEL OF OBESITY

THE SECOND MAJOR IDEA advanced in Gary Taubes's nutritional work is that the root cause of obesity isn't caloric imbalance but hormonal irregularities. We get fat not because we're lazy or stupid or weak-willed, but because something specific has thrown some of our hormone levels out of whack. Obesity is a regulatory disorder, Taubes argues, just like any other growth defect. His theory of how and why animals get fat is somewhat more nuanced than the oversimplified calories-in, calories-out model, but it's just as easy to grasp once we have a working knowledge of a few key physiological concepts.

Let's start with some terminology. The word "fat" commonly is used to refer to two different things, body fat and dietary fat. As we all know, dietary fat is the stuff found in our food and body fat is the stuff that jiggles when we do our naked jumping jacks in front of the mirror every morning. Body fat (adipose tissue) is primarily composed of cells called lipocytes. The name comes from the fact that the cells are primarily composed of lipids, a class of molecules that includes both fatty acids and triglycerides. Fatty acids and triglycerides are closely related to one another: the latter are composed of the former. More specifically, each triglyceride molecule is made up of three (*tri-*) fatty acids (*-ides*) and a single molecule of a sugar alcohol called *glycerol* (*-glycer-*).

Importantly, all of the fat in our fat cells is stored in the form of triglycerides, not as fatty acids. This means that most of the dietary fat we consume also comes in the form of triglycerides (after all, we may call the strip of fat on the outside of a New York strip steak "dietary fat," but back when it is was actually inside of a cow, it was just "body fat"). The reason why the fat in our fat cells is stored as triglycerides and not as fatty acids is simple: triglycerides are relatively large molecules and the membranes enclosing fat cells are only permeable by fatty acids, not by the larger triglycerides. So, in order to stay contained within a fat cell, three fatty acid molecules must stay bound together as a single triglyceride. And, in order to enter or exit a fat cell, triglycerides must be broken down into fatty acids.

This is important because it's the fatty acids themselves, and not the triglycerides, that animals metabolize into actual chemical energy. So if we want to "burn" some of our stored body fat for metabolic fuel, what we need to do at a molecular level is to convert some of the stored triglycerides back into free fatty acids, so that they are able to exit a fat cell and re-enter the blood stream. Then they can be shipped off to a distant organ for use in producing chemical energy. Conversely, if an animal wants to increase the amount of fat stored in its body as adipose tissue (such as a ground squirrel does prior to hibernation), it needs to draw free fatty acids into the fat cells and bind them up with glycerol molecules to form triglycerides. This is necessary for long-term fattening because it prevents fatty acids from escaping fat cells and returning to the blood stream.

To a large degree, the number of fat cells in animal bodies remains constant throughout adulthood. So, when body fat levels within an animal rise, what is usually happening is an increase in the *size*, not the number, of fat cells. As we now know, this happens when the amount of triglyceride stored inside a fat cell increases. So what we call "getting fat" is simply what happens when the flow of fatty acids into lipocytes occurs at a faster rate than the flow out—when triglycerides are created more quickly than they are broken down.

It has been well documented that this process of molecular ingress and egress is taking place within our bodies at all times. The conventional wisdom about obesity may suggest that our fat stores grow only when we consume more calories than we really need and shrink only when we consume fewer calories than our bodies demand. But that isn't the case. In reality, fatty acids are constantly flowing into and out of our fat cells. And whether we get fatter or leaner over any period is simply a function of the relative rates at which these flows occur.

As to be expected, our bodies regulate these rates with astounding precision. The regulation occurs primarily through the operation of hormones and enzymes, substances that operate on both a local and a body-wide basis to influence where, when, and how animals fatten. And, according to Gary Taubes, it is this intricate hormonal dance, *and not simple caloric imbalance*, that fundamentally determines whether the amount of fat inside our fat cells is increasing or decreasing at any given time.

Were it not for decades of public health authorities telling us that getting fat is about consuming more calories than we expend—shifting the blame to individuals and saying that getting fat is all about being lazy and overeating—this wouldn't sound remotely counterintuitive. After all, it is widely recognized that hormonal regulation is the primary driver of most other forms of tissue growth. Human growth hormone fuels the furious growth rates we see in children and adolescents. Anabolic steroids trigger growth in skeletal muscles. Why should adipose tissue grow any differently?

Well, if it didn't, it would sure go a long way toward explaining some otherwise-curious fat-related phenomena. For instance, it would explain why males and females, with their different hormonal profiles, tend to fatten so differently: males tend to fatten around the belly while females tend to fatten in the hips and buttocks. It would explain why skinny girls transform (read: fatten) into shapely women during the prolonged period of elevated sex hormones that occurs during puberty. It would explain why obesity runs in families, why twins tend to fatten in similar places, even though, presumably, they aren't adhering to precisely the same diet and exercise schedules. It would explain why hibernating animals fatten seasonally and why they gain and lose fat on schedule, regardless of whether they actually hibernate and regardless of what their diets look like. It would explain why post-menopausal women and neutered male dogs both tend to fatten particularly easily. It would explain why different breeds of dogs (as well as variants of other species) tend to partition incoming calories differently from each other—why, if you overfeed a Chihuahua, it won't grow as tall as a Great Dane, it'll just get fat.

As all these examples make abundantly clear, the truth, it seems, is that hormones *do* play a central role in directing where fat is to be stored within a body and how much of it there should be, just as they do with every other kind of bodily tissue. The way that they do so isn't particularly complicated or controversial, at least not at a conceptual level. Certain hormones and enzymes simply cause fat cells to suck up fatty acids more readily than they otherwise would or they slow down the rate at which triglycerides are converted back into membrane-permeating free fatty acids. It's not necessary to bore you with all the endocrinological details about how this works in the case of each and every one of the substances that influence adiposity; a single example gives a good idea of how the process works.

Consider the case of the sex hormones estrogen and testosterone. One of the many effects that these hormones have on the human body is a tendency to inhibit the expression of an enzyme called lipoprotein lipase (LPL) by certain fat cells. LPL plays an important role in the process by which animals fatten. In Gary Taubes's words, it "sticks out" of different types of cells (muscle cells as well as fat cells) and coaxes lipids into those cells in part by breaking down circulating triglycerides into membrane-permeating free fatty acids. Both estrogen and testosterone have been shown to suppress LPL expression by some fat cells, so these hormones serve to decrease the rate at which those cells take up free fatty acids, thus working to keep the fat cells relatively small and the bodies in which they reside relatively lean.

As we all know, men and women tend to fatten rather differently. Women, at least pre-menopausal ones, tend to get fat primarily in the thighs and buttocks (develop "thunder thighs") and men tend to get fat primarily in the abdomen (grow "beer bellies"). So, if we could look carefully at their adipose tissue we would expect to see men with higher levels of LPL expression in their abdominal fat than in their gluteal fat. In women, we'd expect to see the exact opposite—more LPL expression in gluteal fat than in abdominal fat. And, indeed, this is precisely what experiments conducted over the past few decades have confirmed.

Now, this is just one example of a much wider-ranging phenomenon. None of it is particularly controversial in scientific circles, nor is it particularly counterintuitive. After all, we all know that our genes influence where, when, and how we're likely to get fat.

The next part of Gary Taubes's model of obesity can be tougher to swallow. The long-and-short of it is this: we've confused cause and effect when it comes to understanding why we get fat. In Taubes's words, "[w]e don't get fat because we overeat; we overeat because we're getting fat." When the body begins sucking fatty acids and other nutrients out of the blood stream and stuffing them into fat cells, the number of calories available to be converted into chemical energy in the short run drops. Our bodies sense this change and motivate us to behave in a way that will correct the energy shortage and re-achieve stability (homeostasis), either by consuming more energy or expending less of it. And it's these behavioral changes that produce the caloric imbalance that must attend any growth in adipose tissue according to the first law of thermodynamics, not laziness or lack of dietary discipline, as the calories-in, calories-out model and its champions would have us believe.

If, like many, you find this notion so revolutionary as to seem illogical, Taubes would ask you to think of the children. The standard calories-in, calories-out model plainly doesn't govern the rapid tissue growth that we see in children and adolescents. Everyone knows that young children grow at a prodigious pace. On average, they quadruple in size during their first 36 months of life, then do it again over the next 15 years or so. But no one seriously believes that this growth is a function of how much food a child eats or how much exercise she gets. We all know that her genes (her hormones), and not her environment (calories-in, calories-out), will determine how big she ultimately becomes. Do growing boys eat a lot? Absolutely. But they're not growing because they're eating a lot, *they're eating a lot because they're growing.* Stuffing them with calories beyond what their appetites dictate won't make them grow any taller. And the same holds true on the calories-out side of the equation. Are growing boys lazy? Of course they are. But they're not growing because they're lazy, *they're lazy because they're growing.* Keeping them off the soccer field and preventing them from running around with their friends won't make them grow any taller.

The same concept applies to physiological outliers, such as extremely tall people and extremely small ones. As we all know, gigantism and dwarfism aren't caused by calorie consumption extremes. They're caused by genetic abnormalities that manifest as abnormal hormone levels. And, fundamentally, it's these hormone abnormalities, not simple caloric imbalances, that cause tall people to grow tall and short ones to stay short. Do the big ones eat more than the small ones? Of course they do, but that's not why they've become big.

Still not totally convinced? Then consider perhaps the most persuasive line of evidence of all on this point, the one involving the study of laboratory rodents. A pair of experiments, discussed by Taubes in *Why We Get Fat*, are particularly enlightening. They were conducted in the early 1970s by a young professor named George Wade at the University of Massachusetts. Wade, an endocrinologist, was studying how animals regulate their fat supplies, particularly females when they become pregnant. As part of his research, he surgically removed the ovaries from a group of rats, causing their circulating estrogen levels to plummet. He then divided the subjects into two groups. The first was given free access to food and could eat as much as their little rat hearts desired. After their ovaries were removed, the animals became voracious over-eaters. They gobbled up much more food than they had ever eaten prior to their surgeries. And, in news that will surprise no one, they became obese. This makes perfect sense. Were we merely to observe this first set of subjects in a vacuum, we might simply conclude that removing a rat's ovaries causes it to overeat. This first group might be seen as a perfect example of calories-in, calories-out. After all, the rats overate and they became obese, just as the conventional wisdom on obesity would predict.

But what of the second group? They weren't given free access to food. Instead, they were restricted to exactly the same number of calories as they had been consuming prior to having their ovaries removed. In fact, everything about their environment remained precisely as it was prior to surgery. No added exercise equipment, no added food, *nothing different whatsoever*. And what happened to the second group? If you believe in the standard calories-in, calories-out model then your answer, without hesitation, should be that the animals stayed as they were. After all, they couldn't eat more than they had eaten prior to surgery and they had no new incentives or disincentives when it came to exercise.

Only that's not what happened. What happened to Wade's second group of rats is *they still got just as fat, just as quickly as the free-feeding group did.* They still became obese.

The second group of rats arrived at the same physiological destination as their counterparts in the first group but they followed a completely different route to get there. Since they couldn't overeat, the members of the second group instead became almost completely sedentary after their surgeries. Their activity levels plummeted. Wade didn't provide the second group with external reasons not to exercise and he didn't impose any kind of sedentary lifestyle upon them. Unlike the first group, he just didn't give them access to a huge abundance of food. They couldn't overeat so they became lazy, all on their own. And, as a result, they became just as fat as the overeaters.

So what was going on? The short answer is that hormones were regulating the rats' body fat levels. As we saw earlier, estrogen suppresses LPL expression in fat tissue (thus ensuring that fat cells don't suck up too many free fatty acids). When Wade removed his rats' ovaries their estrogen levels plummeted, and this allowed LPL to be expressed much more readily by their fat cells. All this new LPL expression caused those fat cells to suck up lipids, stuffing the fat cells with fat and causing the rats to become clinically obese in just a short period of time. And as their blood lipid levels plummeted—which happened since their fat cells were now sucking up all the available fatty acids—the rats frantically sought to replace all the vanishing metabolic fuel. The first group made up for the shortfall by overeating. The second group, faced with the same shortfall and unable to overeat, had no choice but to become sedentary. But in all cases, it was the hormonal imbalance that *caused* them to become fat; changes to their calories-in and calories-out were just *effects*.

Wade went on to spend the better part of his career probing the relationship between hormones and adiposity. Throughout most of his work, his subjects have been laboratory rodents. He has castrated male rats and shown that lower testosterone levels cause them to fatten by depressing the rate at which stored triglycerides are converted back into membrane-permeating free fatty acids in their fat cells. He has shown that mating behavior by female rats is suppressed when hormonal manipulation causes their fat tissues to suck up vast quantities of the circulating metabolic fuel that would otherwise be used to power reproduction. He has even sought to identify the neurological pathways by which the unavailability of metabolic fuel that occurs during periods of rapid fattening actually induce behavioral changes such as overeating, diminished physical activity, and modified reproductive behavior. Ultimately, Wade's body of work casts serious doubt on the traditional calories-in, calories-out model of adiposity. As Wade himself has put it, "[c]hanges in food intake are neither necessary nor sufficient to cause some of the body weight changes induced by ... hormones."

Other researchers have drawn the same conclusion from different rodent experiments. Stephen Ranson, director, in the 1930s, of the Institute of Neurology at Northwestern University, and his then-graduate student Albert Hetherington demonstrated that lesions in a brain region called the ventromedial hypothalamus (VMH) cause rats to become obese, regardless of whether they eat voraciously or not. If they are given free access to food, they overeat and get fat. If they are denied food, they become physically inactive and get fat. What's at work, according to Ranson and Hetherington, is a disruption of the intricate hormonal regulation of the rats' fat metabolism, one induced by lesions on their hypothalami. (The VMH is one of the most hormonally active regions in the brain, and experimental manipulation of the hypothalamus has been used to induce sudden and extreme obesity in rats, mice, monkeys, chicken, dogs, and cats; hypothalamic tumors have also been shown to cause morbid obesity in human beings, weight gain that leading experts have described as "not responsive to diet and exercise.")

A similar phenomenon has been observed in hibernating rodents. Like many other species, ground squirrels spend the lean winter months in a state of deep hibernation. And, despite the relatively modest metabolic demands that their bodies make during these prolonged periods of inactivity, they must always begin hibernation with substantial reserves of metabolic fuel on-hand (after all, they won't be consuming a single calorie for months). To ensure that they always begin hibernation with adequately stocked fat reserves, ground squirrels have evolved a nifty adaptation: like clockwork, they always get really, really fat in the months leading up to their hibernating periods.

But that isn't the most interesting thing. What's *really* interesting is how they manage to do it. Just like a rat with her ovaries removed or with lesions on her VMH, pre-hibernation ground squirrels will get fat *regardless of how much food is available to them*. In fact, as Nicholas Mrosovsky, professor emeritus of ecology and evolutionary biology at the University of Toronto, has observed, even when food is plentiful, squirrels will almost always cut back on their food intake immediately prior to hibernation, but they will continue to get fat at the same rate even as food intake declines. As Mrosovsky has written, "the importance of this way of getting fat [overeating] should not be overstressed since food intake slackens well before hibernators reach their peak weights."

So what's the reason that ground squirrels get fat at the same time every year, like clockwork, no matter how much food they are consuming? The prevailing theory, articulated by Mrosovsky and others, is that hypothalamic hormones are at the root of the phenomenon. In the period leading up to hibernation, ground squirrels and other hibernating rodents have been shown to display abnormally high levels of numerous hypothalamus-mediated hormones. And just like with George Wade's ovariectomized rats, it is the elevated hormone levels that cause their fat cells to get fatter by sucking up large amounts of circulating metabolic fuel. Whether they make up the resulting metabolic shortfall (thus re-achieving homeostasis) by eating more, by moving less, or by some other method is entirely secondary to the matter.

***

So what does all this mean for your dog? If obesity is truly the result of hormonal irregularities, and not just caloric imbalance, what can everyday dog owners do about it? A little living room hypothalamus surgery, perhaps? Hardly. In fact, when it comes to understanding why Gary Taubes's theory of obesity says we should all expect modern-day domestic dogs to be fat at epidemic levels, there is just one hormone whose effects we need to understand. And, thankfully, it's one that we can readily manipulate without surgery or any kind of hocus-pocus whatsoever.

***

If you accept, either in whole or in part, the notion that obesity is a product of hormonal irregularities and not simple calorie miscalculations, then there is one hormone whose role in your dog's body you must understand particularly well. That hormone is insulin.

Insulin is what biologists call an anabolic hormone. This means that it works to accelerate the rate at which nutrients are put together to make new tissues within a body. It literally causes tissue growth. Most importantly for our present purposes, insulin increases the rate at which fat cells get fat and increases the likelihood that they will stay fat. For these reasons, and because its effects are so powerful, insulin plays a critical role in determining whether anyone, human or canine, gets fat. As Gary Taubes and others—including Nobel laureates—have written, insulin is the "principal regulator of fat metabolism" in the body.

Insulin's role in the body actually extends well beyond regulating fat mass. Its broader function is to clear circulating glucose from the bloodstream. Glucose is the most important carbohydrate molecule in the body, for a simple reason: just about all forms of ingested dietary carbohydrates have been broken down into glucose by the time they enter the blood stream. As we all know, carbohydrates come in lots of different varieties. Some are "complex," meaning that they are composed of long chains of molecules that usually require a good deal of digestive effort to be broken down into glucose. Others are "simple," meaning they can be converted to glucose quickly and easily. But, ultimately, almost all dietary carbohydrates get broken down into glucose during digestion. When they exit the digestive tract and enter the bloodstream, they do so as glucose.

This isn't an entirely good thing. Because glucose can be toxic. If too much of it stays in the bloodstream for too long (a condition called hyperglycemia), it will cause us to become sick and die. Chronic, relatively mild hyperglycemia can cause lasting, irreversible damage to internal organs. Acute hyperglycemia (a diabetic coma) is a serious medical emergency with the capacity to kill. In other words, any time we eat a non-negligible amount of dietary carbohydrates, we are, in a way, introducing poison into our bodies.

Fortunately, there is an antidote: insulin. When blood sugar levels begin to rise, a specialized set of cells in the pancreas called beta cells immediately begin to secrete insulin. The insulin then floods the bloodstream, bringing about all manner of biochemical reactions, all of which serve to decrease blood sugar levels. Most notably, insulin turns on biochemical mechanisms that suck glucose directly into fat cells and muscle cells, places where the glucose can be stored in stable forms. At the same time, insulin cues muscle cells to begin burning glucose for energy, rather than circulating free fatty acids. To further ensure that glucose (and not fatty acids) are used as metabolic fuel, insulin induces enzymatic changes that prevent fat cells from releasing stored fatty acids back out into the blood stream. And to ensure that there's somewhere to put all the glucose, insulin even works to create new fat cells. (At least this is how it's all *supposed* to work. People with diabetes either lack the ability to produce insulin naturally or their bodies have become so desensitized to insulin's effects that they can't manage blood sugar effectively. Either way, when they consume carbohydrates, these changes don't happen. And, consequently, their blood sugar levels just stay dangerously high until they introduce supplemental insulin into their bodies.)

Insulin's complex, multipronged attack on blood sugar is a wondrous thing to consider, a prime example of the ingenuity inherent in all evolved bodily systems. Or it would be if each and every one of these biochemical effects—the preferential burning of glucose over fatty acids, the increased storage of glucose in fat cells, the creation of new fat cells, and the retention of fatty acids within fat cells—not only served to clear glucose from the blood stream but also served to make us fat.

Insulin is not unique in this regard. As George Wade and his rats have already shown us, many different hormones influence the rate at which animals fatten. But insulin's effects are particularly profound—they are so powerful, in fact, that they dwarf the collective impact of all the others—and they are directly tied to diet. What this means, according to Gary Taubes and his intellectual progeny, is that when it comes to understanding the hormones that make both human beings and dogs become fat, insulin is the one that really matters. And if you want to keep your dog lean, *the first thing you need to think about is how to keep her circulating insulin levels low.* Not how to reduce her total caloric intake, not how to increase the amount of exercise she gets, not how to "keep her metabolism high"—just how to keep insulin out of her blood stream.

So how do you do that? The answer is remarkably simple: just keep carbohydrates out of her diet.

THE CASE AGAINST CARBS

IF WE'RE BEING literal, Gary Taubes's theory of obesity doesn't say that carbohydrates make dogs fat. It says that insulin does. Insulin causes fat cells to suck up circulating lipids and glucose (read: get fat). And it causes those fat cells to hold onto fatty acids so that they can't be used for energy (read: stay fat). To avoid these consequences, we must keep their circulating insulin levels as low as possible. It's as simple as that.

How to do this is no great mystery. Remember that insulin's primary job in your dog's body is to dispose of glucose. It performs this job in a variety of ways, almost all of which contribute to making her fat cells get fatter. So if we want to reduce insulin, we just need to get rid of the glucose that triggers its secretion. We need to get blood sugar levels as low as healthfully possible and then keep them that way. And by far the best way to do this is also one of the most simple: just minimize carbohydrate intake.

Not all foods containing carbohydrates stimulate insulin secretion equally. Different types of carbohydrates affect blood sugar levels differently (although they all cause it to rise), with some leading to an immediate blood sugar "spike" and others having a slower and subtler impact. The worst offenders are the ones that are most easily converted into pure glucose, because they cause massive quantities of glucose to be injected into the bloodstream all at once. In other words, the more quickly and easily a carbohydrate molecule can be digested, the more readily it will contribute to making your dog fat.

In general terms, this means that the carbohydrates we most want to avoid fall into two primary groups: sweets and starches. Other kinds of carbohydrates tend to affect blood sugar levels less dramatically because they take longer to digest. The carbohydrates in green, leafy vegetables, for instance, are bound together with indigestible fiber molecules. It takes a long time and a lot of digestive work to separate the carbohydrate from the fiber. So when the glucose from a cup of spinach eventually hits the blood stream, it does so as a trickle, not a torrent.

This is the reasoning behind the conventional nutrition wisdom that counsels us to choose "complex" carbohydrates over "simple" ones. In this context, complex just means that the carbohydrate molecule is composed of long, repeating chains of glucose, as opposed to simple carbs, which are just one-unit or two-unit molecules. The simple sugar molecule sucrose ("table sugar"), for example, is made up of just one glucose molecule and one fructose molecule; the complex carbohydrate molecule amylose (a starch commonly found in cereal grains) is made up of a linear chain of hundreds of glucose molecules. Because, the thinking goes, it takes longer to break down a chain of many glucose molecules than a chain of relatively few glucose molecules, complex carbs are better carbs.

But this logic is flawed. Some complex carbs actually increase blood sugar levels more dramatically than simpler ones. The starchy carbohydrate amylopectin A (found in wheat), for example, is quite complex, but it is also uniquely digestible. As a result, wheat bread causes violent blood sugar spikes, increasing blood sugar levels even more enthusiastically than pure table sugar.

The reason we know any of this is the same reason that it's not necessary to limit ourselves to broad conceptual categories like "simple" and "complex" when thinking about the fattening tendencies of specific carbohydrates. We can actually do better than broad, qualitative descriptions—we can measure the direct impact of specific foods on blood sugar. And this goes a long way toward telling us the impact of specific foods on insulin levels.

One well-known way to measure the impact of foods on blood sugar is with a tool called the glycemic index (GI). The GI scale was invented by researchers from the University of Toronto and was first published in 1981. It assigns a number, typically between 0 and 100, to specific foods, and the number indicates that food's likely impact on a human being's blood sugar. The higher blood sugar levels are likely to get in the 90-120 minutes after consuming a specific food, the higher the food's GI rating, with 50 grams of pure glucose typically receiving a rating of 100. The original GI study delivered some surprising findings: the GI of whole wheat bread (72) was actually higher than the rating for table sugar (59) or a Mars bar (68), and far higher than the rating for a Snickers bar (41). Rice, sweet corn, potatoes, and millet all scored very high too (72, 59, 70, and 71, respectively).

In the 30 years or so since 1981 all manner of foods have been run through the GI analysis. A quick visit to the website www.glycemicindex.com will tell you the GI score for just about every kind of "people food" under the sun. But, when thinking about what the carbohydrate-insulin model of adiposity has to say about garden-variety dog foods, there are really just a few points to remember. The first is that starchy cereal grains and sweets are by far the worst GI offenders. These foods cause blood sugar levels to skyrocket. The second is that meats, fish, and eggs register scores of around zero—in fact, it's difficult to get a subject to eat enough of them to deliver the 50 grams of carbohydrate needed to even calculate a GI score. And the same goes for most colorful vegetables, as their carbohydrate content is usually bound up with indigestible fiber and diluted with a good deal of water. The GI of these foods is so low as to not matter. Last but not least, legumes such as chickpeas (GI score of 10), red lentils (28), and kidney beans (24) deliver typical carbohydrate heft and satisfaction while tallying significantly lower GI scores than corn, rice, wheat, and the other common cereal grains.

It should be noted that GI scores are calculated based upon the impact of specific foods on *human* blood sugar levels, not canine ones. And, as you would expect, dogs and people don't metabolize energy in precisely the same way. But it's not exactly a matter of apples and oranges either. As a team of French researchers wrote in the *Journal of Nutrition* in 1994, "the same factors account for postprandial glycemic and insulinemic responses in both human beings and dogs." In other words, the same things that tend to ramp up insulin production in humans tend to ramp up insulin production in dogs. And, as the same team wrote just a few years later, just like in humans, "the amount of starch consumed is *the* major determinant of the glucose response of adult healthy dogs." Or, as others summarized the state of the evidence as recently as 2014, "[i]t is accepted that carbohydrates, primarily starches, are the principal nutrients that determine and modify the postprandial glucose and insulin curves in dogs and humans." Just as in their human counterparts, to prevent canine insulin levels from spiking, all we have to do is minimize the intake of starchy carbs and sweets.

While a full-scale canine equivalent of the glycemic index has yet to be constructed, researchers have quantified to a limited degree the impact that specific carbohydrate sources have on canine blood sugar and insulin. And, in light of what we know about the impact of starches and sweets on human blood sugar, the results are about what you'd expect. For one, cereal grains like corn and rice have been demonstrated to produce violent spikes in post-meal canine blood sugar and insulin levels, while legumes such as lentils have somewhat slower and more muted effects. High-fiber diets have also been shown to induce less pronounced blood sugar spikes, though not to drastically lower overall blood sugar levels. But the most glaring finding that emerges from the literature on canine metabolism is the same one that comes out of studies conducted on human subjects: drastically reducing carbohydrate intake, or eliminating carbs altogether, brings blood sugar and insulin levels crashing back down to earth.

***

The carbohydrate-insulin model of adiposity may not be a part of the conventional nutrition wisdom just yet, in either the human domain or the canine one. But the biochemistry behind it (insulin causes fat cells to get fatter, consumption of starches and sweets leads to elevated insulin levels) is not controversial. It was all worked out by no later than the middle of the twentieth century. Indeed, by 1965, Rosalyn Yalow and her colleague Solomon Berson had labeled insulin the "principal regulator of fat metabolism" and explained that "the release of fatty acids from fat cells requires *only* the negative stimulus of insulin deficiency." Yalow would later receive a Nobel prize for this work; Berson surely would have shared the honor had he not died five years earlier.

Other food-focused scientific bigwigs were decrying the fattening tendencies of carbohydrates long before 1965. They may not have known, way down at a biochemical level, exactly *why* carbohydrates make people fat, but they certainly saw that they *do*. Here's how French polymath and incurable foodie Jean Anthelme Brillat-Savarin put it way back in 1825:

> An anti-fat diet is based on the commonest and most active cause of obesity, since, as it has already been clearly shown, it is only because of grains and starches that fatty congestion can occur, as much in man as in the animals.... It can be deduced, as an exact consequence, that a more or less rigid abstinence from everything that is starchy or floury will lead to the lessening of weight.

Here's how William Banting described the matter in his 1864 *Letter on Corpulence*, essentially the first best-selling diet and weight-loss book ever written:

> Bread, butter, milk, sugar, beer, and potatoes … contain starch and saccharine matter, tending to create fat, and should be avoided altogether.

And here's Dr. Benjamin Spock in his global sensation *Baby and Child Care*:

> The amount of plain, starchy foods (cereals, breads, potatoes) taken is what determines, in the case of most people, how much [fat] they gain or lose.

The idea that we can lose weight and keep it off by eating anything we want, *and as much of it as we want*, so long as we avoid fattening carbohydrates, is not new or alien to the modern world of commercial diet fads either. Weight-loss guru Dr. Robert Atkins popularized the strategy back in the 1970s and garnered legions of followers. More recently, as we've already seen, minimizing high-GI carbohydrates while eating lots of fatty meats, fish, and vegetables, is a core tenet of the immensely popular Paleo diet. The elimination of high-glycemic carbohydrates is also a core tenet of the dietary philosophies embodied in books such as Dr. William Davis's *Wheat Belly*, Timothy Ferriss's *The Four Hour Body*, and Arthur Agatston's *South Beach Diet*, all of which—no matter what you think about the seemingly outlandish claims made by their authors—have become blockbuster international bestsellers.

***

And yet, bizarrely, no one who's anyone in the world of veterinary science seems to be paying attention to any of this. The textbooks, research papers, and other major works addressing the problem of canine obesity haven't latched onto the carbohydrate-insulin model at all, not even as an alternative hypothesis. They all just grab the calories-in, calories-out baton and run with it. In the most recent edition of Ettinger and Feldman's *Textbook of Veterinary Internal Medicine* (a leading veterinary text), the authors state that "[t]he cause of obesity as a primary disorder is simply that an animal is receiving more calories than it is expending, and body fat mass increases." Throughout the textbook's chapter on obesity, not a word is devoted to the biochemical nuts and bolts of adiposity, the ones that are not remotely controversial and that every reader of this book now understands. In a recent "Literature Review" on "Canine, Feline, and Human Overweight and Obesity" published by Banfield Pet Hospital, the "clinical bottom line" that emerges is similar: "The root cause of overweight and obesity is an imbalance between dietary intake and energy utilization, leading to a state of positive energy balance and fat accumulation." Terms like insulin, blood sugar, triglycerides, and free fatty acids are nowhere to be found.

You'd think that vets with an interest in obesity might be paying better attention. Because in addition to the variety of clear and convincing arguments that Taubes and others have used to show that the existing nutritional dogma is flawed and that carbs play an outsized role in making many animals fat—from the biochemical to the historical and from the experiential to the theoretical—the biggest and best studies of ultra-low carbohydrate diets consistently have come down in favor of Taubes and his supporters. Long-term, randomized, large-scale clinical trials comparing *ad libitum* (a ten-dollar term for "as much as you want") ultra-low carbohydrate diets against other popular weight-loss strategies have recently been conducted. And, for anyone clinging to the notion that calorie management and "balanced," low-fat diets are the ways to weight loss and better health, these studies make for some very disheartening reading.

***

Probably the best demonstration of the efficacy of low-carb diets comes out of Stanford University and was published in *The Journal of the American Medical Association* in 2007. It was cleverly nicknamed the "A TO Z Weight Loss Study" because it was designed to compare the effectiveness of four different weight-loss diets: (A) The Atkins diet (very low carbohydrate intake but as much fat and protein as desired, with no exercise and no calorie counting); (T) a Traditional weight-loss diet (at least half of all calories from carbohydrates, but less than 30% of calories from fat, with overall calories restricted and regular exercise encouraged); (O) the Ornish diet, named for weight-loss guru Dean Ornish (fewer than 10% of all calories from fat, an abundance of carbohydrates, and both regular exercise and meditation encouraged); and (Z) the Zone diet (30% of calories from fat, 30% from protein, and 40% from carbohydrates, with overall calories restricted).

Despite the fact that the low-carbohydrate Atkins protocol didn't involve any type of exercise or calorie restriction whatsoever, it still thrashed the other strategies, even those that required *both* exercise and calorie-counting. After a year of low-carbohydrate eating, subjects on the Atkins diet had lost nearly *twice* as much weight as those on any of the other plans (10.3 pounds versus 5.7 pounds, 4.9 pounds, and 3.5 pounds, respectively). They also wound up with markedly better blood markers (including cholesterol levels, diastolic blood pressure, and circulating triglycerides) than the others. Summarizing their findings, the study's authors wrote that subjects "assigned to follow the Atkins diet, which had the lowest carbohydrate intake, lost more weight and experienced more favorable overall metabolic effects at 12 months than [all other subjects]." The lead researcher on the project, an avowed skeptic of low-carbohydrate diets and a longtime vegetarian, later described the findings as "a bitter pill to swallow."

Perhaps an even more compelling piece of evidence was published in late 2014, this time in the prestigious *Annals of Internal Medicine*. This one came out of Tulane University and was funded by the National Institutes of Health. It was even simpler than A TO Z: a group of 150 people from all walks of life were randomly assigned to one of two groups, a low-carbohydrate group (instructed to eat fewer than 40 grams of carbs per day) or a low-fat group (instructed to make sure that less than 30% of their daily calories came from dietary fat). Neither group was instructed to exercise or count calories, the researchers just gave them regular counseling about their new diets and watched them for 12 months.

After a year the results came back. They showed nothing less than a comprehensive victory for the low-carb approach. The members of the low-carbohydrate group had lost, on average, about *eight pounds more* than the members of the low-fat group. The low-carb eaters—who, remember, weren't selected for pre-existing obesity or heart disease or diabetes—had also lost considerably more body fat, improved their cholesterol levels to a greater degree, and lowered their triglyceride levels more than the ones on the low-fat diets too. As the study's authors concluded, "[t]he low-carbohydrate diet was more effective for weight loss and cardiovascular risk factor reduction than the low-fat diet."

The conclusion touches on another important point: the long-standing nutritional dogma which says that *ad libitum* low-carbohydrate diets don't just fail as weight loss tools but can actually *cause* health problems has recently been cast into doubt as well. The most well-known aspect of the dogma—that eating lots of saturated fat causes cardiovascular disease—has suffered a particularly gory demise. Beyond the results of the two aforementioned trials, a recent meta-analysis published in the *Annals of Internal Medicine* also concluded, to the surprise of many in the nutritional community, that "current evidence does not clearly support cardiovascular guidelines that encourage ... low consumption of total saturated fats." The study prompted a *Time* magazine cover story (the delicious cover simply read "Eat Butter") and some very public backtracking by TV health personality Dr. Mehmet Oz, a long-time critic of high-fat diets.

It should be noted that these studies aren't obscure, outlying pieces of evidence. They were conducted by doctors at some of the country's top medical schools and published in two of the most well-regarded medical publications on the planet. The Stanford A TO Z study is also the single most-read study in *JAMA*'s long and storied history. And the results of the recent meta-analysis wound up on the cover of *Time* magazine.

And many nutrition experts have already seen enough. The world's leading obesity researchers are increasingly aligning themselves alongside Taubes and against calories-in, calories-out. Dr. David Ludwig, professor of nutrition at the Harvard T.H. Chan School of Public Health, Director of the New Balance Foundation Obesity Prevention Center at Boston Children's Hospital, and a longtime proponent of the carbohydrate-insulin model of adiposity, recently published a diet book, *Always Hungry?*, in which he summarizes the pathophysiology of obesity as follows: "[o]vereating doesn't make us fat. The process of becoming fat makes us overeat." Thus, just like Taubes, Ludwig advises his overweight readers to "forget calories," "focus on the fat cell," and avoid insulinemic carbohydrates. His book has drawn praise from the country's leading nutritional luminaries, including holistic health guru Dr. Andrew Weil, Harvard nutritionist Walter Willett, renowned obesity expert Kelly Brownell, and Mark Hyman, Director of the Cleveland Clinic Center for Functional Medicine.

Dr. Timothy Noakes, one of the world's foremost exercise physiologists, has also joined the revolution, and in particularly dramatic fashion. Noakes, an avid ultra-marathoner, has long counseled runners to use carbohydrates to fuel their long-distance efforts. (His 1985 book *Lore of Running*—considered a distance runner's bible—is largely responsible for popularizing the pre-race "carbo-load.") But since reading Gary Taubes's work Noakes has changed his tune. He has publicly disclaimed his earlier nutritional recommendations and become a fierce advocate of low-carbohydrate diets, even for ultra-distance endurance athletes.

So, for the moment, the bottom line on the science of obesity seems to be this: there are some very diverse and very robust lines of scientific evidence suggesting that starchy and sugary carbs are the primary determinants of whether anyone, human or canine, becomes fat. That evidence has been persuasive enough to initiate what appears to be a cultural sea change (at least in the domain of human nutrition) and to induce some credible and well-informed people to stake some pretty public bets on the matter. According to them, to avoid becoming obese and to keep our hearts as healthy as possible, we don't need to eat less fat, or exercise more, or be more diligent about counting calories. We simply need to cut out the carbs.

WOLVES, DOGS, AND CARBS

FOR A DOG OWNER trying to decide whether to throw his pup on the carbohydrate-insulin bandwagon, the most important line of evidence is one that Gary Taubes hasn't written much about. Over the past 15 years, veterinary researchers have on several occasions compared the fat-fighting efficacy of low-carbohydrate diets against "conventional" diets, using small animals as subjects. Their experiments were conducted both on cats and on dogs. And what did they show? Well, precisely what Gary Taubes would predict.

First, in 2002, a group of veterinary researchers from institutions across Europe conducted an experiment on a group of obese Beagles. They divided the dogs into two groups and fed each a different dietary regimen. One group got a very-low-carbohydrate food (47.5% protein, 5.3% starch), the other got a conventional weight-loss diet (23.8% protein, 23.9% starch). They fed the animals whatever amount of food it took to induce weight-loss at a rate of about 2% per week, adjusting the amount as necessary to ensure a steady rate of weight loss. Once all the dogs had reached their goal weights, the team looked at how they go there.

Their data (published in the *Journal of Nutrition*) showed that while both groups had lost about the same amount of weight, there were important differences in how they lost it. First, the low-carbohydrate group consumed *more* calories than the conventional-diet group during the weight-loss period—on average, 76.2% of calculated maintenance requirements versus 68.0% of calculated maintenance requirements in the conventional-diet group. Nevertheless, and although both groups lost roughly the same amount of body weight, the low-carbohydrate group lost considerably more fat. More specifically, the low-carb dogs lost, on average, about 13% more adipose tissue than those on the conventional diet. In short, the low-carbohydrate diet induced fat loss more effectively than the conventional one, even though the low-carb dogs ate more calories than those on the conventional diet.

A study published in the *International Journal of Applied Research in Veterinary Medicine* documented similar results a few years later. This time its authors (two veterinarians working for Purina PetCare) conducted their experiment on obese cats rather than obese dogs. They divided the animals into two groups and then gave both extruded, dry diets that were "as similar as possible," in all ways but one: in one diet, protein-rich ingredients were substituted for ground corn. So, for one group, about 32% of calories came from carbohydrate sources. For the other, carbs provided about 44% of the calories. Then, just like in the *Journal of Nutrition* study, caloric intake for each cat was adjusted on a regular basis to ensure steady weight loss until a goal weight was achieved for all subjects.

"Despite feeding each cat based on individual calorie allowances, mean calorie intake during weight loss did not differ between groups," the researchers reported. "Likewise, neither rate of weight loss nor total weight loss differed between diets." In fact, about the only thing that differed between the two groups was that the low-carbohydrate cats lost more body fat and less lean body mass than the "normal" ones. In the authors' own words, "[a] significantly ... greater proportion of weight loss was fat in cats fed the [low-carbohydrate] diet. Likewise [low-carbohydrate] cats lost a smaller proportion of lean body mass." As before, less carbohydrate meant more fat loss *without* additional caloric restriction.

In both of these studies, the authors framed their results as validations of a "high-protein" weight-loss strategy. However, in both cases, they might just as easily have framed them as validations of a "low-carbohydrate" strategy (in both cases, about the only difference between the experimental diets was that some of the carbohydrate was traded for protein). But for some reason they didn't. (Notably, both studies predated the publication of Gary Taubes's *Good Calories, Bad Calories.*) Instead the researchers offered hypotheses about the mechanisms that might be linking protein consumption to fat loss. "Perhaps due to its thermogenic effect," the Purina team speculated, protein "provides a superior satiety effect compared with fats or carbohydrates." But greater satiety could not explain their experimental results, as caloric intake was reported to be identical in both of their groups. The carbohydrate-insulin model of obesity, on the other hand, explains their results perfectly.

In 2004, another group of veterinarians conducted a similar experiment, but this time they did focus their analysis on the carbohydrate side of the equation. "Although there are several studies on the effects of low-carbohydrate diets in humans," they wrote in the *Journal of Nutrition*, "there is relatively little information on the effects of these diets in dogs." Thus spurred to action, the researchers conducted by far the most comprehensive examination in existence of the efficacy of low-carbohydrate diets in dogs.

The researchers divided a group of overweight Beagles into two sets. But their study group—a total of 39 dogs—was considerably larger than those in the two experiments discussed above. As before, one group got a relatively low-carbohydrate, high-protein diet (52% protein, 21% carbohydrate), and the other got a "conventional" diet (28% protein, 44% carbohydrate). The two groups were then subdivided so to test the efficacy of another variable, the addition of conjugated linoleum acid. All dogs were then given 85% of their maintenance energy requirements for 12 weeks.

After three months, the dogs on the conventional, calorie-restricted diet had lost, on average, about 5% of their total body weight. The dogs on the low-carbohydrate diet had lost, on average, more than *twice* as much. And, when the researchers looked more closely at what was driving the weight loss, the difference between the two groups must have been obvious. Members of the control group had lost, on average, about 6% of their body fat. The low-carbohydrate group had lost roughly *six times as much* (more than a third of the fat in their bodies). "This study," the researchers wrote, "found no differences in the calories consumed among the groups, whereas the low-carbohydrate groups still lost significantly more weight and fat mass than the high-carbohydrate groups." If the study's title ("High-Protein Low-Carbohydrate Diets Enhance Weight Loss in Dogs") didn't say it all, then its final line certainly did:

Changing the macronutrient profile of a canine weight-loss diet from a high-carbohydrate level to one primarily based on protein can promote greater weight loss without further reductions in caloric intake. This weight loss is driven primarily from an increased loss of fat mass while maintaining lean muscle mass.

It doesn't get much clearer than that.

***

Now recall what we know about the consumption of carbohydrates by wild wolves. Or, more accurately, the lack thereof. According to Daniel Stahler, Abby Nelson, and the rest of Yellowstone's wolf experts, wolves eat meat and basically nothing else. They eat prodigious quantities of the stuff—a 100-pound wolf needs to consume at least nine pounds every day, just to get by—but that's *all* they eat. So while wild wolves may take in a preposterous number of calories, loads of protein, and copious amounts of saturated fats, they consume close to zero carbohydrates. And precisely zero of the easily digestible, high-GI variety.

That wolves have evolved to eat meat and avoid carbs is clear just from looking at them. After all, if they are going to subside exclusively on wild prey, they're going to need the physiological adaptations that allow them to find it, catch it, kill it, consume it, digest it, and metabolize it. Or, as Darwin himself once put it:

> Let us take the case of the wolf, which preys on various animals, securing some by craft, some by strength, and some by fleetness ... the swiftest and slimmest wolves would have the best chance of surviving and so be preserved or selected.

Let's take a moment and catalogue some of the wolf's predatory adaptations. There are the teeth, which include the large, dagger-like incisors and canines, both of which give wolves the ability to stab and hold large, fleeing prey. But even the behind-the-scenes teeth (the molars and pre-molars) are relatively sharp, and they fit together to form ranges of flesh-tearing mountains and valleys. (In contrast, the molars of omnivorous animals like bears, raccoons, and human beings tend to be broad and flat, suited instead for crushing nuts or grinding up vegetation.) Then there's the skull, where a collection of massive, powerful muscles attach to the jaw, acting as powerful levers and giving wolves the ability to bite viciously and hold tenaciously. There are the four powerful legs and the ability to run as fast as a car, or to trot along at an even pace for hours on end. There are the large, forward-facing ears and the elongated nasal cavity, both of which help wolves to locate far-away prey. And there are the eyes, which are set forward in the skull and produce an effect known as "stereovision," which enables depth perception. While an elk or a bison might prefer the larger visual field and better peripheral vision that come along with having their eyes set far apart from each other on opposite sides of the skull—enabling them to scan a wider landscape for potential predators—forward-facing eyes and precise depth perception give wolves the ability to pounce and bite with precision.

There's even more going on beneath the surface. The innate behavioral tendencies of wolves suggest a psychological hard-wiring that is perfectly adapted for carnivory. They chase fleeing animals. They work together in packs. They chew bones. They bite and they tug. They also have a short gut, because that's all the gut they need to digest meat. The constituent parts of plant matter, notably the cellulose that makes up the walls of many plant cells as well as the energy-rich starch, is difficult for mammals to break down. So much so that herbivores have evolved lengthier guts, complex digestive organs, and enzymatic responses that facilitate plant digestion. Wolves have none of these.

Notice how much of this holds true for domestic dogs too, even the breeds that bear little first-glance resemblance to wolves. They've got the sharp canine teeth, the saw-like molars and pre-molars, the powerful jaws, the tendency to chase, chew, and tug, the short gut, the powerful senses of smell and hearing, and the forward-facing eyes.

However, one of the things that separates wolves from dogs is that, unlike wolves, dogs actually *can* digest starches quite well. Recent studies comparing the genomes of dogs and wolves have revealed that dogs produce more (and, in some cases, much more) of a digestive enzyme called amylase. The primary function of amylase is to break starch molecules down into glucose prior to absorption into the bloodstream. (You can see it in action yourself if you keep a piece of bread in your mouth for a minute or so—the amylase in your saliva will start to break the starch molecules down into glucose and make the bread taste sweet.) Because dogs produce amylase more readily than wolves, they can digest starches and effectively draw caloric nutrition from plant matter.

But while dogs are *able* to digest starchy carbs pretty well, that doesn't mean that they can do so without becoming fat, nor that they in any way *need* them in their diets. After all, human beings can digest starchy carbs pretty well too. Indeed, at the moment, carbohydrate is the most commonly consumed nutritional substrate on the planet. But, as Gary Taubes and others have shown, that doesn't mean that humans thrive on them. And they could just as well have made the same point about dogs. Dogs may have evolved the ability to digest starches, but evolution is concerned only with helping animals reach and make good use of their reproductive years, not with ensuring that they live long and healthy lives thereafter.

And unlike proteins and fats, dogs certainly don't need to ingest carbohydrates. If the fact that their lupine ancestors seem to get along just fine without any carbs doesn't bring you around to this conclusion, then just crack open your nearest copy of the *Nutrient Requirements of Cats and Dogs*, a research compilation published by the National Research Council of the National Academies and a text that is so comprehensive as to be the only reference that matters on the topic of canine nutrition. According to the research summarized by the National Research Council, there are dozens of nutrients that dogs must ingest on a regular basis in order to maintain optimal health. They include protein, a host of individual amino acids (the "building blocks of protein"), several essential fatty acids, a dozen essential minerals, and many more essential vitamins.

But they do not include carbohydrates. Not sugars, not starches, not simple carbs, not complex carbs, not *any* of them. This holds true for all life stages (the NRC issues nutrient recommendations and requirements for three life stages: growing puppies, adult dogs, and gestating and lactating bitches), and it doesn't matter what kind of exercise or other activities a dog tends to perform. There may be "essential" proteins and "essential" fats, but according to the NRC, there's no such thing as an "essential" carbohydrate.

***

If you talk to enough dog-lovers about all this, there are a couple of intelligent counterpoints that you are likely to hear. One is that dogs need carbohydrates because they need glucose to power their brain function. Experiments conducted both on humans and on dogs have shown us that when it comes to big-brained mammals, the brain's preferred source of metabolic fuel is glucose. Thus, as the National Research Council wrote in the most recent edition of *The Nutrient Requirements of Cats and Dogs*, "[a]s in humans, there is probably an obligatory requirement for glucose in organs such as the brain of the dog."

But the fact that dogs probably need a limited amount of glucose for brain function doesn't mean that they actually need to *consume* glucose. Much like human beings, dogs do an admirable job of synthesizing the limited amount of glucose they truly need all on their own, from non-carbohydrate sources. Within your dog's body, other common nutritional substrates, including glycerol and amino acids, are continuously being converted to glucose via a biochemical process known as gluconeogenesis. Gluconeogenesis is an ancient and fundamental process that can be seen in action throughout the natural world; it has been documented in plants, animals, fungi, and even bacteria. In mammals like dogs and humans, it primarily takes place in the liver. And, as we would expect, remembering the potentially toxic qualities of glucose, when blood sugar levels become elevated (such as after a carbohydrate-laden meal), gluconeogenesis tends to shut down, maximizing the rate at which blood glucose is utilized. But otherwise the process runs more or less all the time, churning out a steady supply of glucose that is more than sufficient to keep the canine brain humming along at its full—though often endearingly limited—capacity.

We know this because the metabolic functioning of dogs on carbohydrate-free diets has been well studied. In a 1976 experiment, a group of young Beagles were fed carbohydrate-free diets for eight months and then compared against littermates who were fed high-carbohydrate diets. The fasting glucose utilization rates of the carbohydrate-free dogs never dropped below those of the dogs fed carbohydrate-rich diets. Even after eight months without dietary carbs, the dogs still found a way to both synthesize and utilize some 60 to 80 grams of glucose per day, all on their own. Other studies have looked at the effect of dietary composition on the metabolic performance of dogs during exercise. And while they've found that dogs fed high-carbohydrate diets tend to use more glucose than fat to fuel their activities—again, precisely as we'd expect, knowing that glucose must be removed from the bloodstream quickly—they've found no drop-off in performance when dogs are fed zero-carbohydrate diets. Dogs fed a low-carb diet just burn fat and gluconeogenesis-synthesized glucose instead of glucose that has been derived from dietary carbs.

This gets us to a second counterpoint that is sometimes raised by folks who are hesitant to take away their dogs' carbs—active dogs needs carbs "for energy." We'll explore the basis for this widespread notion in the next two chapters. But there are at least three distinct lines of evidence that strongly suggest that it is misguided.

First, the scientists in the aforementioned studies have looked closely at the metabolic performance of exercising dogs fed a variety of diets, including zero-carbohydrate ones. They've traced where their energy comes from and how it is produced. And they've reported that exercising dogs perform just fine without dietary carbohydrates and documented the biochemical pathways that allow them to do so.

A second reason why we know that dogs don't need carbohydrates "for energy" is the fact that professional sled dogs, some of the most physically active dogs that the world has ever known, often don't eat any carbohydrates whatsoever. Sled dogs have a long history of providing functional assistance to their human colleagues. Teams of robust, athletic dogs have been used to haul cargo-laden sleds across vast expanses of snow-covered Arctic terrain for centuries. The late 1800s and early 1900s have even been called the "Era of the Sled Dog," so important were these pups to the Alaskan Gold Rush and the polar explorations of the day. And while the passage of time may have seen the sled dog become somewhat obsolete as a cargo-moving technology, it has also seen him grow popular as an athletic competitor. These days, sled dogs tend to perform their mind-boggling feats of endurance not while aiding gold prospectors, but in the context of multi-day, thousand-mile races such as the Iditarod.

The fact that sled dogs are often, if not *usually*, fed zero-carbohydrate diets during these epic events is well-documented in the scientific literature. And everything from their blood parameters and metabolic functioning to their physical output and outward signs of discomfort have been observed and recorded by researchers. Their data all point to the same conclusion: sled dogs just don't need to eat any carbohydrates. They tend to perform just as well, if not better, without them. So even if your dog is the type of "active" that sees him pull a heavily loaded sled across hundreds of miles of Alaskan wilderness, day after day, for weeks on end, it's safe to say that he'll be just fine without carbs.

The third and final line of evidence suggesting that dogs don't need carbohydrates "for energy" takes us right back to where we began this chapter: it is well-documented that wild wolves, despite being very active animals, usually don't consume any dietary carbohydrates. They tend to travel ten to 20 miles every day, and they punctuate these long, daily walkabouts with spells of all-out physical exertion when hunting and killing prey. And if carbs helped them do it all one iota faster or more effectively, you can bet your last Milkbone that they'd have found a way to cram some grasses, berries, and other plants into their guts at some point over the eons. But they don't. So they haven't.

PREDICTING THE PRESENT

ONE OF THE WAYS scientists evaluate a new theory is by testing its so-called "predictive power." A theory with strong predictive power can accurately forecast the unknown future. A theory with weak predictive power can't. Probably the best-known example of strong predictive power in action was the French mathematical astronomer U.J.J. Leverrier's use of Newtonian laws of motion to predict the existence of the planet Neptune before the planet had been directly observed. When, in September 1846, a year or so after Leverrier made his prediction, astronomers at the Berlin observatory looked through their telescopes and spied for the first time an eighth planet glowing in the dark, it was a victory both for Newton's laws and for Leverrier's interpretation thereof.

In the name of scientific rigor, we might then ask ourselves the following question: when it comes to our dogs, how predictive is the carbohydrate-insulin theory of obesity?

By this point, we know beyond the shadow of a doubt that wolves don't eat carbohydrates. They eat a lot of fat, a lot of protein, and loads of calories. But no carbs. Not any of them. We also know that wolves never get fat and don't suffer in any meaningful way from the obesity-linked diseases of modernity that plague Western canine civilization.

On the other hand, most of our dogs are fat. Pound-for-pound, the average dog has about eight times as much fat in its body as the average wolf. More than half of our dogs are so unhealthy that it's as if they are smoking a pack a day.

So, knowing all this, what do we suppose that a card-carrying proponent of the carbohydrate-insulin theory of adiposity would have to say about the diets of modern-day domestic dogs?

She would probably guess that our dogs are eating copious quantities of carbs. And, as we've seen, it would be a reasonable enough hypothesis. After all, there is an awful lot of evidence that carbohydrate consumption causes obesity. There are the long-understood biochemical links from carbohydrates to blood sugar, from blood sugar to insulin, and from insulin to adiposity. There's the rich history and widely reported successfulness of low-carbohydrate diets. There's the fact that wild, meat-eating animals don't get fat, but that those living in human captivity do. And there's all the recent experimental evidence showing that carb-free living tends to make people lose body fat and improve their cardiovascular health faster than traditional diet-and-exercise routines. Given all that, it might well be the case that an epidemic of carbohydrate consumption is in some way responsible for the epidemic of obesity killing America's dogs.

But making a reasonable-sounding argument is one thing. Using it to make accurate predictions is another.

So just how accurately *does* the carbohydrate-insulin hypothesis of obesity predict the dietary habits of the modern-day domestic dog? To answer that question, we just need to understand what we're all feeding our pets. Unfortunately, as we'll see in the next chapter, that's somewhat easier said than done.

Chapter Four

BIG KIBBLE AND THE CARBOHYDRATE LOBBY

--

"There is an always-significant difference between knowing and believing. We may know
that the earth turns, but we believe, as we say, that the sun rises. We know by evidence, or
by trust in people who have examined the evidence in a way that we trust is trustworthy.
We may sometimes be persuaded to believe by reason, but within the welter of our experience
reason is limited and weak. We believe always by coming, in some sense, to see. We believe
in what is apparent, in what we can imagine or 'picture' in our minds, in what we feel to be
true, in what our hearts tell us, in experience, in stories—above all, perhaps, in stories."

Wendell Berry, "The Melancholy of Anatomy" (2015)

CARBS, RISING

IDAHO'S POTATOES ARE FAMOUS. It says so explicitly on the
state's license plate and nine out of ten Americans agree that we associate the
crop more closely with Idaho than with any other place. The association is
appropriate: Idaho produces more potatoes than any other state in the union,
around 13 billion pounds annually. Potato farms occupy more than 300,000
acres of its territory, and the potato industry contributes about $4 billion to
the local economy every year.

The most popular variety, by far, is the Russet Burbank. With a flat oval
shape, a light brown skin, and a dense, off-white interior, the Burbank is the
prototypical American spud. But Idaho's farmers produce dozens of other
types too. Some even have exotic names, like the All Blue, the Ida Rose, the
Purple Peruvian, and the Russian Banana. Whatever the variety, Idahoans say
their potatoes are the best in the world. According to the Idaho Potato
Commission, the state's "warm days and cool nights, combined with plenty of
mountain-fed irrigation and rich volcanic soil, produce [a] unique texture,
taste, and dependable performance that keeps customers asking for more."

At the moment, Americans are "asking for more" at a rate of about 111
pounds of potatoes per person per year. We mostly treat them as side dishes;

more than 40% of U.S. potatoes become French fries or tater tots and about 30% become chips, "shoestrings," or some form of dehydrated product. On average, Americans consume about 50 calories of chips and 50 calories of fries every day.

Idaho's potato farmers plant their crops in the spring and harvest in September and October, so the fields were quiet as I passed through the Gem State on a brilliant blue-sky day in mid-July. I was heading north in the shadow of the Teton Range, taking the long way from Salt Lake City to Las Vegas, where I was hoping to get the inside scoop on the dietary habits of the modern-day domestic dog. The diversion was intended to provide a brief introduction to the agricultural system upon which the pet food industry relies. So I was a little disappointed by the lack of harvest activity. In a way, I had hoped to be competing for highway real estate with dozens of flatbed trucks piled high with Russet Burbanks.

Still, circumstantial evidence of potato farming was everywhere. As I crept through the tiny town of Ashton, a little green sign announced a local population of just over a thousand, but an old red-and-white billboard proudly proclaimed, "World's Largest Seed-Producing Potato Area!" A bit further south, in the city of Blackfoot, sits the Idaho Potato Museum, home to the Idaho Potato Hall of Fame and the world's largest potato chip.

I pulled off at a rest stop somewhere north of Ashton. After filling up on gas, I checked in at home (the latest news from the home front: Kody had decided to unspool a roll of toilet paper and scatter the shredded remains throughout the house; he wasn't caught in the act but I imagined him skipping down the hall as shreds fell from the sky like confetti and the unraveled paper trailed behind him like a dragon in a Chinese New Year parade). Then I decided to get something to eat. The options were gas station fare and fast food, and I opted for the latter, drawn in by the intoxicating aroma of frozen Russet Burbanks frying in canola oil. There was really only one appropriate choice, an extra-large helping of Idaho's finest.

I ordered and paid the clerk, and in a matter of moments a paper sack was in my hands. It felt warm as I dropped it into my lap and headed back toward the highway. I unfolded the bag and a blossom of warm, delicious-smelling air wafted upward, filling the car and enveloping my senses. The smell reminded me of childhood road trips. I reached in and grabbed a few fries. They were hot and crispy. My mouth was watering before I had taken my first bite.

***

If I've done a competent job of describing this moment, then some interesting things are happening inside your body. For one, you've begun to drool. Without even having to think about it, glands in your mouth and throat have begun secreting saliva. Biologists refer to these kind of unconscious responses to sensory stimuli as autonomic behaviors. They're usually pretty sensible reactions, and drooling is no exception. Saliva lubricates the throat, facilitating swallowing. Also, as we've already seen, spit contains digestive enzymes. So when a meal seems imminent, it makes sense to set the digestive table by ramping-up salivation.

Dogs drool too, of course. Indeed, under intense sensory stimulation, they've been shown to secrete up to ten times more saliva than we do. And, just like us, they'll drool in anticipation of real meals and (as Ivan Pavlov famously showed) imagined ones.

But your body is also reacting to the mental image of French fries by initiating a second autonomic response. And, like drooling, it's something dogs do too. But, according to the carbohydrate-insulin model of obesity, this reaction isn't so benign (sorry about that)—the beta cells in your pancreas are secreting fattening insulin right now.

In one sense, a pre-prandial insulin response is an ingenious physiological adaptation. Remember, glucose can be poisonous; it's insulin's job to remove the potentially toxic substance from your bloodstream as quickly as possible, by any means necessary. So it's wise to flush some insulin through the circulatory system anytime a sizable quantity of glucose is about to be introduced into it.

And the moment before a handful of fries is consumed certainly qualifies as one such instance. That's because potatoes are one of relatively few food products that contain a sizable quantity of starch, the easily digested carbohydrate molecule that has been called "the principal nutrient" responsible for insulin secretion in both dogs and humans. And, like potatoes, the other starchy crops—corn, wheat, barley, oats, and rice—also happen to be foundational elements of our modern food system.

And therein lies the problem with your body's autonomic pre-prandial insulin response: in this day and age, consumption of starches and sweets isn't exactly rare. Indeed, the very crops that tend to ramp up insulin production also happen to be mankind's primary sources of food. According to the United Nations, corn, wheat, and rice alone account for about half the world's calories. Starches and sweets are the primary ingredients in seven of the top eight sources of calories consumed by adults in America today. (Amazingly, grain-based desserts are *the number-one source of calories in America today*. Breads are second, soda is fourth, beer and other alcoholic beverages are fifth, pizza is sixth, pasta is seventh, and tortillas, burritos, and tacos are eighth.) In total, more than 70% of the world's farmland is devoted to growing starchy crops.

***

It wasn't always this way. Not so long ago (in evolutionary terms), starchy crops weren't just uncommon, they were downright rare. The wild ancestors of plants like wheat and corn could be found, but not without considerable effort. Like other wild plants, they grew only in certain climates and only at certain times of year. And their seeds, scattered by wind, water, and animals, would take up in geographically distant clusters, as we see today with wild flowers and all manner of other wild plants.

They were also difficult for our ancestors to convert into food. Wild grains are hard, small, bitter, and only minimally digestible without processing. They possess few qualities that would have made them more attractive foods for our hunter-gatherer ancestors than, say, berries. But all that changed when human beings invented agriculture.

The cluster of technological innovations that we today call "the invention of agriculture" occurred around 10,000 years ago. Before that time, all humans lived exclusively as hunter-gatherers, nourishing themselves on whatever wild plants and fungi they could gather and whatever wild animals they could kill. As critics of the Paleo diet are quick to remind us, it is difficult to say with specificity what a "typical" Paleolithic person (if there ever was such a thing) ate with regularity. But it's not too hard to know what our Paleolithic ancestors most definitely *did not* eat. And that latter list most certainly includes food products that only became widely available once we invented agriculture. That means little or no corn, wheat, oats, rice, or potatoes. For more than 99% of our genetic evolution, it's safe to assume that starchy carbohydrates—the very ones that Gary Taubes blames for the obesity epidemic—played no more than a minuscule role in our diets.

But all that began to change somewhere around 10,000 years ago. Around that time, bands of humans living in close proximity to one another in separate locations around the globe realized, more or less contemporaneously, that the dormant seeds of annual plants would, under the right conditions, grow into new plants. There's still debate as to how people in far-flung locations such as Asia, Sub-Saharan Africa, the Fertile Crescent, and the Americas could all have come up with the same idea independently, although most archaeologists believe that the relatively stable global climate that arose after the end of the last ice age (in about 11,000 BCE) had something to do with it. In any event, our ancestors soon learned how water, sunlight, and soil affected the process of plant reproduction. And, before too long, primitive attempts at irrigation, fertilization, deforestation, and food storage were all being used to help early farmers produce crops more efficiently.

A specific kind of efficiency was paramount to these early forays into the domestication of plants. As anyone who has ever strolled the glittering, Technicolor produce section of a Whole Foods already knows, an impressive assortment of plants can be domesticated using these same general techniques. But, in its early days, the driving force behind breakthroughs in "food technology" was a need to produce as much life-sustaining food as possible, not a desire to offer discerning customers a diverse selection of tasty alternatives or a nutritionally optimal diet. The primacy of this goal led early agriculturalists to focus their efforts on producing crops that were at once high-yield, low-maintenance, and easily stored for long periods of time. It is no wonder, then, that the chief product of each of the main epicenters of agricultural innovation was a cereal grain: rice in Asia, corn in the Americas, wheat in the Fertile Crescent, and sorghum and millet in Africa. Indeed, the very word "cereal" comes from Ceres, the Roman goddess of agriculture.

Cereal grains are grasses, plants characterized by long, narrow leaves that grow directly up from their base. The edible part of the plant is called the "grain," a single unit that incorporates both the plant's seed and a surrounding wall of fruit. Unlike long, slender leaves, grains—think of an individual kernel of corn—pack a significant amount of nutritional heft into a small space. These little bundles of fuel serve a purpose: they help to sustain freshly dispersed seeds until the seeds sprout leaves and begin photosynthesizing their own energy.

The bulk of the concentrated nutritional content comes in the form of starch, the polysaccharide carbohydrate that we've already discussed at length. And this caloric density is one of the reasons why cereal grains made such good crops. After all, a highly concentrated load of fattening carbohydrates may have dangerous health ramifications in a world where cereal grains are over-abundant, but it's not a bad thing if your primary nutritional concern is making sure that your family doesn't starve to death.

Perhaps an even more important reason why cereal grains exceled as crops was their durability. The so-called "durable" crops (cereal grains and legumes) are smaller and hardier than the "perishable" ones (fruits and vegetables). They also have lower moisture contents and tend to respire more slowly. So while an apple or a banana will ripen (and rot) quickly, a rice kernel will not. The durability of cereal grains makes them immensely valuable because it means that they don't have to be eaten immediately after they are harvested. They can instead be dried and stored, to be eaten at a later time when the demand for food has risen or the supply has dropped.

Another nice thing about cereal grains is they can be used to feed livestock. While nomadic hunter-gatherers are free to track protein-rich wild game over long distances, sedentary farmers are very much wed to the physical location of their crops. And so, with the domestication of plants came the domestication of animals. Cereal grains proved their worth here too, as livestock could be selected for, among other things, an ability to thrive on the very plants that early farmers were already growing.

Thus, in relatively short order, men and women around the world went from hunting and gathering their food to growing and raising it. The cluster of cultural changes wrought by all these innovations were comprehensive enough to warrant the moniker "the Neolithic Revolution," a term which archaeologists now use to describe this important moment in human history. The definitive transition was one of lifestyle, from the roaming, nomadic one of hunter-gatherers, to the sedentary one required to cultivate fields of slow-growing crops. But the more culturally significant change may have been that, for the first time in history, long-term food surpluses were possible. People who for ages had lived meal-to-meal, constantly on the hunt for sustenance, could now produce food so efficiently that they had more of it than they could eat, at least in the short run.

The impact that these food surpluses had on the course of human history is difficult to overstate. They led, in one way or another, to unprecedented population growth, to the founding and development of densely populated settlements, to private property and wealth accumulation, and to trading economies. They also helped to bring about labor differentiation and the social stratification to which such specialization inevitably gives rise, as well as centralized community governance, and, perhaps most significantly of all, a rapid acceleration in the accumulation of knowledge, as, for the first time in history, whole groups of people could spend their days thinking, writing, and teaching, while others tended to crops.

It is tempting, in light of the prominent roles that such institutions still play in the modern world, to see the invention of agriculture as having been a wholly positive thing for humankind. It was not. Indeed, Jared Diamond, the UCLA professor who documented the rise and fall of human civilizations over the past 13,000 years in his Pulitzer Prize-winning book *Guns, Germs, and Steel*, has famously called the invention of agriculture "the worst mistake in the history of the human race." But even if you're not willing to go that far, it's hard to disagree that there are dark sides to many of the so-called "advances" to which agriculture has contributed. Increased population density, for example, has dramatically accelerated the spread of infectious diseases. Private property and wealth accumulation have given rise to inequality and poverty. Lack of dietary variety has exposed populations to famines and nutrient deficiencies. And, according to folks like Gary Taubes, a diet built around starchy cereal grains has given rise to a global epidemic of obesity.

Now speed up the tape and fast-forward a few thousand years. Watch as the cultural momentum, both good and bad, set in motion by modern agricultural methods carries onward. Cities rise as the world's human population explodes. Groups of unrelated people band together and form things like countries, corporations, and clubs. Collective reserves of knowledge grow. And, over time, what we today regard as the definitive manifestations of our humanity—arts, sciences, religions, philosophies, legal systems, and, of particular note for our present purposes, *industries*—gradually bubble to the surface. And all this just in the last 10,000 years or so, a period so evolutionarily insignificant that if all of human history were condensed into a single 24-hour day, it would represent just the last few minutes.

THE CARBOHYDRATE LOBBY

IT IS IMPORTANT TO keep this last bit (the minuteness of the fraction of our genetic evolution that has transpired since the invention of agriculture) in mind when thinking about the role that starchy and sugary carbohydrates play in the lives of both modern-day human beings and our canine companions. For while these nutrients have only had a few ticks of the evolutionary clock to work their way into our lives, they certainly have managed to do so. In this day and age, carbs are everywhere.

You can see this for yourself, of course. Just consider the items on offer at your favorite restaurant. Is it a romantic little Ristorante Italiano? If so, then all the delicious dough that goes into its pastas and pizzas will have been made from wheat flour. And any beef, pork, or chicken (and, in these days of farm-raised fish, even seafood) is likely to have been raised on a diet of corn and soy. Or maybe your favorite spot is a little Mexican joint. If so, then the tortillas will have been made from ground wheat or corn, the chips and taco shells are fried corn, and the beans and rice piled next to your grain-fed chicken or beef will be packed with carbs too. Indian, Japanese, or Chinese? Then there's a mountain of rice sitting next to the corn-fed meat in your tikka masala, yakitori, or Szechuan stir-fry. Or maybe you're just into plain old meat-and-taters American fare. Then it doesn't matter if it's breakfast (corn-fed pigs reduced to sausages and bacon, starch-stuffed pancakes and waffles, home fries and hash browns, sticky-sweep syrup), lunch (sandwich bread, French fries, chips), or dinner (a side of potatoes alongside a slab of corn-fed meat, possibly arranged between two slices of starchy bread), carbohydrates are most definitely on the menu.

The story is pretty much the same if you prefer to buy your food at the grocery store. We can start with the obvious stuff—the breads and other baked goods, the pastas, the tortillas, the chips, the crackers, the candy, the cookies, the ice cream, the frozen dinners, the sodas, the beer, the ears of corn, the mountainous piles of Russet Burbanks—but there are plenty of other places where sweets and cereal grains manage to fly under the radar. Most of the cows that produce our dairy products have been raised on a diet of corn and corn by-products. The chickens that lay the eggs are often grain-fed too. As are almost all of the animals that had the misfortune of being turned into packaged meats in your local factory slaughterhouse.

And then there are the condiments. One of the primary ingredients in most of the mass-produced ketchups, barbecue sauces, mustards, mayonnaises, marinades, and salad dressings that we all use to doll-up our meals is high-fructose corn syrup. From yogurts to pasta sauces and from fruit juices to breakfast cereals, your local grocery store is a veritable temple of carbohydrate worship.

And what about convenience destinations, like gas stations, coffee shops, and fast-food restaurants? Oh, puh-lease. Fresh-baked croissants and syrupy-sweet drinks await at the coffee shop. At the gas station, you'll find coolers brimming with sodas, sports drinks, juices, and beer, as well as row upon row of candy and chips. And at the local fast-food joint, it'll be corn-fed meat slathered with sugary condiments, topped with a slice of cheese from a corn-fed cow, and stuffed between two slices of floury bread, to go along with a sugary soft drink and a mountain of fries.

It bears repeating: In this day and age, carbs are everywhere.

***

There are a number of reasons for the ubiquity of carbohydrates in the modern world, not the least of which being that our government has long told us that we should eat them. Like most Americans, I was raised to believe that "heart healthy whole grains" are the cornerstones of a healthy diet. My thinking was shaped in large part by the USDA and its infamous Food Guide Pyramid, which, from 1992 until 2005, counseled all Americans to eat a whopping six to 11 servings of grains and other starchy carbohydrates a day, or nearly as much as the recommended intake of meats, dairy products, fruits, vegetables, and oils combined. In other words, for most of my life, I've been told by the U.S. government to get about half my calories from starchy carbohydrates.

Despite the considerable influence it has managed to exert on people like me, the Food Guide Pyramid (and, more recently, the USDA's MyPlate guide) has been widely criticized by folks who know a thing or two about such matters. Gary Taubes has blasted gaping holes in the flawed science upon which the Food Guide Pyramid is based. But other prominent experts have gone even further than Taubes, arguing that the bad science isn't merely an accident. Indeed, perhaps the most common criticism directed at the Food Guide Pyramid and other national dietary recommendations is that they have been deliberately crafted to protect and promote the interests of the major agricultural industries that have come to dominate the food supply in the 10,000 years or so since the invention of agriculture. As Dr. Walter Willett, the influential Chair of the Harvard School of Public Health's Department of Nutrition, has recently said, the USDA's guidelines tend to "mix science with the influence of powerful agricultural interests, which is not a recipe for healthy eating."

Dr. Willett's criticism points to a second reason why carbohydrates make up such a large part of the modern-day culinary landscape. What he calls "powerful agricultural interests" might instead be called the "Carbohydrate Lobby," so central is the production and sale of sweets and starches to the group's livelihood. And the reason why it might not be a "recipe for healthy eating" for us to follow nutritional recommendations based on the Carbohydrate Lobby's interests is there are some powerful forces motivating the actions of the Lobby that have nothing whatsoever to do with health, not the least of which being the profit-seeking motive baked into the very DNA of the companies of which the Lobby is composed.

***

All apologies to workers in the flesh trade, but the food business is more probably the oldest one on the planet. With the first food swap deal likely to have been struck at some point shortly after the Neolithic Revolution, food production has had more than 10,000 years to become what economists call a "mature industry." Being a mature industry means more than just having been around for a long time. It also means that a few major players have come to dominate the marketplace. And this is certainly the case with the food business, where four or fewer firms typically dominate each industry sub-sector.

Consider food processing. The two largest firms in the food production and processing industry are Cargill, Inc. and the Archer Daniels Midland Company (ADM). Cargill is no less than the largest privately held company in the world, with annual revenues exceeding $120 billion and over 150,000 employees on the payroll. The list of companies that are dwarfed by Cargill is breathtaking. It includes Wall Street titans such as Goldman Sachs and Citigroup, technology giants like Microsoft and Google, as well as Boeing, Lockheed Martin, AT&T, Verizon, Proctor & Gamble, Johnson & Johnson, and many more of the most recognizable companies in the world. ADM is only slightly smaller—with annual revenues exceeding $80 billion, it is number 34 on the Fortune 500 list of the largest companies in America. Firms like Cargill and ADM prove that making food isn't just old business, it is *big* business.

One of the core business functions of these food processing giants is to acquire commodities like cattle and corn and transform them into food ingredients and other consumable products. In the case of livestock, that means buying calves and other animals from ranchers (such as the ones struggling to keep wolves out of their herds in Montana's Paradise Valley), fattening them at company-owned feedlots, and slaughtering them at company-owned slaughterhouses. In the case of crops like corn, wheat, and soybeans, the commodities are purchased from farmers or grown by the company itself, then milled, crushed, de-constituted, re-constituted, or otherwise "processed" into things like flours, oils, syrups, and sweeteners, as well as livestock feed and energy products.

Don't be ashamed if you're not all that familiar with companies like Cargill and ADM. There's a good reason for their lack of notoriety—they don't sell their products to individual consumers. Instead, they sell bulk quantities to other major businesses, companies that, in turn, market their foods to consumers. As Cargill's website proudly declares, "You will not find the 'Cargill' brand on store shelves, but you will find that we are behind many of the brands that you know well." Or, as David Whitford and Doris Burke wrote in *Fortune* magazine in 2011, "[w]hatever you ate or drank today—a candy bar, pretzels, soup from a can, ice cream, yogurt, chewing gum, beer—chances are it included a little something from Cargill's menu of food additives."

What this means, of course, is that Cargill's army of corporate customers are members of the Carbohydrate Lobby too. The list of companies making prolific use of starchy and sugary ingredients includes those behind many of the most recognizable brands in the world. They include Coca-Cola (No. 63 on the Fortune 500 list), PepsiCo (No. 44), McDonald's (No. 110), Kraft Foods Group (No. 165), General Mills (No. 171), and Starbucks (No. 187). These businesses make their money turning carbohydrate-laden ingredients like flour and high-fructose corn syrup into products like soft drinks and snack foods, then selling those products to eager consumers. In the case of restaurants like McDonald's and Starbucks, their foods are sold directly to us. But companies that produce soft drinks and snack foods have to sell their goods in venues like supermarkets and drug stores. Which means that still *other* companies, mammoth businesses like Safeway (No. 84), Walgreens (No. 35), Kroger (No. 20), Costco (No. 18), CVS Health (No. 10), and Wal-Mart (No. 1, the largest company on the planet) are members of the Carbohydrate Lobby too.

It would be cynical to conclude that these businesses are using their trillions of dollars in annual sales as part of a vast conspiracy to make money by any means necessary, even if it means knowingly inflicting a measure of harm on unsuspecting consumers. But it would probably be naïve to assume that the profiteering motive baked into every one of the Carbohydrate Lobby's corporate members doesn't motivate the Lobby to exert its massive influence upon the very lawmakers and governmental agencies that are supposed to be regulating it.

And, indeed, when we examine the record, it appears that the Carbohydrate Lobby has done precisely that. According to the Center for Responsive Politics, the agribusiness industry spent around $130 million on lobbying in 2015 and donated $90 million to political candidates during the 2012 election cycle. The Center has also found that 180 members of the USDA (the primary regulator of the food industry) entered the agency through a so-called "revolving door," either by virtue of prior or contemporaneous affiliation with an industry-specific lobbying organization or private sector firm. Notably, the former Chief of Staff for the USDA was once the president of the most powerful cattleman's lobbying organization on Capitol Hill. As the investigative journalist Eric Schlosser wrote of the USDA in 2004, "[r]ight now you'd have a hard time finding a federal agency more completely dominated by the industry it was created to regulate."

The USDA's starch-promoting Food Guide Pyramid may be the most glaring example of the Carbohydrate Lobby's influence in action. But it's far from the only one. The market for starchy crops like corn and wheat is also propped up by public funds. Corn and wheat are the two most heavily subsidized crops in the country, with corn subsidies from 1995 to 2014 totaling over $90 billion (roughly the GDP of Ukraine) and wheat subsidies over the same period coming in at nearly $40 billion. The effect of all that subsidization has been pretty much what you would expect: of the 300 million or so acres of American soil devoted to growing food, more than 80 million of them are used to grow corn and more than 50 million are devoted to wheat. In comparison, the hundreds of different fruits and vegetables produced by American farmers occupy, in total, about 14 million acres—or only about 10% of the space devoted to corn and wheat alone.

The abundance of these commodity crops represents a very attractive situation for Cargill, ADM, and the other giants of the Carbohydrate Lobby—ready access to loads and loads of cheap, durable cereal grains. They just need to figure out how to make profitable use of them all.

Fortunately for them, starchy cereal grains are extremely versatile crops. As we've already seen, they can be used to produce all sorts of food products, from bread and chips to beer and soda. But thanks to modern-day advances in chemistry and food processing technology, they can do more than that. Much more. In fact, the use of corn in food products is, incredibly, almost an afterthought for agribusinesses. Just slightly more than 10% of the more than 11 billion bushels of corn produced by U.S. farmers every year gets used in food products designed for human consumption. So if you add up all the corn flour, the corn meal, the high-fructose corn syrup, the glucose, the dextrose, the corn starch, the corn oil, and the beverage alcohol (not to mention all the big, beautiful ears of the stuff sold without being converted into a powder or a paste), it will only account for about one out of every ten bushels of corn sold in the U.S. every year. The other nine will be used to make livestock feed or ethanol fuel.

***

There's another reason why the Carbohydrate Lobby loves starches and sweets so much: they're delicious. When they are used in foods, they tend to make those foods "palatable," a term food scientists use to describe the quality in foods that makes us want to eat more of them. Importantly, palatability is about more than just hunger. As Dr. David A. Kessler, former commissioner of the FDA and dean of the medical schools at both Yale and the University of California, San Francisco, has put it, "when scientists say a food is palatable, they are referring primarily to its capacity to stimulate the appetite and prompt us to eat more. Palatability does involve taste, of course, but, crucially, it also involves the motivation to *pursue* that taste. It is the reason we want more."

You don't have to be a hyper-intelligent and morally sensitive collie to know that sweets are highly palatable. One of the most well-established facts in all of the nutritional science literature is that humans *love* sweet foods. We develop the preference as babies and it just grows stronger as we grow into candy-obsessed children. Even as adults we will preferentially choose sweet foods over less sweet ones and, when given an unlimited supply, we will consume more sweets than other foods.

From an evolutionary perspective, this all makes perfect sense—sweets are an efficient food source, packing a lot of caloric energy into a little space. But while our innate preference for sticky-sweet substances may have served us well back before the dawn of agriculture, it is downright dangerous in a world teeming with sweeteners like sucrose, dextrose, glucose, and high-fructose corn syrup. For, as anyone with a sweet tooth and a weight problem already knows, the urge to eat these highly palatable foods arises regardless of hunger. As Kessler wrote in his book *The End of Overeating*, "[w]e once thought that in the absence of hunger, food could not serve as an effective reward [for laboratory animals]. That idea proved to be wrong. ... [A]nimals will work for foods that are high in sugar and fat even if they are not hungry."

If you ask a neuroscientist, she will tell you that there are at least two distinct reasons for this. The first is because the experience of tasting palatable foods is psychologically rewarding. It induces a feeling—the one you get when you take that first bite of your favorite flavor of ice cream on a hot summer day—that simultaneously relaxes us, relieves our feelings of stress, and causes us to feel pure, unadulterated pleasure. The feeling is brought on by the brain's primary pleasure producer, a bit of neurological hardware called the opioid circuitry. Opioids are chemicals that make us feel good. The external sources of these pleasure molecules include drugs like morphine, heroin, hydrocodone, and oxycodone. But our bodies also produce opioids on their own, in response to certain sensory stimuli. Stimuli that notably include tasting a palatable food. In fact, Kessler claims that the simple carbohydrate sucrose (table sugar) is the single most rewarding food substance of all, more so than even fat or salt.

The second reason we are driven to consume sweets is that we feel a strong desire for them. This isn't exactly the same thing as consciously remembering the sensation of pleasure and wanting to feel that way again.

It's something more than that. It's the same reason a smoker feels compelled to smoke even though she "hates the taste of cigarettes" and truthfully claims they make her feel run-down and lethargic. A craving, a wanting, a yearning, a hankering—whatever you want to call the feeling, a neurotransmitter called dopamine is what's responsible for it. Dopamine heightens our sense of anticipation and causes us to focus our thoughts and attention on a perceived opportunity for reward. It places us in a reward-seeking state of mind. As Stanford neuroscientist Kelly McGonigal puts it, this tendency to make us want something, regardless of whether that something will even make us feel good, is "the brain's big lie." It's one of the key neurobiological reasons why alcoholics drink, why it's so hard to tear yourself away from your smartphone when a Facebook "like" or an e-mail is just around the corner, and why so many of us crave sugary and starchy foods.

As any lover of sweets can testify, cravings for palatable foods come from all sorts of places. The release of dopamine can be triggered by all manner of stimuli, from viewing an image of a palatable food to visiting a location where a delicious meal has been served up in the past. Certain aromas can do the trick. And so can palatable tastes—a particularly scary finding, as it suggests a vicious cycle by which eating sugary foods makes us want to eat *more* sugary foods.

All this, it seems, is understood by the Carbohydrate Lobby all too well. For while producing foods that make folks want to eat them even when they aren't hungry might be a recipe for disaster from a public health perspective, it is an undeniably excellent business model.

***

Beyond the influence that it exerts on regulators and its promotion of subtly addictive food products, the Carbohydrate Lobby has also influenced our thinking about the healthfulness of dietary carbohydrates in another, more direct way—with its marketing dollars. Cargill and ADM may not worry too much about how everyday consumers view their products, but Coca Cola, McDonald's, General Mills, and other makers of consumer products sure do.

The amount of money these companies spend on advertising and other forms of marketing is dizzying. According to *Ad Age*, in 2012 alone, McDonald's, Subway, and Walmart each spent more than a half-billion dollars on advertising, placing them all firmly within the top 25 advertisers in the United States. And according to Yale's Rudd Center for Food Policy and Obesity, Coca Cola, PepsiCo, and Innovation Ventures (the company behind 5-Hour Energy drinks) all spent more than $100 million getting their drinks in front of consumers in 2010. There is no shortage of media upon which all that "ad spend" might express itself—from traditional media platforms like television, radio, billboards, and magazines, to more creative approaches like slapping a brand name on the stadium for a major sports team or paying to place a can of soda in the hands of the beautiful star of a major motion picture. And that's all before we get to the plethora of new advertising opportunities available on the Internet. For the members of a Carbohydrate Lobby interested in using its deep pockets to shape and influence consumer perception, the modern world is their oyster.

And not only do they seize the day, but the technical sophistication with which they do so can be both impressive and frightening. Firms use expert tasting panels to determine palatability and eye-tracking technology to understand how consumers view specific advertisements and product packages. The latest advances in behavioral economics—the study of the processes, both conscious and unconscious, by which people make economic decisions—inform their promotional strategies, from loyalty programs that look like giveaways but really lead consumers to spend far more than the value of what they receive in return, to the careful manipulation of environmental atmospherics like background music, store layouts, and lighting. As we've already seen, the mere sight of a highly palatable food (whether in a magazine ad, on a television, or as a free sample) is enough to get the dopamine pumping and cause us to overeat. But fast-food giants don't stop at showing us images of steaming hot slices of pizza dripping with cheese. They also use cosmetic enhancement and chemical flavorings to make things like mashed-up pig parts seem like whole cuts of prime meat (as McDonald's does with its McRib sandwich). Some even use our olfactory sense against us, intentionally flooding the areas around their restaurants with the enticing aromas of potatoes frying in oil or of buttery cinnamon buns rising in an oven.

While discerning adults may be at least moderately well equipped to defend themselves against this onslaught, children most certainly are not. But that's only one of the reasons why kids constitute such a mouth-watering market for the Carbohydrate Lobby. Children are also likely to trail a couple of parents (read: additional customers) along with them when they stop by a restaurant. And, the thinking goes, if you can nab an impressionable child early in life, she may well grow into a lifelong brand loyalist.

Enter Ronald McDonald, Tony the Tiger, and the Trix Bunny. Children as young as three years old (too young to even read!) have been shown to recognize and appreciate corporate cartoon characters. McDonald's restaurants are home to more than 8,000 playgrounds and, in 1997, a British High Court Justice affirmatively ruled that McDonald's advertising programs have "exploited children." Nevertheless, from Happy Meals to collectable games and from tie-ins with major motion pictures to toy giveaways (*Brandweek* called McDonald's 1997 "Teenie Beanie Baby" promotion "one of the most successful promotions *in the history of American advertising*"), kids remain squarely in the food marketer's crosshairs.

And if you think that leaning on regulators, marketing to children, exploiting innate psychological tendencies, and hijacking our senses might be pushing the ethical envelope a bit, then you're not alone. As RAND Corporation scientist Deborah A. Cohen wrote in her recent book *A Big Fat Crisis*,

> [A]dvertising efforts have shifted from persuasion to manipulation. We can be swayed without ever realizing what has happened. When it comes to food, many experiments have demonstrated how irrational, inconsistent, and oblivious to marketing ruses people can be.

In other words, even if you think that you're above all this psychobabble, then you should probably tread carefully. There are some pretty rich and powerful organizations out there that have a very strong incentive to sell you as many of their carbohydrate-packed food products as possible. And, for many of them, whether that's good or bad for your health seems to be little more than an afterthought. So at the risk of sounding like a bit of a conspiracy theorist, be careful, because "that stuff could never work on me" is precisely what they want you to think.

***

Dietary carbohydrates gained the culinary throne with the help of the Carbohydrate Lobby and its relentless pursuit of profits. But there's a sector of the Lobby that we haven't discussed yet, and it's the one with the most direct ties to the story of canine obesity in America. Its members are every bit as wealthy and powerful as the snack food giants and fast food chains that fuel the human obesity epidemic, and they are every bit as aggressive with their marketing and lobbying efforts too. The only difference is that this group of corporate behemoths doesn't concern itself with stuffing cheap carbs down the necks of men, women, and children. It's focused exclusively on our pets. And it is why, for most of the same reasons that starches and sugars have become dietary staples for human beings, carbs have managed to infiltrate (and, indeed, to dominate) the diets of our canine companions as well.

THE DOGS OF THE LAS VEGAS DESERT

THE LAS VEGAS STRIP in the summertime is no place for a dog. With temperatures often rising above 110 degrees, the heat on the street is crippling. The sun is ever-present and burns blindingly bright. It's enough to cook a man right through the best efforts of his highly-evolved system of pores and sweat glands. Dogs, whose self-cooling strategies are more limited than our own, and generally amount to some combination of panting, hiding in the shade, and finding a cool body of water, are really pressing their luck when the mercury tops out above 110 degrees. More so than even us, they're better off just staying away.

The economic super-machine of Las Vegas is, of course, designed to capitalize on the oppressive summer sun. When the desert heat is at its worst, the allure of the mega-casinos is at its strongest, their doors flung open to bathe sweat-dampened pedestrians with waves of machine-cooled air and promises of luxury, excitement, and sex. But, unlike their human counterparts, urged as they are to escape the midday swelter getting rich inside a cool casino or sipping an expensive frozen drink, dogs are generally unwelcome inside the Strip's finer establishments. Unburdened by hopes and dreams and, in many cases, with neither the hygiene nor the manners needed to thrive in polite human society, they're not particularly beneficial to a casino's bottom line. Alas, in Sin City there just isn't much money to be made off of a lowly mutt.

Or so you might think. And yet, on an epically hot day in mid-July there are tens—perhaps hundreds—of thousands of dogs gathered together at the Mandalay Bay Convention Center at the south end of the Strip. At first glance, they seem to form a representative sample of the American canine population. They certainly reflect all the physical diversity for which the domestic dog is renowned: titanic St. Bernards and English Mastiffs lumber along next to wholesome, square-shouldered Labrador Retrievers while dainty, carefully coifed Malteses sit nearby, perched like child emperors on embroidered throw pillows.

But in other ways this group of dogs is special. For one, they're all a little *too* pretty. The black polka dots on the Dalmatians are spaced a bit too perfectly from each other and stand out in unrealistically stunning relief against their bleach-white coats. All the dogs seem to be wearing the same handsome facial expression too—a playful, confident grin, corners of the mouth drawn back, tongue lolling out between nicely aligned teeth. Even the bulldogs, a group of animals that have literally been engineered to be ugly, don't look so bad. Like a television actress playing a pre-transformation ugly duckling, each one seems just a makeover away from becoming a prom queen.

There aren't many representatives of the so-called "aggressive" breeds either, despite their popularity throughout the broader American canine population. Very few German Shepherds. Even fewer Rottweilers. No Pit Bulls whatsoever. It's something I'm particularly quick to note as I wander the convention floor, being a Rottweiler man myself.

But what most distinguishes the thousands of dogs at the Mandalay Bay from the 70 million or so found in living rooms and backyards around the country is the fact that these dogs aren't living creatures. They aren't actual dogs at all, just *images* of dogs.

This goes a long way toward explaining how they can get around the hygiene issue. It also explains why these dogs actually have a role to play in the Las Vegas economy. Because these dogs, these thousands of beautiful, approachable, smiling pooches, are marketing vehicles. They're making their appearances on product packages and advertising banners, alongside snazzy product names, glowing testimonials, gold seals of approval, and money-back guarantees. They're in Vegas because they're part of a larger plan. They're being used by businesses as part of a concerted effort to sell products and services.

This is the SuperZoo convention, one of the largest and longest-running pet products conventions in the world. There are more than 10,000 attendees walking the floor at this year's event. For the most part they are buyers, representatives of mammoth international pet retailers as well as smaller regional operations. They look like businesspeople, like middle-managers well-acquainted with the industry convention experience. They wear blazers or skirt suits and tired, road-weary looks. They carry briefcases doubling as overnight bags.

The exhibitors are more of a mixed-bag. The major dog food brands are all here. They're the household names, the ones that make television commercials and count their annual revenues in billions of dollars. Their exhibition booths are monstrous, sprawling things, with floor-to-ceiling banners, couches and conference tables, and bags of product samples stacked 20 feet high. Each of these outposts is manned by a small army of smiling sales representatives. They are uniformed, with logo-adorned golf shirts tucked into khaki pants. They eagerly distribute glossy sales catalogues to passers-by and engage you in polite, casual conversation when you pause to have a look at their spreads.

The self-styled "specialty" and "premium" dog food manufacturers are also on-hand, with exhibition booths reflecting the curious hybrid status that these unique firms occupy in the marketplace. These are companies that cultivate a staunchly anti-establishment image while enjoying many of the benefits that accrue only to major industry players. Their products are distributed internationally, their advertisements grace some of the country's largest media platforms, and their private equity investors throw dinner parties for top executives and major distributors at Vegas's swankiest eateries. Nevertheless, differentiating themselves from the allegedly substandard products and unethical business practices of the major dog food brands is a cornerstone of the specialty dog food business model. But although their exhibition spaces are smaller and more welcoming than those of the mega-brands, they are adorned with cultured accents that belie the "you can trust us, we're just the little guy" tone of their marketing materials. At one such booth, the display shelves are made out of polished hardwood. At another, a smartly dressed bartender pours glasses of chardonnay while cubes of sharp white cheddar are passed to browsing buyers. After a long day wandering the convention room floor, I find myself feeling grateful for the complimentary refreshments.

Then there are the small manufacturers, the so-called "mom and pops." These folks occupy small booths on the less expensive real estate toward the back of the convention room floor and display products like deer-antler dog chews and hand-stitched plush toys, stuff produced in small batches close to (and sometimes within one's) home. Unlike the larger exhibitors, whose booths are manned by models and slickster salesman-types, the mom and pops are usually represented by the company president, an individual often doubling as the business's founder, accountant, chief financial officer, project manager, and warehouse supervisor. They pass out their product samples and flyers and otherwise try to make their companies look as large and bona fide as they can. Not without good reason, of course—many have dumped their personal savings into their small businesses and have saved all year to splurge thousands of dollars exhibiting at this three-day buyer bacchanal. So while they may not look much like the deep-pocketed mega-brands, they're just like them in at least one crucial way—they're here at SuperZoo *to sell*.

And sell they do. If, like me, you're a dog owner who is accustomed to being treated first and foremost as a consumer (and not as a re-seller), then the experience of being sold to at SuperZoo might feel strange to you. In these sales pitches, the dog-owning consumer is acknowledged to be a relevant character, but only as a kind of absent third-party, not someone privy to the deal itself. As "they," not "you." Rather than telling you why a product will change your life (or your dog's), salespeople say things like "consumers are really going apeshit over this one" and "the packaging really catches the eye" and "honestly, I'm not sure *why* they all care about this so much, but they do."

It's a different dance than the one performed in a mall or a big-box retailer, where the pitch is inevitably focused on the ways that the product will be useful to *you*, the end consumer. Here at SuperZoo, the product qualities to which the sales representatives draw your attention aren't the ones that make the product useful to the end consumer (or his dog), they're the qualities that make the product useful to *a reseller*. Because the buyers here at SuperZoo only want to purchase things that they can resell, they need to be persuaded that their customers will *perceive* the product to be useful. The *actual* utility of the product is something of an afterthought.

"I don't need to tell you that the whole 'grain-free' thing is getting pretty hot right now," a spiky-haired young guy in the typical khakis-and-polo uniform says to me with a chuckle.

All this talk about consumer behavior underscores the fact that there are a lot of dollars riding on the buying habits of America's dog owners. In 2015, Americans spent upwards of $60 billion (roughly the GDP of Kenya) on our canine companions. It is often said that the pet industry is "recession-proof," that we'll spend on our dogs and cats regardless of the nature of the economic environment. And, seeing as how we all consider our dogs and cats to be our kids, it's not hard to understand why. We'll pay over the odds to buy them the things that we think will make them happy and healthy. We're all too willing to spoil them with the latest and greatest toys, treats, and other gizmos. We love nothing more than to pamper them with material manifestations of our love.

And don't the folks at SuperZoo just know it. This whole spectacle—and, indeed, the whole pet products industry—exists only because dog owners feel strong loving emotions for our pets. Succeeding in the world of pet products is basically a matter of convincing dog owners that your products will make their pets uniquely healthy and happy. And from the mega-brands to the mom and pops, everyone at SuperZoo is here making their case. With their emotional television commercials and magazine advertisements, with their handsome canine models and their reassuring product packaging, and with their unending claims that their products are the things dogs both want and need to be as healthy and happy as possible, they're all just trying to make some kind of connection. To create a narrative, a story that taps into the great emotional undercurrent that binds dogs to their masters.

MEET BIG KIBBLE

MOST OF THE MONEY in the pet industry is in food and "treats." Together, this sector makes up more than a third of the industry and accounts for more than $20 billion in U.S. sales every year. The most obvious reason for these big numbers is edible products are designed to be consumed (unlike a leash or a fetch toy). And that means repeat business, month after month, year after year.

As anyone with a dog already knows, it can all add up pretty quickly. In 2015, the average American dog owner spent nearly $2000 on each of her pooches, meaning that if the pet industry was treated as a single retail segment it would be the eighth largest one in the country. We tend to go for kibble, with dry foods outselling canned ones by better than four to one. On the whole, Americans bought more than six million tons of dog food last year.

Five firms dominate the industry, and each one is every bit as large as the fast food and soft drink giants that have come to rule the human food supply. In some cases, they're the very same companies. The current industry leader, by far, is the Nestlé-Purina PetCare Company, the St. Louis-based firm that sells almost a third of all dog food purchased in the United States every year. Its parent company, the Swiss corporation Nestlé, S.A., is the single largest food company on the planet, with annual revenues of over $100 billion and more than 300,000 employees on the payroll. In addition to pet foods, Nestlé sells astounding quantities of things like baby food, cosmetics, candy, bottled water, and coffee. Its Nestlé-Purina division is responsible for a host of recognizable pet food brands, such as Beneful, Dog Chow, Purina ONE, Alpo, and Beggin' Strips.

Trailing just behind Purina on the list of America's biggest dog food producers are a handful of other mega-corporations. Second is Mars, Inc., the seventh-largest privately held company in the United States. It is responsible for about 14% of the American dog food market, with brands including Pedigree (the top-selling dog food brand in the U.S. overall), Cesar, and Royal Canin. Third is the Del Monte Foods Company, another multi-billion-dollar privately held company. Del Monte is responsible for more than 11% of the total market and is the business behind brands like Kibbles 'n' Bits, Milk-Bone, Milo's Kitchen, and Gravy Train. Last year, Hill's Pet Nutrition Inc. (Hill's Science Diet and Hill's Prescription Diet) and the Iams Company (Iams, Eukanuba) basically raced to a tie for fourth place, with each controlling just under 10% of the total dog food market.

The so-called "specialty" brands take a smaller, but still significant, slice of the pie. Blue Buffalo, Natural Balance, and Nutro are all in the top 16 brands overall, with sales of well over $100 million per year. When you include them in the equation, the top ten labels in the pet food industry (Wal-Mart's private label brands and Waggin' Train LLC are also top sellers) account for about 90% of the pet food sold in the United States every year. The top five firms alone control more than 80% of the market.

Although only a handful of firms are producing the bulk of the pet food sold in the United States, those firms have done an admirable job of making it seem as if we have a near-infinite number of choices when we decide what kind of food to buy. Just consider the daunting amount of shelf space devoted to dog foods at your local pet store. Scan the shelves and you're sure to find hundreds of different colorful packages. There will be all manner of different protein sources—lamb, beef, venison, bison, elk, chicken, duck, turkey, rabbit, salmon—and the assortment of enthusiastic marketing pitches with which the products are positioned can appear limitless. Some products claim to be ideal for certain kinds of dogs ("Large Breed Formula!"). Others select one of the dozens of ingredients used to make the food and highlight it (usually it's a wholesome-sounding vegetable, like pumpkin or sweet potato). Some make a point of telling you what's *not* in their formula ("Grain-Free!, Grain-Free!, Grain-Free!"). Others repurpose comforting and fancy-sounding words from the world of human cuisine ("stew" or "feast" or "paté"). And still others use substantive, though often tenuously reasoned, selling points

("Limited Number of Ingredients!" or "Ideal For a Healthy Weight!").

You'd be forgiven for thinking that this is a consumer environment overflowing with meaningful choice. But you'd be wrong. The reality is that there are only a handful of companies making dog food in America today. Moreover, the businesses that actually print their names on the labels often get their ingredients (or, indeed, their ready-made products) from the very same suppliers. Not unlike Cargill and ADM, these suppliers hide in the proverbial shadows and don't worry about marketing themselves to dog-owning consumers. They just buy ingredients, turn them into dog food, and sell those foods to the handful of firms that have the marketing budgets to convince consumers that their products are special and unique, and the distribution networks needed to get those products out into the market.

For the most part, these suppliers sell strikingly similar products to all their clients. The public health advocate and long-serving former chair of NYU's Global Institute of Public Health, Marion Nestle (no relation to Nestlé, S.A.), put it this way in her eye-opening book *Pet Food Politics*:

> [Pet food] recipes may differ in proportions of ingredients, but the basic ingredients are much the same. So the recall produced this revelation: the contents of pet foods are much alike, and the most important difference between one brand and another is not nutrition; it is price.

Nestle made this claim while telling the story of the largest recall in the history of pet food. And it's a story that serves as a scary reminder of the dangers of industry consolidation. In 2007, a supplier of canned pet foods called Menu Foods Income Trust bought a batch of wheat gluten (a cereal grain derivative) from a vendor, that had in turn imported the ingredient from China. At the time Menu Foods was the largest supplier of canned pet foods in the world, and it used the Chinese wheat gluten in products made for clients like Purina, Hill's, Del Monte, Royal Canin, Natural Balance, Blue Buffalo, Diamond, and Proctor & Gamble (at the time the corporate parent of Iams), as well as in many major private-label brands, such as those sold by Wal-Mart. Unfortunately, the Chinese wheat gluten turned out to be tainted with something called melamine, a poisonous substance that causes acute kidney failure in dogs and cats. The melamine went into the food products, the food went out to the big pet food labels, and thousands of unsuspecting American consumers went on to poison their dogs and cats.

The result was nothing short of a nightmare, both for the pet food companies and for the animals that ate their foods. The contaminated products were eventually recalled in what was, at the time, the single largest product recall in the history of the United States. But not before as many as 4,000 pets had died from melamine-induced renal failure. Menu Foods and its vendors shouldered much of the blame, eventually reaching a $24 million settlement in a class action lawsuit brought by pet owners. The company shut down some factories and sold others off (Mars bought one). It lost almost all of its market value and was later acquired, for just pennies on the dollar, by another major pet food supplier, a company called Simmons Pet Food, Inc.

This story highlights some of the most glaring problems associated with the modern pet food market. For one, the industry is so consolidated that if just one supplier drops the ball it can spoil a whole host of pet food products. The 2007 recall also shows just how opaque the supply chain for most major pet food products really is. That opacity has hardly been corrected in the years since the recall. After all, Simmons Pet Food—the supplier that acquired Menu Foods in the wake of the 2007 scandal—still "supplies all or a meaningful portion of the private-label wet pet food products sold by 9 of the top 10 and 35 of the top 40 North American food retailers."

But all this industry consolidation gives rise to another problem too: for all the choice that appears to exist in the pet food market, the products that are available to consumers are far more similar than they are different. And, when it comes to the story of canine obesity in America, they are similar in one particularly notable way. Essentially all of the dry dog foods on the market today are built primarily around a single nutritional substrate. In evolutionary terms, it's pretty new to the global food landscape. And, as we've already seen, wolves don't eat it and dogs don't need it. But thanks to modern farming techniques, it is profoundly inexpensive.

There's just one problem: according to Gary Taubes and company, it's also causing a global epidemic of obesity.

WHY BIG KIBBLE LOVES CARBS

IF GIVEN THE CHOICE, dogs will mostly avoid carbohydrates, as a series of experiments conducted in the United Kingdom recently demonstrated. The scientists behind the studies, which were published in 2013 in the journal *Behavioral Ecology*, crafted several different kinds of dietary "self-selection" situations and exposed a host of different dogs to them. Each of these different scenarios provided the dogs with an opportunity to choose how much of each of the major macronutrients (protein, fat, and carbohydrate) they would consume. The researchers used five different breeds—Papillons, Miniature Schnauzers, Cocker Spaniels, Labrador Retrievers, and Saint Bernards—and let the dogs choose time and again exactly what proportion of protein, fat, and carbohydrate they wanted to eat.

In the end, the animals chose, on average, a ratio of 30% protein, 63% fat, and only 7% carbohydrate. The researchers noted the "remarkable consistency" with which the 30/63/7 ratio held across the five observed breeds, a finding that dovetailed well with previous nutritional self-selection studies in dogs. The domestic dog, it seems, is pretty averse to carbohydrates.

Unfortunately, most kibble recipes do little to honor the dietary preferences of the domestic dog. According to an *ad hoc* committee convened by the National Research Council in 2006, most dry dog foods are composed of somewhere between 46% and 74% carbohydrate. So the foods that some 80% of us are feeding to our canine companions every day contain about *ten times* as much carbohydrate as those dogs would eat if left to their own devices.

To understand why carbohydrates play such a prominent role in dog foods, it is important to understand the history of mass-marketed kibble. The story is said to have begun in the mid-19th century with a man named James Spratt. Spratt was an American, and an entrepreneurial one at that. While visiting London to promote a lightning conductor that he had recently patented, he is said to have happened upon a pack of dogs squabbling over some kind of food. Upon closer inspection, the food was revealed to be a chunk of hardtack, a tough biscuit made from a simple mixture of flour and water. Despite being something of a chore to consume (the word "tack" was slang for "food," so it is probably safe to assume that "hard-tack" was more than just pleasantly crusty), hardtack was popular in navy campaigns of the day, as it was (1) very inexpensive to produce and (2) very long-lasting. Knowing all this, and observing the hungry dogs fighting over the "sea biscuit," Spratt had an idea.

He introduced Spratt's Patent Meat Fibrine Dog Cakes in 1860. They were flour biscuits whose ingredients apparently included some type of meat (or, more likely, a meat by-product), though, setting the tone for an industry that is still less than forthcoming about its ingredients, he is said to have kept the meat ingredient a secret, even until his death in 1878. But whether they were made with beef or beef blood doesn't seem to have been too important to consumers, because Spratt's new meat-flavored dog biscuits were a hit. His company grew large and its products spawned imitators. Among them were F.H. Bennett, a cracker-baker who introduced his "Malatoid Milk-Bones" shortly after the turn of the century, and also a grain distributor named William H. Danforth, who founded his own firm in 1894. When picking a name for his new dog biscuit company, Danforth chose to pay homage to a quackish self-help fad of the day, one that claimed that a purer race of human beings could be achieved if people avoided nefarious activities, such as eating watermelons, and focused instead on a few essential guiding principles: **R**egime, **A**ctivity, **L**ight, **S**trength, **T**emperation, **O**xygen, and **N**ature. Like most of the under-regulated huckster health fads of the late 19th century, "Ralstonism" didn't stand the test of time. But Danforth's Ralston Purina Company sure did. Today, its corporate successor, the Nestlé-Purina PetCare Company, is the largest dog food manufacturer in the world.

***

I wanted to understand how much (or how little) has changed in the world of dog food over the past century, so I asked Purina for a tour of one of their factories.

Not that it's any great secret how dry dog food is made. Unless Purina had recently developed a top-secret, proprietary kibble-producing machine, the company is probably employing some variant of the very same process that just about all dry dog food manufacturers use to produce their foods. It's called extrusion processing.

Making dry dog food via extrusion processing is like baking little nubs of meat-infused pasta. First the ingredients are combined in a massive mixing vat. Those ingredients will vary depending on the formula but there are a few things you can count on. The recipe will almost certainly include some kind of animal-based product (or by-product). This is as much to satisfy consumer expectations and create a marketable product as it is to deliver protein and essential amino acids—one imagines that dog owners wouldn't exactly be lining up to buy a dog food whose protein content comes from, say, soybeans. The second thing you can count on is that there will always be a significant amount of a starchy cereal grain or some other carbohydrate ingredient. The need for starches arises in the second step of the process, when the mixture is heated. Heating is typically done in two stages, first in a pre-conditioner, where the mixture is steamed, and then in an extruder barrel—the defining piece of machinery in the process, it looks like a giant conical meat-grinder—where it is baked. Just like with bagels, biscuits, pancakes, muffins, cinnamon rolls, cupcakes (can you feel the dopamine flowing yet?), or any other kind of baked good, a substantial amount of starch must be added to the mixture in order to give volume to the dough and ensure that it retains its shape as it is heated.

After the mixture is heated, it gets squeezed ("extruded") through a shaping nozzle and then cut into individual kibbles. The little nuggets are then dried, making them shelf-stable. And, last but not least, the kibbles get sprayed with some kind of "flavor-enhancer," in order to maximize palatability.

I contacted Purina because I was interested in seeing extrusion processing first-hand. The company seemed like an appropriate choice; after all, it sells more dog food than anyone else in the world. Unfortunately, after sitting on my request for a few days, an anonymous Purina representative wrote me back, politely informing me that the company didn't offer factory tours to outsiders. No attempt was made to explain the justification for the policy. They just said no.

So I tried the Blue Buffalo Company, perhaps the best known of the self-described "premium" dog food brands, and one that fashions itself as a kind of anti-Purina. Historically, Blue Buffalo's advertisements have been characterized by aggressive, explicit criticisms of "big name" pet food manufacturers. Its website tells dog owners to "Love Them Like Family" and "Feed Them Like Family." The suggestion is that we should avoid the Purinas of the world and instead feed our dogs one of Blue Buffalo's many different "healthy" and "holistic" formulas, all of which are made with only "the finest natural ingredients." Surely if any manufacturer was going to break ranks with Purina and let me inside the kitchen it would be Blue Buffalo.

Alas, it was not to be. A few days after receiving my request, a Blue Buffalo representative named Belinda sent me the following curt reply:

Hi Daniel,

Thank you for taking your time to contact BLUE. At this time there are no factory tours.

Take care,
Belinda
Blue Buffalo Co.

Perhaps I shouldn't have been all that surprised that Blue Buffalo didn't want to show me how its products are made. For one, its "you can trust us, we're just the little guy" image is more marketing ploy than reality. In its early days, the company's explosive growth was fueled by generous investment from the Invus Group, a leading private equity firm. When, in 2015, Blue Buffalo went public, it raised $677 million in its very first day of trading on the Nasdaq Stock Market. Its homespun brand identity notwithstanding, Blue Buffalo isn't exactly your local butcher.

It also appears that Blue Buffalo's foods aren't quite as unique as it would have us believe. In 2014, Purina filed a multimillion-dollar false advertising lawsuit against the company, alleging that Blue Buffalo has lied about what's in its pet foods. Purina claims to have independently tested some Blue Buffalo products and found that they contain things like "poultry by-product meal," eggshells, and feathers—precisely the stuff that Blue Buffalo claims to avoid. Over the course of the litigation, some pretty damning e-mails have come to light. They seem to corroborate Purina's allegations, highlighting the "massive product recalls," "market share loss," and "enormous" liabilities that were likely to result from the presence of by-products in Blue Buffalo's foods. The e-mails have been proven prescient: in 2015, Blue Buffalo finally bit the bullet and agreed to pay more than $30 million to its misled customers. The whole episode has played out in the media, rendering Blue Buffalo's self-cultivated identity rather bogus.

Of course, it's also possible that Blue Buffalo doesn't actually control all of the factories where its foods are produced. It certainly didn't as of 2007, when it got caught up in the Menu Foods scandal. Unfortunately, the company also wouldn't provide me with any information about its vendors. So, just to complete the loop, I reached-out to as many "white label" pet food manufacturers and suppliers as I could find (like Cargill and ADM, these firms have every interest in keeping a low profile with consumers, so they're not all that easy to identify), and asked each one for a quick tour. They all denied my requests. CJ Foods, Inc. ("We are the home for custom contract manufacturing services for the Super Premium pet food industry") said no. American Nutrition ("The biggest brands in pet food partner with American Nutrition") said no. Mountain Country Foods ("[W]e are one of the largest pet treat manufacturers in the United States") said no. Simmons Pet Food (the contract manufacturer that bought Menu Foods after the melamine scandal) didn't even bother to respond.

In other words, getting one's self inside a dog food factory is not as easy as you might hope—I've been trying for the better part of four years and have yet to succeed. And the willingness of dog food companies to make outlandish claims about the quality of their products far exceeds their willingness to provide facts about those products and let you reach your own conclusions. As Marion Nestle observed in the wake of the Menu Foods scandal, for all the feel-good messaging to be found on the surface of the pet food industry, what lies beneath is still shrouded in opacity.

***

There are several reasons why extruded products dominate the dog food market so comprehensively. In comparison with other types of dog foods, kibble is a convenient product. It keeps well, doesn't make much of a mess, and is simple to prepare—just scoop and serve.

And, more importantly, it is inexpensive. To understand the astounding degree to which this is so, compare the per-calorie price of a "premium" kibble against one of the cheapest restaurant-prepared foods you can find in America today, the McDonald's Quarter Pounder with Cheese. If you stop by your local McDonald's and order one of their undeniably delicious burgers, you will be asked to pay about $4.25 for the privilege of eating it (at least that's the current price in my neighborhood). In exchange, you will receive about 540 calories of nutritional sustenance. When you do the math, this works out to about 80 cents for every 100 calories of nutrition. Not bad—probably less than the per-calorie cost of a Coke.

But now let's compare that against the per-calorie cost of a fancy kibble, such as one from Blue Buffalo's curiously named "Life Protection" line. Regardless of how "premium" the ingredients in Blue Buffalo's foods actually are (however Purina's lawsuit ultimately pans out), the company prices its foods as if they are some of the best in the market. If you buy from the online retailer Chewy.com, a 30-pound bag of "Life Protection Formula Chicken and Brown Rice Recipe with LifeSource Bits" will run you $46.79, making it one of the more expensive kibbles money can buy. And, according to its label, when you add up all the servings in that 30-pound bag of kibble, you'll wind up with just about 50,000 calories of total nutrition. Whip out your calculator and do the same math we did earlier with our Quarter Pounder with Cheese and you'll see that this works out to less than ten cents for every 100 calories of nutrition—or about 10% of the per-calorie cost of a Quarter Pounder with Cheese.

Yes, you're reading that right. A calorie of one of the most infamously junky foods ever created costs about 700% more than a calorie of Blue Buffalo's fancy, "holistic" kibble. Don't let all the images of fresh, whole vegetables and deliciously marbled steaks fool you—even "premium" kibbles are still some of the cheapest edible substances you can find anywhere on the planet today.

So why can dry dog food manufacturers sell their products for such insanely low prices? It's simple: the products are incredibly inexpensive for them to produce. The most infamous strategy for keeping kibble ingredient costs low is the use of animal by-products instead of actual meat to give a food product its protein content and aura of meat-ness. As Blue Buffalo's massive consumer class action settlement shows, this practice elicits strong feelings of disgust from many dog owners (although it must be said that you don't hear too many complaints from their dogs). Still, it's hard to deny that, as an economic matter, it is highly efficient. Essentially, animal by-products are what's left of slaughtered animals once all the meat is gone. Some examples are blood meal (made from the blood of slaughtered cows), chicken by-product meal (made from undesirable carcass parts like intestines, undeveloped eggs, and feet), bone meal (made from rendered skeletons), as well as arguably grosser things like chicken feathers and fetal pigs. Although many of these by-products contain some nutritional value (some caloric content, some quantity of protein), they're so disgusting to human beings that most of us have no interest in eating them. They would all be treated as waste if it weren't for modern food production techniques that allow them to be salvaged and processed into ingredients to be used in products like dog foods.

The business of converting animal by-products into things like pet food ingredients is called rendering, and it is a critical part of modern agribusiness. As much as 50% of beef, 44% of swine, and 30% of all poultry tissues will never be used in human food products. These tissues would amount to nearly 50 billion pounds of waste a year if they weren't processed into things like pet food ingredients, which about a quarter of them reportedly are. Blue

Buffalo's claim that its products contain only "real meat" is another way of saying that they don't contain meat by-products. And Purina's lawsuit is a way of challenging that claim.

Just about any food made with animal by-products is going to cost less to produce than one composed of real meat. But there's an even more glaring reason why all dry kibbles—no matter how "premium" their ingredients—are so inexpensive to produce. And that is because, regardless of whether the protein comes from egg shells and feathers or USDA Prime filet mignon, it is certain to be combined with sizable quantities of corn, wheat, rice, potatoes, or some other kind of starchy agricultural product. And these crops—the very ones Gary Taubes and company blame for the obesity epidemic—are *by far* the least expensive edible substances to be found anywhere on our planet.

WHY IS THIS NEWS?

CONSIDERING HOW EMOTIONAL dog owners are about our dogs, it's not all that surprising that we can get pretty worked up about something as simple as dog food. The consumer outrage associated with the 2007 Menu Foods recall was thunderous (at least for a time; many seem to have already forgotten some of the important lessons taught by the scandal). And with websites like "The Truth About Pet Food" and books like *Not Fit For a Dog!*, consumer activists regularly level loud and vociferous criticism at dog food manufacturers for all manner of perceived transgressions. The use of meat by-products instead of actual meat, the importing of ingredients from foreign countries with substandard health regulations, the notion that many dog food products don't deliver enough of the micronutrients that dogs need for optimal health—and those are just the tip of the iceberg.

But for all that vitriol, something you don't hear too much about is the idea that dietary carbohydrates play an outsized role in making dogs fat and that the excessive carbohydrate content of dry dog foods may be playing a large role in perpetuating one of the largest animal welfare crises in the world today.

So why not?

For one, the idea that carbs play an outsized role in making us fat runs against the current nutritional dogma and, for that very reason, it's going to be an uphill battle to get it into the mainstream. The underlying science may not be new or controversial, but folks like Gary Taubes, William Davis, Loren Cordain, Tim Noakes, and David Ludwig—the individuals who have done the most to raise public awareness about the science—have done the bulk of their work in only the last 15 years or so. And some of the most persuasive pieces of evidence which are used to make the case against carbs—like the Stanford A TO Z study—are even more recent than that.

15 years may sound like a long time, but compare it to the history of

smoking in the United States. Human beings have been smoking tobacco since ancient times. But it wasn't until 1929 that a pathologist in Germany made the first statistical link between smoking and lung cancer. And the first major studies definitively linking lung cancer to smoking weren't published until 1950. Anti-smoking initiatives began to gather pace in the wake of the 1950 publications, as the scary findings slowly began trickling into the American public's consciousness. In 1964, the Surgeon General of the United States issued his damning "Report on Smoking and Health." And, by 1970, Congress had finally removed all cigarette advertising from television and radio.

But, despite the compelling scientific findings, the consistent efforts of public figures to draw attention to this newfound health hazard, the many legal challenges, and the widespread federal regulatory backlash, it wasn't until about 1970—two decades after the publication of the landmark studies linking smoking with cancer—that per-capita cigarette consumption began to decline in earnest in the United States. Even today, there are more than 40 million smokers in the United States. It's *still* one of the leading causes of preventable death in our country.

You can probably guess one of the main reasons why it's been such slow going. By the second half of the 20th century, as the scientific community was uncovering the dangers of smoking, tobacco was already a colossal American industry, one selling billions of cigarettes to American consumers every year. And mammoth corporations like Phillip Morris and RJ Reynolds fought the emerging anti-smoking measures tooth and nail, steadfastly denying the health dangers of their products and dumping huge sums of money into marketing and legal defense. While the truth about the dangers of smoking is now well understood by American consumers, winning the publicity war against Big Tobacco has been a slow and arduous process. And many lives have been lost along the way.

Is something similar going on right now with Big Kibble and its dry dog food products? As firmly entrenched members of the Carbohydrate Lobby, these mega-corporations have vested interests in preserving the reputations of "heart-healthy whole grains" and the other starchy carbohydrates of which their foods are primarily composed. And just like the corporate giants responsible for most of the food eaten by modern-day humans, Big Kibble also has the budget to exert its influence upon regulators, veterinarians, and the public-at-large. In other words, Big Kibble has both the means and the motive to obscure the fact that it uses immense quantities of dietary carbohydrates in its dog foods and to downplay the significance of scientific findings suggesting that that's a bad thing for canine health and longevity.

Of course, means and motive aren't enough to convict. This may all sound reasonable enough, but before we jump to any conclusions about the role that Big Kibble plays in shaping how we all think about canine health and wellbeing, we need to look for actual evidence of funny business.

***

In order to begin evaluating that evidence, I reached out to Dr. Tiffany Bierer, lead author of the 2004 *Journal of Nutrition* study that we discussed in Chapter Three, the one in which low-carbohydrate dogs lost six times as much fat as dogs on traditional diets. When considering the case against carbohydrate-laden pet foods, Dr. Bierer's 2004 trial is likely the most important piece of scientific evidence presently in existence. But her experiment hasn't made nearly the impact one might expect. It has been cited in only a handful of subsequent studies, none of the major veterinary nutritional textbooks spend much time discussing it, and Dr. Bierer herself hasn't followed it up with any related work.

That all struck me as strange, seeing as the study's findings are wholly inconsistent with the ubiquitous calories-in, calories-out model of obesity. Either calories-in, calories-out is wrong or Dr. Bierer's conclusions are wrong; the two simply can't coexist. And I had begun to wonder whether Big Kibble—with its vested interest in preserving the sanctity of calories-in, calories-out—could somehow be involved in the study's otherwise-inexplicable low profile. So I decided to send Dr. Bierer an e-mail.

She wasn't hard to find. In an effort to facilitate the public's understanding of scientific works, most academic journals publish contact information for their authors. And *The Journal of Nutrition* was no exception. Dr. Bierer's e-mail address was printed right there in her paper, alongside her forceful conclusions about the fat-fighting efficacy of low-carbohydrate diets.

I put together a short message. It expressed my admiration for her work, described my own project, and requested an opportunity to discuss her experiment further. I fired it off and I waited. Several weeks passed. But I never heard back from her.

This too seemed strange. I had contacted dozens of scientists in connection with my research. And just about all of them had been anxious to speak with me, if for no other reason than to tout the significance of their work. And, as the author of an important (and widely overlooked) piece of scientific research, Dr. Bierer seemed like someone who'd be particularly keen on answering journalistic interview requests.

So I tried to reach her again, this time using Twitter. After a bit of online sleuthing, I discovered that she maintained an active presence on the social media platform, regularly posting new informational content and otherwise interacting with her animal-loving followers. I sent her a few polite messages, explaining who I was and why I was interested in communicating with her directly.

And then I waited.

But, again, no response. Over the days that followed, I watched my Twitter account far more closely than is healthy. And although Dr. Bierer made several new posts, she never responded to any of my messages.

I was disappointed to receive the cold shoulder. She didn't even feel like I deserved a "no comment" or a "thanks, but no thanks"? It felt like an indictment, both of my project and of me. Still, I was prepared to let the whole thing go when one morning a week or so later an e-mail finally showed up in my in-box. The subject line read, "Tweet to Dr. Tiffany Bierer." But when I opened the message I discovered that it wasn't from Dr. Bierer herself. It was from a woman named Angel, a "corporate communications manager" for Mars PetCare—the Big Kibble firm responsible for brands like Pedigree, Iams, and Cesar. Her message was short and to-the-point:

> Hi Daniel,
>
> I am writing in response to a tweet from you to Dr. Tiffany Bierer regarding a request to speak to her about a pet obesity book you are writing. Would love to understand more about your project.
>
> Thanks,
>
> Angel

I was dumbstruck. I had requested to interview the author of an important piece of journal-published scientific research and, rather than receive a response from her directly, a public relations representative for a company with a vested interest in the study's findings had responded on her behalf. This was, to say the least, not consistent with my previous experience interviewing research scientists.

But when I looked a bit more carefully into Dr. Bierer's record, I began to glean what was going on. I came to learn that Dr. Bierer was an employee of Mars PetCare. And not only had her study been conducted while she was an employee of one of Mars's corporate predecessors, but the study itself was sponsored by the firm, as was the symposium at which the paper was originally presented. Mars's fingerprints were all over the research. And it seemed the company was—at least in my case—exerting a measure of control over the scientist who had produced it.

I put together a response to Angel's e-mail, explaining who I was and why I was interested in interviewing Dr. Bierer. I highlighted some of my perspectives on canine obesity and outlined the contents of my book. I made it clear that I wasn't seeking any of Mars's trade secrets or other confidential information. I was just interested in Dr. Bierer's perspectives on her own published research. Then I sent the message off and I waited.

No response.

I sent another e-mail.

Nothing.

I never heard back from Dr. Tiffany Bierer. But my numerous failed attempts to reach her were enough to pique my interest in the relationship between Big Kibble and the veterinary research community. Were Dr. Bierer and her 2004 study just an example of a larger phenomenon? Exactly what role does Big Kibble play in shaping how dog owners—veterinarians and laypeople alike—understand the science of obesity? More than ever, I was motivated to learn more. And, as I'd soon discover, there was more to learn.

Much more.

Chapter Five

TRUTH, FICTION, AND VETERINARY NUTRITIONAL DOGMA

--

"I believe nicotine is not addictive, yes."
William Campbell, President & CEO, Phillip Morris USA,
Sworn testimony before Congress (1994)

———————

NUTRITION EXPERTS?

BECOMING A VETERINARIAN is a long and challenging process. For most, just getting into school is an insurmountable obstacle. There are only 30 AVMA-accredited veterinary schools in the United States and their admissions processes are notoriously selective. To even be considered, applicants usually will have excelled at the undergraduate level, even while completing rigorous math and science coursework. They'll have aced the GRE. And many will have spent time working at a veterinary practice or volunteering at an animal shelter before applying. Even so, the majority of vet school applicants will be denied admission.

One of the reasons why the barriers to entry are so high is that rising veterinarians are expected to become experts in a wide range of topics. Animals are remarkably complicated organisms. Their bodies are composed of between nine and 12 different organ systems (depending on how you define things), all of which work together with symphonic intricacy. And not only must aspiring veterinarians demonstrate their knowledge of each system—by completing a rigorous, four-year graduate degree program and passing a 360-question interstate licensing examination—they must understand how each functions in all manner of diverse species.

Melissa Tucker knew all this—she never expected vet school to be easy. Still, having excelled throughout her life, she arrived confident. The eldest of five children, Melissa was born and raised in Tobaccoville, North Carolina, a sleepy postage stamp town on the outskirts of Winston-Salem. Today, she describes the town's prevailing economic conditions with a shrug and a quip:

"Folks get most of their clothes from Goodwill." Like many Americans raised in rural communities, animals—dogs, cats, sheep, horses, a goat named Molly—were part of Melissa's life from a young age. And, through regular exposure and a regimen of daily chores, she gradually developed an affinity for the simple-minded peacefulness and charming eccentricities of her four-legged companions. By the time she went away to college she knew that she wanted to be a vet. Fortunately, she had spent her childhood cultivating a sense of discipline and a strong work ethic. At college, she excelled in her studies and eventually gained admission to one of the most selective and prestigious veterinary schools in the country.

Graduate programs in veterinary medicine are overseen by the AVMA's Council on Education, which employs a curriculum policy as part of its rubric for determining whether a school is worthy of accreditation. So curricula tend to look pretty similar from one school to the next. At most schools, the first year is about fundamentals, with courses that introduce students to the inner-workings of animal bodies and the biological boundaries that separate one species from another ("Veterinary Anatomy I," "Veterinary Physiology I"). These courses tend to be large, multi-credit affairs, structured around lectures, labs, and textbook learning. Lecture courses feature in the second year too, but they tend to focus on particular groups of animals, organ systems, and pathologies ("Clinical Toxicology," "Small Animal Medicine and Surgery," "Food Animal Medicine"). Over the third and fourth years, students are gradually exposed to even more specific topics ("Shelter Medicine," "Camelid Practice"), along with electives and clinical experience. In this way, schools allow for a degree of specialization. But while individual students gravitate toward individual subjects, everyone is expected to be at least reasonably expert on just about everything.

There is, in other words, a lot of information to process. At times, Melissa found the experience to be like drinking water from a fire hose. "There was *so much* to learn," she remembers. "If you're an animal person, then it's hard not to enjoy the work. But, my God, there was a lot of it."

The across-the-animal-kingdom nature of the curriculum played a particularly significant role in keeping the work volume turned up at all times. "From early on, I was sure that I would be going into small animals," Melissa says today, using the industry term for pet cats and dogs, "but I still had to spend a tremendous amount of time learning about wildlife and food animals." To accentuate the point, she tells me about how she and some fellow students spent a semester training for and entering a cattle show. (They mostly competed against schoolchildren. Sadly, their cow, a Holstein named Ginger, took last place.)

In the final analysis, however, Melissa found that the robust intellectual challenge more than made up for the lack of free time. Talking with her today, it is clear that she remembers her veterinary school experience with great affection. "My professors were wonderful, the other students were bright and motivated, the courses were fun and interesting and challenging." Indeed, she seems to have only positive things to say about vet school, with one notable exception.

***

They say that an ounce of prevention is worth a pound of cure. But for every dollar spent on human health care, only a few cents go toward prevention—most of it is spent on treatment. And the economics that govern the practice of small animal veterinary medicine in the United States are much the same. In fact, they may be skewed toward treatment even more heavily.

"I'd say that precisely zero percent of our business comes from preventive care," says Dr. Jordan Scherk, the medical director of a specialty veterinary clinic in Salt Lake City, Utah. "In the world of specialty veterinary medicine, well visits are extremely uncommon," he continues. "They just don't happen." In smaller, non-specialty practices, vaccinations and dental cleanings are somewhat more common. But on the whole, veterinary medicine is an industry focused primarily on treatment, not prevention.

Vet school curricula tend to reflect this reality. "My courses definitely focused on clinical care and treatment," Melissa remembers. "Pathology, toxicology, diagnostics, that kind of stuff." This is, of course, a perfectly reasonable way to prepare rising veterinarians for a world in which preventive care will make up only a fraction of their daily responsibilities. It's just not a particularly good way to prepare them for a world in which "the number one chronic health concern in our canine companions" is obesity, a condition best managed via preventive care.

A broader survey of America's veterinary schools hammers the point home. At the time of writing, only three schools in the United States require their students to complete anything more than a single nutritional science course. Most don't even require that. In one-third of the veterinary schools in the country, students receive their degrees without having to complete any graduate-level nutrition coursework whatsoever. Moreover, when a nutrition course is required, it is in almost all cases a one or two credit-hour experience, putting it on the same level as hyper-specialized subjects like "Ornamental Fish Medicine" and "Equine Dentistry."

In that one short course, most students are taught everything they will ever be expected to know about canine obesity. But they'll also cover much more than that. The course will address *all* aspects of canine nutrition, not just how the phenomenon relates to obesity. And it won't focus exclusively on dogs either. In a single course, students typically will cover all aspects of nutritional science with regard to all animal species—cats, gerbils, horses, cows, fishes, snakes, birds, and everyone else that managed to stake out some space on the ark.

The net result, to hear Melissa Tucker tell it, is not a particularly detailed or rigorous examination of veterinary nutritional science. "Honestly, our nutrition course was a joke," she says.

Like many others, Melissa's veterinary school didn't have a board-certified veterinary nutritionist on its faculty. So one was flown in from an off-site location to teach the course. The instructor appeared a grand total of three times: once for each of two separate one-week teaching blocks and once, later, to administer the final exam.

No textbook was required either. Some ten years after completing the course, Melissa showed me the photocopied pamphlet that served as its only required reading. Emphasizing the across-the-animal-kingdom nature of its contents, the cover of the pamphlet was decorated with hand-drawn images of a ram, a cow, a horse, a dog, and a cat. It was about 80 pages long. It featured a short outline of the course (total classroom time: 22 hours) and a one-page discussion of obesity, but not a single academic citation.

Dr. Ernie Ward was apparently subjected to something similar during his own professional education, a couple of decades earlier. "In veterinary school, I'd been taught how to treat diseases, not prevent them," he writes in *Chow Hounds*. "No one taught me to view food as medicine or how nutrition could preserve health." To his eyes, the result of this tendency to focus on treatment rather than prevention has been predictable—a nation of veterinarians with a remarkably unsophisticated understanding of basic nutrition and other wellness issues. "Here's a secret few veterinarians (or human doctors) will let you in on," he has written, "most health professionals haven't the faintest clue how to interpret a food label."

***

This is not to say that veterinarians are doing anything wrong. After all, they're not responsible for developing their own educational programs. And academic administrators deserve some sympathy too. Given the sheer quantity of information relevant to the practice of veterinary medicine, it only makes sense to skim over some subjects in the general curriculum and rely on specialization to make up the difference—to selectively sacrifice depth for breadth. This is a strategy that the human medical community has long embraced and the veterinary medical community has been coming around to since at least the 1970s. As Dr. Willem Becker, a board-certified veterinary surgeon, recently told me, "the practice of veterinary medicine is increasingly becoming a niche profession. The days when one vet would be responsible for seeing all patients, all problems, all animals—those days are disappearing."

In other words, if you want to become a true expert on canine nutrition, your best career move is to seek board certification as a veterinary nutritionist. The American College of Veterinary Nutrition is the organization that provides such certification, and it requires at least two years of nutrition-focused clinical, teaching, and research experience, plus passage of a written examination, before it is willing to certify any new diplomate.

The only problem is that no one actually wants to be a board-certified veterinary nutritionist. At the moment, fewer than 80 of the more than 100,000 vets in the United States are ACVN diplomates. That works out to less than one-tenth of 1% of the total veterinary population. The other 99.9% of vets probably just got Melissa Tucker's "it was a joke" nutritional course, if that.

And before you go looking to see if there's a board-certified veterinary nutritionist in your neck of the woods, let me offer you some advice based on my own personal experience: don't get your hopes up. I recently reviewed the ACVN's directory, looking for a local expert to help me understand how to optimize my own dog's nutrition. I found not a single board-certified veterinary nutritionist practicing anywhere in my home state of Utah. Unfortunately, there weren't any to be found in any of the neighboring states of Nevada, Wyoming, Montana, or Idaho either. I was able to locate two in Colorado, from whom I am separated by only about seven hours of mountain driving. But, upon closer examination, I learned that only one would actually be available to help me. The other had recently passed away.

My research revealed another problem too. Many of the board-certified veterinary nutritionists practicing in America aren't local vets, the kind that provide nutritional advice to everyday pet owners and clinical care to everyday pets. In fact, according to the ACVN, there are fewer than ten board-certified veterinary nutritionists in private practice in the United States today. Academic work is more common. And, unfortunately, so is working for Big Kibble. In fact, about 20% of the world's veterinary nutritionists currently work for pet food manufacturers.

But this is just one example of a far broader trend. Indeed, when trying to understand why the veterinary community has been so slow to embrace the carbohydrate-insulin model of obesity, it's hard to escape the conclusion that Big Kibble—a vested member of the Carbohydrate Lobby—is playing a leading role.

BIG KIBBLE GOES TO VET SCHOOL

Since dog owners get the bulk of their nutritional advice from veterinarians, it makes good business sense for Big Kibble to form close relationships with America's vets. After all, convincing 70 million dog owners that a product is special (or even nutritionally adequate) might border on impossible, even for a multinational corporation. But motivating 100,000 influential people to get your message out via word-of-mouth? That just might work.

The strategy of marketing dog food through veterinarians was pioneered by Hill's Pet Nutrition, a company that went from rendering animal byproducts and packing meat (it once specialized in horse meat) in the early 20th century, to making "premium" pet foods for the household products giant Colgate-Palmolive by 1976. As the journalist Tara Parker-Pope wrote in the *Wall Street Journal* in 1997, Hill's borrowed the marketing practice from the toothpaste side of Colgate, where a similar strategy recently had been used to successfully sell toothpaste through dentists. Colgate, in turn, had borrowed the strategy from the pharmaceuticals industry, where wooing doctors has long been seen as the best way to market new drugs. "It's just like taking drugs," according to John Steel, Colgate's former senior vice president of global marketing and sales. "You go to the doctor and he prescribes something for you and you don't much question what the doctor says. It's the same with animals."

Is it ever. By focusing on marketing to vets rather than to consumers, Hill's grew explosively, from $40 million in annual sales in 1982 to nearly $900 million by 1997. And it did so on a marketing budget that was dwarfed by many of its Big Kibble competitors. But those competitors gradually took notice. These days, it seems you're nobody in the world of Big Kibble unless you're marketing your products through trusted veterinarians.

***

Like most rising veterinarians, Melissa Tucker was something of a cash-strapped young animal lover during veterinary school. "We weren't exactly shopping at Goodwill anymore, but we were definitely living on a budget," she remembers. Back then, she and her husband shared their small house with three dogs and a cat. And, with Melissa struggling just to keep her head above the rising academic waters, they shared a single income stream too.

Vet school is expensive. The average tuition approaches $50,000 for each year of a four-year program, and that's before books, housing, and other expenses. As a result, the average graduate enters the workforce with more than $135,000 in student loan debt. In this regard, Melissa was no exception—she relied on a combination of scholarships, financial aid, and student loans to pay for her professional education.

But she also relied on a curious kind of corporate benevolence to help make ends meet. On her first day of classes, she was grateful (if somewhat surprised) to discover that Big Kibble's efforts to get in good with America's vets begin during veterinary school. "At my school we had a student store," she remembers, "and, since practically all veterinary students have pets, one of the things that the store carried was pet supplies—foods, treats, flea and tick meds, all that." The products were offered at deeply discounted "student rates," low prices made possible because of heavy subsidization by Big Kibble suppliers. "Everything was like 80 or 90% off," Melissa remembers. "It was amazing." For a family with four pets, the savings were too good to pass up.

She soon learned that Big Kibble was also interacting with veterinary students in another way—the student store was staffed by on-campus representatives of major dog food companies. These individuals—usually senior veterinary students—were not typical clerks. In exchange for financial aid, they were responsible for answering product questions, passing out logo-adorned corporate goodies and educational literature, and otherwise representing their employers in front of young veterinary students. (Melissa considered working as a rep for a year, but ultimately decided to focus on her classes instead.)

And subsidizing pet food purchases and employing on-campus advocates are not the only ways that Big Kibble has managed to infiltrate the veterinary academy. Companies fly their own salaried nutritionists out to schools to put on extracurricular lectures and nutrition labs. They even provide funding directly to veterinary schools. In 1996, Purina announced that it would be donating $550,000 to fund a nutrition professorship at the University of Missouri-Columbia College of Veterinary Medicine. As of 1997, Hill's was funding a nutrition professorship in nearly half of the veterinary schools in the country.

And then there are the legendary "resident/intern dinners." After graduating from veterinary school, Melissa and her family moved to the Pacific Northwest, where she began a residency in internal medicine at a major veterinary teaching hospital. One of the extracurricular highlights of the experience was an annual dinner put on for all the hospital's residents and interns by Purina Pet Care. It was a swanky affair. "All you can eat, all you can drink, bring your spouse, all that," as Melissa remembers it. The event was staged at the most expensive restaurant in town and there were, of course, cases upon cases of complimentary Purina products on hand.

***

Exactly how much food Big Kibble donates to the veterinary community every year is anyone's guess, but with thousands of veterinary students in school at any given time and with thousands of other caregiving and research institutions benefitting from Big Kibble's largesse as well, it's safe to assume that many thousands of tons of kibble are being given away every year.

The cost of all these giveaways is not insignificant. Indeed, as John Steel has said of Hill's marketing expenses, "the *bulk* of our expenditure goes to the veterinary community." Even at ten cents for every hundred calories, giving away thousands of tons of product every year is going to add up.

So do these considerable financial sacrifices amount to an exercise in corporate altruism? Are these significant expenses being incurred for the purpose of supporting America's rising veterinarians and feeding its sick and needy pets? You'd hope so, at least on some level. Though it's hard to imagine that these campaigns would have any staying power if, in the final analysis, the additional sales they produced didn't outweigh their costs.

More importantly, is it all working? Is Big Kibble actually managing to shape the way that our vets emerge from school thinking about nutrition? The meteoric rise of Hill's during the 1980s and 1990s certainly suggests so. And some folks, such as Anne Martin, the author of *Food Pets Die For*, and the trio of veterinarians behind the book *Not Fit For a Dog!* have issued scathing indictments of the arrangement. Martin has written that, as a result of their exposure to specific brands during vet school, vets are actually being "brainwashed into thinking they have to recommend these commercial foods." The authors of *Not Fit For a Dog!* have gone even further, calling the whole set-up unethical and arguing that "when the full extent of it is realized, the reputation of the veterinary community will be compromised."

Among the vets I interviewed in connection with this book, the most common opinion expressed was that Big Kibble's efforts didn't actually sway the *conscious* loyalties of practitioners. The effects were subtler than that. The brands that took the time to form relationships with vets simply became more visible to them. They increased their "share of mind" with young vets and improved the likelihood that those clinicians would remember specific brands (and, indeed, remember them fondly) when the time came to talk with their patients about dietary decision-making.

Whether there's anything wrong with such an arrangement is hard to say. On the one hand, we like to believe that professionals are more than capable of thinking for themselves. On the other, it's hard to imagine that a similar arrangement would pass the "smell test" if it involved human medical doctors and, say, McDonald's. Right or wrong, one thing is clear: Big Kibble's wooing has, in one way or another, influenced the way that many veterinarians—folks who have had little nutritional training in the first place—think about the most basic issues of diet and nutrition.

***

If that strikes you as a dangerous recipe for institutional bias, then you'll be disappointed to learn that the problem extends well beyond classrooms and clinics. It has made its way into the laboratory too. In fact, Big Kibble's influence is particularly profound in the world of veterinary nutrition research. The closer you look at what vets are being taught about canine nutrition—the studies and textbooks that set forth the information itself, the experiments that supposedly reveal scientific truth—the more often you'll see

Big Kibble's name stamped all over it.

It's a phenomenon that starts all the way at the top. Big Kibble finances some of the most influential veterinary medical organizations in the world. The AVMA, the organization whose stated objective is "advancing the science and practice of veterinary medicine," recently received a $1.5 million donation from Hill's, a founding member of the AVMA's "Platinum Partners Program." Similarly, the World Small Animal Veterinary Association (a kind of global AVMA) sits a "Global Nutrition Committee," which is endorsed by three sponsors: Hill's Pet Nutrition, Nestle Purina, and Royal Canin. In exchange for their financial support, representatives from each of the three companies—all leading dog food manufacturers—are granted direct access to the operations of the Global Nutrition Committee.

Beyond sitting at the most influential policy-setting tables in the veterinary world, Big Kibble's influence also trickles to the ground level, down into the labs where small animal nutrition research is actually being conducted. Funding for companion animal research is notoriously hard to come by. As the AVMA has written, "funding for health-related research dedicated to companion animals (dogs and cats) and horses is virtually nonexistent in comparison to research funding for human and livestock animal health." In 2005, the Association of American Veterinary Medical Colleges estimated that the total annual investment in companion animal and equine research was about $16 million. In comparison, the National Cancer Institute alone provided about $4.9 *billion* worth of cancer research funding in 2014—or about 300 times more than the total amount given to fund all aspects of companion animal and equine research in 2005.

Most of the companion animal research that actually is done takes place in one of two kinds of places—academic institutions and corporate research facilities. And in both cases Big Kibble plays a prominent role in the work.

When it comes to research conducted at veterinary schools, industry sources and other private donors fund a hefty portion of the research. In 2003, private donors and corporations provided more than $55 million for research projects conducted at vet schools, more than the amount contributed by all state agencies *combined* and more than was provided by the USDA. Big Kibble is also usually among the most prominent partners of the non-profits devoted to raising money for animal research, organizations such as the Morris Animal Foundation and the AKC Canine Health Foundation. Since 2013, Hill's, Blue Buffalo, and PETCO have all donated more than $100,000 to the Morris Animal Foundation. In 2013, Purina was the AKC Canine Health Foundation's single largest donor (other than the AKC itself), contributing more than $1,000,000.

When small animal nutrition research isn't conducted at a veterinary school, it is usually conducted at a private research facility. And almost all of these facilities are owned by—you guessed it—Big Kibble. Examples include the Waltham Center for Pet Nutrition (owned by Mars, the parent company behind the Cesar and Pedigree brands) and the Nestle-Purina Pet Care Center. These facilities provide veterinary researchers with the laboratories, equipment, funding, and other resources they need to carry out their work. And a sizable chunk of the published small animal nutrition literature comes out of them.

It's hard to say exactly how much. Because they are run by corporations (as opposed to public agencies), hard data on these private research centers is hard to come by. In a 2005 report on the state of veterinary research in the United States, a committee convened by the National Academy of Sciences wrote that "considerable research on companion animals is conducted by pet-food companies" but that "the committee was unable to quantify any of the resources devoted to those activities because of lack of data." In other words, Big Kibble is keeping much of its private research close to the vest. A paper recently published in the *Journal of the Science of Food and Agriculture* put it nicely when it called all this private research "proprietary." The results of the research belong to Big Kibble, and it's up to Big Kibble to decide what to submit for publication in a peer-reviewed journal and what to keep for itself.

Not that Big Kibble is any stranger to the publishing industry. In fact, two of the most popular nutrition textbooks currently in use in America's veterinary schools were essentially written by dog food companies. Three of the four editors of *Canine and Feline Nutrition: A Resource for Companion Animal Professionals* were employees of Proctor & Gamble (once the company behind the Iams and Eukanuba brands) at the time of publication. In the case of *Small Animal Clinical Nutrition*, two of the book's four editors and more than 15 of its contributing authors were Hill's employees at the time of publication. On the back cover of *Small Animal Clinical Nutrition*, one can even find a testament to the role that Big Kibble played in creating the book: a shiny gold logo and the words "Compliments of Hill's."

***

Is there anything inherently wrong with Big Kibble playing such a prominent role in shaping how the scientific community learns about and understands small animal nutrition? That much is up for debate. On the one hand, giving money to socially valuable causes is a good thing. And corporations should be commended when they use their money to help advance our understanding of important medical issues.

But, on the other hand, you'd have to be pretty naïve to think that Big Kibble doesn't cave to self-interest at least *some* of the time when self-interest comes into conflict with specific research hypotheses. (Again, just try to imagine the public backlash that would ensue if it were revealed that McDonald's owned the research facilities producing much of the world's

nutritional science and wrote the textbooks being used in medical schools.)
And, given what we know about the health dangers of adiposity and the
carbohydrate-laden recipes used by most pet food companies, it's hard to
deny that there is a direct and fundamental conflict of interest between Big
Kibble and any research that might suggest that carbohydrates make dogs fat.
If those conflicts of interest are motivating Big Kibble to drive the research
agenda—to shape what research gets funded and what doesn't, to influence
what gets published and what remains "proprietary"—well, then it's a lot
harder to commend them for it.

PROBLEMS WITH PET FOOD LABELS

Several different entities participate in overseeing the production and sale
of pet foods in the United States. But, at the federal level, the process is
regulated primarily by the Food and Drug Administration. The FDA
discharges its duties pursuant to the *Federal Food, Drug, and Cosmetic Act*, a
piece of federal legislation which, at a high level, requires that all pet foods be
safe to eat, be produced under sanitary conditions, contain no harmful
substances, and be labeled truthfully.

When regulating pet foods, the FDA works closely with an entity called
the Association of American Feed Control Officials, a private organization
that Dr. Ernie Ward has called "arguably one of the most important animal
food organizations in the world." AAFCO has no explicit regulatory or legal
authority and is not a part of any government, state or federal. Still, it
manages to exert considerable influence over how pet foods are sold in
America today. In fact, it probably plays an even more important role in the
process than the FDA itself does.

AAFCO's stated goal is to ensure that animal food markets are safe and
fair. It pursues this goal by publishing a detailed rules framework that
governs the sale of animal food products—what nutrients *must* certain kinds
of foods contain, what ingredients *can* such foods contain, how should food
packaging be labeled, and so forth. In the case of dog foods, these rules take
the form of model bills and regulations that AAFCO publishes and then
lobbies individual state legislatures to enact. Most states have adopted
AAFCO's model bills and regulations wholesale and many others have
written them into their consumer protection laws to a significant degree. As a
result, dog food manufacturers looking to sell nationwide really have no
choice but to comply with AAFCO's model rules and regulations.

Unfortunately, the veterinary community has long been highly critical of
AAFCO's model rules, particularly those regarding nutritional labeling. To
begin to understand why this is so, consider the following chart, which
summarizes in AAFCO's required nutritional labeling format the contents of
a snack regularly enjoyed by millions of human beings.

GUARANTEED ANALYSIS

Crude Protein (Min.):	0.5%
Crude Fat (Min.):	2.1%
Crude Fiber (Max.):	0.4%
Moisture (Max.):	83.6%

Calorie Content (ME): 736kcal/kg
Figure 1 (a).

How's that look? Not so bad, right? Not much protein—but not much fat either. Perhaps a little heavy on the calories. But, then again, how many calories are you supposed to consume in a day anyway? If you don't know the answer to that question off the top of your head, this summary won't do you much good because it doesn't include recommended daily allowances. Moreover, even if you do happen to know your recommended daily caloric intake by heart, you'll need to weigh your snack before you know how many calories it really contains. That's because the chart only describes caloric content on a per-kilogram basis. On the whole, it's a pretty oblique and cumbersome way to summarize nutritional content, but what little information we can glean seems to suggest at least a reasonably healthy snack.

Now consider the nutritional contents of the very same snack, as summarized in the way that the FDA requires producers to label their "people food."

Nutrition Facts

1 servings per container

Serving size	1 Snack

Amount Per Serving

Calories 820

	% Daily Values*
Total Fat 24g	37%
Saturated Fat 3.5g	18%
Trans Fat 0g	
Sodium 310mg	13%
Total Carbohydrate 153g	51%
Dietary Fiber 5g	20%
Total Sugars 86g	
Includes 86g Added Sugars	172%
Protein 6g	12%

*The % Daily Value (DV) tells you how much a nutrient in a serving of food contributes to a daily diet. 2,000 calories a day is used for general nutrition advice.

Figure 1 (b).

125

86 grams of sugar? A third of your daily fat? *Half* your carbs? Yikes. It's the same food in both summaries, but it feels quite a bit worse the second time, doesn't it? And the way you feel after seeing the second summary is probably the way you *should* feel about this snack. Because, just like with the first summary, the snack described here is a large Coke and a large fries from McDonald's. But you'd probably never have guessed that if you'd just seen the first summary.

This example exposes some of the shortcomings of the "Guaranteed Analysis" panel, the AAFCO-imposed dog food equivalent of the "Nutrition Facts" panel found on your favorite bag of chips. The required terms of the Guaranteed Analysis panel are defined by AAFCO and they have been on the receiving end of much criticism from the veterinary community. For one, as Dr. Ernie Ward explains in *Chow Hounds*, the nutritional data in the panel is inherently misleading because it does not provide nutritional information on what's called a "dry-matter" basis. Instead, the percentages are calculated on what's called an "as-fed" basis. This is an important distinction with serious ramifications.

Describing nutritional content on an "as-fed" basis means that any water contained in a food gets factored into percentage-based expressions of the food's nutritional content. This is why the fat and protein numbers in the first example seemed so small. Lots of foods (dog foods and human foods alike) contain lots of water. But water isn't really food—it doesn't provide any caloric nutrition whatsoever. If a food product is 83% water (such as in the example above), then only 17% of the product is actual calorie-containing food. So while only 2% of that *product* is fat, the percentage of the *calories* that come from fat is considerably higher. And this same phenomenon applies to all the other information contained in the Guaranteed Analysis panel too.

A far more helpful way for dog food to be labeled would be on what's called a "dry-matter" basis. When nutritional content is reported on a dry-matter basis, moisture isn't factored into the equation. So percentage-based statements are fair and accurate representations of a food's true nutritional content.

Of course, you can convert the as-fed information into dry-matter information on your own—just subtract out the stated moisture content and then recalculate the nutritional content (for a step-by-step primer on how to make use of the Guaranteed Analysis panel, see Chapter Eight). But you probably weren't aware of that until just now, and the fact that AAFCO doesn't just do the calculations for you is perplexing. It has also wrought much confusion over the amount of protein, fat, and other nutrients that dog food really contains.

From an anti-obesity perspective, another problem with AAFCO's nutritional labeling rules is that they don't require producers to tell consumers enough about caloric content. In fact, until recently, AAFCO didn't require many producers to include any calorie information whatsoever on their labels. But, in 2014, in response to consumer backlash, the model regulations finally started requiring calories to be mentioned on the label.

Unfortunately, the required calorie information isn't all that helpful for consumers. Most consumers have no idea how many calories their dogs actually burn on a daily basis and, although AAFCO has a decent idea, it doesn't require manufacturers to tell us. So, unlike the Nutrition Facts panel, which provides consumers with a rough frame of reference for how many calories they should be consuming on a daily basis, AAFCO just requires a naked, stand-alone statement of the number of calories in the product. Better than nothing? Of course. But not all that helpful when the number of calories a dog actually burns on a daily basis is far from obvious to most consumers.

But the most glaring problem with the Guaranteed Analysis panel is one that Gary Taubes would be particularly quick to notice: it doesn't say a single word about carbs. Nothing about the percentage of calories from carbohydrate sources. Nothing about the amount of sugar. Nothing about the amount of starch. Not a single word. In AAFCO's eyes, the dietary carbohydrate—the very nutritional substrate that dogs will avoid if given the option, the one that their bodies don't need, that wolves don't consume, that likely plays an outsized role in causing obesity, and that just happens to make up the bulk of almost every kibble sold in the world today—doesn't even warrant a mention on a dog food label.

***

On one level, these shortcomings are perplexing. If AAFCO's goal is to keep the pet food market safe and fair, why not make a few simple and obvious changes to the rules regarding nutritional disclosures?

In answering this question, we ought to recall Walter Willett's criticism of the USDA's Food Guide Pyramid. Remember, in Dr. Willett's eyes, the Food Guide Pyramid was unreliable because it tended to "mix science with the influence of powerful agricultural interests, which is not the recipe for healthy eating." And, just as it has done with the USDA, the Carbohydrate Lobby seems to have invested considerable time and energy building inroads of influence within AAFCO as well. Today, representatives from Cargill, ADM, Purina, the Pet Food Institute (the primary lobbying group for Big Kibble), and both the American Feed Industry Association and the National Grain and Feed Association (two other Carbohydrate Lobby groups) all sit either as AAFCO committee members or AAFCO "industry advisors." When it comes to labeling requirements, it seems that Big Kibble is, quite literally, regulating itself.

The results of which have been much as we would expect. Over the past two decades, progressive, commonsensical pet food labeling requirements have often been considered by AAFCO's Pet Food Committee. But these new rules have always had to fight against an industry-inspired current of dilatory tactics and other opposition.

Consider, for instance, the painfully slow evolution of AAFCO's calorie disclosure requirements. Calorie labeling has been required on certain human foods since the early 1990s. A 2001 study revealed that 80% of pet owners and 97% of veterinarians wanted calorie information on pet food labels too, and AAFCO formed a working group to consider the issue in 2005. But the group spent nearly a decade noodling over the matter before finally deciding to mandate a limited form of calorie disclosure. And the primary reason for the foot-dragging was the one that most of us would expect: industry advisors from the Carbohydrate Lobby adamantly and consistently opposed the new regulations throughout committee deliberation. As Dr. William Burkholder, the FDA's Veterinary Medical Officer and a long-time AAFCO Pet Food Committee member, put it in a 2010 committee meeting, when it comes to calorie disclosures, "regulators appear to be in favor of the proposal, industry opposes it."

A similar pattern now seems to be playing out with respect to carbohydrate disclosures as well. In response to consumer pressure, AAFCO's Pet Food Committee formed a "Carbohydrate Working Group" in 2010. For the past six years the group has been toying with the idea of mandating some form of carbohydrate disclosure on pet food labels. But, to date, no such requirements have seen the light of day.

CARBOHYDRATES,
THE BIG KIBBLE PERSPECTIVE

LEANING ON REGULATORS, writing textbooks, buttering-up veterinarians, and incentivizing researchers are all just indirect ways for Big Kibble to influence how dog owners think about nutrition and obesity. But there are also plenty of ways in which it can—and does—speak directly to us. When it does so, it almost always hides the ball about the outsized role that carbohydrates play in its recipes. Moreover, as you would probably expect from a member of the Carbohydrate Lobby, when Big Kibble has the opportunity to discuss the healthfulness of dietary carbohydrates, it tends to take some liberties with the scientifically verified truth.

As we've already seen, starchy carbohydrates are the primary nutritional substrate found in just about *all* dry dog food products. With some very minor exceptions, there's really no getting around that fact. But Big Kibble certainly tries. In an attempt to deflect attention from the overwhelming carbohydrate content of most dog foods, manufacturers employ a host of clever product packaging and marketing strategies.

First is something we've already discussed—the fact that under AAFCO's model regulations, dog food manufacturers are not required to explicitly disclose the amount of carbohydrate in their foods. The Guaranteed Analysis panel simply doesn't include a line item for carbs. Can a consumer calculate the total carbohydrate content of a specific food using the information on the label? Yes. She just better bring a copy of this book and a calculator when she goes shopping. And if she'd like to know how much sugar or starch is in a product, then she's basically out of luck altogether.

If you take a stroll down the dog food aisle at your local pet store you might notice a second way that Big Kibble is disguising the carbohydrate content of its products. It's a kind of product packaging shell game that dog food manufacturers seem to be playing with their customers. The game is simple: regardless of which starchy carbohydrate ingredients *are* in a recipe, use product packaging to highlight whichever starchy carbohydrate ingredients *are not* in the recipe. Is the food built around corn? If so, then its label will scream "Gluten Free!" Built around wheat? Then it'll be "No Corn!" Built around potatoes? "Grain Free!" Built around rice? You get the idea.

These are not lies. But combine them with the lack of explicit information about carbohydrate content and you can imagine how a consumer could get the impression that a "grain free" food, particularly one whose label features a red "X" drawn across an image of an ear of corn, might be low in carbohydrate content—even when it's not. Not lies, but not exactly straightforward declarations of truth either.

A third carb-obscuring strategy is the widespread use of warm and fuzzy marketing jargon to describe dog food products. Although they're plastered all over Big Kibble's marketing materials, you might be surprised to learn that terms like "holistic," "wholesome," "species-appropriate," "premium," "super premium," and even "*ultra* premium" all mean precisely the same thing— *nothing*. Not one of these terms is defined in AAFCO's *Official Publication*, the document that AAFCO uses to regulate pet food labels. What this means, essentially, is that the terms can mean whatever Big Kibble wants them to mean. Or, as the ACVN has written (a good bit more peaceably), the definitions of these terms are "dependent on the philosophy and marketing strategies of the individual manufacturer." As a result, Big Kibble can slap these meaningless terms onto whatever products it wants, regardless of their recipes.

Is there anything wrong with the widespread use of meaningless but vaguely comforting words like "holistic"? Again, there's probably nothing about the practice that amounts to fraud. Still, I'd wager that I'm not the only one who would expect a wholesome, holistic, species-appropriate, ultra-premium dog food to be on the lower end of the carbohydrate content spectrum. Unfortunately, there's no guarantee that that's the case. Indeed, it is far more likely *not* to be the case.

The last noteworthy way that Big Kibble downplays the abundance of carbohydrates in its dry dog food products is by highlighting and exaggerating the supposed nutritional benefits of carbohydrates. Perhaps the best example of this common practice is the use of terms like "heart-healthy whole grains" and "wholesome whole grains" to describe certain starchy carbohydrate ingredients. As cardiologist William Davis has documented in considerable historic and scientific detail in his book *Wheat Belly*, in the world of human nutrition, the expression "heart-healthy whole grains" isn't considered false advertising because it conforms with an antiquated, oversimplified scientific dogma by which carbohydrates were considered better for a person's heart than dietary fats, simply because the carbs were less calorically dense. As we've already seen, that dogma has been cast aside as our scientific understanding of nutrition and obesity has improved over the past 50 years. But the phrase "heart-healthy whole grains," a powerful marketing tool for the Carbohydrate Lobby, has still managed to stick around.

The notion of the "healthy" whole grain also reflects the fact that whole grains (those that include the entire grain kernel—the germ, the endosperm, and the bran) are generally less bad for health than refined ones (those, like white flour and white rice, that contain only the endosperm). So, while both whole grains and refined grains are bad for health, the former are, well, *less bad*. By this logic, to borrow an analogy from Dr. Davis, processed grains are a bit like high-tar cigarettes and whole grains like low-tar ones. For what seem like obvious reasons today, federal law prohibits cigarette companies from marketing low-tar cigarettes as "healthy" alternatives to higher-tar ones. And yet the "heart-healthy whole grain" remains a staple of the Carbohydrate Lobby's marketing materials.

***

Big Kibble's practice of exaggerating the health benefits of carbohydrates actually goes further than just describing its starchy ingredients as "wholesome" and "heart-healthy." Oftentimes Big Kibble manufacturers also take to their websites to launch more sophisticated defenses of the carbohydrates that dominate their food products. (Perhaps "more sophisticated" isn't really the best way to describe these writings, but they do involve more words than typical advertisements.) When they do so, their statements tend to be vague, lacking in scientific validity, and, frankly, somewhat insulting to the intelligence of the average dog owner. Here are a few highlights:

From Purina's Website: "Carbohydrates in nutritionally complete and balanced diets provide energy!'"

From Purina's Website: "Wheat is a valuable pet food ingredient. Wheat is an excellent source of carbohydrates for energy, as well as a source of protein."

From Blue Buffalo's Website: "Carbohydrates are a key source of energy for dogs and cats. Whole grains, like brown rice, barley and oats, are excellent low-fat sources of highly-digestible complex carbohydrates."

From Hill's Website: "Corn is an excellent ingredient because of the benefits it brings to the product."

From Eukanuba's Website: "Starch is abundant in the seeds of cereal grains and tubers (potatoes) and represents up to 70-80% of a grain's dry matter. It plays an important role in the nutritive value of diets consumed by dogs since it is the primary source of energy for many body functions and is necessary for the synthesis and metabolism of other nutrients."

From Royal Canin's Website: "Cats and dogs can live without carbohydrates in their food…. The intake of carbohydrates does, however, greatly improve the body's functioning ability."

See what I mean? Not lies, at least not precisely. But not exactly straightforward, meaningful information either. (If ever there was written a more mealy-mouthed, pseudoscientific expression than "the body's functioning ability" then I have yet to see it.) Indeed, a fair and unbiased summary of the scientific evidence concerning the nutritive value of carbohydrates brings the disingenuousness of these statements into dramatic relief. For your convenience, one follows.

Just like humans, dogs can and will metabolize carbohydrates for energy, if *and only if* carbohydrates are made to be part of their diets. But regardless of whether your dog is an Iditarod winner, an obedience wizard, or an ordinary house pet, his body does not *need* carbs. Not for brain power, not for physical activity, not to "improve the body's functioning ability." Not for anything. Nevertheless, highly processed, starchy carbohydrate (usually in the form of rice, wheat, barley, potato, or corn) is almost *always* the single most common nutritional substrate to be found in commercial dry dog foods. We have explored the myriad reasons for this strange phenomenon over the past two chapters. But, in a way, they can all be traced back to a single fact—starchy cereal grains are attractive ingredients for dog food manufacturers because they are fantastically inexpensive. Which would be fine, were it not for the fact that a large and growing body of evidence suggests that highly processed starchy carbohydrates are unique in their ability to make animals fat. And, because being fat has been shown to be epically harmful to a dog's health, if the evidence supporting the carbohydrate-insulin model of adiposity strikes you as more convincing than not, then you should probably consider cutting the carbs out of your dog's diet altogether.

WHY NOTHING REALLY CHANGES

ON A BLUSTERY MORNING in early March I found myself entering the sterilized confines of the Doubletree Suites in downtown Salt Lake City. I was there to spend a morning away from the disembodied, faceless information contained in textbooks and journal articles. I wanted to see what it was like to be taught canine nutrition the old-fashioned way: by an actual person. More specifically, by a paid representative of Big Kibble.

I was there to attend a one-day nutritional seminar for veterinary technicians. According to the National Association of Veterinary Technicians in America, a vet tech is "the veterinarian's nurse, laboratory technician, radiography technician, anesthetist, surgical nurse, and client educator." To hear veterinarians tell it, techs are exceedingly valuable to the modern-day veterinary healthcare system. Those among them who work at small animal clinics and veterinary hospitals get to spend a lot of face time with pets and pet owners. They conduct physical exams, take X-rays, collect blood samples, answer questions, and provide emotional support to worried pet owners during the tense exam-room moments between a patient's admission to a clinic and the veterinarian's arrival. As one vet tech put it when describing her job in an interview with *U.S. News and World Report*, "[w]e do everything except diagnose, prescribe, and do surgery."

While there are only 30 AVMA-accredited veterinary schools in the United States, there are nearly ten times as many vet tech programs. And there are more in Canada. These programs are offered primarily by community colleges and technical schools, and both in-person and "distance learning" options are available. All of which means that there are many more veterinary technicians in the United States then there are veterinarians. And the ranks of the techs are swelling—according to the Bureau of Labor Statistics, the number of vet techs in the country is expected to surge by almost 30% between 2012 and 2022.

In many states, techs must pass a licensing exam and earn a number of continuing education credit-hours every year. And the event at the Doubletree was an opportunity for Utah vet techs to earn seven of them. Melissa Tucker, by this time a practicing veterinarian at a specialty hospital in Salt Lake City (one that, amazingly, was acquired by a Mars subsidiary only a few months prior to publication of this book), had learned about it from one of her clinic's technicians and she had mentioned it to me during one of our interviews. "If you're really interested in seeing how health care professionals learn about diet and nutrition, you should check it out," she said.

It was scheduled to be an all-day affair. But it was free of charge and lunch was going to be provided. The tab was being picked up by the organization responsible for choosing the informational content to be taught, as well as preparing the take-home materials and naming the lecturers—Hill's Pet Nutrition, Inc.

Two men ran the show, a Hill's veterinarian named Scott Carter and a sales representative named Brady Farley. I had exchanged e-mails with Dr. Carter prior to the event and he had initially tried to dissuade me from attending. "This is a meeting for veterinary clinic employees," he wrote. "I have taught classes in the past for pet owners, but this meeting will be more in-depth."

I showed up anyway and he was gracious and welcoming as we chatted in a conference room in the build-up to the first presentation. Brady, his counterpart, was bearded, funny, and eminently likable. He had greeted me with a casual "sup, man?" and a firm, confident handshake.

The other attendees (of whom there were perhaps three dozen, most under 30 years of age, and all but myself and two others women) filed in and took their seats at long tables under the glow of buzzing fluorescent lights. Neat stacks of written materials awaited us—our own copies of the forthcoming slideshows, some flow charts, a lengthy *Nutrition Reference Manual*, a binder of materials entitled "Keys to Clinical Nutrition," detailed information about various Hill's products, plastic-wrapped Hill's notepads, a glossy, one-page document on which a Boston Terrier looked to be taking his first ravenous bite of food and a headline screamed "**Pet Parents are Raving About the New Prescription Diet—Stews!**," and "Hill's Technical Information Services Nutritional Nuggets," one-page summaries of specific nutritional issues. Cute photographs of dogs and cats were everywhere. Bowls of Jolly Ranchers and pens embossed with the Hill's logo had been scattered on the tables.

We took turns standing to introduce ourselves to the group. Everybody already seemed to know Brady. "I'm the fabulous sales rep that comes around and sees you guys," he joked, before telling us about his four pets (two dogs, a cat, and a snake) and showing us a video of a shark-shaped, remote-controlled blimp chasing a terrified Beagle around a living room. Dr. Carter cut a more authoritative figure, tall and barrel-chested with angular, rimless glasses and a neat haircut. He wore a button-down shirt tucked into slacks and planted his hands on his hips as he delivered his introduction. He'd been with Hill's for 11 years. His primary responsibility was teaching nutritional seminars at veterinary schools and technical colleges. He had one pet, a dog named Boog.

The all-day seminar would be divided into several presentations, each led by one of the two Hill's reps. But, as Dr. Carter had assured me shortly before kick-off, the afternoon would be devoted primarily to clinical case studies and a prolonged discussion of specific prescription diets. Most of what I was interested in (how to feed my own dogs in order to keep them as lean and healthy as possible in the long-term) would come in the morning, during the presentation on "basic nutrition." Between that and a free lunch that I didn't feel I deserved—not being exactly the presentation's intended audience—I resolved to duck out after the morning session was complete.

Dr. Carter led the session and began with a short history of Hill's Pet Nutrition. He told us about Dr. Mark L. Morris, Sr., the veterinarian who founded the company back in 1948, shortly after founding the second small-animal practice in the entire world. He recounted Dr. Morris's experiences with service dogs and explained how the Science Diet line was launched in 1968. He mentioned that the company's name came from the Morris hospital's merger with Hill's Pet Nutrition (ignoring the bit about that company's history with horse meat). And he mentioned that Colgate-Palmolive had eventually acquired the company and remained its corporate parent to this day (ignoring the bit about how the strategy of marketing its products through healthcare professionals, such as was being done at this very seminar, was borrowed from Colgate's successful experiences marketing toothpaste through dentists).

After the short introduction, I was encouraged to see that Dr. Carter's very first slide was aimed at precisely the topic I'd come to hear about: obesity. The headline, "**What is the most common type of malnutrition in pets today?**," was set above a collection of photos of grossly obese cats and dogs. Dr. Carter did nothing to play down the significance of the problem—it was the very first substantive issue on his list and later he discussed the various studies that proved that obesity is both deadly and widespread. He made it very clear that he viewed obesity as the single most important nutritional problem facing dogs in America today.

And this was admirable. But also, to my mind at least, it was to be expected. The evidence documenting the dangers of obesity is unassailable. A presentation on canine nutrition that ignored what is almost certainly the most significant canine nutritional disorder in the country would come off as rather incomplete.

What was no less expected but somewhat less commendable were the portions of Dr. Carter's presentation that offered explanations as to *why* so many dogs today are so fat. His presentation embraced the standard calories-in, calories-out model of obesity (and its various implications—count calories, eat less, exercise more) as a kind of unchallenged scientific fact. The carbohydrate-insulin model of adiposity—the notion that easily digestible carbohydrates induce insulin secretion, and that insulin causes fat cells to become fatter—was not mentioned, not even as an alternative to the standard hypothesis. The studies proving carbohydrates to be uniquely fattening nutritional substrates were nowhere to be found. The evidence that hormones (particularly insulin) play a crucial role in determining where, when, and how animals fatten was not mentioned.

Instead, a significant portion of the presentation actually seemed to be devoted to protecting or enhancing the reputation of the dietary carbohydrate. One slide showed a multi-tiered pyramid with each of six classes of nutrients—vitamins, minerals, fat, protein, carbohydrates, and water—occupying its own level. Next to the pyramid the word "**ENERGY**" was written in a starburst with an arrow pointing to the carbohydrate level. Later, when discussing a slide with a headline that read "Carbohydrates," Dr. Carter explained that "the whole purpose of carbohydrates" in pet foods was "to provide energy without any detrimental effects."

"Dogs are just like us," he explained, "they are omnivores. You can feed a dog a vegetarian diet and it will do very well, just like a human." It was a statement that, if you defined things just right, didn't amount to an outright falsehood. While the domestic dog is a member of the order *carnivora* (the order of mammals which also includes cats, bears, wolverines, weasels, and other animals with claws, sharp teeth, and other predatory adaptations) it is probably true that if you fed your dog enough soybeans to satisfy his protein requirements, he wouldn't *require* meat in his diet. (Cats are different. They are "obligate carnivores" that require a regular dose of taurine, an amino acid found only in animal meat). And dogs are certainly capable of digesting and drawing caloric energy out of grains and other plant matter. But whether that means that a dog fed a vegetarian diet will "do very well," probably depends on what that outcome means to you.

The same goes for the comment that dogs are "just like us." Sure, they can digest starches, just like humans can. But does that mean dogs are really "just like us"? If you're anything like me, you might think that just about every aspect of a dog's outward appearance (not to mention its genetics) suggests that it has a good deal more in common with some other types of animals. Like, say, wolves.

But Dr. Carter had a way of dealing with that objection too—according to him, wolves actually do eat plants. In addition to meat, he explained, "wolves actually eat a lot of plant material. But you don't see that on TV because it isn't exciting enough for the Discovery Channel." He didn't cite any evidence in support of this claim, which was flatly contradicted both by the biologists I had met in Montana and the dozens of scientific papers they had published over the years.

All the talk about wolves and dogs had come up in response to a question about a recent Blue Buffalo television commercial, one that had some wolves in it. Apparently, the wolves were (to Blue Buffalo, at least) a reason to buy Blue Buffalo kibble instead of some other brand. Dr. Carter and Brady scoffed at what they considered a marketing ploy. I scoffed too. I thought it was ridiculous for Blue Buffalo to suggest that its carbohydrate-laden kibbles resembled in any way the diet eaten by a typical wolf. It only later became clear that the guys from Hill's were insulted by something else. They thought that Blue Buffalo was actually doing some carbohydrate ingredients a disservice because of the company's tendency to bash whatever carbohydrate ingredients *weren't* used in a formula while refusing to mention all the carbohydrates that *were* used. They claimed that this was a disingenuous attempt to enrage consumers over ingredients that were, in reality, perfectly safe. My participant manual drove the point home, with headlines that read *"No Grains?* **Is this idea about Marketing or Nutrition?"** and **"Gluten Free? Reality or <u>Marketing Gimmick?</u>"**

"You hear a lot about corn," Dr. Carter said, chuckling, "but a lot of people just don't understand what their pets really need." Apparently, what their pets really need is corn. Because the participant manual that was provided to the techs at the nutritional seminar was practically bursting with corn propaganda: **"Corn—An Amazing Grain"** read one Nutritional Nugget. **"CORN—a terrific ingredient for pet foods"** read another. At one point, a sequence of Nutritional Nuggets explained why corn was **"Better nutrition for cats than spinach ... sweet potato ... and kelp."** The reason why the Hill's participant manual was so pro-corn wasn't revealed until the end of the manual: **"As good as gold,"** it read. **"Corn is a well-rounded nutritional package and an ideal choice as a pet food ingredient. No other ingredient is as versatile as this golden grain. That's why you'll find corn in most Hill's ® Science Diet ® brand pet foods."**

***

After the morning's session concluded, I pulled Dr. Carter aside and asked him to level with me about the real value of carbohydrates in pet foods. Throughout his presentation, he had emphasized the importance of viewing small animal nutrition with a focus on nutrients (carbohydrates, protein, vitamins) rather than ingredients (corn, beef by-products, kelp). I thought this perspective might predispose him to admit something that was well-established in the relevant literature but largely glossed-over during his presentation—the fact that dogs don't really need dietary carbohydrates for anything. That carbs were, if not uniquely fattening, at least unnecessary.

I presented him with a hypothetical situation: if we could craft a diet that provided a dog with precisely the right amount of all the essential nutrients—exactly the right amounts of protein, essential fats, and all the various essential vitamins and minerals—what would happen if we just left carbohydrates off the menu? His response was strained. No, dogs don't "technically" need carbohydrate, he explained, but too few carbs would mean too little energy. And if we made up the energy deficit with fats and proteins? That would, in turn, result in too *much* energy (and, thus, the possibility of weight gain), because fat is a particularly energy dense macronutrient. Too few calories or too many—without carbs, a dog just couldn't win.

In the end, the Hill's nutritional seminar did little to dispel the notion that you're unlikely to get straight talk from the representatives of your local multinational corporation, at least not when there are serious financial interests involved. If you go to Big Kibble for nutritional advice, you're probably not going to hear outright falsehoods, but you are likely to get answers that cast its carbohydrate-stuffed products in the best light possible. There will be tenuously reasoned defenses of the importance of carbohydrates to canine nutrition. Any evidence suggesting that carbohydrates are uniquely fattening nutrients probably won't get mentioned at all. And the problem of canine obesity will probably be cast as a function of owners who are lazy (not giving their dogs enough exercise), uneducated (feeding their dogs more calories than they really need), or weak-willed ("loving their dogs to death"). You'll probably be told that Big Kibble has no responsibility whatsoever for the canine obesity epidemic. That it's all on the dog owners.

At least those were the messages that I took away from the Hill's nutritional seminar. But one other message, less a substantive Nutritional Nugget and more an ethical appeal, had come through too: building the nutritional literacy of America's pet-owning public was up to the veterinary healthcare professionals in attendance. There's a lot of bad information out there, attendees were told, and if we want to save dogs and cats from nutritional ruin, healthcare providers would need to play an activist role in transmitting nutritional knowledge to pet owners. They would need to spread the Big Kibble dogma far and wide.

Dr. Carter had made a point of highlighting this time and again during the seminar. "There are a lot of people out there who go to the veterinarian and ask what to feed their pets," he had noted. But it was up to vets and vet techs to actually answer their questions. To bolster the point, there was a slide with a couple of pie charts on it. "**90% of pet owners want a nutritional recommendation**," it read, "*But ... only* **15% perceive they receive one**." One of the pies was shaped like PacMan and had the figure "**85%**" written on it, next to which was written the word "**Opportunity!**"

In Dr. Carter's view, transmitting nutritional information—specifically, the tenuously reasoned material presented as fact throughout the seminar—through trusted veterinary professionals was the only good way to shape the pet-owning public's understanding of vital issues like what we should be feeding our dogs. It was really the only way to reach them. Or it was at least better than something like, say, reading a book about it. "When you buy a book," Dr. Carter had explained to us, "nothing really changes."

Chapter Six

THE MAGIC OF EXERCISE

--

"Do what you love. Know your own bone; gnaw at it, bury it, unearth it, and gnaw it still."

Henry David Thoreau,
Letter to H.G.O. Blake (1848)

―――――

BO KNOWS FITNESS

MY FIRST ENCOUNTER with Crystal McClaran and her dog Bo took place at the 2013 DockDogs World Championships in Dubuque, Iowa. It was a big day for Crystal, and it showed. She grimaced as she elbowed her way through a throng of spectators and led the dog towards me. Her steps were choppy. Her eyes darted nervously.

Her anxious mood was understandable. Dock-diving is the fastest-growing canine athletics competition in the world, and Crystal and Bo are two of the sport's fiercest competitors. They live in Florida and had driven thousands of miles to be here. In just a few hours they would be taking to the dock to compete in the most important event of their season, the one for all the marbles.

The team had trained hard for this day. Early mornings, two-a-day workouts, a strict dietary regimen, and considerable personal sacrifices on Crystal's behalf were the price they had paid to compete at the very top of their sport. And expectations were high, both within their camp and throughout the broader dock-diving community. Bo was an exciting young phenom, one who had set the sport alight throughout the summer, winning qualifying competitions and racking up numerous new records in the process. Though a relative newcomer to dock-diving, Bo was one of the favorites to win at Worlds.

But if he was feeling the pressure, the dog didn't show it. He ambled along beside his mommy, tail slowly swinging back and forth. Casually taking in the spectacle, he made his way through the crowd, pausing to lick little children and have his flanks stroked by adoring fans. When he reached me, he launched into one of his signature behavioral quirks, a charming attention-seeking ritual in which he gradually leans his standing frame more and more heavily into the thighs of a nearby human admirer, until he is practically balanced on two legs. The leaning doesn't stop until his new buddy gives in and makes with the petting (or loses his balance altogether). "Yeah, Bo's a real leaner," laughed Crystal anxiously, as I began stroking the dog's ears.

He is a large and strikingly beautiful animal, the product of a Doberman Pinscher and a Treeing Walker Coonhound, with the structure of the former and the coloration of the latter. His body is incredibly lean and well-muscled. Graceful but powerful, he moves in much the same way that the tennis great Roger Federer glides across a court. And with his shiny tricolor coat and towering frame he bears more than a passing resemblance to a painted horse.

As his gait and physique suggest, Bo is a supremely talented athlete. Indeed, at the time of writing he is arguably the best canine athlete on the planet. In 2013, at only two years of age, Bo had already risen through the dock-diving ranks to become one of the sport's most decorated competitors. Going into the 2013 Worlds competition, he was the top-ranked Iron Dog Titan in the entire field. Being the top-ranked Iron Dog in DockDogs' Titan group is like being the top-ranked golfer on the PGA Tour. The sport of dock-diving is organized and governed by several different organizations, the largest and most influential of which is DockDogs, Inc. Under DockDogs rules, teams of dogs and their handlers are stratified by ability into different classes, and they compete in up to four different events: Big Air, in which dogs leap off a dock for maximum distance; Speed Retrieve, in which they swim to reach a lure at the end of a pool as quickly as possible; Extreme Vertical, in which they jump for maximum height; and Iron Dog, in which competitors are graded by their aggregate scores from the three sub-disciplines. The Iron Dog competition is thus a bit like the decathlon, a true measurement of all-around physical ability. And the Titan group is composed of the most accomplished Iron Dogs in the field.

I was seated in one of the front rows when Bo competed at the 2013 DockDogs World Championships. Catching his first glimpse of the pool upon entering the arena, the dog's laidback, Joe Cool demeanor evaporated. He instantly lost all semblance of self-control and was transformed into a nervous bundle of energy, baying excitedly as he jumped around and tugged at the end of his lead, his tail wagging furiously. It was clear that the pool, the dock, and the lures all signified that something positively wonderful was about to take place. He was overjoyed. Crystal held his lead with both hands and sat with her weight against it. She ground the soles of her shoes into the floor for traction. It was all she could do to keep the dog from breaking free and lunging into the pool ahead of his turn.

Bo performed well in the Big Air and Speed Retrieve legs of the competition, finishing near the top of his heats in both events. But, with his explosive power and towering height, the Extreme Vertical event is where he really shines. In Extreme Vertical, a lure is hung from an apparatus eight feet off the front of the dock. Dogs barrel down the dock at top speed before leaping into the air, grabbing for the dangling lure, and plunging into the pool. As the competition progresses, the lure is inched higher and higher with each successive jump. The dog that snatches it from the highest height wins.

During the summer leading up to the 2013 Worlds competition, Bo had set and broken numerous Extreme Vertical world records. Crystal joked that, unlike her co-competitors, she didn't bother printing Bo's accomplishments onto trading cards and other promotional materials during this period because the dog's personal-best results kept improving week after week. Such was the remarkable rate of his ascendency through the dock-diving ranks as he climbed onto the dock in Dubuque.

In his first jump, Bo popped off the dock and easily snatched the lure from a height of well over seven feet, a mark that all but a few of the tens of thousands of other DockDogs competitors can only dream of. By the time the lure had reached eight feet four inches, there were only two competitors remaining, Bo and a Belgian Malinois named Grizz. Both dogs barely managed to snatch the lure. (For reference, eight feet four inches is higher than the current men's high jump world-record. Although in Extreme Vertical the lure is hung eight feet off the front of the dock, so Bo's and Grizz's jumps are far more impressive than any ever performed by a human being.)

At eight feet six inches, Grizz narrowly missed, leaving Bo to jump for the World title.

He held at the start of the run-in, muscles twitching as he waited for Crystal's command. Suddenly, the cue: "Go get it!" The dog accelerated down the dock, exploded off the lip, and flew high into the air. His body became vertical as he stretched for the lure. With what seemed to be the last fiber of his being he knocked it free. Dog and lure tumbled into the pool together. The crowd erupted in applause. Crystal shrieked with delight. Bo won.

And he didn't just win the Extreme Vertical leg. He won the whole enchilada—the 2013 DockDogs Iron Dog Titan World Championship. But once the scores from all the sub-disciplines were tallied it became clear that Bo hadn't just won the Iron Dog; he had also set a new world record in the process. He hadn't only produced the highest Iron Dog score of the year; he had produced the highest Iron Dog score *ever recorded*. So, on that blustery November day in Dubuque, Bo wasn't just the best canine athlete in the world, he was the best canine athlete *in the history of the world*.

HALF THE BATTLE?

I LIKE TO THINK THAT Kody is a pretty athletic dog. But he is a mere mortal, not a demigod like Bo. We exercise a lot, but he doesn't compete in athletic competitions, not at any level. Nevertheless, I took something important away from watching the best canine athlete in the history of the world ply his trade—although it's probably not what you would expect. To begin to understand what it is, and why, ultimately, physical activity is so important for dogs, let's take a step back and review the conventional wisdom about the relationship between exercise and obesity.

These days, it's commonplace for health gurus to talk about weight loss as being driven by two equally important factors, diet and exercise. This notion is based on the calories-in, calories-out model and it reflects that model's appealing cleanliness and simplicity—lower the number of calories-in by eating better, raise the number of calories-out by exercising more, and *voila!*, you'll lose some weight. Simple and memorable. It's no surprise that most well-known weight loss strategies have both a diet component and an exercise component.

The idea that exercise is a critical part of weight management is such a pervasive notion that it has spilled over into the canine realm. "Effective weight reduction," according to a recent Banfield Pet Hospital literature review on canine obesity, requires "careful attention to diet, exercise, and regular monitoring as part of a coordinated weight management program." For his part, APOP's Ernie Ward devotes a considerable portion of *Chow Hounds* to a discussion of canine exercise. "If you're reading this book," he writes, "there's a good chance your dog needs additional exercise and (a lot) less food." And Big Kibble, motivated as it always is to shift the blame for the canine obesity epidemic away from its products, is particularly fond of framing adiposity as the natural consequence of the inactive lifestyles that sedentary dog owners are imposing upon our pets.

There's only one problem: the evidence supporting the notion that exercise will help anyone get lean and stay that way is modest, at best. Despite its ubiquity in the mainstream health and fitness press, and despite the fact that more people than ever are packing into health clubs for daily workouts and crowding the starting lines of marathons, exercise has a decidedly poor evidentiary track record as a long-term weight-loss strategy, at least in the human domain.

Several groups of experts have recently gotten together for the purpose of reviewing the published literature on the fat-fighting effects of exercise regimens. And each time the same conclusion has emerged: if exercise has been shown to have any long-term impact on adiposity whatsoever, it is minimal. In 2000, two public health researchers from Finland's University of Helsinki completed a meta-analysis of the relevant literature on the link between exercise and adiposity. Their conclusions on the matter are best summarized by the last line of their study, published in the journal *Obesity Reviews*: "the [fat-fighting] effects of a prescribed exercise programme remain very limited." A few years later, a panel of experts from around the world convened in Bangkok for the purpose of reviewing the evidence and formulating a consensus position on the fat-fighting power of exercise for the International Association for the Study of Obesity. They concluded as follows:

> The current physical activity guideline for adults of 30 minutes of moderate intensity activity daily, preferably all days of the week, is of importance for limiting health risks for a number of chronic diseases including coronary heart disease and diabetes. However, for preventing weight gain or re-gain, this guideline is likely to be insufficient for many individuals in the current environment.

On separate occasions, similar meta-analyses were also conducted by a Brown University professor and two doctors from the Medical College of St. Bartholomew's Hospital, in London. But both reviews used the same word to characterize the body of evidence suggesting that exercise leads to long-term leanness: "modest." The Nutrition Society (the largest academic society for the study of nutrition in Europe) has weighed in on the matter too: "The majority of studies suggest that low levels of activity are only weakly associated with future weight gain." And the American Heart Association and the American College of Sports Medicine recently updated their official activity recommendations for adults to highlight the relative lack of evidence:

> It seems reasonable that persons with relatively high daily energy expenditures would be less likely to gain weight over time, compared with those who have low energy expenditures. So far, data to support this hypothesis *are not particularly compelling....* [T]he effect of physical activity on weight loss over the long term remains unclear.

As for the reason why exercise doesn't fight fat quite as well as many of us would like to think, that depends on whom you ask. If you ask Gary Taubes (who, by the way, is a former boxer and college football player who exercises every day), he'll tell you that when we exercise we "work up an appetite" and thus wind up eating more (or moving less) than we otherwise would, thereby making up whatever caloric difference would otherwise result from the bout of exercise and re-achieving homeostasis. As always, he'll say that avoiding insulin-induced fattening should be the primary focus of our efforts to stay lean. Exercise be damned.

But even if you don't buy what Taubes is selling, and you insist on clinging to the traditional calories-in, calories-out paradigm, there's still a problem with the notion that exercise has a crucial role to play in managing your dog's weight: it falsely suggests that, when it comes to body composition, diet and exercise are equally influential and thus equally important. In truth, they are not. Even the most ardent fan of physical exercise (which I might in fact be, for reasons we'll get to shortly) must admit that it doesn't tend to move the caloric needle all that much, even if we don't compensate by eating more after our workouts. Even if we take the poor evidentiary track record of exercise-as-weight-loss-strategy off the table, and even if we disregard the various lines of evidence suggesting that hormones, not calorie management, are the root causes of why anyone becomes obese, we're still left with the fact that exercise isn't a particularly efficient way to manage calories. Dietary changes simply have a more profound impact on net energy balance.

To see what I mean, consider the following example.

Let's say that your dog, Rufus, is a 50-pound, lightly muscled mixed-breed. He's three years old and lives a moderately active existence. According to the National Research Council, that means he probably burns around 1,350 calories per day just knocking around the house. Now let's say that we incorporate a daily workout into his life in an effort to increase the total number of calories that he burns on a daily basis. Maybe we've got a glut of time on our hands and maybe we're fairly fit and active ourselves (two not-altogether-realistic assumptions in the first instance, but bear with me), so we decide that we'll spend 30 minutes of every single weekday morning taking Rufus for a walk. Because we're so fit, we can travel at the relatively speedy rate of four miles per hour, meaning that we'll cover about two miles during our daily walk.

What will this relatively significant expenditure of time and effort do for our buddy Rufus, calorically-speaking? Not much. According to the NRC, he'll probably burn about 70 additional calories propelling his 50-pound body over the two-mile route.

How much is 70 calories? Well, let's see what it looks like on the calories-in side of the equation. Using traditional calories-in, calories-out math, in order to effectuate the same net change to Rufus's energy balance as our 30-minute walk, we will have to remove the equivalent of 70 calories worth of food from his daily intake. This translates into roughly one-fifth of one cup of Blue Buffalo's Life Protection Formula Healthy Weight Chicken & Brown Rice Recipe for Adult Dogs, or about a third of an Extra-Large Milkbone.

See what I mean? We could have had the same impact on Rufus's daily caloric balance just by breaking off a chunk of his daily treat or withholding a few nuggets of food from his daily ration, rather than waking up early and spending 30 minutes of our morning taking him for a fast-paced walk. And that's a conservative example. It's not hard to imagine a diet that's so bad that no amount of exercise could make up for it.

To look at it another way, consider that, at four miles per hour, a 50-pound dog like Rufus would need to walk about 100 miles in order to burn just a single pound of adipose tissue (at about 35 calories per mile and around 3500 calories per pound of fat). So if about a third of his 50-pound body is adipose tissue, as many canine bodies in America today are, we would need to cover about 1150 miles in order to get him down to the 10% body fat typical of even the fattest wild wolf. *More than a thousand miles.* That's further than the distance from New York to Miami. And, even if we get out for 30 minutes of brisk walking every single weekday morning, with no exceptions, it would still require several *years* of work, even assuming that Gary Taubes is completely wrong about stuff like hormones, homeostasis, and compensatory eating.

***

All this is just a longwinded way of saying that, even if you reject the carbohydrate-insulin model of adiposity, it's hard to deny that diet has a much more direct and efficient impact on energy balance and fat loss than exercise. Dietary changes simply require less effort. When it comes to getting lean and staying that way, exercise is definitively *not* half the battle. Diet is the real key.

This is particularly the case when it comes to our dogs (and our other pets too; there may be someone out there creative and patient enough to introduce bouts of structured exercise into the lives of America's millions of overweight cats, but, alas, it's not me). If we're talking about the lifestyle changes that will most effectively modify the composition of our human bodies, both changing how we eat and changing how we exercise will require discipline, willpower, and ongoing effort. Forcing yourself out of bed at 6:00 AM to go for a jog on a cold, rainy morning is tough, but so is resisting the sensory seduction of a freshly baked chocolate chip cookie when you haven't eaten for a few hours. But while exercising our pets usually requires that we expend some of our own willpower alongside them (by, say, tying on the running shoes or loading Rufus into the car for a trip to the park after a long day of work), making changes to how our pets eat requires remarkably little out of us. Sure, we have to do some front-end thinking, a few minutes of calculating. And we have to deal with the twinge of guilt that pops up when we deny our dogs some food that they're expecting. But, for most of us, the 15 minutes of critical thinking and the occasional discipline needed to overcome little surges of emotional pain pales in comparison to the amount of willpower needed to consistently deny ourselves something we really want once strong desire takes hold.

In addition to its relative ease and efficiency, there's a second reason why, when it comes to changing body composition, diet beats exercise every time: exercise is more limiting. For some dogs—seriously obese ones, seniors, brachycephalic breeds, and those with movement-limiting disabilities— exercise can be difficult or even dangerous, certainly more of a threat to overall health and longevity than a benefit. And the same goes for dog owners. Some of us simply lack the time or the physical tools necessary to exercise alongside our dogs.

A third reason: in all likelihood, calorie management isn't quite as simple as the previous example makes it sound. Gary Taubes and his ilk have given us all sorts of reasons to believe that calories-in and calories-out are not independent variables. When we increase the number of calories that we burn through exercise, they say, we're probably going to find ways to get at least some of those calories back. All of which points in the same direction: if you're serious about helping your dog lose body fat, start by getting her diet dialed-in and think of exercise more as the icing on the weight-management cake.

Then again, if exercise is such a risky, limiting, and inefficient drag, then what are we doing spending an entire chapter talking about it? I'm glad you asked. The answer, of course, is that it's not a drag at all. It's just that in the war against canine obesity, the evidence says that diet is a much more powerful weapon, regardless of whether you accept the carbohydrate-insulin model of obesity. But that doesn't mean that exercise isn't absolutely wonderful in its own right. In fact, no matter how much your dog may love to eat, exercise can probably enrich her life in ways that her diet never will. For starters, while cutting down on the amount of fat in her body may be an excellent strategy for increasing the *quantity* of time that your dog gets to spend on this planet, a dose of regular exercise seems to be a great way to improve the *quality* of that time. If you've got any interest in making your dog's life as enjoyable as reasonably possible, adding some daily exercise to the mix is probably the perfect place to start.

JOYFUL MOTION

IT'S THE SAME THING every morning. I wake and stumble, bleary-eyed, into the kitchen to retrieve the day's first cup of coffee. My appearance rouses Kody from his slumber, usually taken curled up in a corner of the sofa. I return to bed with a mug and a book—my usual morning ritual—and the dog hops down off the couch and follows me back into my bedroom. He climbs onto the bed, eases down beside me, and sets his chin on his big paws. It would be a relaxed pose were it not for his eyes, which remain wide-open and fixed upon me. Each time I turn a page or set the mug down on the bedside table he reacts—his head pops up, brow arching, ears forward. He's not relaxed; he's full of twitchy anticipation.

Once I've shaken off the cobwebs I rise. He immediately follows suit, springing to his feet as his stump begins to wiggle. I trade pajamas for pants and a shirt, make the bed, and sit down to put on socks and shoes. At this point he usually loses the ability to contain his enthusiasm. He barges into me, thrusting his big head into my lap and preventing me from getting my shoes on. His stares up with the wide, rounded eyes of a child as his stump beats excitedly back and forth. I can't help but tease him a little, provoking an even more animated reaction: "You want to go *outside*, bud?" I ask, drawing out the key word and using a goofy voice usually reserved for entertaining infants. He bounds off toward the front door, leaving me to finish getting dressed.

By the time I gather the leash and some toys he is waiting by the door, his whole body now wiggling with excitement. He knows exactly what's about to happen. And he's really, really jazzed about it.

To understand why a bout of daily exercise has been a part of just about every day of Kody's life since he was a puppy, the place to start is with one of the most pervasive clichés of modern-day pet ownership, the one that tells us that well-exercised dogs tend to be well-behaved dogs. Like most clichés, the evidence supporting this one is more anecdotal than scientific. Perhaps the only peer-reviewed study to systematically examine the relationship between exercise and behavior in dogs, summarized in a paper published in the journal *Comparative Medicine* in 1997, found that 20-minute bouts of exercise had relatively little impact on the behavior of adult male Beagles over a 12-week study period.

But the lack of hard scientific evidence hasn't stopped many scientifically minded folks from trumpeting exercise as an important technique for managing undesirable canine behavior. The team of researchers at the Animal Behavior Clinic at Tufts University's Cummings School of Veterinary Medicine "believe that 'a tired dog is a happy dog'" and recommend daily exercise to help manage unwanted canine behaviors. Celebrity dog trainer and self-styled "dog psychologist" Cesar Milan has famously described a bout of daily exercise as the single most important strategy for preventing unwanted canine behaviors. And both Ernie Ward and the psychologist Alexandra Horowitz (author of the bestselling book *Inside of a Dog*) have written of the therapeutic effects of the daily walk too. Combine all this with an appealing narrative about how exercise works its behavioral magic—by siphoning off anxiety and other forms of nervous energy—and it's easy to see why many folks view it as a venerable wonder cure for all the challenges presented by misbehaving, stubborn, and destructive dogs.

Count me among their ranks. Kody, like many Rottweilers before him, has always been a dog that requires some "owner assistance" in order to conform his outward actions to the expectations of polite human society. His younger years were dotted with bouts of destructive behavior and many a fancy gadget met its untimely demise between his jaws. Even as an adult he retains what the American Kennel Club's breed standard for the Rottweiler describes as "an inherent desire to protect home and family." Oftentimes, when a strange person or dog appears at the door (or, more humorously, on the television) his hackles bristle and a low growl emanates from his throat. On the balance, he's much more love bug than guard dog, but with his considerable size and strength any aggressive tendencies are a serious liability. I'm no dog trainer, and I profess no expertise when it comes to the inner workings of the canine mind, but it has certainly been my experience that a bout of daily physical exhaustion helps to curb these unpleasant social gaffes.

We usually opt for something with an interactive element. This is easy, because most forms of canine exercise are built upon the interaction between dog and owner—fetch games, herding games, training for competitive canine sports, on-lead walking, the list goes on. These activities involve the exchange of cues for behaviors, reward transmissions, teamwork, collaboration, communication, and constant eye-gazing, all of which serve to deepen the emotional bond between dog and owner. In other words, if you're struggling to improve your relationship with an untrusting new dog, a few new collaborative exercise activities might be just what you need to make a breakthrough. And even if you're perfectly happy with your relationship with your dog, what better way to celebrate that relationship than by engaging in some mutually enjoyable exercise?

Assuming that it's actually enjoyable for dogs to engage in physical exercise. It's not particularly helpful to approach the topic of canine psychology with the kind of skepticism that serves us so well in separating fact from fiction in most other scientific domains. It's just not that easy to know what's going on between the ears of a non-verbal animal—what are you going to do, ask her how she feels?—particularly when it comes to subtle experiential states like the ones we call "happiness" and "pleasure." If you're simply out to play devil's advocate, you probably won't have too much trouble rebutting someone who tells you that his dog feels really good when he's exercising, or doing anything else for that matter.

So long as you don't mind having your dinner party invitations declined. I mean, *come on.* Sometimes—Kody wiggling excitedly at the front door, Bo straining to jump into the pool, or any of the hundreds of YouTube videos of dogs bursting with goofy excitement when they sense that some outdoor playtime is imminent—the truth is right under our noses.

In Alexandra Horowitz's estimation, for a dog, "happiness is novelty—new toys, new treats—in a safe, well-known place." And many of the activities that provide this combination of novelty and familiarity involve dynamic interaction with a dog's local environment, with people and toys and squirrels and other dogs. Note how these are activities which dogs that lack basic physical fitness are largely prevented from doing. Because exercise improves metabolic fitness (unlike dietary weight management), it enables dogs to do many of the things that most excite and stimulate them. It opens a door to fun activities.

More than that, most dogs also seem to enjoy the very work itself. There are exceptions to this rule, of course, but for the most part the types of activities that provide your dog with a metabolic workout are exciting, stimulating, and downright fun for the animal too.

This perspective on the psychic benefits of canine exercise is consistent with the substantial and growing body of evidence documenting a somewhat easier-to-measure set of phenomena—the myriad positive ways that exercise has been shown to impact *human* well-being. Over the past few decades, studies have consistently shown aerobic exercise to be an easy, natural, and highly effective fix for all manner of psychological disorders, from depression and anxiety to cognitive decline stemming from chronic stress and aging. In his recent book *Spark: The Revolutionary New Science of Exercise and the Brain*, Harvard psychiatry professor John J. Ratey touts exercise as "the single most powerful tool you have to optimize your brain function." A body of evidence that Ratey describes as "hundreds and hundreds of research papers," most published over just the past decade, supports his prescription that, to stay sharp and happy, we should all get out for a bout of aerobic exercise every day (and we should probably mix in some strength training for good measure).

Of course, this will hardly come as news to anyone who has ever completed a workout of his own. Working up the motivation to go to the gym can be a struggle, and suffering through the pain of pushing past physical limits may be torturous, but it's tough to deny that some good, old-fashioned sweating generally leaves everyone feeling pretty good in its wake.

While these psychological phenomena may be a good deal harder to measure when it comes to non-verbal animals like dogs, you'd have to be a fool to say that Kody doesn't look the part of overjoyed exerciser during our outside time. He is, if the raised-hackle expressions of his protective instincts are ignored, never in his life so invigorated as during our play sessions.

***

As we make our way toward the park he carries a ball in his mouth and pulls eagerly on the leash, doing his best to ensure that our route will take us exactly where he wants it to go. He drops the ball at my feet as I unclip the lead. His stump is beating furiously as his rapt attention darts from ball to ball-thrower and back again. I cue him to "heel" and he springs to my side and sits dutifully, coiling his body into a tight ball of potential energy, a sprinter in the blocks. I launch the ball toward the horizon line and he thunders off after it, galloping at full-tilt. He catches up to it after a few bounces then performs that amazing trick which all dogs, with their amazing visual acuity, can do better than even the most skilled human athletes—he closes on the bouncing ball, runs for a moment alongside it, then in a single swift motion snatches it in his jaws. With ball in mouth he bleeds off some speed making a wide turn, then sets a beeline course back to the ball-launcher. He bucks and prances as he runs, cutting a figure of proud and joyful self-celebration. He returns and drops the ball at my feet, I cue him to "heel," he heels, and we begin the happy cycle again.

We continue until he has slowed to a trot on the return and is panting and twitching while he waits for the next throw. Sometimes we finish the session with a round of jumping exercises, the rough canine equivalent of an exercise routine that CrossFitters call "box jumps." The idea is to string together a set of explosive jumping movements in quick succession until muscular exhaustion is achieved. Unlike CrossFitters, who can be instructed by a coach to leap onto a tall box and then back down again a set number of times, as fast as possible, I have to use a little trickery with Kody. I hold a ball at my eye level, a height that he can reach with a sufficiently explosive jump, then cue him to "get it!" He springs upward and outward (I'm mindful of making sure that his leaps are mostly outward, to minimize the possibility of him landing awkwardly and to decrease the amount of force that shockwaves through his body with each return to earth). Just as he's about to snatch the ball, I move it outside the reach of his snapping jaws. His leap carries him past me and he lands squarely, balanced over all four feet. He then wheels around and comes back for another attempt, because I have immediately reset the ball to a height that he can reach if he jumps with sufficient "pop." He does his best but I again move the ball just in the nick of time. He comes down, wheels around, and comes back again, and again and again—surely a strange dance for any eye-witness to behold. Each leap represents something close to the maximum amount of explosive force he can generate at the time, so each one bleeds a bit more energy out of his muscles. Once his best efforts are only carrying him a few feet off the ground (usually only a dozen jumps or so, an amount that is sufficient to make me dizzy from all the wheeling around), I let him have it. He snatches the ball cleanly and I shower him with effusive praise and try to regain my balance. He wags his tail and pants (and, I'd swear it, grins) as I tussle his ears and tell him what a good dog he is.

If it were up to Kody, these play sessions would probably go on forever, interrupted only by meals. But, as my world is often overstuffed with other responsibilities, we usually keep them brief. Kyra Sundance, celebrity dog trainer and author of the *101 Dock Tricks* series—and, as an accomplished ultra-marathoner, someone who has plenty of first-hand experience with the "runner's high" and the other psychic benefits of exercise—once told me that she advises clients to try to find just 20 minutes a day to devote to exercising their dogs. In Kyra's estimation, that represents a fair balance between the hectic schedule of the typical modern-day human and the needs and desires of the typical modern-day domestic dog. In any event, it's often about all the time that Kody gets. If it's not a fetch game, it's probably a workout with his herding ball or a purposeful on-leash walk around the neighborhood. Sometimes, when my schedule is more permissive, we go for long walks. But, whatever it is, one thing's for sure: his stump will be wiggling the whole time.

MEANWHILE, BELOW THE NECK

THIS BOOK IS PRIMARILY about obesity, a condition that has been shown to be absolutely horrible for a dog's health. And we've seen that, whether you buy the carbohydrate-insulin model of obesity or not, exercise is, at best, only marginally useful in getting a dog lean and keeping it that way. It is undoubtedly good for the animal's mind, but unless you reject the carbohydrate-insulin model as a conceptual matter *and* you've got both the time and the energy to devote a significant amount of time to exercising your dog every day, managing her diet is always going to be a far more efficient way to manage her weight. That being said, it should also be noted that there is a body of evidence which suggests that regular exercise is uniquely good for your dog's physical health, even if we disregard its somewhat limited utility as a fat-fighting technique. That evidence, as is too often the case when it comes to canine health, comes primarily from studies of human subjects. Still, it warrants a brief discussion.

It manifests as two distinct theories, both of which have at least reasonably strong evidentiary support. The first is that exercise improves cardiac health and decreases the risk of heart disease (even if it doesn't help us lose weight), simply by making us more metabolically fit.

As hard as this may be for younger readers to believe, this is a relatively new idea. Though the notion that exercise is "good for us" is positively ubiquitous today, as recently as the 1970s aerobic exercise was widely considered to be *bad* for heart health. Speaking at a medical conference in the fall of 1976, Dr. Paul Milvy, an epidemiologist and biophysicist at the Mt. Sinai School of Medicine, explained that "until just a few years ago, the conventional wisdom was that strenuous exercise was bad for you." But by 1977 a new conventional wisdom had burst onto the public consciousness. As *The New York Times* reported in that year, "[t]he new conventional wisdom—that strenuous exercise is good for you—has propelled millions of Americans into an *exercise explosion.*"

Obviously, the popularity of recreational exercise has only grown since the 1970s. Today the notion that regular aerobic exercise is good for heart health is not at all controversial; it's very well established by the relevant literature. In 2009, for instance, a meta-analysis examining the link between cardiorespiratory fitness (a measure of one's ability to tolerate rigorous physical exercise) and cardiovascular disease as well as all-cause mortality was published in the *Journal of the American Medical Association*. The authors looked at data from more than 30 other studies, featuring, in total, more than 100,000 subjects. They found a clear and significant inverse correlation between physical fitness and both cardiovascular disease and all-cause mortality. Translation: fitter subjects were less likely to get heart disease and die.

Unlike the calories-in, calories-out model of adiposity, which gives us two separate avenues by which to reduce body fat—diet (calories-in) and exercise (calories-out)—there is, conceptually, only one way to improve cardiorespiratory fitness: with exercise. So it should come as no surprise that not just fitness, but exercise itself, has been shown to improve heart health. As a team of researchers recently wrote in the *American Journal of Cardiology* after conducting a meta-analysis of their own on the links between exercise habits and heart disease, "long-term aerobic exercise has clear cardioprotective effects." By 2007, the American Heart Association and the American College of Sports Medicine had made it official, publishing an update to their official physical activity recommendations for adults—it was the same document that described the evidence linking exercise with weight loss as "not particularly compelling"—and concluding that, to optimize cardiovascular health, adults should perform "moderate-intensity aerobic activity" (a brisk walk) for at least 30 minutes five times per week or "vigorous-intensity aerobic activity" (jogging or the equivalent) for at least 20 minutes three times per week.

The precise mechanism(s) by which exercise exerts its cardioprotective effects is not yet a matter of broad agreement. The epidemiological evidence shows that "vigorous exercise" is more cardioprotective than "moderate exercise," but, as the AHA/ACSM's expert panel wrote in 2007, the reasons why this is the case remain "unclear at present." Still, the evidence is voluminous and compelling enough to suggest that exercise has a role to play in optimizing human cardiovascular health, if not necessarily in keeping anyone lean.

It should be noted, however, that dogs don't suffer from heart disease at nearly the same rate as their human companions. According to the CDC, heart disease is the number-one cause of death among adults in the United States today. This is why measures to improve human heart health—quitting smoking, reducing stress, exercising—are usually among the most emphasized public health recommendations. Improving the cardiac health of the nation would go a long way toward improving its overall health.

But when all types of heart problems—congestive heart failure, congenital diseases, arrhythmias, etc.—are lumped together and considered as a single phenomenon, they kill, in total, only about one out of every ten adult dogs, a rate that is far outstripped by the rate of death by heart disease among adult Americans. This is perhaps part of the reason why there seem to be precisely zero peer-reviewed epidemiological studies documenting the cardioprotective effects of exercise in dogs, let alone meta-analyses of dozens of such papers, such as have been conducted in the human domain. (That being said, a group of doctors from the Medical College of New York and Yale University has found that aerobic exercise increases the release of nitrites in the coronary vessels of dogs, a physiological response that some researchers believe to be the mechanism primarily responsible for the cardioprotective effects of exercise.) Still, the robust body of evidence showing that exercise helps protect human beings from heart disease is, if nothing else, at least worth remembering the next time your pup is sitting at the front door with a leash in his mouth.

Another way that regular exercise has been suggested to improve long-term health is by helping subjects build and maintain lean muscle mass and the muscular strength that tends to come along with it. Diet may be the more efficient way to lose fat, but exercise, particularly *resistance exercise*, is about the only way to build skeletal muscles.

It's a fact of life that as we (both human beings and dogs) age, our skeletal muscles will gradually waste away. In general, the older we get, the faster the deterioration occurs. And if the atrophy is allowed to proceed unimpeded for long enough it will lead to a clinical disorder called sarcopenia, a widespread condition characterized by having ominously low levels of skeletal muscle mass. Picture a frail grandmother who isn't strong enough to walk up the stairs on her own—she is the face of sarcopenia. In human beings, sarcopenia has been shown to reduce day-to-day functionality, increase the likelihood of injurious falls, disrupt healthy metabolism (skeletal muscles are a "sink" into which circulating glucose and triglycerides can be dumped, otherwise those molecules will just hang around in the bloodstream or get sucked up into adipose tissue, making that tissue become even fatter), and diminish the body's ability to cope with disease-related heightened metabolic demands. Fortunately, there's a way we can stop the rot—with resistance exercises and other forms of strength training.

Conceptually, resistance exercises are so simple that a body-builder could do them. Just use weights or some other apparatus to load muscles with more resistance than they would usually need to overcome during contraction, then force them to contract a few times anyways, give them some time to recover from the effort, and repeat. Over time, this process has been definitively shown to cause muscles to grow both larger and stronger. And this is why athletes and other folks who have a professional interest in being strong and muscular tend to spend so much time in the weight room.

But the strength and muscle-building benefits of resistance exercise have important implications not just for athletic performance, but for long-term health as well. Studies have consistently shown that both muscular strength and resistance training itself are associated with living longer and avoiding chronic diseases, particularly in the elderly (among whom sarcopenia is most common). Having enough skeletal muscle in your body, it seems, is critical for living a long and healthy life. There is, however, an important difference between the documented health benefits of muscular fitness and those associated with aerobic fitness. In the case of the cardioprotective benefits of aerobic fitness, the evidence suggests what's called a "dose-response relationship" between fitness and heart health. That, in essence, more is better—the fitter you are, the healthier your heart is likely to be. But in the case of muscular fitness, the evidence seems instead to show what's called a "threshold effect"—if you have too little muscle then you're in trouble, but as long as you're at least moderately muscular, you'll enjoy the same long-term health benefits as someone who is *very* muscular. To become strong enough to enjoy these benefits, as the ACSM and the AHA put it in their 2007 update to their official activity recommendations, adults should perform resistance exercises twice per week. The prescribed regimen is simple: (1) pick eight to 12 exercises, aiming to hit all major muscle groups; (2) use enough resistance so that the relevant muscles can only perform eight to 12 repetitions of each movement without having to rest (over time you'll get stronger, so you'll gradually need to increase this amount); (3) do each movement until you're more or less out of steam, then take a short break and move on to the next movement; then (4) give yourself a few days rest and do it all again.

As always, the evidence showing that it's healthy to maintain sufficient amounts of lean muscle mass throughout life is less robust in the canine domain than in the human one. Still, enough doggy-specific data does exist to leave us reasonably comfortable that the concept translates from one species to the other. Several different technologies and methods (including CT, ultrasound, and carcass analysis) have been used to document age-related muscle wasting in dogs. Researchers have also found positive correlations between overall body weight and post-diagnosis survival time in dogs diagnosed with heart failure and chronic kidney disease. These findings suggest that, as in humans, the amount of muscle mass in a dog's body at the time of a chronic disease diagnosis will go a long way to determining how long it lives. Add this to the robust body of evidence showing that maintenance of lean body mass helps human beings live longer and healthier lives and you can see why Tufts University veterinary nutritionist Lisa Freeman recently wrote that sarcopenia is increasingly being recognized as an "emerging syndrome of importance in dogs and cats."

As the AHA has shown us, when it comes to combating age-related muscle wasting (as opposed to disease-induced muscle wasting, a distinct phenomenon called cachexia), there's really only one way to get the job done: with resistance exercise. Unfortunately, dogs are not particularly good at the most common form of resistance exercise, weight-lifting. They tend to struggle with gripping barbells. Many aren't smart enough to understand instructions like "use enough resistance so that you can only perform eight to 12 repetitions." And, try as I might, I've never been able to get Kody to swing a kettle bell. So if you want to approximate with your dog the type of strength training regimen recommended by the American Heart Association (a few sets with each major muscle group, using enough resistance so that only eight to 12 reps are possible, two times per week), you'll have to get creative.

This is how jumping exercises came into Kody's life. Just as with CrossFitters performing box jumps, the pull of gravity upon his sizable body is a form of resistance that his muscles must overcome in order to propel that body into the air each time he tries to grab the lure. By holding the lure at a height that is barely higher than his best jump, I'm doing my best to coax a maximally explosive effort out of him with each jump. What this usually means is that, after a dozen or so jumps, he'll have lost a good deal of his "pop"—a reasonable if unscientific proxy for the AHA's "eight to 12 repetitions, to the point of muscular failure" recommendation.

Of course, there are plenty of other ways to use gravity to load some resistance onto your dog's muscles. Send her up a steep hill or a flight of stairs in pursuit of a fetch toy or repeatedly cue her to climb up onto some kind of obstacle, for example. And while no one has yet come up with Nautilus machines designed for canine bodies, some innovative entrepreneurs have invented other ways for dogs to pump iron. Weight vests can be used to increase the amount of weight that must be moved when walking, running, or jumping. Harnesses can be used to attach dogs to heavy loads (simulations of the sled-pulling that many dogs have done for centuries). Resistance exercise isn't the easiest thing in the world to do with your dog, but with a little creativity it's certainly possible.

Moreover, in this regard, any kind of exercise is better than nothing. Studies have definitively shown that the heavy resistance recommended by the AHA—enough so that all you can muster is about a dozen repetitions of a movement—is by far the best for growing and strengthening skeletal muscles. But at least some amount of resistance is overcome in the performance of just about any kind of physical activity, from a slow walk to a heavy bench press. Any kind of weight-loaded activity (even if it's just *body weight*-loaded) foists at least some amount of resistance onto canine muscles. So just about any form of exercise will help to fight the effects of sarcopenia to some degree. In fact, when thinking about what kind of exercise to incorporate into your dog's life, the most pressing inquiry of all may not be *what's the most efficient way to stimulate muscle growth?* It may be something else altogether: *what form of exercise will my dog actually enjoy?*

FINDING YOUR DOG'S "THING"

AS DOGS GO, KODY IS a personal trainer's dream. He possesses a near-insatiable appetite for any kind of physical activity—fetching, herding, jogging, jumping, learning new behavioral cues, navigating agility courses, exploring new places, meeting new people. He loves doing and he never seems to tire. I sometimes wonder what sense all these activities make to him—what he thinks he's accomplishing when he's pushing his herding ball around in circles for 20 uninterrupted minutes; how, for that matter, concepts like "doing" and "accomplishing" exist at all in his non-verbal mind—but usually I just feel grateful for the fact that he doesn't require a lot of encouragement in order to perform healthy physical activity. He's at his best when he's exercising and he'd do it all day long if he could.

To hear Crystal McClaran tell it, Bo is the same way. "Bo has incredible drive," she says, referencing a canine personality quirk that trainers use to describe a dog's appetite for physical work. "It's off-the-charts. The pool is his favorite, of course. But he really loves it all. If it wasn't dock-diving, it would probably be frisbees or the agility course. He's a dog who really just shines when he has a job to do."

Kody and Bo are not alone in their affection for work. Many (if not most) dogs have a thirst to perform at least some type of human-directed physical activity. In fact, it's baked into their DNA. The functional utility of certain behaviors was a driving force in the dog's domestication, and a willingness to perform those behaviors was a trait that humans consciously selected when breeding their canine companions. "When we think of dogs, we tend to think of animals that were selected for behavior performed in the service of people," wrote professors Raymond Coppinger and Richard Schneider in a recent paper describing the evolution of modern working dog breeds. "Dogs pull sleds, guard property, herd sheep, guide the blind, track and retrieve game, and so on." Notice that each of these behaviors—pulling, guarding, herding, etc.—is not just useful, but also physically demanding. In many cases, we have tinkered with the genetic makeup of our dogs to make sure that they are receptive to physical work.

But not in all cases.

***

Kody has a stepsister (my "fur stepdaughter," I suppose). Her name is Lucy. She was gifted to my wife more than a decade ago, and the two had already lived together for more than six happy years by the time we all met. For the better part of the past decade, however, we've all been one big family.

Lucy is an English Bulldog, and if there is such a thing as a textbook example of a geriatric bulldog's temperament, she's got it. The American

Kennel Club's breed standard for the English Bulldog—the document that spells out the "official" bulldog look and personality—has been much maligned. In a 2011 cover story for *The New York Times Magazine*, the journalist Benoit Denizet-Lewis described the experiential travails that supposedly come along with being a modern-day bulldog and explained why many folks believe that the dogs live unnaturally short and unpleasant lives as a result of unhealthy physical attributes promoted by the breed standard. Even if you share his sentiment, it's hard not to give credit to the Bulldog Club of America (the group that holds the copyright on the standard) for one thing: its description of the bulldog's temperament as "resolute" and "pacific" is a truly fine example of lyrical artistry. A less poetic breed organization might just have used the words "stubborn" and "lazy" to describe what are surely the breed's two most famous personality traits.

All of which is to say that Lucy is not exactly an exercise buff. She doesn't do much moving, let alone working. And she often spends as much as 23 out of every 24 hours asleep.

Still, we love our little "Nugget" very much and we want to keep her around for as long as possible. And, because we've seen the evidence documenting the health benefits of regular activity, we've tried our best to incorporate exercise into her life. We've tried everything: walks (50 yards, max), fetch games (nope), herding games (no way), jumping (oh, please). And we've experimented with just about every form of motivation: affection (ha!), praise (don't touch me), food (meh). I'm not one for quitting in the face of opposition, but Lucy proved to be a pretty tough nut to crack. In fact, I had just about given up when my wife first told me about "the flashlight game."

If you're not familiar with the flashlight game, do yourself a favor and block off some personal time, search YouTube for "flashlight game dog" or "flashlight game cat," and prepare to be entertained. The idea is simple: because some small animals can be led to believe that an erratically moving flashlight beam is a stimulus worthy of rabid pursuit, a handheld flashlight can be used to spurn them into vigorous (and hilarious) chase behavior.

Apparently Lucy was one of them. I was skeptical, but my wife persisted. So I grabbed a flashlight from the car, shone its beam on the floor, woke up Lucy, and gave the device a wiggle.

The transformation was instantaneous and Lazarus-ian. She was on her feet in a heartbeat, scrambling for purchase on the hardwood floor, bellowing and darting off after the beam. I skated it across the floor and she charged it down immediately, more bull than bulldog. I ran the beam back to the other end of the room and up the wall a bit. Another scramble, then rapid acceleration and more baying. I ran it up the stairs and she charged up the stairs. I ran it up on the couch and she sprung onto the couch. It was hard to believe your eyes.

After ten minutes or so she began to show signs of fatigue so I switched off the beam. We did a little celebration and gave her some water. In a few moments she was back asleep again. But we'd clearly found her "thing," a form of vigorous exercise that was right in the wheelhouse of our lazy, stubborn, geriatric bulldog.

These days, the flashlight comes out on a regular basis. Sometimes we use the couch or the stairs to add a bit of resistance to the mix, other times we keep four on the floor. Lucy doesn't have Kody's metabolic engine so she runs out of gas after only a short while. But, if she could manage it, I think she'd chase the flashlight beam all day. Does that mean she enjoys it? I'm no "dog psychologist"; all I can report is that our time with the flashlight is Lucy at *by far* her most energetic. To my inexpert eye, she appears to have a serious love for the flashlight game.

So is it doing her any good? A 2010 study published in the *Journal of Small Animal Practice* reports that the average lifespan of a bulldog is about six years (one of the shortest lifespans of any breed). At present, Lucy is more than twice that age. She has already lived longer than just about every one of the 841 bulldogs in the *Journal of Small Animal Practice* study. As purebred dogs go, bulldogs are infamously unhealthy. But Lucy has, knock on wood, managed to avoid chronic diseases and surgeries for almost 14 years. And, though she's not the world's most energetic dog, she can still make a good accounting of herself from time to time (given the right stimulus). She's also very much the world-class character she's always been.

But the role played by our little exercise program in contributing to her good health is debatable. In the final analysis, the evidence that inactive lifestyles are to blame for the canine obesity epidemic just isn't that persuasive. Do modern-day domestic dogs tend to be less active than wild wolves? Absolutely. *Far* less so, in fact. As we've seen, wolves often walk and trot upwards of 15 miles every day. And they punctuate those daily odysseys with kill-or-be-killed struggles with big game (read: vigorous aerobic work and muscle-building resistance exercise). Most dogs, on the other hand, are lucky to get a quarter-hour of fetch a day. Nevertheless, if half of the dogs in America are "too heavy," then the other half are *not*. And though no one has published the study that documents the amount of exercise enjoyed by America's dogs, the idea that the 30 million or so who *do* manage to maintain appropriate body conditions do so only because they're performing wolf-like amounts of daily exercise seems a bit fanciful. Lucy and Kody, for their part, always get a daily dose of tongue-wagging exercise. But it's usually brief, vigorous, and to-the-point. And, though it's surely working in the right direction, for us, it's as much about having fun as it is about getting fit.

In the end, we may never know exactly how much of Lucy's current body condition is attributable to exercise (as opposed to diet, genetics, or something else). But something we *can* feel pretty confident about is the role her lean body condition has played in helping her live a long, healthy life.

Because, unlike the role of exercise in managing canine obesity, that is a topic that *has* been well studied. And to understand the relationship between canine body condition and health, all we need to do is have a look through the scientific evidence underlying the final (but arguably most important) topic in this book: *how fat should a dog really be?*

Chapter Seven

HOW FAT IS *TOO* FAT?

--

"The history of science, like the history of all human ideas, is a history of irresponsible dreams, of obstinacy, and of error. But science is one of the very few human activities— perhaps the only one—in which errors are systematically criticized and fairly often, in time, corrected. This is why we can say that, in science, we often learn from our mistakes, and why we can speak clearly and sensibly about making progress there."

Karl Popper, *Conjectures and Refutations: The Growth of Scientific Knowledge* (1963)

STARVING, SUFFERING, AND SIGHTHOUNDS

STEVEN BECKERMAN'S FIRST sighthound was a little Italian Greyhound named Dee. It wasn't his first dog. His boyhood companion had been a large, blue Standard Poodle named Sashi. But allergies pushed him away from dogs as a young man and kept him away for much of his life. Then, in 2006, he met and fell in love with a young veterinary student named Christina, a dog lover who shared her home with a rescue dog. Love can do strange things to people and Steven suddenly found that his allergies had become manageable again. The couple added another dog—a shaggy Spinone Italiano they named Gavi—during their first year of marriage. Then came Dee. And then another sighthound, a Silken Windhound named Honey.

Sighthounds make up a unique part of the canine kingdom. There is considerable physical variation among them—the smallest varietal is the Italian Greyhound, dogs like Dee, that typically weigh in at less than 20 pounds and stand only a foot tall at the withers; the largest is the Irish Wolfhound, the tallest of all the AKC-recognized breeds and often taller than Shaquille O'Neal when standing on their hind legs. But there is also a commonality of physical appearance that differentiates them from all other dogs.

The sighthound look is best exemplified by the Greyhound, the quintessential representative of the group. Greyhounds are the fastest dogs in the world, having been clocked running at speeds of over 50 miles per hour. Because a pack of dogs chasing a lure around a track at highway speeds makes for both exciting spectating and good speculating, greyhound racing has been both a pastime and a commercial industry in the United States for nearly a century. Though the heyday of modern greyhound racing is likely behind us now—there was a time, according to the Greyhound Hall of Fame, in Abilene, Kansas, when a dog named Downing was *twice* made the subject of in-depth *Sports Illustrated* features during his lifetime—the activity is still popular in certain corners of the world. And, when you watch a greyhound race, it's not hard to see why. The dogs move with the frenetic pace of a rallied ball in a professional tennis match, so quickly as to be difficult to track with the naked eye. When aided by super-slow-motion replay, it becomes clear that they are wearing expressions of rapt determination, eyes bulging, teeth exposed, ears flattened back. The pack moves as a single unit and kicks clods of mud high into the sky as it tears around the corners of the oval, hugging the curves tightly. They gallop so furiously as to flatten their bodies almost completely at the top of each stride cycle. In these moments they are arrows in flight, hind legs kicked back in the wake of powerful, thrusting strides, forelimbs reaching out for a point, still some distance away, where the next stride cycle will begin.

The Greyhound's physical attributes have given the breed a monopoly in this competitive environment. They are lithe and aerodynamic, from the tips of their long snouts clear through to their ropey tails. Their narrow, deep-chested bodies are carried on legs that are spindly, disproportionately long, and capable of generating immense power. And unlike blockier dogs—such as Rottweilers like Kody—whose skeletal musculature naturally tends to develop outward into what we call "bulk," greyhounds tend to develop the long, sleek muscles typical of Olympic swimmers. They are at once slight and powerful, an ideal combination of speed racing traits.

All sighthounds possess this set of physical attributes, though usually not to the same degree as the Greyhound. Some are marginally narrower or wider through the shoulders and hips. The length and color of their coats varies. There are tremendous differences in height. But, once you know what you are looking for, you can always spot a sighthound: just look for the dogs who are particularly long and lean.

All hounds descend from hunters and trackers. But, unlike most hounds, sighthounds were bred to track by sight (rather than scent), and to overcome prey with flashes of incredible speed (rather than hours of persistent chasing). And, with a little assistance from humans, they've gradually developed the cluster of physical traits which allow them to excel at this unique hunting style—the sharp eyes, lean bodies, narrow hips, deep chests, and long, powerful legs that make them so readily identifiable.

But while sighthound aficionados tend to appreciate all this, these attributes can create a very different impression in the untrained eye. Specifically, sighthounds strike many laypeople as unhealthily skinny, even malnourished. They stand out among other dogs, being so lean while most dogs are so fat. And because their dogs look different than most, the owners of sighthounds tend to get singled out for negative treatment by other owners. They get criticized for having lean dogs.

It's a phenomenon with which Steven Beckerman is well acquainted. Even today, taking Dee and Honey to the park or for a stroll around the neighborhood is likely to produce a litany of comments. "Whoa, what's wrong with your dogs, man?" and "Oh, these poor guys must not be getting enough to eat!" and "Don't you think you should be feeding them more? They're going to starve to death!"

Perhaps someone who was raised with sighthounds would have grown accustomed to the barrage by the time he had become an adult, but it took Steven by surprise. "The frequency with which I got those sorts of comments was baffling to me," he remembers.

But he didn't just think the comments were surprising, he thought they were wrong. "I didn't think there was anything wrong with my dogs. I thought they looked like they should. Frankly, I was proud of their body condition—they were well-muscled and lean, just like they were bred to be. I mean, how could they be malnourished? My dogs are muscular—a body can't support the development of muscle mass without adequate nutrition, can it?"

Fair point. Not that it's exactly surprising that the typical American dog owner would hold uninformed or even nonsensical opinions about the healthiness of a canine body. According to polling conducted by Dr. Ernie Ward and the Association for Pet Obesity Prevention, almost half of the dog owners in the United States will readily admit that they have no idea how much their dogs really ought to weigh. Even worse, most of those who think they do know are *wrong*. Indeed, more than 90% of the clinically obese dogs in the United States belong to owners who wrongly believe their dogs are in "normal" condition. Dr. Ward and his colleagues call this lack of knowledge the "Fat Gap" and they say that it goes a long way toward explaining why more than half the dogs in America today are overweight. "The Fat Gap is rampant and we believe it's the primary factor in the pet obesity epidemic," says APOP board member Dr. Joe Bartges.

Steven Beckerman knows all about the Fat Gap and APOP's polling. But expert opinions and hard data can be cold comfort when your friends and neighbors honestly believe (wrongly or not) that you're hurting your best friends by keeping them "so skinny." So in April of 2014 Steven decided to take matters into his own hands. He did something smart: he sought to surround himself with other folks who shared his outlook on canine body condition, dog owners who were proud of their lean, fit dogs—just like he was. And he leveraged the tools of the Internet Age to ensure that he made the most of the endeavor. He created a Facebook group for dog owners who felt unfairly criticized by the under-educated outside world.

Steven called the group "No, It's Not Starving." He kicked it off with a few photos of Dee and Honey and some anecdotes about the trials and tribulations of sighthound ownership in the Fat Gap Era. Then he spent a little time promoting the group to some of his personal friends. He made the group public, so that anyone could join. But, privately, he just hoped that a few other sighthound people would relate to his plight and join him from time to time for some friendly, therapeutic online griping.

It's fair to say that Steven underestimated the resonance of his message. Within a few weeks, No, It's Not Starving had more than 3,000 members. Today there are more than 15,000 of them.

They're a pretty active bunch. New photos of dogs show up most every day—dynamic action shots of dogs running and playing and portrait-style arrangements of family pets being lovingly embraced by their people. Members converse energetically with each other too. They talk about their dogs, about their latest achievements in conformation shows and athletic competitions, about their dietary philosophies and exercise regimens, about training and obedience, and, more than anything else, about their experiences living in a world where what they consider thoughtful canine parenting is often considered by others to be a mild form of animal abuse.

When you scroll through the member posts, one of the things that jumps out is how diverse the dogs are. If their photos are anything to go by, then practically every corner of the canine world is represented in No, It's Not Starving's constituency. Big, burly pit bulls flex their veiny muscles as they swing from tree-hung truck tires. Retrievers and spaniels go careening into ponds, splashing frantically in pursuit of some unseen attractant. Napoleonic Chihuahuas chase chipmunks and proudly mangle neon-colored rubber toys. The domestic dog may be a physically diverse species, but any dog, it seems, can be really fit.

Another thing that is immediately apparent is these dogs are a remarkably active bunch. Many are working dogs—local law enforcement K-9s, military operatives, members of search and rescue teams, avalanche dogs, and all sorts of others whose professional duties require the performance of vigorous exercise and the maintenance of tip-top physical condition. Many others compete in recreational canine athletics, where physical prowess may not be required, but it is rewarded. Crisp, dynamic images from sports like lure coursing, agility, fly-ball, weight-pulling, and dock-diving fill the group's feed, like a dog-themed ESPN pictorial. It's not clear that exercise is what's keeping No, It's Not Starving's dogs lean, but it is clear that most of them happen to be both very active and very lean.

And that's the last, and most obvious, thing about the dogs in Steven

Beckerman's Facebook group. They're all admirably lean. Not unlike selfie-snapping celebrities, members usually share only the photos that put their dogs' most impressive paws forward. Still, these dogs are a sight to behold. In the case of the shorthaired ones, particularly the Pit Bulls, their skeletal musculature is as well defined as any Thoroughbred horse. Even from some distance away, you can see where each muscle ends and the next begins. You can see the swirling vasculature. You can see each piano key of the ribcage. Running full-tilt across a grassy expanse, they look like professional athletes do—positively rippling with striated muscles. Not exactly the body condition possessed by your garden variety house pet.

Now, 15,000 is a pretty big number. But it represents only a minute fraction of America's more than 70 million dog owners. And though the folks in Steven Beckerman's Facebook group may think they have a good sense of just how lean their dogs ought to be, APOP's polling shows that many of America's dog owners freely admit that they have no idea. The polling also shows that those who *do* think they know are—at least in APOP's eyes—usually wrong.

So who's right about body condition? Is it Steven Beckerman and his legions of canine fitness advocates? Dr. Ward and APOP? Someone else altogether? We know that being *really* fat kills dogs—that much is pretty obvious. But just how lean should we keep our dogs if we want to minimize their health risks and help them live as long as possible? There's only one good way to answer that question, and that's to seek out whatever relevant facts have been revealed through peer-reviewed scientific experimentation and then apply a little logical reasoning to make sense of them all. And that endeavor is precisely what this chapter is about.

***

For obvious reasons, the "how fat is too fat?" question doesn't get much attention in your typical human-use weight-loss book. In those cases, the reader usually is assumed to be a good deal fatter than he ought to be and the book's implicit promise is to get him back to reasonably good condition. Truly optimizing the reader's body condition isn't too relevant—when you're having trouble achieving even a baseline of health, it's not particularly helpful to know that it would be *even better* to get *even leaner*.

In a book about dogs, though, it's a different story. As the big-brained custodians of our canine companions, we get to make decisions on their behalf. And one of the benefits of this agency relationship is we are removed from some of the emotional forces that can compel bad weight management decision-making. (Not all of them, as we saw in the last chapter, but many of them.) So, for most of us, it's easier to help our dogs lose weight then it is to lose weight ourselves.

For that reason, it's worth trying to understand what it means for a dog to be in truly "optimal" condition. When it comes to our dogs, optimization isn't an unreasonable a goal. And, if there really is such a thing as optimal canine body condition, why not aim for that? After all, if a longer life is a good reason for your dog to lose a few pounds, isn't an even *longer* life a good reason to lose a few more?

WHY BODY WEIGHT DOESN'T MATTER

DR. ALEXANDER GERMAN is one of the world's foremost experts on obesity in small animals. Since 1998 he has authored or co-authored more than a hundred academic articles on one aspect of the subject or another. He is an editorial board member or an official reviewer for numerous nutrition and obesity journals. He is an internationally recognized speaker, a professor at the University of Liverpool, and a recipient of the British Small Animal Veterinary Association's Woodrow Award (given annually for outstanding contributions in the field of small animal veterinary medicine). Much of what we know today about why being fat is so bad for dogs goes through Dr. German's work if we trace it back far enough.

Writing in 2006, Dr. German had occasion to comment on the existing state of scientific knowledge surrounding the "optimal body weight" for a dog. He observed that recently published reports classified "cats and dogs as overweight when their body weight is >15% above their 'optimal body weight,' and as obese when their body weight exceeds 30% of optimal." But he cautioned that these reports and others like them *"have not been confirmed with rigorous epidemiological studies."* In other words, the body weight breakpoints used in these studies were arbitrary. Later in the article, Dr. German explained that when it comes to dogs and cats, "limited data exist on the nature of an optimal body weight."

This last line is nothing if not a wry understatement. Because the truth is that the published data on the "optimal" body weights for dogs are not just "limited," they are non-existent. The studies have not been done. As yet, no one has devised a scientifically validated method for identifying the optimal body weight for any individual dog (including the millions that don't fall neatly into one breed or another), let alone published any data derived from such a methodology.

Among the reasons for this, an obvious one is that dogs are a remarkably diverse bunch. In fact, because of their unique evolutionary history—a history into which human beings rather presumptuously injected ourselves—the domestic dog is the most physically diverse species on the planet. (We might occasionally find a large but healthy man who is twice as large as a small but healthy man. But big dogs can easily be more than *forty times* as large as little ones. Try imagining how that same ratio would play out if applied to human beings.) This tremendous physical diversity makes it incredibly difficult to make claims about how much any individual animal should weigh. The amount of lean body mass just varies too much from animal to animal— while some are thick-boned, wide, and muscular, others are narrow, long, and lithe. And millions fall somewhere in between. It would take *a lot* of scientific work before we could begin to say how much they all ought to weigh. And no one has done the work yet.

Think about the implications of this reality for a minute. How many times in your life have you been told how much your dog "should" weigh? Did the breeder or rescue organization that gave you your puppy instruct you what body weight to aim for when she grew up? Is there an overbearing know-it-all at the local dog park who loves to offer unsolicited opinions on the matter? If you have a purebred dog, Google her breed along with the phrase "ideal body weight" and take a look at all the writers and organizations that claim to know the healthiest weight for your dog. Surely, if nothing else, your local veterinarian has told you exactly how much he thinks your dog ought to weigh.

Here is the truth: In every single one of those instances, no matter how authoritative or confident or scientifically inclined the speaker may have seemed, her recommendation *was not based on statistical analyses or any other kind of published scientific research*. She may have had the best of intentions, but if she claimed to know the healthiest weight for your dog then she wasn't telling you anything resembling a scientifically proven fact. (Don't believe me? Put down the book, call up your vet, and ask her to refer to you to a single peer-reviewed publication that uses a consistent methodology to assign an "optimal" weight to any breed of dog. I recommend that you do not hold your breath while waiting for a response.)

So where *did* all the "optimal body weight" recommendations you've received in your life come from? The short answer is that most of them arose from a single phenomenon, one that is at once totally unscientific, explicitly unconcerned with matters of health and longevity, and (in my view, at least) kind of ridiculous. That phenomenon is the conformation dog show.

***

The long answer dates back to man's domestication of wolves, several hundred centuries ago. Once our ancestors recognized how useful (and, presumably, how fun) it could be to have a large, approachable canine around, it's hard to imagine that it took them long to start selectively breeding their new companions for specific traits. There are many ways in which a dog can physically outperform a human. It will run faster over short distances, it is better at detecting subtle scents and sounds, it can inflict more damage with a bite. And there were just as many ways that those qualities could be put to use by our scheming, big-brained ancestors. A smeller could help with tracking game, a runner could help with corralling livestock, a biter could protect against predators and enemies. The evolutionary descent of the modern-day domestic dog, in all its myriad shapes and sizes, is largely the story of man's attempts to selectively breed for the specific traits—both behavioral and physical—that suit his many diverse wants and needs.

Now fast-forward a few thousand generations and observe the domestic dog in Victorian England. He can be found in hundreds of different forms, displaying almost all of the physical diversity that we know today: there are big dogs and there are little dogs; heavy-coated dogs and hairless dogs; excitable ones and aloof ones. This impressive diversity reflects the many ways that dogs have proven their value to humans. But diversification has also been accelerated by another, less practical concern. The more rarified classes of the Victorian era have begun using dogs as status symbols. And just as the supposed purity of certain bloodlines has given rise to race-based social stratification in 19th century England, so eugenic thinking has launched an obsession with "purebred" dogs. Outwardly observable traits, verifiable lineages, and closed breeding practices have been used to define hundreds of different dog "breeds." Breed-specific "kennel clubs" have been formed to draw and enforce the lines between the pure and the impure. And, in the upper echelons of Victorian society, to own a certain kind dog—one that hews closely to a breed standard—is considered a marker of refinement.

It was against this backdrop that the conformation dog show was born. While some of the details have changed over the past 150 years or so, the basic idea is much as it always was; it is a beauty contest for dogs. But unlike in human beauty pageants, where, for all their unique and charming personal attributes, the competitors are pretty physically similar (it is a rare case indeed when one entrant is, say, twice as large as another competitor), dogs are so physically diverse that a roundabout system must be used in order to meaningfully compare one animal against another. In that system, judges evaluate individual dogs for conformance with published "breed standards," written guidelines that set forth the characteristics that the ideal representative of each breed ought to display. By ranking competitors based on their relative conformance with breed standards, judges can make defensible judgments about which dog is most beautiful, even in a competition featuring representatives of many different breeds. The dog that best conforms to its respective breed standard wins.

Each breed standard is created and maintained by an organization devoted to the preservation and promotion of a specific breed. For example, the breed standard used by the American Kennel Club to evaluate Golden Retrievers is published by the Golden Retriever Club of America, a group composed of breeders, hobbyists, and other folks who really like Golden Retrievers. Breed standards only refer to outwardly observable qualities, such as an animal's physical appearance, movement, and temperament. But, for those qualities, the standards represent the ideals that breeders should, in the eyes of the relevant breed association, seek to achieve in their stock. Each standard includes body dimension guidelines for both males and females, and those usually include specific height and weight recommendations. And *that* is where any notion of an "ideal" body weight for a specific breed comes from.

***

It should be emphasized that breed standards are not scientific documents. Indeed, with their ties to eugenics, fashion, and culturally contingent notions of beauty, they have a decidedly *un*-scientific heritage. Moreover, as we've already seen, there simply isn't any published research to guide kennel clubs in setting weight standards. There are just groups of folks—people who, admittedly, have a great deal of experience with specific breeds—offering largely anecdotal observations on how representatives of a breed ought to look in order to best achieve the purposes for which the breed was originally developed.

In the interest of intellectual honesty, we still might ask whether body weight recommendations grounded in breed standards nevertheless serve as reasonable guides for determining how much our dogs truly ought to weigh. They might not be overtly scientific, but they're better than nothing, right? After all, the folks at the Golden Retriever Club of America have surely seen enough Golden Retrievers to have developed a good idea of how much one ought to weigh, even if their informal observations lack the sheen of credibility that adorns published scientific research.

Well, perhaps. But there are a few reasons why relying on breed standard-based body weight recommendations might not be such a good idea.

First is the fact that many breed standards have come under intense scrutiny from veterinary researchers and animal welfare activists for affirmatively promoting decidedly unhealthy traits. As documented in the scathing and scandalous BBC One production "Pedigree Dogs Exposed," many breed standards explicitly encourage breeding for traits that, while they may "protect and advance the interests of the breed" (whatever that means), do so while seriously jeopardizing the health and happiness of individual dogs. Traits like the English Bulldog's flat, brachycephalic face; the Pug's tail, which should be "curled as tightly as possible" (despite the fact that this tends to produce spinal deformities); and the Cavalier King Charles Spaniel's unnaturally small skull (the reason as many as a third of all Cavaliers develop the crippling neurological condition syringomyelia). Alas, what qualifies as beauty in the show ring and what constitutes good health is not always the same thing.

Moreover, there is at least some affirmative evidence that the body weight recommendations found in breed standards tend to be too high. Dr. Christine Zink, one of the world's foremost experts on performance and working dogs, has written that show dogs "don't win in the conformation ring unless they are fat." In her estimation, "if your dog is winning in the conformation ring, it is probably about 8 to 15 pounds overweight." Dr. Zink's observations are consistent with a recent study conducted by Dr. German and one of his University of Liverpool colleagues, in which they found that more than a quarter of top-ranking dogs from a national dog show were overweight.

Another problem with body weight recommendations based on breed standards: they are often so imprecise as to be utterly useless. As just one example, in the case of the Newfoundland, the AKC's official breed standard recommends a weight of between 100 and 150 pounds—a full 50% difference between the lightest recommended weight and the heaviest one! This is no more helpful than being told that an American of European descent should weigh somewhere between 150 and 225 pounds. Which is to say not helpful at all. Some breed standards don't even include quantitative body weight recommendations—they just use vague qualitative descriptions, such as "proportionately tall" or "solid and big for his inches." And, of course, they're of little help when it comes to the millions of dogs that don't fit neatly into one breed category or another.

But perhaps the most cogent criticism of breed standard-based body weight recommendations is one that has nothing to do with the specific recommendations themselves. Evaluating total body weight just isn't a particularly good way to determine the amount of fat that a body actually contains. Body fat is a weighty substance, to be sure. But all other bodily tissues—muscle, bone, digestive organs—are too, and the total weight of those tissues can vary dramatically dog-to-dog, even when the total amount of fat does not. Higher body weight doesn't always mean more body fat.

For all these reasons, in order to understand what it means for a dog to be in truly optimal condition, we need to start with something better than body weight recommendations based on antiquated and widely criticized breed standards. Fortunately for us, there is something better.

CANINE BODY CONDITION SCORING SYSTEMS

IN THE VETERINARY COMMUNITY, the standard method for analyzing canine body condition does not require a scale, a tape measure, or a breed standard. Instead, it involves the use of visual and tactile evaluation protocols. Sounds a bit complicated, but the basic idea is pretty simple: just see how a few specific parts of a dog's body look and feel and then use written guidelines to determine what those observations mean about the total amount of fat in her body. Several such protocols (usually called "Body Condition Scoring" or "BCS" charts) have been scientifically validated, including the two popular ones shown below.

9-CATEGORY BCS CHART

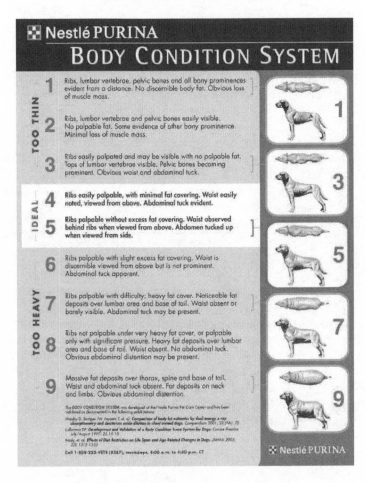

Figure 2(a).

7-CATEGORY BCS CHART

Waltham S.H.A.P.E.™ Guide for Dogs

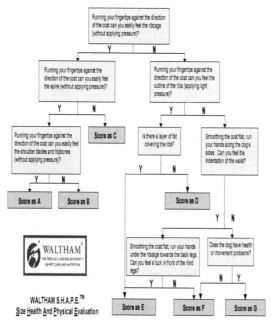

WALTHAM S.H.A.P.E.™
Size Health And Physical Evaluation

S.H.A.P.E.™ Score	Description
A	**Extremely Thin** Your dog has a very small amount or no total body fat. Recommendation: Seek veterinary advice promptly.
B	**Thin** Your dog has only a small amount of total body fat. Recommendation: Seek veterinary advice to ensure your dog is offered the appropriate amount of food. Reassess using the S.H.A.P.E.™ chart every 2 weeks.
C	**Lean** Your dog is at the low end of the ideal range with less than normal body fat. Recommendation: Increase food offered by a small amount. Monitor monthly using the S.H.A.P.E.™ chart and seek veterinary advice if no change.
D	**Ideal** Your dog has an ideal amount of total body fat. Recommendation: Monitor monthly to ensure your dog remains in this category and have him/her checked by the veterinarian at your next visit.
E	**Mildly Overweight** Your dog is at the upper end of the ideal range with a small amount of excess body fat. Recommendation: Seek veterinary advice to ensure your dog is offered the appropriate amount of food and consider increasing activity levels. Avoid excessive treats and monitor monthly using the S.H.A.P.E.™ chart.
F	**Moderately Overweight** Your dog has an excess of total body fat. Recommendation: Seek veterinary advice to implement safely an appropriate weight loss plan including increasing activity levels. Reassess using the S.H.A.P.E.™ chart every 2 weeks.
G	**Severely Overweight** Your pet has a large amount of excess total body fat that is affecting its health and well being. Recommendation: Seek veterinary advice promptly to introduce a weight loss plan to reduce your dog's weight, increase activity levels and improve health.

NB: Some breeds and different life-stages may have different ideal S.H.A.P.E scores. Consult your veterinarian if you are unsure.

TM Registered Trademark © 2005 Mars, Incorporated

Figure 2(b).

As you can see, they are delightfully simple. They take no more than a minute or two, don't require any special training or technology, can be performed in the comfort of your living room, and, in a matter of moments, will produce a tidy conclusion about your dog's overall body condition. Analyzing fluffy or long-haired breeds is a bit more challenging because their bodies are hidden beneath dense coats. Fortunately, both popular BCS protocols also provide at least some degree of guidance for using tactile evaluation (how body parts feel, as opposed to how they look) to make judgments about overall body condition. So, in theory, BCS protocols can be used with just about any dog.

But do they work? Does your dog's BCS score actually tell you something meaningful about the condition of the animal's body? This deceptively simple question raises a few separate issues. And in order to understand how useful BCS protocols are for evaluating canine body condition we'll need to look briefly at each one.

***

Let's begin by asking whether a BCS score actually gives us a good idea of how much fat is inside a dog's body. Here, the answer is simple and unequivocal—yes, it does. We know this because the two most popular BCS protocols have both been subjected to scientific scrutiny. And both have passed with flying colors.

The first scientifically validated canine BCS system (the nine-category protocol depicted in Figure 2(a)) was developed in the mid-1990s. It was the brainchild of a veterinarian named Dottie Laflamme, who produced it while working as an employee of the Ralston Purina Company (a corporate predecessor of Purina PetCare). For the same reasons we've already discussed, Dr. Laflamme recognized that a simple body weight measurement would never be a particularly good way of assessing obesity in dogs. So she came up with something better, adopting a method with a proven track record of accurately evaluating the relative adiposity of cattle and other production animals and modifying it for use with dogs.

In 1997, Dr. Laflamme published a paper defending her new canine BCS system. In her paper—published in a little-known journal called *Canine Practice*—she explained how a team of six operators had used her new system to score the body conditions of 255 dogs, mostly Labrador Retrievers, German Shorthaired Pointers, and English Setters. She then used a sophisticated body-scanning technology called DEXA to measure the fat mass of each animal directly. And she found that "[t]he correlation between

BCS and percent body fat determined by DEXA was linear and highly significant," with body fat increasing by about 5% for each one-unit increase in BCS.

In other words, her new system worked well as a diagnostic tool. The dogs who wound up in the same body condition categories all had about the same amount of fat in their bodies. The dogs scored as BCS 5 (the high end of the "ideal" category) tended to contain, on average, a little less than 20% body fat. Those scored as BCS 7 ("too heavy") tended to contain closer to 30% body fat. And the DEXA-measured body fat percentage of most dogs fell within a few percentage points of the average for each of the nine BCS categories.

AVERAGE BODY FAT % (9-CATEGORY BCS SYSTEM)

BCS Score	Males	Females
1	N/A	N/A
2	3.7%	2.6%
3	8.2%	8.4%
4	12.7%	14.1%
5	17.2%	19.9%
6	21.7%	25.7%
7	26.2%	31.4%
8	30.7%	37.2%
9	35.1%	43.0%

Figure 3(a).

Similar things can be said for the seven-category BCS protocol (Figure 2(b)). This system was developed in 2006 by Alexander German and his colleagues at the University of Liverpool. Unlike the nine-category protocol, the seven-category one operates as a flow chart that directs users to a final score by guiding them through a series of yes-or-no questions. In contrast, Dr. Laflamme's nine-category system operates as a matching exercise involving just a single step.

Like the nine-category system, the accuracy of Dr. German's seven-category protocol has been evaluated using laboratory technology. And the results of the evaluation were similarly good. Dr. German asked both experts and laypeople to use his flow chart to score a group of over 70 dogs of a wide variety of breeds, ages, and body conditions. Then, like Dr. Laflamme, he used DEXA technology to crosscheck the results. On average, the bodies of the dogs that were scored as BCS D ("ideal") tended to contain, on average, about 17% body fat. Those scored as BCS F ("moderately overweight") tended to contain, on average, about 35% body fat. And, again, most dogs fell within just a few percentage points of the average for each category.

AVERAGE BODY FAT % (7-CATEGORY BCS SYSTEM)

BCS Score	Body Fat %
A	N/A
B	0.28%
C	8.84%
D	17.39%
E	25.95%
F	34.50%
G	43.06%

Figure 3(b).

The two protocols have also been tested for user friendliness. And in both cases they performed well. When Dr. Laflamme's nine-category protocol was used by two different operators to score the same dog, their scores matched up remarkably well with one another. And when the same operator used the system twice to analyze the same dog (with the two observations separated by a few days), the scores matched up even better.

Dr. German also looked at the reproducibility of the scores derived from his BCS system. He asked both inexperienced dog owners and trained experts to separately analyze each dog in his study group. And he found that their conclusions agreed in most cases and, when they disagreed, only did so to a small degree:

The scores of the owners using the [new seven-category system] agreed on 29 of 38 (76%) and 30 of 38 (79%)

occasions with those of the experienced operators... When scores disagreed, they were always within 1 integer category of each other, and owners over- and underestimated scores an approximately equal number of times. Other than on 2 occasions, the disagreement was between assigning integer scores of 6 and 7.

These findings all suggest that a BCS analysis is a pretty good way to measure the total amount of fat inside a dog's body. No matter which BCS protocol we use, we can feel confident that it's going to tell us something pretty useful. Scores won't be perfect in all cases. But they'll provide reasonably good measures of adiposity.

Unfortunately, that's not the whole story. Before we run off and start relying on BCS charts to guide us through determining the optimal body condition for our dogs, there's one more issue we need to consider. And it's a vital one.

***

A BCS analysis can undoubtedly help us to understand how much fat is inside a dog's body. But knowing how much fat *is* in a dog's body is only useful if we also know how much fat *should* be in her body. Otherwise, well, what's the point of the analysis?

The popular BCS protocols claim to be helpful in this regard too. Both make implicit conclusions about optimal canine body condition by assigning short qualitative descriptions—"too fat," "too thin," "ideal," etc.—to each of the condition categories. So, if I score my dog as a "D" on the seven-category protocol, the chart suggests that he is in ideal condition. If he scores an "E" or above, he's too fat. And if he scores a "C" or below, he's too lean.

But are these judgments trustworthy? Is it true that a dog with about 17% body fat is in "ideal" condition (as the seven-category BCS protocol suggests)—and that leaner dogs actually need to *gain* some fat?

As both popular BCS protocols have been analyzed in peer-reviewed scientific papers, we'd hope that answers to these important questions could be found with a minimum amount of fuss. Unfortunately, that isn't the case. As much as I'd love to report that there is ample scientific evidence supporting the recommendations made by both major BCS protocols, the truth is quite the opposite. The studies in which the protocols were published and analyzed do not include any discussion whatsoever of how the BCS category breakpoints were chosen. There is no discussion of why the authors think that a dog scored as a "D" has an ideal amount of fat in her body or why a dog scored as a "C" is too lean. There are no studies cited and there are no epidemiological data mentioned. In both cases, no attempt whatsoever has been made to explain the rationale behind the chosen classification frameworks. The breakpoints for differentiating an "underweight" dog from an "ideal" one seem to have been chosen arbitrarily.

Dr. German and his colleagues at least admit as much: "[M]ore structured epidemiological studies are required to confirm whether the current body condition recommendations are optimal for all breeds, ages, and genders of dogs and cats." But Dr. Laflamme chose not even to address the issue. Despite devoting an entire paper to explaining the statistical methods used to ensure repeatability in her new nine-point BCS system, she didn't devote a single line of text to explaining *why* her new system considered a BCS score of 5 to be "ideal" and a BCS score of 4 to be "underweight."

What this means is, if we want to understand whether BCS charts can be used to accurately diagnose whether our dogs are overweight or not, we'll need to dig a little deeper. We'll need to take our own look at the published scientific record and see what it can teach us about what it means for anyone—man or dog—to really be "too fat."

A SHORT CULTURAL HISTORY OF HUMAN ADIPOSITY

THERE'S ONLY ONE PLACE TO BEGIN an effort to understand what it means to be too fat. That's with the most authoritative public health body on the planet, the World Health Organization. The WHO doesn't concern itself with dogs, mind you. Its work is devoted exclusively to people. But its role in the world of human health is second-to-none and, as you may have heard, obesity is something of a problem for modern-day human beings too. According to the WHO, more than 1.9 billion adults worldwide—about a third of the planet's population—are overweight. Perhaps even more troubling, more than 40 million children under the age of five are already overweight or obese. The human obesity epidemic is, in the words of the WHO, a "leading risk for global death." So it's not hard to see why it has gotten the organization's attention.

The WHO defines obesity as "abnormal or excessive fat accumulation that may impair health," a definition that includes three separate elements:

(1) fat accumulation,
(2) of an abnormal or excessive amount,
(3) to the point that it may impair health.

Conceptually, this gets right to the heart of the matter—being obese means having so much fat in your body that it's bad for your health. But for our purposes, there's a problem with the definition: it is incredibly vague. Words like "abnormal" and "excessive" are only meaningful if they are paired with a reference point, something against which we can evaluate specific cases to determine whether they fall into the group we're seeking to define. Otherwise we're just left asking "excessive *of what*?"

The main reason for the ambiguity in the WHO's definition is a lack of consensus as to exactly how much adipose tissue should be inside a body at any given time. The scientific community understands very well that having *a lot* of fat in a body is bad for health. And it understands that at least *some* is necessary for a body to function properly. But between these two endpoints things get murky. And a more helpful bright-line definition of obesity has largely proven elusive, both for dogs and for people.

***

That's not to say that no one has tried. Indeed, armchair diagnosticians have been judging the relative chubbiness of their friends and neighbors for millennia. In many corners of the world, the amount of fat that a person's body contains is—and has long been—a reflection of his or her social standing. Thus, time and again, specific body condition norms have evolved to reflect the unique cultural circumstances under which they arose.

Prior to the invention of agriculture, our hunter-gatherer ancestors occupied a world in which the food supply was precarious and ample fat reserves were a marker of evolutionary advantage. Artifacts from this period seem to suggest that chubbiness was, at the time, seen as a desirable trait. Notably, a collection of limestone statuettes dating back to Stone Age Europe more than 20,000 years ago (including the famous "Venus of Willendorf") depict women bearing signs of gross obesity—love handles, pendulous breasts, bulging bellies, and wide thighs pressed tightly against one another. Scholars believe that these figurines represent ideal Paleolithic women, or even goddesses. And given the relative scarcity of food in the Paleolithic, it's not hard to see why.

Even after the invention of agriculture, chronic food shortages, hunger, and malnutrition persisted as global norms for several thousand years—a period lasting well into the last few centuries. Much of the art produced during this long period of widespread scarcity again suggests that portliness was widely considered a quality to be strived for and sought after. The fleshy bodies of Michelangelo's renderings of Biblical characters in his Sistine Chapel frescoes and Peter Paul Rubens's, well, Rubenesque nudes would all qualify as "overweight" by today's standards. According to Nobel laureate Robert W. Fogel, it wasn't until the technological advances of the Industrial Revolution that food shortages began to subside and whole populations began to grow bigger and stronger, thus easing the pressures that once made chubbiness fashionable.

But cultural significance is one thing and medical significance is another.

Even prior to the Industrial Revolution, perceptive thinkers had begun to identify the links between adiposity and disease. And while the masses of the day may have been itching to bolster their reputations by adding a few extra inches to their waistlines, those who cared about the health consequences of obesity could see the tragic folly of this pursuit. In 400 BC, no lesser a figure than the Greek physician Hippocrates flatly observed that "persons who are naturally very fat are apt to die earlier than those who are slender." Some 400 years later, his Roman disciple Celsus of Alexandria agreed: "Many of the obese are throttled by acute disease and difficulty breathing; they die often suddenly which rarely happens in a thinner person." Even Benjamin Franklin once observed that "[t]o lengthen thy life, lessen thy meals."

By the 19th century, as the advances of the Industrial Revolution loosened the global straightjacket of hunger, the prevailing social norms and popular medical wisdom finally began to align against adiposity. And it was during this time that body fat began to earn widespread notoriety as both unfashionable and unhealthy.

The alignment began in Europe, and is exemplified by the publication there of the world's first diet books, including William Banting's *Letter on Corpulence* (1864), William Wadd's *Comments on Corpulency* (1829), and Cecil Webb-Johnson's *Why Be Fat?* (1923). The popularity of these titles reflected a growing awareness about the dangers of obesity—Banting's was a long-running best-seller and was so influential that the word "Banting" is still occasionally used as a synonym for "dieting."

It wasn't long before fat's bad press made its way stateside. By 1924, a doctor writing in the *Journal of the American Medical Association* observed that "[t]o be thin is fashionable." Quintessentially American diet fads, miracle cures, slimming devices, and other efforts to commercially exploit this blossoming preference for thinness followed in due course. (Not surprisingly, the first major surge in modern eating disorders wasn't far behind.) By World War II, "you can't be too thin" had largely replaced "husky is healthy" as the conventional American wisdom on body condition.

This ideological shift occurred at a time when the scientific study of obesity was still in its infancy. The transition was fuelled more by fashion, commerce, and other cultural forces than by scientific breakthroughs. But in 1943 a breakthrough of sorts finally did occur. And while it would be nice to report that it was spearheaded by an insightful, socially aware young scientist with dreams of extinguishing a pervasive and under-appreciated health problem, the truth is that it arose from a decidedly less sexy source—the American insurance industry.

HEIGHT, WEIGHT, AND ILLNESS

IN 1943, EXECUTIVES WORKING on behalf of the Metropolitan Life Insurance Company conducted the world's first serious effort to quantify the amount of fat that a person's body really ought to contain if that person is interested in maximizing his or her lifespan. Using the reams of data at its disposal, the company determined the average mortality rates of its policyholders, depending on their body weight, gender, height, and "frame size." The company then created tables showing the "desirable" body weight (i.e., the weight corresponding with the lowest average mortality rate) for each group. Thus, for the first time in history, MetLife's "height-weight" tables allowed all individuals to quickly and easily identify their proper body weight.

METLIFE "HEIGHT-WEIGHT" TABLES

Desirable Body Weight – Women, Ages 25 and Over

Height	Weight in Pounds		
	Small Frame	Medium Frame	Large Frame
5'0"	105-113	112-120	119-129
5'1"	107-115	114-122	121-131
5'2"	110-118	117-125	124-135
5'3"	113-121	120-128	127-138
5'4"	116-125	124-132	131-142
5'5"	119-128	127-135	133-145
5'6"	123-132	130-140	138-150
5'7"	126-136	134-144	142-154
5'8"	129-139	137-147	145-158
5'9"	133-143	141-151	149-162
5'10"	136-147	145-155	152-166
5'11"	139-150	148-158	155-169

Figure 4(a).

Desirable Body Weight – Men, Ages 25 and Over

Height	Weight in Pounds		
	Small Frame	Medium Frame	Large Frame
5'2"	116-125	124-133	131-142
5'3"	119-128	127-136	133-144
5'4"	122-132	130-140	137-149
5'5"	126-136	134-144	141-153
5'6"	129-139	137-147	145-157
5'7"	133-143	141-151	149-162
5'8"	136-147	145-156	153-166
5'9"	140-151	149-160	157-170
5'10"	144-155	153-164	161-175
5'11"	148-159	157-168	165-180
6'0"	152-164	161-173	169-185
6'1"	157-169	166-178	174-190
6'2"	163-175	171-184	179-196
6'3"	168-180	176-189	184-202

Figure 4 (b).

It was an admirably logical first attempt to answer the question of how fat a person ought to be. But it didn't settle the matter outright.

The most obvious shortcoming of the tables was the variable they used to represent adiposity—body weight—is not a particularly good indicator of the amount of fat a body actually contains. As we've already discussed, higher body weight doesn't always mean more body fat.

And there was another problem: the weight recommendations were all too high. As *descriptive* reports, the MetLife tables were spot-on. As far as we know, the company correctly crunched its data and accurately reported the body weights that corresponded with the lowest mortality rates. But if the tables were used *prescriptively*—to identify the ideal body weight for any one individual—they were inherently skewed toward the heavy side. Why? Because some of the deadly diseases that killed MetLife's policyholders also caused significant weight loss. In those cases, people with low body weight died relatively young, but low body weight wasn't the *cause* of their diseases, it was an *effect*. Had those individuals been omitted from the data sets, the ideal body weight ranges would have dropped significantly as a result.

Despite these shortcomings, MetLife's height-weight tables were widely used to evaluate human body condition, right up until the 1980s. They only fell out of favor once a new and better body condition tool came along. This alternative way of expressing adiposity quickly rose to prominence with obesity researchers and is still widely used today. It has historical roots stretching back nearly 200 years but was recently dusted off, statistically validated, and given a catchy new name—the Body Mass Index (BMI).

***

The metric that we now call BMI was originally formulated in the first half of the 19th century by the Belgian mathematician and sociologist Adolphe Quetelet. Quetelet was, by all accounts, an eccentric and an obsessive. (While still in his early twenties, he apparently persuaded the government of Belgium to build an astronomical observatory for his personal use, then later to issue him a grant so that he might travel to France and actually learn some astronomy.) But his new method of expressing body condition was simple and elegant, at least in the metric units of 19th century Brussels:

$$BMI = Weight\ (kg) / Height\ (m)^2$$

Even with clunky U.S. customary units, it's only a bit less tidy:

$$BMI = (Weight\ (lbs)\ x\ 703) / Height\ (in)^2$$

Quetelet was an ambitious scholar and a prolific writer, but he had no interest in obesity. He devised his ratio—called the "Quetelet Index" during his time and in the decades that followed—not as part of any effort to identify optimal body condition but as a tool to support his true passion, the use of probabilistic methods to analyze the demographic and anthropometric characteristics of *l'homme moyen* ("the average man"). He made no attempt to apply it to the epidemiological study of obesity.

In fact, it wasn't until 1972 that the Quetelet Index was demonstrated to be a valuable tool for evaluating adiposity. In July of that year, the metric was excavated from obscurity and elevated to prominence with the publication of a well-known paper by the American scientist Ancel Keys. Keys was one of the leading diet and nutrition researchers of the 20th century, a true science superstar whose image once graced the cover of *Time* magazine. In their 1972 paper, Keys and colleagues showed the Quetelet Index to be a more accurate representation of adiposity than any other ratio of weight and height. (They examined the correlations between various weight-to-height ratios and two direct measurements of fatness—skin-fold thickness and body density. And they found that the Quetelet Index correlated more closely with the direct measurements than any other weight-to-height ratio.) Then they rebranded the formula with the snappy moniker that we still use today, the Body Mass Index.

The name stuck. And, over time, its influence grew. Today, BMI is widely used by public health organizations as a tool for tracking and evaluating fatness. The WHO has published BMI-based obesity guidelines, which have been adopted by organizations such as the National Institutes of Health and the CDC, as well as more than a few foreign public health bodies.

It is not hard to see why. As a team of researchers recently wrote in the *American Journal of Epidemiology*, BMI is a "simple, inexpensive, safe, and practical" way to evaluate body condition. From a public health perspective, the ease with which a health variable can be measured by the public-at-large is important. We're much more likely to evaluate ourselves if we can do so from the comfort of our living rooms. And calculating BMI requires little more than a scale, a tape measure, and, perhaps, a calculator.

Still, it's just an approximation. Like the height-to-weight ratios underlying MetLife's life expectancy tables, BMI is a way to make an educated guess at how much fat is in a body without actually measuring the fat directly. Is it subject to errors—even dramatic ones—in individual cases? Absolutely. As an extreme example, Jay Cutler, the four-time IFBB Mr. Universe bodybuilding champion, typically weighs in at around 275 pounds on the day of his competitions. So, standing at 5'9," Cutler has a BMI of over 40, a score which the WHO considers morbidly obese. But world-class bodybuilders like Jay Cutler aren't morbidly obese—quite to the contrary, on competition day, they are among the leanest human beings on the planet.

***

Despite its shortcomings, BMI has been fully embraced by the WHO. To supplement its three-element conceptual definition of obesity, the organization has also published specific guidelines that define obesity in BMI terms. The WHO's International Classification of Adult Underweight, Overweight, and Obesity According to BMI are reproduced in full below.

WORLD HEALTH ORGANIZATION'S INTERNATIONAL CLASSIFICATION OF ADULT UNDERWEIGHT, OVERWEIGHT, AND OBESITY ACCORDING TO BMI

Classification	BMI
Underweight	<18.50
Severe Thinness	<16.00
Moderate Thinness	16.00-16.99
Mild Thinness	17.00-18.49
Normal Range	18.50-24.99
Overweight	≥25.00
Pre-Obese	25.00-29.99
Obese	≥30.00
Obese Class I	30.00-34.99
Obese Class II	35.00-39.99
Obese Class III	≥40.00

Figure 5.

One thing to notice about the WHO's BMI guidelines is that, like both popular canine BCS protocols, they imply that the relationship between adiposity and health is U-shaped. In fact, this is a characteristic of just about all modern-day body classification systems, formal or otherwise. They all implicitly regard "optimal" or "normal" body condition as being a kind of happy medium between "too fat" and "not fat enough."

The WHO's U-shaped BMI guidelines were the result of a major research initiative, one in which more than 100 leading obesity experts spent two years working to evaluate the existing scientific evidence linking adiposity and health. In 2000 the group published an extensive report, documenting their findings and making specific body condition recommendations to the WHO. According to the report, having a BMI of 25 ought to be considered "overweight" because that's the point at which obesity-related health risks begin to rise. Having a BMI of 30 or greater should be considered "obese" because at that point the risks become particularly severe.

On these issues, the WHO was evaluating a scientific record that is about as unassailable as it gets. There is an enormous body of evidence suggesting that the fatter a person is, the greater her risk of developing cardiovascular disease, diabetes, and many forms of cancer (in 2007, two dozen of the world's leading cancer researchers published a 500-page analysis of the links between cancer and obesity, concluding that "convincing evidence" showed that "greater body fatness" is a cause of kidney cancer, endometrial cancer, postmenopausal breast cancer, colorectal cancer, and pancreatic cancer). There's also a reasonably robust body of evidence suggesting that the risk of developing Alzheimer's disease, gallbladder disease, hypertension, and osteoarthritis increases as well.

But in all these cases the relationship between adiposity and disease is *not* U-shaped. The risk of disease simply rises as one gets fatter—the fatter you are, the greater your risk; the leaner you are, the lower your risk. Period.

So why the U-shaped pattern? There's an answer to that question but it's not a simple one. And to understand it, we first need to understand what's so bad about excessive body fat. We need to understand how fat really works.

HOW FAT WORKS

AS RECENTLY AS 50 years ago, the medical research community had almost no idea why having lots of adipose tissue in one's body was so bad for health. Despite the mounting epidemiological evidence linking adiposity with deadly diseases, by the 1960s the mechanisms by which fat kills had yet to be explained. In his 1960 paper "The Pathology of Obesity," W. Stanley Hartroft, chief pathologist at St. Louis Children's Hospital and chairman of the pathology department at the Washington University School of Medicine, described the murky mechanisms by which fat causes disease as "ill-understood," speculating that "abnormal forms of fat storage," such as infiltration of the heart and pancreas by adipose tissue, could be the cause of obesity-related diseases.

Hartroft was self-aware enough to recognize that his ideas were products of his time and place, and subject to displacement by technological and ideological progress. "Perhaps with the advent of more precise tools and their application to the autopsy procedure," he admitted, "the pathologist will be able to detect true pathologic changes in mild stages of obesity. But, at present, lesions can only be linked to the advent of diabetes or to stages of obesity where sheer mechanical embarrassment from overcrowding produces organ dysfunction and provides correlation with clinical findings associated with excessive adiposity." In other words, as of 1960, the best explanation we could come up with for how fat harms health was that, at really high levels, it crowds other organs.

By the 1990s we were doing better. By then, the scientific advances that Hartroft had wished for in 1960 had been achieved. They occurred in the field of molecular genetics and were put to use on the study of adiposity by a young scientist named Jeffrey Freidman, whose work at the Rockefeller Institute would forever change the way we understand obesity.

Freidman was born in Florida and raised in New York. A precocious talent, he received his medical degree at only 22 and was given his own lab at the Rockefeller Institute shortly after turning 30. There he focused his work on mapping the genome of the *ob/ob* mouse, a rare breed of laboratory rodent with a single recessive gene mutation that causes it to overeat voraciously and become incredibly obese (often weighing *three times* as much as a normal mouse). The *ob/ob* mouse fascinated Freidman, so genetically similar was it to other mice and yet so morphologically different. So, over a period of eight years, he and his colleagues worked patiently to identify the precise genetic mutation that led to morbid obesity in the *ob/ob* mouse, as well as the way that that mutation expressed itself at the cellular level.

In 1994, Freidman and his team published their findings in the journal *Nature*. What they had discovered was that *ob/ob* mice are different from normal mice in just one way: as a result of the genetic mutation, they don't encode a single 167-amino acid hormone. Freidman and his colleagues dubbed the new hormone "leptin," after the Greek word for "thin," which probably gives you an idea of what it does in the body. They found that circulating leptin interacts with receptors in the hypothalamus, a region deep within the brain, to produce a feeling of satiety and fullness. In this way, leptin serves to suppress hunger and regulate energy balance. Because the *ob/ob* mice couldn't produce leptin, they never got full. And that made them overeat, so much so that they became morbidly obese.

But while leptin's specific role in the body is a nice example of the link between hormones and obesity, its role in regulating energy balance isn't particularly important to this part of our story. What is important is the fact that leptin—a hormone with the power to exert significant influence over both health and behavior—*was being produced by fat cells*. Freidman's study proved that adipose tissue isn't just an inert stockpile of metabolic fuel waiting to be consumed (or, as is more often the case when it comes to both dogs and humans in America, *not* consumed) according to the body's energy demands. It's also the largest endocrine organ in the body. Just like the pancreas, the pituitary gland, the adrenal glands, the ovaries, the testes, or the thyroid gland, body fat actively secretes hormones and hormone precursors. And these secretions make their way into the bloodstream, travel throughout the body, interact with distant organs, and cause all manner of reactions. In this way, adipose tissue is constantly communicating with the rest of our bodies.

***

The discovery of leptin revolutionized our understanding of adiposity and earned Jeffrey Freidman a Lasker Award, one of the world's most prestigious science prizes. It also launched hundreds of other studies, papers that would highlight the myriad ways that body fat actively communicates with and influences the brain and other organs. These studies have shown that leptin isn't the only substance secreted by adipose tissue. Far from it. Indeed, since the publication of Freidman's 1994 *Nature* paper, dozens of other body fat secretions—collectively, they have come to be known as "adipokines"—have been identified. Adipokines are the media by which body fat sends messages to other parts of the body and triggers physiological responses in those other organs. And they are central to our current understanding of why fat makes us—dogs and humans alike—sick.

Essentially, it seems that the messages adipokines communicate to our other organs are often bad ones, impossible-to-ignore orders to do things that harm the body. In lean bodies, circulating adipokine levels are relatively low, so the orders aren't delivered very forcefully—more like a whisper than a scream. But as the amount of adipose tissue in a body grows, the concentration of adipokines in the bloodstream grows too. And, as it does, the volume of these deadly orders gets louder and louder.

More specifically, the dominant theory currently being used to explain why fat is so bad for health is that many adipokines cause or worsen disease by hijacking the body's inflammatory responses. Inflammation is the term used to describe the body's primary emergency response to injury, pain, illness, and stress. When something bad happens in the body, inflammation kicks in. It comes in two flavors, "acute" and "chronic," and the distinction between the two is critical. Acute inflammation is observable as the increased blood flow (i.e., redness), fluid buildup (swelling), and loss of function (pain) that results when you suffer a localized injury, like a sprained knee or a bump on the head. It facilitates the healing of acute injuries, both by flooding the injury site with tissue repair agents and by encouraging you to act in a way that protects the site and avoids exacerbation. It's a tremendously useful and completely intuitive function—if you were to build a living organism from the ground up, you'd do well to give it an acute inflammatory response system not unlike the one operating in your own body.

But chronic inflammation is another story altogether. When the body's inflammatory response becomes chronic and systemic, the hormonal switches that trigger the response just stay in the "on" position all the time, albeit at a lower volume than in acute cases. So a process that's supposed to ramp up only in the presence of an acute injury is instead running constantly, all throughout the body. This is a bad thing, for several reasons.

First, many of the immune agents deployed in an inflammatory response are highly destructive. It's their job to attack and kill cells, kick-starting the healing process by purging the body of damaged cells so that newly created, healthy ones can take their place. In the context of a localized injury, this cell warfare is an undeniably good thing—we need to sweep out the damaged cells to make way for new healthy ones as part of the healing process. But in a chronically inflamed environment these destructive immune agents flood the body and run amuck, damaging scores of otherwise healthy cells.

Second, chronic inflammation contributes to the development of cardiovascular disease by promoting the build-up of arterial plaque and the formation of atherosclerotic lesions. Arterial plaque is one of the cornerstones of cardiovascular disease. It's the gunk that builds up over time in our blood vessels, causing them to harden, narrow, and become blocked, leading to heart attacks and strokes. And not only does chronic inflammation stimulate the accumulation of arterial plaque, but the stuff is largely *made up of* spent white blood cells, the very immune cells that get deployed to defend the body in connection with an inflammatory response. Arterial plaque has other biochemical ingredients too, but to a large degree the stuff clogging our arteries is, quite literally, a remnant of systemic inflammation.

And, last but not least, chronic inflammation seems to promote tumor growth. In the words of University of California, San Francisco cancer researchers Lisa Coussens and Zena Werb, inflammation creates "an attractive environment for tumor growth, facilitating genomic instability and promoting angiogenesis [the formation of blood vessels needed to supply rapidly growing tumors with nutrients]." In other words, inflammatory adipokines act like tumor fertilizer, creating a microenvironment conducive to cellular proliferation, survival, and migration—precisely the setting you'd look for if you were actively trying to grow a tumor.

To appreciate the strength of the connection between chronic inflammation and cancer, consider that obesity is far from the only inflammatory condition linked with the disease. Some other well-known examples are colorectal cancer stemming from inflammatory bowel diseases, liver cancer caused by Hepatitis C infection, and cervical cancer arising from human papilloma virus infection. Recent epidemiological data suggest that as many as 25% of all cancers are associated with some form of chronic inflammation.

Killing our healthy cells, clogging up our arteries, and fertilizing nascent tumors—chronic inflammation is the pits. It is a phenomenon that any rational, health-conscious individual would work hard to avoid. And it is brought about by, among other things, the mere presence of adipose tissue in the body. The more adipose tissue we have in our bodies, the more pro-inflammatory adipokines that tissue secretes. And the greater the concentration of pro-inflammatory adipokines circulating in our bloodstream, the more severe the body's systemic inflammatory response. Which is why fat people (and fat dogs) are almost *always* in a constant state of chronic inflammation. And it's why they so often seem to get sick.

***

So what about individuals with a moderate or "normal" amount of adipose tissue in their bodies? Does the pathophysiology of adiposity suggest that even they should try to reduce their body fat levels if they want to improve their health? If we accept that fat means adipokines, that adipokines mean inflammation, and that inflammation means disease, are we forced to conclude that *minimizing* the amount of fat in our bodies really is our best health strategy?

Not according to the WHO. In its 2000 report on obesity and health, the WHO's Consultation on Obesity concluded that a BMI below 18.5 ought to be considered "underweight." In other words, according to the WHO, if your BMI is below 18.5 then you're too lean. You probably need to fatten up a bit.

At first glance, this seems like a strange recommendation—if obesity is defined as having so much fat in your body that it's bad for your health, and if the fatter you are the greater your disease risk, how come the WHO's recommendation isn't just "the leaner the better"?

The answer: Because while very low BMI individuals are particularly impervious to chronic diseases, their all-cause mortality risk is higher than that of their somewhat fatter peers. Having a very low BMI won't increase your risk of developing coronary heart disease, diabetes, cancer, or any other chronic disease (to the contrary, it's well-established that your risk of acquiring these killer diseases *rises* if your body condition changes from "underweight" to "normal"). But it seems that it will still increase your overall risk of dying.

How strange.

PARADOX OR ILLUSION?

THE CURIOUS LINK BETWEEN low BMI and high mortality risk has appeared often enough in the published literature to have earned its own nickname—the "Obesity Paradox." It is a topic that tends to provoke something resembling tribal warfare between its supporters and detractors. Experts on both sides of the debate have published their share of critical editorials in leading academic journals. But, thus far, no one seems to be budging much.

Among the factors weighing in favor of the paradox's detractors, one is particularly compelling: at present there is no overwhelming consensus as to *how* adiposity is supposed to reduce mortality risk. There is limited evidence suggesting that adipose tissue absorbs dangerous chemicals that might otherwise find their way into vital organs. There are some suggestions that overweight patients receive better medical care. And some experts have speculated that a few adipokines actually do good things within the body.

But the most common explanation for the Obesity Paradox is the more general idea that, while a bit of excess body fat may be a bad thing when you're perfectly healthy, it becomes useful if you're battling a deadly disease. In this way, as Dr. Kamyar Kalantar-Zadeh, a professor of medicine at the

University of California, Irvine, has written, fat is a bit like a dodgy friend:

> Metaphorically, we can liken such cardiovascular risk factors as obesity to a friend who is a negative influence, causing the two of you to misbehave and be sentenced to jail, but once imprisoned, the friend remains loyal and protects you against poor prison conditions and other inmates.

The idea that body fat acts as a buffer against disease-induced metabolic demands is consistent with one of fat's most fundamental and well-understood functions in the body, to serve as a metabolic fuel silo. As we all know, our stored body fat helps us to weather periods of reduced energy supply (famine) as wells as periods of heightened energy demands (disease). In this way, when contending with the vicissitudes of life, ample reserves of metabolic fuel are decidedly good things. We should fully expect fat individuals to handle diseases better than their lean neighbors.

Or should we? According to some leading experts, there is a problem with this theory: It accidentally confuses lean muscle mass with body fat. And, they say, once we sort through our confusion, what looks like an Obesity Paradox reveals itself to be nothing more than an illusion.

The Obesity Paradox's critics don't deny that trauma and disease heighten metabolic demands. When trying to manage a serious illness, it is unquestionable that the body's metabolic appetite grows. What they do deny is that fat has much to do with it. They say that what a body really needs to fight off a disease isn't fat—it is protein.

The cells that make up our most important organs—the heart, the brain, the liver, etc.—are composed largely of proteins. These molecules are locked in a perpetual process of degradation, constantly being broken down into amino acids and getting dumped into the blood stream, where they are replaced with fresh, new proteins synthesized from other amino acids. The constant degradation and replacement of cellular proteins enables our bodies to adapt to changing circumstances. It also allows us to sweep damaged, mutated, or denatured proteins out of our cells and to replace them with new, high-quality ones.

So where do all the new amino acids come from? If not from our diet, then from our muscles. As Dr. Robert R. Wolfe, Director of the Center for Translational Research in Aging & Longevity at Texas A&M University has put it, the skeletal muscles are the body's "principal reservoir" of amino acids:

> Muscle plays a central role in whole-body protein metabolism by serving as the principal reservoir for amino acids to maintain protein synthesis in vital tissues and organs in the absence of amino acid absorption from the gut and by

providing hepatic gluconeogenic precursors.

In this way, the skeletal muscles fuel the ongoing maintenance of the heart, brain, and other vital organs—a process that Dr. Wolfe has fairly described as "essential to survival."

When there isn't enough protein to go around, the body chooses the vital internal organs over the skeletal muscles. So when the rate of protein turnover exceeds the rate of new protein ingestion and synthesis, skeletal musculature tends to get sacrificed. We can see this phenomenon for ourselves in at least three different situations. The first is in cases of fasting and starvation, where dietary protein intake drops so low that muscles (and protein-rich internal organs as well) shrink significantly in size. The second we've already discussed. It is sarcopenia, the muscle wasting which often occurs in the elderly as muscle-building physical activity gradually slows with age.

The third place to see muscle wasting in action is the most important one for our present purposes. It is with cachexia, a well-documented medical phenomenon in which musculature shrinks rapidly in individuals battling deadly illnesses. When the body is in an acutely stressed state—most notably in cases of traumatic injury and advanced cancers—its demand for amino acids rises stratospherically. During these periods of severe stress, more protein than usual is needed in order to power immune responses and accelerate wound healing. Often, the demand is so great that no amount of dietary protein intake can make up the shortfall. Accelerated muscle protein degradation leads to diminished musculature and the frail, atrophied look often seen in those battling for their lives. And as protein reserves gradually run dry, vital organs and the bodily processes they enable begin to tremble and sputter, before eventually failing altogether. In this way, there is a clear physiological link between skeletal musculature and a person's capacity to respond to both aging and deadly diseases—the more muscle in a body, the better.

***

This is a good time to remind ourselves that BMI is just a way of approximating fatness. At the population level, it does its job admirably. But it doesn't do nearly as well with individuals. As professor Jonathan C.K. Wells put it in his excellent treatise *The Evolutionary Biology of Human Body Fatness*, BMI "has a relatively poor capacity to rank individuals accurately in terms of body fat level."

As our earlier bodybuilder example demonstrated, one of the principal reasons for this failing is that, in the eyes of the Body Mass Index, all weighty tissues are the same. So heavily muscled people tend to wind up with relatively high BMI scores (whether or not they are fat), and scrawny people tend to wind up with relatively low scores (whether or not they are fat).

Some experts believe that this hiccup can explain the otherwise puzzling U-shaped relationship between BMI and mortality. They contend that when it comes to body condition, there are at least two separate factors that influence health and longevity: the amount of fat in a body and the amount of fat-free mass (muscle) in a body. And, they claim, if we could only measure these variables independently—instead of relying on BMI to approximate them—we'd see that they tend to have opposite effects on how long we live: fat-free mass tends to help us live longer while fat tends to kill us.

This hypothesis has been tested numerous times over the past 20 years. And the results suggest that it may well be right on the money. Specifically, researchers have measured the body fat mass and fat-free mass of individuals directly, before analyzing the relationships between those variables and overall mortality risk. In these studies, total fat-free mass has almost always been shown to have a direct, negative relationship with mortality—the more muscular an individual, the better, just as the pathophysiologies of cachexia and sarcopenia would predict. On the other hand, total body fat tends to show a direct, positive relationship with mortality—the leaner an individual, the better, just as the pathophysiology of obesity would predict.

The implications of these findings are profound. As one team concluded in 2004, "[o]ur findings suggest that BMI represents joint but opposite associations of body fat and FFM [fat free mass] with mortality. Both high body fat and low FFM are independent predictors of all-cause mortality." Or, as another put it in 2002, "[t]hese results support the hypothesis that the apparently deleterious effects of marked thinness may be due to low FFM and that, over the observed range of the data, marked leanness (as opposed to thinness) has beneficial effects." Or, still another, "[t]he apparent U-shaped association between BMI and total mortality may be the result of compound risk functions from body fat and fat free mass."

More research is needed to resolve the issue once and for all, but there are already a litany of independent reasons to believe that the Obesity Paradox is really just an illusion. The pathophysiologies of obesity, starvation, sarcopenia, and cachexia all strongly suggest as much. The undeniably positive (not U-shaped) relationship between BMI and all of the leading obesity-linked comorbidities does too. And when we measure body fat and fat-free mass directly, we tend to see that leanness and muscularity are both associated with longevity, while scrawniness and adiposity are both associated with greater mortality risk. Add all this to the evidence suggesting that many low BMI scores are caused by deadly diseases (as opposed to the other way around) and you can't help but wonder whether there really is such a thing as being "too lean" after all.

ON THE DIFFERENCE BETWEEN "LEAN" AND "STARVED"

STARVATION IS NOT a pleasant thing to think about. The experience is, by all accounts, horrific. Joseph Conrad reminds us that starving men can be driven to cannibalization, and (gulp) worse:

> No fear can stand up to hunger, no patience can wear it out, disgust simply does not exist where hunger is; and superstition, beliefs, and what you may call principles are less than chaff in a breeze.

It is also a difficult topic to study scientifically. Recruiting subjects who are willing to expose themselves to such profound suffering is no mean feat. So the published literature on the subject is sparse, to say the least. Indeed, at present it is mostly composed of a single, impressively detailed study, one conducted in the shadow of World War II by Ancel Keys, the same scientific bigwig who made the Body Mass Index relevant.

By 1944, war-induced famines had already swept across Poland, the Soviet Union, the Netherlands, and Greece, killing millions. Millions more were being deliberately starved in Nazi concentration camps. As Allied victory inched closer, it became clear that understanding the physiological effects of extreme starvation, as well as the recovery therefrom, would be key to furthering the relief effort in war-torn Europe. Enter Ancel Keys. In a stroke of creativity, he recruited 36 conscientious objectors to serve as subjects in his comprehensive starvation study. They were men who, like Keys himself, believed that the knowledge gained through their significant suffering would advance a worthy cause—alleviating the suffering of millions of others.

And suffer they did. Working largely from a dingy basement below a football stadium at the University of Minnesota, Keys systematically starved the men for a period of six months. They were not denied food altogether but they received far less nutrition than their bodies needed. Keys drastically restricted the amounts of carbohydrate, fat, and protein that the men ate (feeding them about half the daily calories that they needed to maintain their bodies and less than half of the protein they were consuming prior to the experiment).

Physically, the men changed dramatically over the 24-week period of deprival. The average body weight of the group fell from 152 pounds to 115. Some of the weight loss came from the catabolization of fat stores—the average body fat percentage of the subjects dropped from 14% to 5% during the experiment. But others tissues also shrank dramatically as the men catabolized their skeletal muscles and other vital organs to make up for the lack of protein in their diets. The subjects' hearts shrank by an average of about 17%. The circumferences of their uppers arms decreased by about 25%. The circumferences of their thighs decreased by about 20%. Average abdominal circumference shrunk by about 10%. Average calf circumference by about 12%.

Their bodies also changed in how they functioned. Average internal body temperatures dropped from 98.6 degrees to 95.8 degrees as bodies lowered their thermostats to conserve energy. Average heart rates slowed from 55 beats per minute to only 37. In total, the men dropped their total oxygen consumption by more than a third, from 228.1 cubic centimeters per minute to only 139.2, a decrease that far outstripped any attendant loss in overall body weight. Their bodies were not only shrinking, they were conserving what limited energy they had. Observing the subjects in the final week of their six-month fast, Major Marvin Corlette, a doctor and witness to the atrocities committed in Nazi concentration camps, likened the men to the very individuals they were trying to help: "Most had gaunt pinched faces and the peculiar sallow color that those of us who had seen the concentration camps had learned to associate at a glance with starvation."

But perhaps the most glaring changes induced by Keys's starvation experiment were behavioral ones. Most of the subjects began the experiment robust, hearty, and eager to save the ailing world. But once starvation began, they quickly became weak, fatigued, and unwilling or incapable of performing physical work. One man was so weak by three months into the starvation period that he got stuck in the revolving door at a department store, as should probably be expected from a man whose body had been eating itself for a quarter of a year. Profound psychological deterioration followed, manifesting as acute depression, disagreeableness, a perverse preoccupation with food, and a loss of interest in just about everything else. Keys took his men right up to the edge of life, dragging them through harrowing bouts of depression and madness as their bodies gradually fell apart. By any measure the experience was hellish.

***

We should remember, however, that leanness does not equate to starvation. Indeed, it's not hard to find examples of people functioning remarkably well—excelling both physically and psychologically—while maintaining bodies that are every bit as lean as those of Ancel Keys's starving subjects.

Consider, for example, a group of individuals close to my own heart: endurance athletes. In the world of competitive endurance sports leanness is critical. Professional runners, cyclists, triathletes, and the like are in the business of moving their bodies from Point A to Point B as quickly as possible. And because a heavier body is harder to move than a lighter one, an extraordinarily lean physique is considered a job requirement for a top-level racer. According to Matt Fitzgerald, endurance sports nutritionist and bestselling author, the average body fat levels of competitive male cyclists and triathletes are often as low as 6%. World-class male rowers are usually less than 8% body fat. And top-class male runners tend to be the leanest of all, with one study finding that elite marathoners carried, on average, only about 7.3% body fat while competing. Perhaps the greatest marathoner of all time, Ethiopian Haile Gebrselassie, set a world record in 2008 while racing at a body weight of only 117 pounds. And according to an article published in *Scientific American*, the American short-track speed-skater Apolo Anton Ohno competed at the 2010 Vancouver Winter Olympics at a body fat percentage of lower than 3%. (Ohno won three medals at the 2010 Games, brining his career tally to eight, the most ever won by a United States Winter Olympian.)

Whether these reported measurements are precisely accurate is beside the point. If they are even reasonably representative of the truth, then it's fair to say that the world's best endurance athletes compete at about the same level of fatness experienced by Ancel Keys's subjects as they wallowed in the depths of depression. And while Keys's subjects wound up so weak that one of them couldn't even turn a revolving door in a department store, folks like Haile Gebrselassie and Apolo Anton Ohno energetically inserted themselves into the Pantheon of the most decorated athletes in history.

While the world's top endurance athletes are extraordinarily lean, they bear little other physical resemblance to the gaunt and listless subjects of Keys's starvation experiment. Unlike Keys's subjects, the bodies of professional athletes tend to be racked with striated muscles. After all, skeletal muscles are at the root of the mechanical processes that they use to power their bodies to the finish line. They are the very tools of the endurance athlete's trade.

World-class endurance athletes tend to live longer than the rest of us too. A study published in the *International Journal of Sports Medicine* in 2011 showed that riders of the Tour de France, perhaps the most challenging endurance race on the planet, live an average of eight years (more than 17%) longer than age-matched non-competitors. And that study isn't an outlier—many others have also shown a similar longevity benefit to high-level endurance training. So while Keys's subjects wound up as the very definition of poor health and malaise, knocking on death's door within a half-year, top-class endurance athletes tend to be paragons of good health and vitality.

Similarly stark contrasts arise when we compare Keys's conscientious objectors with other groups of notably lean individuals. For example, up until the middle of the 20th century, the native residents of the Japanese island of Okinawa made up what was essentially the leanest population on the planet.

(Studies suggest that prior to the end of World War II the average Okinawan had about the same BMI as current citizens of the famine-plagued Democratic Republic of Congo, more than two-thirds of whom are clinically malnourished.) At the same time, they were also unquestionably the longest-living population on the planet. (Astoundingly, the odds of a midcentury Okinawan living to 100 years old were about *five times better* than a current resident of the Untied States.) Quality of life among Okinawa's senior citizens was also astoundingly good, with more than 80% remaining functionally independent at 92 years of age and roughly two-thirds still functionally independent at the ripe old age of 97. For midcentury Okinawans, being very lean and being very healthy went hand-in-hand.

Similar things can be said about proponents of the modern-day lifestyle philosophy known as "calorie restriction." At its essence, calorie restriction theory is as simple as it sounds—if you want to live a particularly long and healthy life, always eat fewer calories than your body would seem to need in order to maintain energy equilibrium. As any would-be dieter confronted with a hot plate of fries knows, calorie restriction may not always be the most workable strategy in a world overflowing with delicious, calorie-rich foods. But, when its directives have been followed, calorie restriction has a truly remarkable track record of success. The practice has been shown to extend average lifespan in all manner of species, including rats, mice, fish, flies, worms, yeast, monkeys, and, most notably for our present purposes, dogs. As Okinawa Centenarian Study researchers Bradley J. Willcox and colleagues have written (the traditional Okinawan lifestyle inspired the calorie restriction movement) drastically cutting calories "is the most robust and reproducible means of reducing age-related diseases and extending life span."

Why it does so is still a matter of debate. But the simplest and most commonsensical explanation is one we've already discussed: it tends to make you really lean. As researchers from the Albert Einstein College of Medicine have recently pointed-out, "marked reduction in fat mass is the main phenotypic expression of calorie restriction in animals." And, given all we have learned about the role of fat as an endocrine organ, doesn't it make perfect sense that a decrease in fat mass would be the primary physiological mechanism through which calorie restriction would benefit its practitioners? That's certainly what the team from Albert Einstein thinks. Here's how they described their outlook in a recent paper:

> [A]ll of the benefits of [calorie restriction] on the neuroendocrine system and those related to the improvement in glucose homeostasis can be attributed to decrease in adipose cells and their products [i.e., adipokines].

Over the years, improved longevity through calorie restriction has garnered its share of believers, despite the superhuman willpower that it would seem to demand. The Calorie Restriction Society, a confederation of calorie restriction devotees founded in 1994, has more than 7,000 members. Overall, there are likely to be more than 100,000 practitioners of the philosophy worldwide. Most of them are jaw-droppingly thin. (Calorie Restriction Society President Brian M. Delaney says that he is so skinny that "I don't recognize what I see in the mirror as me.") But, because they eat sufficient quantities of protein and micronutrients, maintain adequate skeletal musculature, and don't suffer from wasted organs and depleted energy stores, they may be lean but they're not lethargic. To the contrary, as Calorie Restriction Society member Paul McGlothlin, 61, has said, "we live like we're about 20 years younger than our real chronological age."

***

The primary difference between Ancel Keys's conscientious objectors and these groups of lean-and-thriving individuals is the nutritional adequacy of their diets. Are they consuming enough of what their bodies need in order to live well? In the case of Keys's subjects, the answer was no. In the case of endurance athletes, Okinawan centenarians, and calorie restriction devotees, the answer is yes. This is the difference between being lean and being starved.

As we've already seen, one component of nutrition goes a particularly long way toward separating the starved from the healthy—dietary protein intake. Unlike Keys's subjects, who were denied sufficient protein to maintain their muscles and vital organs, professional endurance athletes tend to follow precise nutritional regimens, programs deliberately crafted to help them achieve very low levels of body fat while simultaneously maintaining impressive musculature. Evidently, similar things can be said of midcentury Okinawans and calorie restrictors too.

Of course, like the amino acids of which muscles are composed, the lipids composing adipose tissue are also used to power essential bodily processes. And body fat reserves will be catabolized to make up for insufficient fat and glucose intake, just like muscles will be catabolized during periods of insufficient protein intake.

But, in this regard, there are at least two important ways in which fat is different from muscle. First, a little fat goes a long way. A single example ought to demonstrate the point. Let's say you're a lean, mean, 125-pound woman, with a body fat percentage of around 20% (giving you a BMI that is likely to be well below the WHO's recommended range). It is likely that your body uses about 1500 calories' worth of energy every day powering its vital functions. Even though you are already an exceedingly lean person, you still have about 25 pounds' worth of adipose tissue in your body (125 pounds x 20% BFP). Now, remember that each pound of the stuff contains about 3500 calories of metabolizable energy. In other words, despite the fact that you are already leaner than the WHO thinks you should be, you still have enough caloric energy in your body fat to fully power your vital bodily functions for *two whole months* without eating a single morsel of food.

A second thing to note: the amount of body fat necessary to forestall undesirable physiological changes is exceedingly low. Adipose tissue performs a number of beneficial functions in the body; after all, if it had no meaningful role to play then we wouldn't have evolved the capacity to get fat in the first place. Many of these—protecting internal organs from violent trauma, keeping us warm in cold temperatures, fueling the body during periods of enforced starvation—are not particularly relevant to the modern world.

But others—powering physical activity, modulating immune function—are. Accordingly, it is widely accepted that a body must contain a certain amount of fat, even if its other nutritional needs are being met. Rather than cross this lower threshold, the body will preferentially catabolize lean tissues, energy levels will wane, and other emergency physiological responses will kick-in, all to help the body retain whatever fat remains.

So how much is it? Very little. So little, in fact, that it's highly unlikely that anyone reading these words will ever have to worry about it. In human men, the lower limit looks to be about 3-5% of total body weight. What does a man with only 5% body fat look like? If he is muscular, then he looks like a professional body-builder on competition day—striated muscles covering every inch of his body, bulging veins, all that. If he is less muscular, then more like a recently liberated concentration camp survivor—a thin layer of drawn, sunken skin pulled tight over a knobby skeleton.

In women, a similar amount of fat (3-5% of body weight) is generally considered to be essential. But there's another factor to account for: women may have to fuel their bodies through pregnancy, lactation, and the other metabolically demanding activities associated with having a baby. Because reproduction is such a metabolically taxing enterprise, most obstetricians believe that a woman's body will automatically steer her away from pregnancy by temporarily suspending menstruation if her body fat levels get too low. (And if it's not leanness *per se* that serves as the physiological trigger for the suspension, then they probably believe it's something similarly indicative of metabolic scarcity—excessive levels of physical activity, insufficient nutrition, etc.)

Ultimately, this means that there is an additional sex-specific amount of body fat that women must carry in their bodies in order to maintain fertility. The exact amount isn't universally agreed-upon by researchers, but it is commonly thought to be at least an additional 5% or so, bringing the healthy lower threshold for women up to about 10%.

Such individuals are more or less as lean as can be realistically imagined. To voluntarily achieve this kind of body is all but impossible. It requires constant vigilance and otherworldly discipline, particularly in a modern-day nutritional environment teeming with fast foods and sweets. For mere mortals, it is a limit that is so low as to be all but unattainable.

What this means is that mortals don't have to worry too much about getting so lean as to starve their vital organs of the lipids they need to function at a high level. If you're fatter than a competitive bodybuilder—and so long as you are consuming enough protein and other essential nutrients—then you may be lean, but you're probably not starved.

A DOG THAT'S "TOO LEAN"?

Obesity seems to work about the same in dogs as it does in people. Not that dogs are unique in this regard. When it comes to adiposity, animals that look hardly anything like human beings—mice and rats—have taught us much of what we know about how and why we get fat. (Think back to Jeffrey Freidman and his discovery of leptin, probably the most important breakthrough in the history of obesity research—his experiments were performed on mice, not men.) We've learned much of what we know about human obesity by observing other kinds of fat animals.

When a non-human animal is used to shape our understanding of a human health phenomenon it's called an "animal model." Experiments involving animal models are common in science because they give us an opportunity to improve our understanding of harmful diseases without subjecting human beings to them. (Whether it's right or wrong to use non-human animals for these purposes is another question, but that's the rationale.) While rodents are by far the most common animal model of obesity, domestic dogs (along with pigs and non-human primates) have at times also been used to help advance our understanding of why and how people get fat. Some scientists even believe that dogs present a unique and underused animal model of obesity. In 2008, a team of researchers from the University of Aberdeen wrote that dogs "have clear potential as a study model for human obesity," largely because of our advanced understanding of the canine genome. The team predicted that the "potential for the use of dogs to inform us about obesity in humans should be realized during the coming decade."

In order to understand how fat a dog really ought to be we must, at times, do the inverse of animal modeling—we must use the robust body of research on human adiposity to fill in the gaps in the sparse literature on canine adiposity. Human modeling of canine obesity, if you will.

This is hardly a novel approach. Even the most well-regarded canine obesity researchers in the world commonly rely upon the study of human obesity to shape their conclusions about dogs. For this very reason, however, there's something we'd do well to keep an eye on when trying to understand how fat our dogs really ought to be: we should watch for cases in which scientific error has spread from the study of human obesity to the canine side.

We've already covered several ways in which error has come to infect the science of human obesity—problems stemming from the Body Mass Index's conflation of adipose tissue and lean body mass, the tendency of cultural forces to color our scientific perspectives, an overreliance on and misinterpretation of epidemiological data. As Jonathan C.K. Wells wrote in *The Evolutionary Biology of Human Body Fatness*, when it comes to human beings, "much that is written about 'obesity' may have only a tenuous basis in the biology of adipose tissue." If we want to help our dogs live as long and healthfully as reasonably possible, we're obligated to ensure that our knowledge is built upon a firmer foundation. With that precaution in mind, let's take a look at what the scientific literature has to say about the impact of adiposity on canine health and longevity.

***

The seminal study on the impact of obesity on dogs was carried out by a team of American researchers over a period of two decades, beginning in the mid-1980s. Their methods were simple. 48 Labrador Retrievers were paired within their litters by sex and weight at six weeks of age. A member of each pair was then randomly assigned to one of two lifelong feeding strategies—"control feeding" or "restricted feeding." The difference between the two strategies was small but significant: while all the dogs ate exactly the same foods, the dogs in the restricted-feeding group were only allowed to consume 75% as much as their control-feeding counterparts. The researchers then followed the dogs for their entire lives, monitoring health markers like body weight, BCS score, muscle mass, bone density, disease presence, and lifespan.

As you would probably expect, the restricted-feeding group wound up lighter than the control group. Once they reached adulthood, the restricted-feeding dogs maintained average body weights of just about 75% of their control-fed counterparts, in parallel with their food intake.

They wound up leaner too. Average BCS scores (using Dr. Laflamme's nine-category system) were 4.6 for the restricted-feeding group and 6.7 for the control group. On average, fat made up between 30% and 35% of the tissue in the heavier dogs, while the average body fat level of the leaner dogs was between 15% and 20% for most of their lives.

Something important to note here is that none of the dogs in the study wound up particularly lean. People with as much fat in their bodies as the dogs in the heavier group (body fat levels of 30-35%) would have rung up

BMIs of well over 30 and unquestionably been deemed "obese" by the WHO. But, with adipose tissue still making up some 20% of their bodies, the dogs in the restricted-feeding group weren't all that lean either. According to a study recently published in the *British Journal of Nutrition*, a 30-year old man with 20% body fat would probably have a BMI of around 25 and be classified by the WHO as "overweight." Most Okinawans, calorie restriction practitioners, and competitive athletes are *far* leaner.

To frame the issue slightly differently, consider that wild canines also tend to be far leaner than the dogs in the study's "lean" group. As we've already seen, wolves, foxes, and coyotes all typically maintain body fat levels of lower than 10%, meaning that the study's leaner dogs were about twice as fat as the typical wild canine. And, in this regard, wild canines aren't the outliers. A recent study of species typically consumed by feral cats—which included gophers, moles, voles, Norway rats, roof rats, and birds—found average body fat levels of about 11%. Similarly, in a paper presented at the 1967 research symposium "Body Composition in Animals and Man," an analysis of 49 different animal species from a host of geographic locations revealed that wild animals tend to contain, on average, well under 10% body fat (despite the fact that hibernating rodents, with BFPs of over 35%, tended to skew the data toward the fat side). So while one group of dogs in the experiment wound up significantly leaner than the other, both were considerably fatter than most wild animals, as well as the healthiest and longest-living human beings. It's fair to say that none of them would have been a good fit for Steve Beckerman's Facebook group either.

But what of the experimental results? For one, the dogs with less fat in their bodies lived a lot longer: the average lean dog lived for 13 years, while the average control dog only lived to 11. The average lifespan of the leaner dogs was about 16% longer than the average lifespan of the control-fed dogs. And on the day that the last of the 24 control-fed dogs died, more than a third of the dogs in the leaner group were still alive.

Those are some very significant findings. To put them in perspective, consider that, on a percentage basis, the life expectancy difference between the leaner dogs and the fatter ones was greater than the difference in life expectancy between lifelong smokers and lifelong non-smokers. Or between citizens of the United States and citizens of places like North Korea and Syria. The leaner dogs lived *a lot* longer than the fatter ones.

But the difference in average life expectancy was far from the only meaningful finding that emerged from the study. The fatter dogs also started losing their skeletal musculature far earlier than the leaner dogs. The leaner dogs showed better insulin sensitivity and lower circulating blood insulin levels than the control group. The leaner dogs showed slower and less severe immunological deterioration as they aged. And, while the causes of death did not differ significantly between the two groups (ultimately, members of both groups fell victim to the same kinds of diseases), the timing differed dramatically—on average, treatment for chronic disease was not needed until 20% later in life for the leaner dogs.

So if we want our dogs to live as long and healthfully as possible, this study serves as compelling evidence that they'd be better off maintaining a BCS of between 4 and 5 (out of 9) than one between 6 and 7. What that means is that, to the best of our knowledge, the qualitative labels used in the major canine BCS protocols are probably at least half-right. It is the case that dogs with relatively high BCS scores aren't as healthy as dogs with scores in the middle of the BCS spectrum. It is fair and accurate to use a label like "too heavy" to describe a dog with a BCS above 5/9 because, in all likelihood, the overall health and longevity of that dog can be improved by reducing the amount of fat in his body.

This conclusion has been confirmed time and again in studies that compare disease prevalence rates among relatively fat dogs and relatively lean ones. From osteoarthritis to pancreatitis and from cardiovascular disease to cancer, just like with humans, dogs with a lot of fat in their bodies are almost always more likely to get sick than their somewhat leaner counterparts.

The primary mechanism by which fat makes dogs sick seems to be the same one that's at work in their human companions. Here's how Dr. Joseph Wakshlag—a professor at Cornell University and one of the country's leading canine obesity experts—and colleagues described it in a recent paper:

> Advances in obesity research suggest that adipose is not an inert tissue, but rather it releases a variety of adipokines that drive the chronic inflammatory response in peripheral tissues, thereby exacerbating many disease processes.

We don't yet understand which specific adipokines are most harmful to dogs and why. But enough research has been done to show that some version of this process is likely behind the fact that relatively fat dogs tend to get sick and die earlier than relatively lean ones. As in humans, body fat begets adipokines, adipokines beget inflammation, and inflammation begets disease.

***

The fact that fat dogs die young underscores the significance of epidemiological studies examining the prevalence of canine overweight and obesity in America and elsewhere. Depending on which researcher you ask, some 30% to 50% of dogs today are overweight. If you are concerned about matters of animal welfare this should worry you—*one-third* to *one-half* of the dogs in America are suffering from a deadly, debilitating, and largely avoidable health problem.

To further contextualize the social significance of the issue, compare it to smoking, one of humanity's most pressing public health concerns. According to the CDC, smoking is "the leading cause of preventable disease and death in the United States." It is considered such a serious and pervasive public health problem that the federal government spent upwards of $300 million on anti-smoking initiatives in 2014 and 2015 alone. In 2015, states spent a further $490 million on tobacco control. That same year, funding from tobacco settlements and taxes exceeded $25 billion.

It was money well spent. As we've seen, a lifetime of smoking is roughly as bad for a person as having a BCS of 6/9 is for a dog, which is to say absolutely horrible. But smoking is *far* less common among American humans than obesity is among American dogs. As of 2014, fewer than two out of ten of Americans were smokers, making canine obesity at least twice as common.

And, somewhat incredibly, this math probably *under*-estimates the true costs of the canine obesity epidemic. For when we dig a little deeper into the scientific record, it becomes clear that our notion of what it means to be an "overweight" dog may well be outdated. Indeed, there are several diverse strands of evidence—some concerning dogs, others derived from the study of human beings—suggesting that dogs ought to be even leaner than researchers had once believed. And if, as the WHO tells us, obesity is an "abnormal or excessive fat accumulation that may impair health," then canine obesity may be an even more common phenomenon than even our most pessimistic estimates suggest.

***

In experiments designed to evaluate the relationship between canine health and adiposity, obesity is usually defined in terms of BCS. Researchers decide whether a dog is overweight simply by following whatever BCS protocol they happen to have selected for their study. Using Dr. Laflamme's nine-category system, for instance, a dog counts as overweight if he has a BCS of 6/9 or above. And, as in the oft-cited study discussed at the beginning of this section, experiments typically compare one group of "overweight" dogs with a similarly defined group of "ideal" dogs.

This is a perfectly reasonable approach if your only goal is to compare these two body conditions. But it doesn't tell us much about the costs and benefits of any other body types. If we want to understand the health consequences of being, say, as lean as the typical wild wolf (a BCS of perhaps 2/9), we need an experiment that examines a whole range of different body conditions.

In the underfunded world of small animal research, such experiments are uncommon. But they have, on occasion, been performed. And, when they have, their findings tend to look a lot like the ones that emerged from studies of human adiposity: the leanest dogs seem to have *by far* the lowest risk of developing the deadly, chronic diseases that are plaguing America's dogs.

One such study was published in 2007 in the *American Journal of Veterinary Research*. Aiming to understand the links between obesity and cancer in dogs, the study's authors examined medical records of tens of thousands of dogs that had been treated at the veterinary medical teaching hospital at the University of California, Davis, over a five-year period beginning in 1999. Each dog in the study group had had its BCS measured by a trained veterinarian at its first visit to the hospital. Because some of those dogs went on to be diagnosed with cancer, the study team was able to use statistical tools to calculate the likelihood that different BCS scores would be associated with specific cancer diagnoses.

The researchers used Dr. Laflamme's nine-category BCS protocol and their paper focused on comparing cancer rates in "ideal" dogs (BCS 4/9 or 5/9) with cancer rates in "overweight" dogs (BCS 6/9 or 7/9) and "obese" dogs (BCS 8/9 or 9/9). But the data they compiled also revealed something that the researchers didn't spend much time discussing in their paper: the leanest dogs in the study group (scored BCS 1/9 or 2/9 and labeled "extremely thin" by the study's authors) had by far the lowest cancer risk in the study. The so-called "ideal" dogs were about twice as likely as the "extremely thin" ones to be diagnosed with sarcomas and a whopping ten times (*ten times!*) more likely to be diagnosed with carcinomas. On the whole, the leanest dogs in the study were the least likely of any body condition group to be diagnosed with cancer, the number-one killer of dogs in the United States. No other group even came close.

The study also revealed a second interesting thing about very lean dogs. And, given the well-known link between cancer and death, this one shouldn't be all that surprising: the lean dogs had the best odds of living very long lives. Dogs in the "underweight" category (BCS 3/9) made up a disproportionately large fraction of the oldest dogs in the study. And dogs in the "extremely thin" group were overrepresented among the elderly to an even greater degree. In each of the "ideal," "overweight," and "obese" classes, only about 1% of dogs were 15 years or older when they were evaluated. Among dogs in the "underweight" and "extremely thin" groups, *the rates were three and seven times greater*, respectively. In other words, for the thousands of dogs in the study, the leaner they were the longer they tended to live.

Similar findings were documented in another recent study. This one was published in the *American Journal of Epidemiology* and focused on the relationship between canine adiposity and breast cancer, one of the most common forms of cancer among American dogs. The study was conducted by a team of researchers from veterinary schools around the country and was aimed at unearthing the links between canine breast cancer and various common behaviors and health variables, including adiposity. The researchers looked at three groups of dogs—those diagnosed with breast cancer, those diagnosed with other forms of cancer, and cancer-free dogs. Each group contained about 150 animals, and they were all matched for known breast cancer risk factors. Then, as part of their statistical analysis, the team divided the dogs into four body condition groups—"thin," "average," "slightly overweight," and "overweight" (the study took place before the publication of a scientifically validated canine BCS system, so they used these descriptors instead of BCS scores)—and compared disease prevalence rates.

What they found when they looked at their data was that lean dogs were *far* more common in the control group than in the experimental group. Only 7.4% of the dogs with breast cancer were classified as "thin" at 9-12 months of age, while more than *three times as many*—more than 23%—of the cancer-free dogs were thin when they were young. According to the researchers, "a thin body conformation at 9-12 months of age reduced the risk of breast cancer among spayed dogs by 99 percent." Yes, you read that right: *a ninety-nine percent reduction in one of the most common killers of dogs in the United States.* And, according to the research team, being thin reduced breast cancer risk even among dogs that weren't spayed: among intact dogs, being thin at 9-12 months of age reduced breast cancer risk by a full 40%.

***

These findings are at odds with the conventional wisdom about canine adiposity. That conventional thinking—embodied in both of the scientifically validated canine BCS protocols—presumes that the health effects of canine adiposity are subject to the same U-shaped pattern that we saw earlier in our discussion of human beings. It suggests that very fat dogs are "too fat" and that very lean dogs are "too lean."

According to Dr. Alexander German's seven-category BCS system, owners of dogs scored as a BCS "C" (around 18% body fat) should "increase food offered" and "seek veterinary advice" if their dogs don't fatten up on their own. Dogs scored as a BCS "B" (around 10% body fat, about the same as wolves and most other wild animals) are considered emergent cases—their owners are advised to proceed immediately to the vet for doctor-assisted fattening. The same idea can be seen in Dr. Dottie Laflamme's nine-category BCS system—dogs on the leaner half of the body condition spectrum are considered to be *un*-healthy.

As we saw at the beginning of this chapter, however, the body condition categories in these protocols aren't based on any stated rationales. Both protocols were defended in peer-reviewed scientific papers, but neither paper spent any time discussing the evidence supporting specific body condition recommendations or analyzing how much fat should be in a dog's body. The protocols and their authors simply seem to have assumed that the U-shaped conventional wisdom about human adiposity is grounded in fact and then roughly translated that conventional wisdom into the canine realm.

Over the course of this chapter we have reviewed the evidence on body condition. And what we've seen is that the U-shaped model of adiposity is no longer the article of faith that it once was. In fact, when it comes to our canine companions, there are at least seven different reasons to doubt whether it's the best way to think about the relationship between adiposity and health.

First, our best pathophysiological explanation for why body fat is bad for health (in both dogs and in humans) is difficult to square with the U-shaped model of adiposity. It makes little sense that the inflammatory adipokines secreted by fat tissue would be beneficial for health at some levels but detrimental to health at others. It may be the case that moderate levels of inflammatory adipokines are not *that bad* for health and that only very high concentrations pose profound health risks. But it's hard to come up with a reason why this most fundamental characteristic of adipokines—whether they are beneficial or detrimental to health—would depend in some way on their concentrations in the body. To accept such a rationale requires, if nothing else, some competing pathophysiological explanation to account for it.

Second, no such explanation has yet been advanced. We know that very lean individuals aren't more susceptible to life-threatening diseases than their fatter counterparts. (In fact, we've seen that the leanest people in the world have the lowest risk of chronic health problems like heart disease, diabetes, and cancer.) And we know that very lean people aren't at risk for immunological deterioration and starvation, so long as they maintain sufficient amounts of lean body mass and consume enough protein and other essential nutrients. In short, no one has come up with any explanation for *why* being very lean would be so bad for canine health—at least not one that stands up to a critical, evidence-based examination.

The third argument against the U-shaped model of adiposity is the fact that some of the most sophisticated epidemiological studies of human beings suggest that the leanest people in the world also happen to live the longest, so long as they maintain sufficient amounts of musculature and other lean tissues. If we remove scrawny individuals from study samples, the U-shaped pattern that otherwise governs the relationship between adiposity and longevity in humans seems to vanish. If we just look at folks who have sufficient amounts of lean tissue in their bodies, then the leanest people in the world are simply the longest-living people in the world, period.

Fourth, when we pull our heads out of the peer-reviewed literature for a moment and take a look around the "real world," we see that the leanest people on the planet really do seem to be the healthiest and longest-living people on the planet. From the native inhabitants of Okinawa to professional endurance sports athletes and the ultra-lean practitioners of calorie restriction, folks who keep their bodies very lean really do seem to be exceptionally healthy.

Fifth, animal models of obesity have done much to confirm the view that the less adipose tissue there is in a body the better that body is likely to function. Surgical removal of fat tissue from mice not only improves their circulating adipokine levels, it also improves their health markers, helps them avoid chronic diseases, and causes them live longer. Moreover, extreme calorie restriction—a surefire way to help an animal achieve a lean physique— is regarded as "the most robust and reproducible means of reducing age-related diseases and extending life span in short-lived animals." When it comes to mice, rats, and other small laboratory animals, one thing we know for sure is that getting them very lean helps keep them very healthy, regardless of whether diet or surgery is used to make them that way.

Sixth, while we know that many of the fundamental attributes of adipose tissue are the same in dogs as they are in animals like humans and mice, studies of very lean dogs also show that they too are particularly impervious to chronic diseases. Unfortunately, these papers are somewhat few and far between. Fat dogs are so common and lean ones so rare that, most often, when researchers examine canine adiposity, they do so by comparing a cohort of very fat dogs with a cohort of somewhat less fat dogs. But in the few cases where very lean dogs have also been added to the mix, we see that they tend to be astoundingly healthy.

The seventh and final reason to doubt the dogma about canine body condition is one that takes us right back to where we began this book—with the domestic dog's wild ancestor, the grey wolf. Even the fattest wild wolves are nowhere near as fat as what the conventional veterinary wisdom calls an "ideal" dog. (Nor are the fattest coyotes, nor are the fattest foxes. Indeed, as we've seen, other than "functionally fat" animals like whales and hibernators, there are very few documented cases of wild animals with body fat levels above 10%.) To believe that an optimally healthy dog really ought to be a good deal fatter than practically every other species to walk the earth (other than human beings, of course), is to suggest that we've somehow outsmarted millions of generations of evolutionary adaptation. Such hubris is rarely rewarded.

ALL DOGS ARE OBESE

Toward the end of my research for this book, I reached out to Dr. Dottie Laflamme and Dr. Alexander German, the veterinarians most responsible for promoting the conventional wisdom about canine adiposity. I wanted to ask them to expand upon the reasoning behind their canine BCS protocols. What was the scientific evidence in favor of the U-shaped model of adiposity that they had both endorsed? How did that evidence influence their thinking about body condition? They were both good enough to respond to me.

Dr. Laflamme continued to defend the U-shaped model of adiposity, calling optimal canine body condition a "sweet spot" between underweight and overweight. She explained that her thinking was based upon epidemiological studies suggesting that being lean *was* bad for a dog's health, rather than any pathophysiological explanation for *why* that would be so. As she put it, "large population data from humans" showed that "mortality is lowest with a body mass index between about twenty-two and twenty-eight."

She also directed me toward evidence supporting this conclusion. The handful of studies she cited included several of the same papers discussed earlier in this chapter. And she was right, they *did* show a U-shaped relationship between BMI and mortality in humans.

But this is ground that we've already covered. We've seen that confounding factors (notably, the tendency of deadly diseases to cause weight loss and the tendency of the Body Mass Index to confuse muscle with fat) are likely responsible for bending the otherwise-linear relationship between fatness and mortality into what looks like a U-shaped curve. Dr. Alexander German, the University of Liverpool professor who created the other widely-used canine BCS protocol, actually highlighted both of these phenomena in an e-mail he sent me explaining his thinking about canine body condition: "Much of the association [between thinness and an increased risk of mortality] is likely to be due to the dog having developed a disease, then lost weight," he wrote, before adding that "in short, you must consider lean mass, not just fat." In the context of our broader and more nuanced understanding of the relationship between health and adiposity, studies documenting a U-shaped relationship between human BMI and longevity don't tell us anything that we don't already know.

But Dr. Laflamme also sent me some interesting studies involving elderly cats. Studies that, rather than depicting a U-shape in the relationship between body condition and mortality, actually showed a *positive* relationship between mortality and various body condition measures, including lean body mass, overall body weight, and body fat mass. She explained that these studies also suggested that one really can be "too lean," because something about being lean was causing these cats to live shorter lives than their fatter peers.

At first glance, these studies just seemed bizarre. Being fat was associated with living *longer*? That seemed to run counter to just about everything that science has taught us about how obesity works. But then I dug into the studies a bit. Their authors made it clear that what they were observing wasn't that being lean was causing cats to become sick, it was the opposite— being sick was causing them to become lean. In their own words, the positive correlation between body fat and longevity "likely reflects the onset of chronic disease and more rapid utilization of body tissue reserves during disease states."

A closer look at their data supports this thinking. Over the course of their lives, the cats in these studies maintained more or less constant levels of body fat—the fat ones stayed fat and the lean ones stayed lean. But near the very end of their lives, their body fat levels suddenly and dramatically fell off. The end result, when viewed as a graphical association between fat mass and age, was a largely flat line that took a steep plunge downward over the last few years. Thus, while average mortality rate increased as fat mass decreased, it would not be at all fair to infer that being lean actually *caused* cats to get sick. The reality, as the study's authors explained, was quite the opposite—being sick was causing them to become lean. And that makes sense. Indeed, it is one of the main conclusions that emerged from our analysis of the link between body condition and health in humans. But it doesn't really suggest that a dog can actually be "too lean."

**

I was grateful for Dr. Laflamme's thoughtful responses. But, I wasn't persuaded to abandon my skepticism about the U-shaped model of adiposity. She was saying things we already know. She wasn't introducing anything new to our analysis of how lean a dog really ought to be.

Until, that is, she sent me something I had never seen before. It was an article that she had written herself. The short piece was something of an overview of the science of canine adiposity, not a summary of any experiment she had performed. For the most part, its content would look familiar to anyone who has read this book—the metabolically active nature of body fat, the prevalence of obesity in pet dogs, etc. But one aspect of the piece was completely new and original, at least to me.

Dr. Laflamme apparently had gotten her hands on the raw data from the landmark study discussed earlier in this chapter, the one in which a group of relatively lean Labrador Retrievers were shown to live longer and stay healthier than their comparatively fat littermates. And she had gone on to conduct her own analysis of that data by using regression techniques to determine the mathematical relationship between body condition score and lifespan among all of the dogs in the study. In an e-mail she sent me, she described this analysis as showing a "fairly clean break" between dogs with a BCS of less than 5/9 ("ideal") and those with a BCS of 5/9 or above—a finding that would support to a limited extent the U-shaped model of adiposity.

Only that's not what the data looked like to me. Not at all. Looking at a graph of the data, a few things caught my eye. First of all, the dog with the leanest body condition in the entire study (a BCS of about 2/9) lived longer than all but one of the more than 40 other dogs. Second, just about all of the dogs with a BCS of lower than 4/9 (supposedly "too thin") lived longer than all of the dogs with a BCS of 5/9 (supposedly "ideal") or higher. On the whole, the graph from Dr. Laflamme's paper looked exactly like what a proponent of the "leaner is better" school of thought would expect—a near-linear negative relationship between body condition score and lifespan:

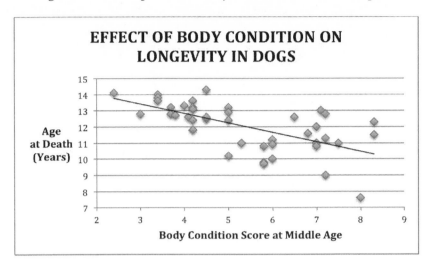

Figure 6.

In fact, Dr. Laflamme had actually done the math and figured out the equation that most accurately summarized the relationship between body condition score and lifespan in the study. This is the equation she came up with:

Expected Lifespan (Yrs.) = 15.208 – (0.589 x BCS)

According to Dr. Laflamme, the relationship between body condition score and lifespan in the study was *linear.* According to her formula, dogs with a BCS of 7/9 ("too fat") were likely to live about 11 years. Dogs with a BCS of 5/9 ("ideal") were likely to live a bit longer (about 12 years). And dogs with a BCS of 2/9 ("too thin") were likely to live even longer than that (about 14 years).

***

In the end, try as I might, I just couldn't escape the notion that Dr. Laflamme's BCS system (and the conventional wisdom about canine body condition to which it has contributed) didn't really reflect the truth about the relationship between canine adiposity and health. Her original paper didn't cite any evidence supporting the U-shaped model implicit in her BCS protocol. And even after making a good faith effort to consider her additional evidence—none of which, it should be noted, could have influenced her BCS system in the first place, because it was all published long *after* she had formulated and published her system—I was left unpersuaded.

It seemed more likely to me that her BCS protocol was an honest attempt to create a useful diagnostic tool for veterinarians and dog-owners, but one that was now (some 20 years after its creation) in need of some updating. For the moment, canine BCS protocols continue to be abundantly useful in helping us determine how fat our dogs *are*. But they're just not too helpful in teaching us how fat our dogs *ought to be*.

The good news: you don't even need a BCS chart to figure out if your dog is "too fat." You can just follow a simpler rule instead: the leaner the better. As long as she has sufficient musculature on her frame, there's really no such thing as a dog that's "too lean." If, as the WHO tells us, obesity is what happens when there is more fat in a body than there really ought to be, then the truth may seem counterintuitive but it's also incredibly simple: just about all dogs are obese.

Chapter Eight

THE OPTIMAL DOG

--

"I have always thought the actions of men the best interpreters of their thoughts."

John Locke,
An Essay Concerning Human Understanding (1689)

BUILDING THE OPTIMAL DOG

When I first started writing about canine obesity, I called my blog *The Optimal Dog*. I thought it had a nice ring to it. It also conveyed my ultimate goal with respect to my own dogs—to make decisions that would optimize their health and well-being in the long run.

But over the years I've grown to dislike the name more and more. It now seems to shine with the surgically enhanced radiance of a faddy diet book—as if I am so foolishly overconfident (or dishonest) as to believe that everyone who takes my advice will wind up with the perfect dog.

Alas, such perfection just isn't possible in the real world. Living organisms are complex, as is the world in which we live. In matters of health, guarantees are rare. The scientific evidence informing our understanding of canine obesity remains in many ways incomplete. And even if it weren't— even if we really could do everything "right"—unforeseen consequences would still have a knack for showing up and ruining our best-laid plans. (See this book's epilogue for my first-hand experience with this.)

Still, if I were you, I think I'd want this book to include a summary of the conclusions that have emerged from its author's half-decade study of canine obesity. I'd want him to tell me exactly what he thinks I should be doing in order to give my dog the best life that I can. It's all well and good to document a quest to understand an epidemic, to report on experiences and let readers weigh the extent to which those experiences carry weight in their own lives. But summarizing what's been learned along the way still seems to have its place.

What follows is an actionable summary of my interpretation of the scientific evidence on canine obesity. It takes the form of five simple principles, each one pertaining to a separate topic (diet, exercise, etc.). To help you make use of them all, I've also added a few rules, guidelines, and tips—a little toolbox that ought to help you with your own dogs.

It should be noted that these are the same principles I use to make decisions for my own dogs. That's because I really do love my fur babies as much as anything in the world. I really do want to give them lives that are as long and happy as reasonably possible. And this really is how I go about pursuing that goal.

PRINCIPLE # 1:
KEEP NORMAL ADULT DOGS AS LEAN AS POSSIBLE WHILE MAINTAING MUSCULATURE AND ENERGY

In the end, the evidence shows that body fat is, in effect, poisonous for dogs. Thus, anyone who wants their dogs to be as healthy as possible should try to minimize the amount of fat in their bodies, so long as (1) doing so doesn't cause them to lose any muscle mass, (2) they don't show signs of lethargy, and (3) they're not ill, making or nursing puppies, or puppies themselves.

In Chapter Seven, we saw that not everyone agrees with this strategy. The mainstream health and wellness press won't recommend it, either for dogs or for humans. But while there is valid evidence both supporting it and refuting it, for the reasons discussed throughout Chapter Seven, I believe the weight of the evidence tips pretty heavily in its favor. The U-shaped model of adiposity seems to be a pervasive but flawed intellectual relic, one built upon our limited ability to measure how much fat is inside an organism and our failure to understand how fat really works. From both a pathophysiological and epidemiological perspective, leaner really does seem to be better. So that's the rule I've used to guide my decision-making for my own dogs.

(If you don't agree with my interpretation of the evidence on this matter, that's fine too. I'm not offended. Your primary alternative is the U-shaped model of adiposity, the same one that underlies all of the various published canine BCS protocols. To see what proponents of that model consider to be an "ideal" or "optimal" canine body condition, just take a look at the protocols themselves. They are self-explanatory and you can find copies elsewhere in this book.)

Unlike the U-shaped model of adiposity, which asks us to use measurement tools to pin our dogs to precisely the right body condition, the "leaner is better" paradigm doesn't require precise measurement. You don't need a BCS chart to understand what your dog's ideal body condition looks like. Subject to the few aforementioned caveats, leaner is simply better. A BCS rubric may be useful for diagnostic purposes—by grading your dog's body condition it can give you a good idea of how fat your dog *is*. Just ignore its qualitative recommendations about how fat your dog *should be*.

Now, a few words about the caveats to the general rule. Most importantly, remember that being lean is good for dogs because it helps them avoid deadly chronic health problems, like cancer. But there are times in their lives when other health concerns outweigh the benefit of chronic disease avoidance. These include periods of serious illness, pregnancy and lactation, and growth, when bodies require considerably more metabolic fuel than usual in order to maintain functionality. Leanness should, of course, take a back seat to other concerns under these unique circumstances. If you're interested in optimizing your dog's body condition during one of these periods, go find a board-certified veterinary nutritionist and talk to her before making any changes to your dog's lifestyle.

Secondly, remember that in Chapter Seven we saw that muscle wasting and a lethargic, listless affect are the primary outward manifestations of starvation. And while we want our dogs to be lean, we certainly don't want them to be starved. So, in your quest to optimize your dog's body condition, watch to make sure she doesn't lose her skeletal muscles or become lethargic and unenthusiastic in her interactions with everyday stimuli.

I don't believe that we need to measure with exacting precision in order to monitor these indicators. Personally, I don't use any formal measurement framework in either case. I may not trust my ability to intuit what is "ideal" for my fur babies (controlled experiments and voluminous data will beat my intuitions every time), but, like all parents, I do like to believe that I know when something is "off" with them. I have a lot of experience with my kiddos and I'm able to detect subtle changes that most third parties would miss. When my dogs are losing bulk or not displaying their usual *joie de vivre*, I like to think that I'm the first to know.

In that regard, I've found that continued fat loss becomes tough sledding at around a BCS 2/9, when dogs have a BFP of perhaps 7% to 12%. Beyond that point—which happens to be, surprise, surprise, right about the same level that most wild canines maintain—further fat loss becomes a struggle and dogs appear strikingly lean. When viewed from above, they have an hourglass figure—shoulders and hips wide with musculature and waists that are only about half as wide as their rib cages. From the side, a steep and pronounced abdominal tuck becomes visible, as does the outline of the ribcage. But, up until that point, "leaner is better" is all the guidance I use.

PRINCIPLE #2:
AT LEAST ONE BOUT OF EXERCISE EACH DAY

As the experimental evidence described in Chapters Three and Six shows, it is certainly possible to reduce the amount of fat in a body without a targeted exercise program. Even if you subscribe to the calories-in, calories-out model of obesity, weight loss does not at all require daily exercise—if you're not using exercise to add to the number of calories-out, then just reduce the number of calories-in accordingly.

But so what? Exercise has been tied to all manner of tangible benefits—both psychological and physiological—that go far beyond fat fighting. Moreover, dogs tend to love it, it helps to manage undesirable behaviors, and it opens the door to more food (if you increase the number of calories-out, then you can also increase the number of calories-in while maintaining the same caloric deficit), something dogs tend to support. Exercise clearly has a role to play in a dog's daily life.

I aim to provide each of my dogs with at least one bout of tongue-wagging exercise per day, using Kyra Sundance's 20-minutes-a-day rule as a minimum requirement. To maximize the effectiveness of the session, I usually opt for something that is as vigorous as safely possible. With Kody, that means a fast-paced fetch game or a frenetic session with his herding ball. I mix in some stimulating cue-response work too—"heel," "stay," "take it!"—just to keep things interesting. Every two or three days I throw resistance exercise into the mix. Some jumping, or hill-running, or (in Lucy's case) charging up a flight of stairs. And perhaps once a week, whenever my schedule is most permissive, we dial-down the intensity and go for a nice, long walk instead. I don't get too regimented—outward signs of fatigue like panting and sluggishness are treated as indicators that we've done enough and there's no workout schedule tacked to my wall. I just aim for at least 20 minutes a day and try to keep things fresh.

It's harder to make the case for exercise if your dog doesn't seem to enjoy it. So you may have to experiment a bit to find your dog's thing. Maybe her preferred form of vigorous exercise involves wrestling with other dogs at the park or at a daycare facility. Maybe it's swimming. Or training for dock-diving, agility, weight-pull, or one of the other canine athletic competitions that have recently become popular. Just aim for something that your pup is enthusiastic about and that leaves her visibly pooped by the time it's over.

PRINCIPLE #3:
AS FEW STARCHY AND SUGARY CARBS AS POSSIBLE

There are several reasons why I'm persuaded by Gary Taubes's theory of obesity. I think the experimental evidence is compelling (the biggest and best studies show that *ad libitum* low-carbohydrate diets tend to make people leaner than diet/exercise combo plans that involve caloric restriction, discipline, and regular exercise). The biochemistry of how fat works supports the carbohydrate-insulin model more than the alternative. I think the population-level epidemiological evidence is convincing (carb-free wolves don't get fat, carb-stuffed dogs do; pre-agricultural societies weren't fat, modern-day Western ones are; poor people are more likely to eat carbs and more likely to get fat; etc.). And I think that broader contextual arguments suggest that Taubes and company are more right than wrong (in evolutionary terms, both dogs and humans only began eating starches and sweets very recently, but these inexpensive and highly palatable ingredients are favorites of the mega-corporations that make foods for us and our dogs, so in our modern world they are as ubiquitous as obesity itself). For all these reasons, I am convinced that consumption of starches and sweets plays an outsized, if not dispositive, role in determining whether a dog will or will not get fat.

If you feel the same way, then the fundamental way to help your dog get lean and stay that way is obvious: reduce the amount of carbohydrate in her diet, or eliminate carbs altogether. There are a number of ways to do this and, while you can probably figure most of them out on your own, I've included a few words about each below.

(If, on the other hand, you're not convinced by the carbohydrate-insulin model of adiposity, you can skip ahead to the next section, where we'll cover how to do old-fashioned calories-in, calories-out calculations for your dog.)

Cut the "Treats"

Perhaps the most effective way to cut starchy and sugary carbohydrates from your dog's diet is to simply eliminate dog biscuits, ingestible chews, and other forms of packaged "treat" rewards. Dr. Ernie Ward calls these canine junk foods "Kibble Crack," and it's not hard to see why. Just like cookies, brownies, cakes, and other sugary-sweet human deserts, they are often crammed with prodigious quantities of starches and sweeteners.

Starch is a necessary ingredient in dog biscuits and other baked treat products for the same reason that it's a necessary ingredient in dry dog foods—it binds the dough together during baking. And, because of their extreme low cost, cereal grain products like flours and corn meal are by far the most popular way to add this starchy heft to dog biscuit dough. So you're virtually assured that some kind of cheap cereal grain will play a prominent role in your dog's biscuit of choice.

Sweeteners are ubiquitous in treats for a different reason—they're delicious. Dogs have been shown to prefer foods spiked with table sugar (sucrose). And plenty of other mammalian species have been shown to prefer foods laced with some combination of sugar, fat, and salt. So it isn't too surprising that Big Kibble, with its vested interest in selling as many of its products as possible, often uses sweeteners in treat recipes. What's more surprising is the utterly dominant role that those ingredients tend to play.

Take Snausages Snaw Somes! Beef & Cheese Flavor, for example. The first four ingredients in this treat product are *all* starches or sweeteners— wheat flour, corn syrup, sugar, and crystalline fructose. In total, more than 90% of the food matter in each Snaw Some! is digestible carbohydrate. Or consider Pedigree's large Jumbone, where the first *six* ingredients are all starches or sweeteners—rice flour, glycerin, sugar, wheat flour, propylene glycol, powdered cellulose—and, in total, about 85% of the more than 600 calories per treat come from digestible carbs. These products are every inch as packed with starchy and sugary carbohydrates as a cream-filled donut or a big slice of rich chocolate cake. They are true canine junk food.

So how do you eliminate them from your dog's life? First of all, remember that treats are not the only way to reward a dog. Just as she is psychologically "hard-wired" to be pleased by palatable foods, your dog is also hard-wired to enjoy things like affection, play, and physical touch. And any of these other pleasurable stimuli (or a combination of them) can serve as a worthy replacement for edible treats. The fact that things like verbal praise, physical affection, and tug games are 100% free also means that making the switch to treat-free living can also be good for the wallet.

Removing treats from your dog's life altogether won't compromise nutrition either. Under AAFCO rules, commercially prepared pet foods must fulfill *all* of a dog's daily nutrient requirements. You can't sell a pet food under AAFCO's regulations if the food must be supplemented with a treat in order to fulfill a dog's nutritional needs. Moreover, because treats are not even considered "pet foods" under AAFCO rules, they don't have to contain vital nutritional substances like micronutrients, amino acids, and essential fats. Under the AAFCO framework, foods must provide all the necessary nutrition. Anything extra that comes from treats and supplements is a bonus.

Still, for many of us, giving treat rewards is a practice that we have trouble abandoning entirely. Not only do our dogs enjoy their Kibble Crack, but it plays an important role in their behavioral training too. It's hard to deny that dogs tend to be more motivated by food than by any other kind of positive reinforcement.

If you'd rather not cut out the treats altogether then at least consider making the switch to a very low-carbohydrate product. You have a few options. If commercially prepared products are your thing, there are several styles of treat products that are composed entirely of animal-based ingredients, including freeze-dried all-meat treats, jerkies, and frozen raw meat treats. Be mindful of not simply choosing products based on their names— some "jerky" products are still spiked with sweeteners—and instead make a habit of reviewing the ingredient list to make sure that starches and sweeteners play little role, if any, in your choice.

On the other hand, if you don't mind putting a little elbow grease into preparing your dog's snacks, homemade, low-carbohydrate treats are also an option. Small slices of bacon or sausage, chicken morsels, and crumbled ground meats all make for easily refrigerated and easy-to-feed carbohydrate-free rewards.

For chewers, there's another option: paying a visit to your local butcher and procuring some sliced-up beef bones. (Pork bones and chicken bones fracture much more easily than beef bones. They pose a choking hazard and should *not* be fed to dogs under any circumstances.) Butchers often treat bones as waste products, so they can generally be procured from your neighborhood meat counter at a very low cost. They can also be frozen indefinitely, and they contain precisely zero carbohydrates. All good things. That being said, feeding your dog bones from the butcher also presents some unique challenges. And that segues nicely into a second carb-reduction strategy.

Go Raw

Once upon a time in the not-too-distant past, a new player emerged on the commercial dog food scene. Unlike the dry kibble products that have long dominated the pet food market, the new guy's foods actually bore a meaningful resemblance to those that wild wolves typically eat. The macronutritional content was similar—lots of protein, lots of essential fats, very few carbs. The ingredients were similar—almost nothing but animal meat, with just a trace of minimally processed plant matter. And the underlying cooking process, or, more accurately, the lack thereof, was similar too—just like the meat consumed by Yellowstone's wolves, these new dog food products were designed to be served up *raw*.

The popularity of raw dog food has grown explosively in recent years. Today, zealous proponents of raw feeding practices populate Facebook groups boasting hundreds of thousands of active members. Dozens of blogs and books offer dog owners pointers on how to "go raw" with their dogs. Advocates for various sub-disciplines enthusiastically recommend one specific style of raw diet or another. And just as with the human ancestral health movement, it's hard to deny that the notion of honoring one's evolutionary heritage has a good deal of logical appeal here too. Our dogs ate nothing but raw meat for eons. All else being equal, why change that?

Raw diet devotees tend to tout a number of health benefits that supposedly come along with going raw: better dental health, fewer digestive problems, and less severe skin allergies are among the most common. But other, tougher-to-measure health advantages are often attributed to raw diets too. As Dr. Jean Dodd, a so-called "holistic veterinarian" who describes herself as "one of the foremost experts in pet healthcare," wrote on her blog in 2012: "Many of us in the veterinary community, including myself, have seen first-hand the health and vigor of dogs and cats fed raw diets. These animals just 'shine' in all respects." According to this logic, raw-fed dogs just, well, *seem* healthier.

The AVMA, the ACVN, and the American Animal Hospital Association have all looked at the evidence and weighed-in on the supposed health benefits of raw food diets. And they're not exactly buying the hype. Not one of these influential organizations acknowledges that raw diets are in any way beneficial. All of them are decidedly against the practice of raw feeding. The AVMA writes:

> There are many anecdotal reports of benefits associated with feeding raw foods—including easier weight management; reduced dental disease; healthier coat and skin; elimination of allergies; improved health and immunity; and more—but there is no scientific evidence to support these claims.

The ACVN strikes a similar chord:

> Advocates of raw diets claim benefits ranging from improved longevity to superior oral or general health and even disease resolution (especially gastrointestinal disease). Often the benefits of providing natural enzymes and other substances that may be altered or destroyed by cooking are also cited. However, proof for these purported benefits is currently restricted to testimonials, and no published peer-reviewed studies exist to support claims made by raw diet advocates.

It's all escalated into a rather spicy debate between the health authorities and the raw food advocates. But a critical look at the evidence on either side of the debate is beyond our focus here. Why? Because, regardless of whether raw diets improve nutrient absorption and enzyme uptake or do nothing of the sort, *they most definitely* are *very low in total carbohydrate content*. And the voluminous scientific literature supporting the carbohydrate-insulin model of adiposity suggests that that's a very good thing for canine health. (Curiously, the ACVN, the AAHA, and the AVMA seem not to have considered that literature when they made their bold, across-the-board pronouncements about the lack of peer-reviewed evidence supporting raw diets.)

The primary reason raw diets don't contain much in the way of carbohydrates is that, unlike dry dog foods, raw foods don't need to stay bound together during any kind of baking process. No baking means no starch. No starch means minimal insulin secretion. And, according to the carbohydrate-insulin model of obesity, minimal insulin secretion is a good thing for your dog's waistline. How good? *Very* good. Switching your dog from a garden-variety dry food to a raw diet will dramatically reduce her daily intake of carbohydrates. Recall that dry dog foods are typically composed of somewhere between 1/2 and 3/4 carbs. Raw foods tend to contain effectively none of them. In terms of carbohydrates, the space between a typical Big Kibble formula and a commercially prepared raw food product is massive. And given what we've seen about the relationship between carbohydrate intake and adiposity, as well as the disastrous health consequences associated with being fat, it's a space that is vital too.

There are, however, a few buts. In the real world, where healthfulness is just one of many factors that influences which foods we choose for our dogs, there are a few other things about raw diets that one should keep in mind. The first is that while no baking means no starch, no baking also means a short shelf life. The epic shelf life of dry dog foods is one of their primary selling points. Raw meat obviously spoils much faster.

Fortunately, raw food manufacturers have come up with a few different strategies for minimizing the spoliation problem. One is to freeze-dry their foods, removing almost all of the moisture content so that foods may be stored at room temperature for long periods without spoiling. Another is to distribute and sell frozen raw meat products. As long as it stays frozen, even raw meat isn't at risk of spoiling.

These innovations are clever. But they demand a bit of work from consumers. Feeding your dog a dry food is as simple as "scoop and serve," but feeding a commercially prepared raw food involves a few extra steps. In the case of freeze-dried foods, nuggets must be broken up and then re-hydrated prior to feeding. And in the case of frozen ones, patties must be thawed in advance. Nothing so difficult as, say, hunting and killing an elk, but a bit more involved than simply feeding a bowl of kibble.

These innovations also relate to a second notable drawback of commercially prepared raw foods: they are much more expensive than dry dog foods. Because more work goes into raw foods—both during manufacturing and, in the case of frozen products, distribution— manufacturers must charge more to cover their costs. And these comparatively high prices are likely to induce a good bit of sticker-shock in new customers. At the moment, each calorie of commercially prepared raw dog food will likely cost you at least *five to eight times* as much as each calorie of "ultra-premium" kibble. Yes, you read that right. Unless you have a very small dog, making the switch from kibble to a commercially prepared raw food is going to bump up your monthly dog food bill pretty dramatically.

Importantly, this is *not* to say that these products are particularly expensive. It's just that, as we've seen, dry dog foods are astonishingly cheap. And if you've built your notion of a "reasonable" dog food price around products that cost 10% as much as a McDonald's cheeseburger, you're going to have to readjust your expectations a bit if you want to make the switch to something meaningfully less junky.

One last drawback to raw dog foods is they are susceptible to contamination with food-borne pathogens in a way that dry dog foods generally are not. Whether it is sold for human consumption or canine consumption, raw meat is prone to contamination with bacteria and the various other microscopic pathogens that can cause food poisoning. And although decontamination technology and regulatory oversight is steadily improving, contaminated meat manages to slip between the regulatory cracks all the time. According to the USDA, more than 140 million pounds of ground beef was recalled in the United States between 1995 and 2000. And more than 90% of that meat was only recalled due to potential contamination with the deadly *E. coli 0157:H7* bacteria. When it comes to less deadly but more common food-borne bacteria such as *Salmonella*, recalls are rare and contaminated meat and eggs are regularly allowed to go to market. Indeed, up to 25% of the broiler chickens sold in the United States are estimated to be tainted with *Salmonella* bacteria. As a result, approximately one million cases of *Salmonella* food poisoning occurred in the United States every year between 2000 and 2008. During this same period, food-borne pathogens killed more than a thousand people per year in the United States.

Thoroughly cooking meat will kill food-borne pathogens and eliminate the risk of illness. On the other hand, the consumption or handling of raw or undercooked meat (such as occurs when a bowl of raw food is prepared for a dog) may present a health risk to humans. It should be noted, however, that this is almost entirely a human problem—not a dog problem. While dogs are susceptible to infection by common food-borne pathogens such as *Salmonella*, infection very rarely results in illness or any kind of clinical symptoms. Dogs ate nothing but raw meat for millions of generations and seem to have evolved the ability to manage most meat-borne infections without becoming sick. But humans have not. And the risk of infection with *Salmonella* and other food-borne pathogens—transmitted either through improper handling of contaminated raw meat or by coming into contact with a dog's pathogen-shedding fecal matter—has been enough to lead many prominent veterinary health authorities to warn against feeding dogs foods containing raw meats. These authorities include the AVMA, the ACVN, and the AAHA—basically anyone who's anyone in the world of veterinary medical policy.

In one sense, their warnings seem sensible. Although there is scant evidence of *Salmonella* infection actually harming pets, numerous studies have documented the increased prevalence of *Salmonella* and other bacteria in the feces of raw-fed dogs.

But in another sense, the warnings seem to be unjustifiably shrill. As of writing, very few cases of dog-to-human *Salmonella* infection have ever been documented, anywhere in the world. And, as the authors of one meta-analysis put it, when it comes to the public health risk posed by contaminated raw foods, "there have been no studies conclusively documenting the risk to either pets or owners." It is certainly possible that raw dog food could wind up making you sick, but it is not at all likely.

In any event, if you do decide to go raw, the strategies for minimizing the risk of infection are obvious enough. Carefully wash and disinfect all hands, dishes, and surfaces that come into contact with raw meat products, diligently ensure that all humans (particularly children) avoid contact with dog poop, and always store raw products appropriately.

Before we wrap-up this brief introduction to raw dog foods, a few words of caution about the practice of feeding home-prepared raw diets. Some raw diet devotees recommend avoiding commercially prepared raw foods altogether, either because they're too expensive or because, just like with baked foods, the manufacturing processes used to limit the pathogens in these products also limit the number of valuable enzymes in the products. These folks urge dog owners to prepare meals for their dogs at home, using raw meats and other store-bought ingredients.

I'd hope that this would strike any dog owner as a serious undertaking, one at least worthy of an in-depth personal consultation with a board-certified veterinary nutritionist prior to its inception. Anyone who has made it this far in a book with such a reverence for scientific evidence probably doesn't need to be reminded to be skeptical of self-appointed experts, folks long on impressive-sounding back stories but short on valid evidence supporting their positions. Still, the world of home-prepared raw food diets is brimming with such individuals, and many of them are eager to teach you how to begin making your dog's meals at home.

If you are considering preparing your dog's meals yourself, there is at least one danger (other than food contamination) of which you should be particularly cognizant—the risk of improper micronutrient intake. According to both AAFCO and the National Research Council's Committee on Animal Nutrition, dogs require a daily ration of several *dozen* different vitamins and minerals (in addition to still more essential amino acids and fats). When it comes to some of these nutrients, daily intake must exceed a minimum threshold in order to prevent the development of chronic vitamin deficiencies. But others must be consumed in specific ratios in order to avoid other acute nutritional disorders, such as the developmental bone defects that may result in puppies with improper calcium/phosphorous intake ratios.

Commercially produced foods sold with AAFCO's blessing (whether they be dry or raw ones) need to meet AAFCO's nutritional specifications in order to call themselves "complete and balanced" pet foods. Obviously, home-prepared diets need not do so. Moreover, according to a study published in the *British Journal of Nutrition* in 2011, they oftentimes *do* not do so. There, the various homemade raw foods fed to dogs by a cohort of German dog owners were analyzed for compliance with the NRC's recommended daily micronutrient allowances. And about 60% of the foods failed to meet one or more of the NRC's recommendations. That study isn't an outlier either—a critical review of the evidence both in favor of and against raw diets published in the *Canadian Veterinary Journal* in 2011 highlights several others where vitamin deficiencies were also documented. Whether or not any specific diet will provide your specific dog with the right amount of specific micronutrients can only be determined on a case-by-case basis. But, as these studies show, meeting the nutrient recommendations set forth by AAFCO and the NRC isn't always a simple endeavor. So if you do decide to make your dog's food at home, approach the process with care and seriously consider bringing a board-certified veterinary nutritionist into the process.

Switch to a (Relatively) Low-Carb Kibble

For readers accustomed to feeding their dogs a garden-variety Big Kibble dry dog food, a less jarring change than going raw might be switching to a low-carb kibble. Of course, bear in mind that the term "low-carb" is only appropriate here by way of comparison. At the time of writing, about one-third of the nutrition in even the lowest-carbohydrate kibble still comes from digestible carbohydrates. And starch, sugar, and Glycemic Index disclosures aren't required by AAFCO's labeling regulations. So it's not always easy to understand exactly how much fattening carbohydrate is in your dog's food. Still, given the high prices of raw food products (and their other disadvantages), a low-carb kibble may still be the best fit for many Taubesian dogs.

Fundamentally, there are two ways to make such products. The more common one is to replace some of the digestible carbs in the formula with indigestible ingredients. This is the process used to create almost all of the "light," "lite," "weight-loss," and "low calorie" kibbles on the market today. The idea behind them is simple: some types of carbohydrates—notably the dietary fiber found in ingredients like cellulose—do a serviceable job of binding other ingredients together while also being impossible for dogs to digest. So they keep kibble together during the extrusion process but they pass through a dog's digestive tract without any caloric energy being absorbed. In this way, swapping some digestible starch for some indigestible cellulose significantly lowers both the digestible carbohydrate load of the product as well as its metabolizable energy content (so these products make sense as a weight-loss vehicle regardless of whether you accept the carbohydrate-insulin model of adiposity).

Kibble products that use indigestible ingredients in this fashion are easy to find in the marketplace. Just look for three qualities: (1) a catchy weight-loss name, (2) low caloric content (AAFCO requires that any dry dog food product labeled as "light" or "lite" contain fewer than 3,100 calories per kilogram, which is easy to achieve since all the indigestible material adds zero digestible calories), and (3) a significant amount of crude fiber in the Guaranteed Analysis panel (likely 10% or more on a dry-matter basis). If fed in appropriate amounts, these products will undoubtedly induce fat loss in your dog; their effectiveness has been demonstrated in study after study. And, as gut distention is thought to play a role in inducing feelings of fullness, many folks suggest that they're a particularly humane way to get your dog lean.

Whether these types of products appeal to you or not will probably depend on how you feel about feeding your dog something other than food. Ingredients like powdered cellulose and wheat bran will pass straight through your dog without being digested or absorbed. Not unlike cardboard, they are, quite literally, not food. Nevertheless, if used correctly, products containing these ingredients will almost certainly result in fat loss, and there is no evidence that they are harmful in any way to the health of normal, adult dogs.

But if the idea of feeding your dog non-food isn't that attractive to you, then perhaps consider the second type of low-carb kibble—that made by replacing high-glycemic carbohydrate ingredients with lower-glycemic ones. This is the primary way that I've minimized the role played by carbohydrates in my own dogs' lives. We feed Kody and Lucy a kibble called Orijen, made by a company called Champion Petfoods. Champion is a smallish Canadian manufacturer with an uncommon commitment to the carbohydrate-insulin model of adiposity. Recently, its Orijen product was named the Glycemic Research Institute's "Pet Food of the Year" for three consecutive years. Here's how the company describes its views on the nutritive value of dietary carbohydrates:

> Carbohydrates are an empty calorie, which means they have no essential function in the body and provide only sugar for energy, which converts quickly to glucose in the blood. If carbohydrates are provided in excess (as they often are), they convert easily into body fat.

Might as well be Gary Taubes, huh? Certainly a far cry from Hill's "Golden

Grain" propaganda.

Orijen is a relatively expensive product, currently somewhere between $75 and $100 for a large bag (about $0.15 to $0.20 for every 100 calories), depending on which protein you choose. So more than a garden variety Big Kibble product but far less than any commercially prepared raw food. And far, *far* less than a typical fast-food meal.

What do you get for your money? When it comes to carbs, at least two things. First, a low overall carbohydrate content. Since AAFCO doesn't allow manufacturers to explicitly state the carbohydrate content of their products in Guaranteed Analysis panels, you have to do a little math in order to figure out exactly how much is in there. But once you do, you can see that only about 30% of the calories in Orijen's dry dog foods tend to come from carbohydrate sources—much more than a wolf would eat, but far less then is found in many garden-variety Big Kibble offerings.

The second thing you'll get for your money is low-glycemic carbohydrate ingredients. In Orijen dry foods, the most abundant carbohydrate ingredients tend to be legumes (lentils, chickpeas), rather than the potatoes and cereal grains that are more commonly found in kibbles. Legumes register far lower Glycemic Index scores than cereal grains and their derivatives. Red lentils (the most abundant non-animal ingredient in the Orijen "Regional Red" formula) score a 21 on the index. Chickpeas (the second most abundant non-animal ingredient) score a 10. As a frame of reference, remember that meats usually score zero, pure glucose scores 100, and cereal grains and potato derivatives tend to score in the 60s, 70s, and 80s. The reason for this discrepancy is simple—while cereal grains and potatoes tend to be composed primarily of easily digestible starch, legumes like lentils and chickpeas contain almost no starch whatsoever.

It's also worth noting that of all the manufacturers I contacted seeking a facilities tour in connection with my research, Champion was the only one that said "yes." (I have no affiliation with the company other than the fact that I feed its products to my dogs.) The company owns its own factories and sources its own ingredients and, unlike the folks at Blue Buffalo and Purina, its representatives were more than willing to let me see their manufacturing process in action. Make of that what you will.

Reduce Overall Food Intake

The last way to reduce your dog's overall carbohydrate intake is the simplest strategy of all: just feed him less. If you're currently feeding your dog a garden-variety Big Kibble dry dog food, any material reduction in daily serving size will also result in a meaningful reduction in total carbohydrate intake. Less dry dog food, by definition, means fewer carbs.

How much less? I'm glad you asked.

PRINCIPLE #4:
CALCULATE SERVING SIZES WITHOUT RELYING ON MANUFACTURER RECOMMENDATIONS

If you arrive at this juncture as something of a "hard" believer in the carbohydrate-insulin model—if you believe that minimizing carbohydrate intake is the *only* dietary strategy that will cause your dog to lose body fat—then what follows probably won't interest you much. If you're of that intellectual camp, then you don't need to count calories. Just switch your dog to a zero-carbohydrate food and feed her as much as her little heart desires (and your pocketbook can manage).

But if you either reject the carbohydrate-insulin model of adiposity altogether or if you're just a "soft" believer, someone who believes that carbohydrates play some kind of outsized-but-not-exclusive role in shaping whether dogs become fat, then at some point in your quest to optimize your dog's body condition you're going to have to count some calories.

Your primary goal will be identifying the number of calories that your dog should consume each day in order to lose or maintain body fat over time. But that won't be your only goal. You'll also be trying to pick a calorie number that doesn't cause any harm. Removing some fat from your dog's body is a great idea, but you don't want to torture her or compromise her other nutritional needs in the process. Starvation is a very real and very unpleasant phenomenon and it's hardly worth helping our dogs lose some body fat if they're going to have to starve in order to do it. If it was, we could just reduce caloric intake to zero and be done with it.

Instead, our ultimate calorie-counting task might be summarized as follows: figure out the number of calories our dogs should consume each day in order to achieve the best body condition possible without suffering and without losing out on any vital nutrition. In other words, we're looking to construct a diet that satisfies each of three elements: (1) loss or maintenance of body fat; (2) minimal suffering; and (3) fulfillment of all other nutritional needs.

Any honest primer on canine calorie-counting must begin with the following disclaimer: the veterinary community has yet to come up with a formula that definitively links a dog's energy requirements with easily measurable variables like body weight, age, and physical activity. As I write these words, there just isn't great agreement among scientific researchers as to how quickly dogs burn calories. Scientists have spent plenty of time studying the subject—there have been at least two dozen studies published since 1990—but the formulas that they've come up with differ dramatically from one to the next. As Dr. Richard Hill wrote in the *Journal of Nutrition* in 2006, at the moment, canine calorie-counting equations "are only an educated guess of the actual energy requirement for an individual animal and may be incorrect by a substantial margin." And, to understand what Dr. Hill means by "a substantial margin," consider how the National Research Council recently described the accuracy of these equations:

> At present, the energy requirements of an individual dog cannot be more than an educated guess and can easily miss the true requirements by 50 percent.

In the end, there are loads of variables that influence the rate at which animals use caloric energy—physical activity, size, diet, climate, age, health status. There's just too much stuff to cram into one tidy little equation. If we want to accurately estimate our dogs' true caloric needs, we'll need a process that accounts for that reality. Fortunately, I think I can articulate one.

Step One: Estimate Baseline Maintenance Needs

Start by choosing whichever of the following equations best describes your dog and his typical daily activity level. (Please note that very different equations are used to calculate the metabolic needs of growing puppies and gestating bitches, but because you shouldn't worry about helping your dog lose body fat at those times, I've chosen not to include them here.) This will be your estimate of your dog's baseline maintenance caloric needs.

BASELINE MAINTENANCE CALORIC NEEDS

Inactive Dogs (little to no daily exercise; minimal pacing or other nervous activity throughout the day)	95 kcal/kgBW$^{0.75}$/day
Active Dogs (regular or semi-regular exercise; stimulated to movement on occasion throughout the day)	130 kcal/kgBW$^{0.75}$/day
Highly Active Dogs (lots of intense daily exercise; constant pacing and other movement throughout the day)	180 Kcal/kg BW$^{0.75}$/day

Figure 7(a).

Example (Step One): Kody weighs 90 pounds (40.82 kilograms). He spends most of his day lounging indoors and doesn't pace or fidget too much, so he is probably best described as an "inactive dog." Accordingly, his daily maintenance baseline is about **1534 kcal/day** *(95 × 40.82kg$^{0.75}$ = 1534).*

Step Two: Factor in Targeted Exercise

It may be the case that your dog performs more physical exercise on some days than others. And she will burn more calories on more-active days than on less-active ones. While there's significant disagreement among researchers as to exactly how quickly exercising dogs burn calories, most of their findings seem to cluster around the following equations:

ENERGY REQUIREMENTS OF EXERCISE

Standing	3 kcal/kgBW/hour
Forward Motion	1.5 kcal/kgBW/km

Figure 7(b).

As you can see, the number of calories burned is a function of distance, not speed. In other words, it takes roughly the same amount of energy to run two miles as it does to walk two miles (all else being equal, running will actually burn slightly fewer calories, because your dog will be on his feet for a shorter length of time). Also note that, when it comes to dogs, exercise often occurs in the form of fetch games or erratic dog-park chase routines, rather than straight-line distance running. So you may have to do a bit of estimation in order to figure out the approximate number of miles your dog covers during your 30-minute morning play routine.

Example (Step Two): Today, Kody and I play fetch for 30 minutes, during which I estimate that he covers 2.0 miles (about 3.2 kilometers). Using the equations above, we can see that he burns about 61 calories (3.0 × 40.82kg × 0.5 hours) by standing instead of lying down during our 30-minute fetch game. In addition, using the equations above, we can see that he burns about 196 calories by running 3.2 kilometers during our game (1.5 × 40.82kg × 3.2km). Thus, the total number of additional calories burned during our 30-minute fetch game would be 61 + 196, or 257 calories. Add this to his usual caloric output of 1534 calories/day (from Step One) and we have a total daily output of about **1791 calories.**

Step Three: Calculate Protein Requirements

Protein-derived compounds are put to a variety of critical uses within a dog—maintaining vital organs, growing skeletal muscles and other new tissues, producing glucose through gluconeogenesis, the list goes on. As you'd probably guess now that you know that wolves tend to consume at least nine pounds of meat a day, protein is an absolutely essential ingredient in a dog's diet. (Indeed, few facts are more clearly established by the scientific literature than this one. It has been 200 years since French physiologist Francois Magendie first demonstrated that diets composed exclusively of sugar (carbohydrate) or olive oil (fat) would not even keep dogs alive.)

For these reasons, it is imperative that your dog ingests a sufficient quantity of protein every day, even if you are attempting to reduce the amount of adipose tissue in her body. According to the *Nutrient Requirements of Dogs and Cats*, a dog's recommended daily allowance of crude protein can be calculated using the following equation:

$$3.28 \text{ grams protein/kgBW}^{0.75}$$

Unlike dietary fats and carbohydrates, which are broken into other compounds and stored within bodily tissues when consumed in excessive quantities, excess amino acids ordinarily are not stored within your dog's body. The waste products of protein metabolism just get filtered out of the blood stream and excreted. Consequently, unlike many other nutrients, the National Research Council has not established a "safe upper limit" for crude protein consumption by dogs. According to the NRC, there's no such thing as "too much protein" for a dog.

Nevertheless, the fact that the waste products of protein metabolism are filtered and excreted by the kidneys seems to be the basis for a stunningly pervasive doggy health myth—the idea that feeding "high protein" foods to dogs raises the likelihood of kidney disease and failure.

This myth has been roundly debunked by more than 30 years' worth of published science. Of particular interest, a 1986 study published in the journal *Kidney International* showed that high levels of dietary protein consumption had no correlation with either renal failure or deterioration of renal function in dogs, even after the subjects had 75% of their kidney mass surgically removed. Even with only a quarter of their original renal capacity, dogs that got more than *half* of their calories from protein for more than four years suffered no ill effects.

In a 1991 review paper published in the *Journal of Nutrition*, Dr. Kenneth C. Bovée of the University of Pennsylvania School of Veterinary Medicine concluded that previous evidence did "not support the hypothesis that feeding a high protein diet had a significant adverse effect on renal function or morphology." Seven years later, Dr. Bovée delivered a paper at the Purina Nutrition Forum entitled "Mythology of Protein Restriction for Dogs with Reduced Renal Function." In the paper, he tracked the pernicious myth all the way back to the 1920s, following it through the emergence of competing theories based upon the unique physiology of rats before analyzing the results of ten separate experimental studies on dogs. His conclusion? "Results of the 10 experimental studies on dogs have failed to provide evidence of the benefit of reduced dietary protein to influence the course of renal failure." The evidence simply does not support the myth.

So why do veterinarians and laypeople alike continue to endorse the idea that copious protein consumption causes or exacerbates kidney disease in dogs? For Dr. Bovée, the answer is simple: Big Kibble is shaping veterinary nutritional dogma. He concluded his impressively erudite paper—which cites Carl Jung, W.B. Yeats, and Mortimer Adler—as follows:

> If we as professionals are uncertain about the facts concerning a controversy, we are likely to put ourselves in someone else's hands who appears to have authority. Power to command this authority is in the hands of commercial advertisements that promote [low-protein foods marketed as treatments for kidney disease] with misleading messages. Marketing is aggressively aimed at veterinarians and owners alike. There is a profit motive for veterinarians to sell these diets. ... The situation can remind us that we are part of an uncritical profession with little review or standards. When scientific proof fails to justify a practice, a false myth may likely live on.

In other words, protein isn't something to be afraid of. Indeed, if you're actively trying to grow your dog's muscles with resistance exercise, she'll need even more dietary protein than her maintenance requirements would otherwise call for. And the same goes for older dogs. In order to slow the accelerating effects of age-related sarcopenia, which, as we've seen, has strong ties to longevity and survival rates in aging dogs, the *Nutrient Requirements of Dogs and Cats* suggests that older dogs consume as much as 50 percent more protein than they would otherwise require. Though precise guidelines have yet to emerge, Dr. Lisa Freeman, likely the world's leading authority on canine sarcopenia, has also suggested that protein intake which exceeds the recommended daily allowances "may be more optimal" for elderly dogs.

Example (Step Three): Kody weighs 90 pounds (40.82 kilograms). Accordingly, he requires **at least 53 grams of crude protein per day** *(3.28 × 40.82kg$^{0.75}$ = 52.97 grams).*

Step Four: Pick Your Starting Caloric Deficit and Plan Your Dog's Daily Menu

In laboratory environments, small animal weight loss is usually effected at a rate of about 1% of body weight per week. In a 2005 paper, Dr. Dottie Laflamme and a colleague reported that a loss of 1% of total body weight per week "supports safe weight loss" in cats. Dr. Laflamme has also used the same rate (1% of total body weight per week) when effectuating weight loss in laboratory-housed dogs. In his book *Chow Hounds*, Dr. Ernie Ward recommends that his readers aim for their pets to lose 3% to 5% of total body weight each month. A rate of 1% to 2% of total body weight per week was also used in canine weight loss studies published in the *Journal of Nutrition* in both 2002 and 2004. While the reasoning underlying these rates wasn't made particularly clear in any of those cases, you can rest assured that, all else being equal, weight loss at a rate of 1% of body weight per week has been widely used by experienced veterinarians.

But a more rapid rate of canine weight loss has also been effectuated in a laboratory setting, with no ill effects reported. In a 2004 study entitled "Rapid Weight Loss with a High-Protein Low-Energy Diet Allows the Recovery of Ideal Body Composition and Insulin Sensitivity in Obese Dogs," researchers cut the total caloric intake of a cohort of Beagles by about 50%, causing weight loss at a rate of 2%-3% of total body weight every week. On average, their obese subjects (who were all fed a restricted number of calories from a high-protein, low-carbohydrate, "complete and balanced" diet) reached their goal weights in about three months. The researchers remarked that their highly restrictive diet "allowed a very satisfactory weight loss in obese dogs, quantitatively and qualitatively." So there's reason to believe that weight loss in excess of 1% per week is probably just fine for a dog too.

Standard calories-in, calories-out math provides that a pound of body fat contains about 3,500 calories worth of metabolic energy. By this logic, daily caloric deficits must be as follows in order to effectuate weight-loss at 1%, 2%, or 3% of body weight per week.

CALCULATING DAILY CALORIC DEFICIT

Body Weight	Targeted Weekly Weight Loss and Needed Daily Caloric Deficit		
	1%/week	2%/week	3%/week
10 lbs.	50 kcal/day	100 kcal/day	150 kcal/day
20 lbs.	100 kcal/day	200 kcal/day	300 kcal/day
30 lbs.	150 kcal/day	300 kcal/day	450 kcal/day
40 lbs.	200 kcal/day	400 kcal/day	600 kcal/day
50 lbs.	250 kcal/day	500 kcal/day	750 kcal/day
60 lbs.	300 kcal/day	600 kcal/day	900 kcal/day
70 lbs.	350 kcal/day	700 kcal/day	1,150 kcal/day
80 lbs.	400 kcal/day	800 kcal/day	1,300 kcal/day
90 lbs.	450 kcal/day	900 kcal/day	1,450 kcal/day
100 lbs.	500 kcal/day	1,000 kcal/day	1,600 kcal/day

Figure 8.

To determine how quickly you want your dogs to lose weight, you must balance two factors: (1) the duration of the weight-loss program and (2) how much you want to challenge your dog. How to balance these factors is not a question that science can answer. You'll have to weigh them for yourself, using your own subjective decision-making process. But bear in mind that the specific food you've chosen will play a part in shaping your decision. If it's a relatively low-protein formula, you may not be able to restrict daily calories very much without dipping below your dog's minimum protein requirement. *Don't do that.* Without sufficient protein, very bad things will happen to your dog's body. If you can't give her enough protein, you'll either need to switch foods or change your chosen caloric deficit.

Once you've chosen a food and a daily caloric deficit that you're happy with, read the calorie information on the food label to determine the volume of food to feed your dog each day. (Remember that all foods, including treats and table scraps, must be factored into the equation.) Once you have the daily food volume figured out, throw a measuring cup in your food bin so you'll know exactly how much your dog should be getting every day. Feeding the correct portion size will be a matter of habit before you know it.

Example (Step Four): I choose to aim for 1% total body weight loss per week with Kody. He currently weighs 90 pounds and my target weight is 85 pounds. That means I'll aim for him to lose 0.9 pounds per week, and try to achieve his goal weight in about 6 weeks. Looking at the chart above, that amounts to a caloric deficit of about 450 calories per day. From Step One and Step Two, I know that his daily energy requirement is about

1791 calories/day. So his new daily caloric intake will be **1341 calories/day** *(1791 - 450 = 1341 calories/day).*

According to its label, 38% of the calories in Kody's food come from protein (on an as-fed basis). The label also shows that the food contains 468 calories/cup. According to these figures, Kody needs to consume **2.86 cups of food per day** *(1341/468 = 2.86 cups per day) during his weight-loss program. Because 38% of these calories come from protein, and because protein provides metabolic energy at a rate of about 3.5 calories per gram, 2.86 cups of food will supply Kody with about* **146 grams of protein per day** *(1341 calories × 0.38 = 510 calories worth of protein per day; 510 calories of protein / 3.5 calories of protein per gram of protein = 145.7 grams of protein). This is well in excess of his daily minimum protein requirement, so we're all good there.*

Accordingly, I calculate that Kody should receive **2.86 cups of food per day** *during his six-week weight-loss program.*

Step Five: Observe and Adjust

According to traditional calories-in, calories-out math, there are a great many variables that influence the rate at which a dog will gain or lose body fat. These include the amount of adipose tissue in the animal's body at any given time. Because this variable will, we hope, be changing throughout the course of your dog's weight-loss program, you will likely need to recalculate his serving sizes as the program progresses. Specifically, you'll probably have to feed him progressively less as you go.

Moreover, as we've already seen, canine calorie counting is notoriously imprecise. Although the equations above are considered state-of-the-art by scientific standards, they're not perfect. They may very well miscalculate your dog's true caloric needs in the first instance.

For both of these reasons, you'd be wise to monitor your dog's weight loss progress and make dietary adjustments as necessary. Checking body weight and BCS every one to four weeks ought to do the trick. But remember to be precise—a little kibble goes a long way.

Adjustment is also necessary once your dog reaches his goal weight. Once you reach the end of the rainbow, you will need to recalculate daily food intake so that your dog maintains his body composition going forward. Congrats in advance.

PRINCIPLE #5:
BE A PARENT, NOT JUST A BEST FRIEND

For most of us, helping our dogs lose weight is easier than actually losing weight ourselves. In our modern world, if we want to get our own bodies lean and keep them that way, we've not only got to make smart decisions, we've got to *execute* them. Opportunities to make unhealthy choices abound. And if resisting temptation was merely a matter of being well-informed then obesity probably wouldn't be "a leading cause of global death." Most fattening foods are devilishly delicious. And reminders of their deliciousness—sights, smells—lay in wait for us around every corner. It takes willpower to do what we know is right.

With our dogs this is a less important issue—weight loss is mostly about owner knowledge. Still, it's not *all* about cold, levelheaded decision-making. Managing impulses and emotions does play a role, if perhaps a limited one, in keeping our dogs healthy.

This is something that anyone raising human children already knows all about. Our kids are more similar to our dogs than we might like to admit. Both are slaves to their emotions and their gut-level impulses, forming desires and making decisions based on short-term benefits, not long-term ramifications. If you share your home with a couple of children, ask yourself if they would voluntarily do things like finish their homework, eat their vegetables, or go to bed early if left to their own devices. Of course they wouldn't. They'd do what feels best in the moment, not what's most likely to work out best in the days, weeks, and months ahead.

Dogs aren't all that different. Like kids, they'll take as much junk food (read: short-run pleasure) as they can get. They just can't grasp the downside that human adults, with our big, rational brains, know is waiting somewhere down the line. And just like with our kids, whose environment is teeming with reminders of all the delicious fast food, soda, candy, and snacks just waiting to be enjoyed, most dogs are well aware of all the doggy junk foods that their masters control. And they know just how to leverage their behaviors in order to manipulate ours.

It's something I'm all too familiar with. My dog Kody is, indeed, a dog. But he's something else too—a pig. He is wholly obsessed with eating. He whirls feverishly when a meal appears on the horizon. He is drawn to everyday household events that raise even a remote prospect of a morsel of food falling to the floor (see me as the face of rejection as he refuses my affections and sits patiently in the kitchen, watching my wife chop carrots). And, of course, he begs.

I'd wager that your dog isn't all that different. He probably loves to eat too. He probably knows that people like you play an important role in influencing what and when he gets to eat. And his behavior has probably been shaped to milk that connection for all it's worth. He's probably at his most disarming when he wants something from you. And you probably feel a little pang of heart-melting emotion whenever he's at it.

So what to do? How do you avoid "loving your dog to death" while still, well, loving your dog? How do we square the fact that it feels good to give our dogs all the delicious food they want with the fact that doing so isn't particularly good for them?

First of all, know that you've got options. There is a list of alternatives to traditional treat-style rewards earlier in this chapter. If you're not willing to work on simply saying no, then you might at least consider making your dog's treats as healthy as possible.

Beyond that, remember that your dog is very much a creature of habit. And just as bad dietary habits can lead to the expectation of junky food rewards, healthy habits can reverse that expectation. If you suddenly remove food rewards from your dog's life, he may be unpleasantly surprised, but he'll get over it in time. I promise.

Another thing to keep in mind when your resolve is tested by your dog's big, sad eyes, is that, as worldly sensations go, there's a big difference between hunger, on the one hand, and cravings for specific foods, on the other. Hunger is a special kind of suffering, a feeling that arises slowly and builds over time, until it becomes so painful and impossible to ignore that it pushes all other feelings and motivations into the experiential periphery. The reason that the sensation of hunger can be so powerful and unpleasant is that the consequences waiting for us if we fail to act upon it are particularly dire. Hunger is the signal that our bodies are not taking in enough of the nutrition that they need to operate. That we are becoming starved. And, as Ancel Keys and friends have already shown us, that isn't a path that anyone (man or dog) wants to go down.

Cravings are different. They arise when we *want* to eat something but, physiologically speaking, don't *need* to eat it. They are commonly triggered or enhanced by sensory stimuli, either direct ones ("betcha' can't eat just one!") or indirect ones ("I hear a person in the kitchen, that means table scraps!"). Your dog's cravings, as we discussed in Chapter Four, are particularly susceptible to manipulation by the folks trying to sell you as much dog food as possible. And, while your dog's desire to consume a highly concentrated bite of hyper-palatable goodness is real in every sense of the word, I think it's fair to say that the kind of suffering experienced when that desire goes unfulfilled is not of the same ground-shaking severity as true hunger. Your begging dog isn't starving, she's just craving something that tastes good.

The last thing to remember about managing begging-induced guilt is the difference between your fur baby's happiness in the short-run and her happiness in the long-run. Just like our human children, our dogs will beg for fattening foods because they can't weigh the delicious benefit of those foods in the short-run against their deadly costs in the long-run. Alas, they're just not smart enough to think it all through.

But you are. Yes, you—just sitting there, processing these big words with your highly evolved, forward-thinking brain. You can educate yourself about what's really in your dog's best interests. You can weigh the evidence. You can craft a plan. You can carry that plan through to fruition. In fact, you're about the only one who can. Your dog certainly isn't going to do it on her own.

I hope that this book, with its emphasis on evidence and scientifically verified truth, will help you. Because, in the end, it's a book designed to help people, not dogs. Now, don't get me wrong—I like dogs! But what's particularly rewarding to me is the idea of helping the *people* to whom those dogs matter so much. Folks like Melissa Tucker, Crystal McClaran, Abby Nelson, my mother, and the millions of other Americans who love their dogs as much as I love mine. Folks just like you. As a reader, I'm grateful for books that reveal things about the world that are both true and valuable. And this book has been my attempt to contribute something truthful and valuable to your relationship with your canine companion.

After all, such relationships—the ones that bind us to our fur babies—are sources of both great joy and great sadness. We grow profoundly attached to our dogs only to watch as they slip away from us just a few years later. My goal with this book has been to give you some of the tools that your big, powerful brain needs to delay that tragedy for as long as possible. I hope you've found it helpful. And I wish you and your dog the longest and happiest of lives together.

EPILOGUE

--

"Philosophers have always tried to show that we are not like other animals, sniffing their way uncertainly through the world. Yet after all the work of Plato and Spinoza, Descartes and Bertrand Russell, we have no more reason than other animals do for believing that the sun will rise tomorrow."

John Gray,
Straw Dogs (2007)

I've already told you the story of the first time I thought my dog was going to die. Now I want to tell you about the second time. It's a much more serious story.

Much had changed in the years between the first time and the second. I resigned my job as an attorney only a short while after stumbling upon the canine obesity epidemic. A few months of feverishly following the research rabbit hole was all that it took to convince me that the epidemic was a vastly underappreciated problem, and that raising awareness about the problem would be a worthy professional pursuit. So, in late 2011, I left my job in order to found a company called Varsity Pets, an organization whose mission it is to end the canine obesity epidemic.

My new gig seemed to be serving Kody and Lucy well. As my understanding of nutrition and adiposity developed over the years, it led my wife and I to completely overhaul their diets. Where once I had fed Kody a "premium" kibble topped off with sugary treats and chews, I now fed him the least starchy dry food on the market, supplemented with raw veggies and some occasional raw, meaty bones. And, since I now worked from home, we had much more time for exercise too. I could make regular progress chipping away at his insatiable appetite for fetch games. And we could spend our free time enjoying long, leisurely walks together.

The changes looked to be paying off. As I've written throughout this book, for my money, the best science effectively says that your dog can never really be "too lean." But Kody may have been pushing it. He had been

240

forged into a solid block of muscle, with veiny forelimbs and a handsome hourglass figure. Most importantly, he seemed to be as happy as he'd ever been—as docile and well-behaved as I could reasonably expect, and regularly doing things that he enjoyed with the people that he loved.

Right up until the second time I was confronted with his mortality.

It was summer, a time of year when the heat of the Utah desert is nearly as oppressive as that which stifles the Las Vegas strip. It only reluctantly permits outdoor activities like baseball games and outdoor barbecues, such as the one we were enjoying on a sunny Saturday afternoon in mid-July. I had woken early to light the smoker, and by the time guests began arriving the pork shoulder had developed a nice, crunchy bark and the intoxicating aromas of burning hickory and slowly cooking meat had settled upon our back yard. Stacy had prepared coleslaw and a summer salad. Some friends had arrived and we were playing yard games under the brilliant summer sun.

Kody was soaking it all in. He had been making the rounds, mopping up affection and coaxing guests into throwing the ball for him, wiggling his stump and showing off. And now he was lying in the shade of an awning, getting some rest and watching all the goings-on. He rose to greet new guests and take in their scents before returning to his shady spot and lying back down. But when a young couple from Stacy's hospital arrived at our back gate just as the afternoon heat was breaking, he tried to get up but did something else instead—he did not get up. He began to stand but promptly pitched over his front legs and toppled to the ground.

I saw it happen. And, at first, it didn't really alarm me. My initial reaction was that he had probably been lying awkwardly on his legs and had managed to accidentally restrict the blood flow and "put them to sleep" (the irony of this phrasing did not strike me until I wrote these words some time later). But other people noticed it too, and they were more worried than I was. They looked to me for a reaction. I went over and sat down on the ground next to the struggling dog. I teased him, expecting the problem to resolve itself quickly: "Oh, what's wrong bud? I think you've got something wrong with your wimpy little legs. *Poor puppy.*" I tussled his ears.

But the problem didn't resolve itself. It got worse.

Within a minute or so he had lost all control of his limbs. If he tried to emerge from a prone position he'd topple over, bashing his shoulder or his head in the process. If I stood over him, looped my hands under his ribcage, strained to pick him up, and straightened the limbs for him, he'd teeter on them for a moment, straight-legged and swaying, before beginning to wobble more dramatically and then collapsing into a heap. He turned his big eyes up at me, unable to understand and desperate for help.

Stacy is a nurse and she works in the intensive-care unit of a major hospital. She managed to stay composed as the gravity of the situation revealed itself. She was the one who immediately located and got on the phone with the nearest emergency veterinary clinic. She was the one asking our guests to give Kody some space. She was the one telling me to comfort the dog, to stay calm and keep him from struggling. And it's a good thing that she was so calm and collected, because I was a mess. My chest was too tight to breathe. I bit my lower lip and couldn't stop flapping my hands. A reel of speculative thoughts spun in my head. Was he bitten by a rattlesnake? Did he drink antifreeze? Weed-killer? A bug bomb?

There were no answers yet as we left for the emergency vet a short time later. I gathered the big dog up in my arms, his formidable musculature now dead weight, like a big sack of potatoes. I carried him out to the Jeep, Stacy put the third row of seats down, and we covered them with a blanket. We laid him on his side and sped off for the clinic.

When we got there we brought him in and laid him down on the tiles in the waiting room. He had stopped struggling, either because he had accepted whatever was happening or because he simply couldn't move at all. He just lay there on his side. He didn't even look around, just fixed his gaze straight up at the ceiling and panted. Then the night crew came to get him. We got him on a cart and they rolled him back into the clinic. Stacy and I sat on hard plastic waiting room chairs and tried to tell each other why everything would be fine.

In time the attending doctor came out. He still didn't know exactly what was wrong. Something, they weren't yet sure what, was interfering with the transmission of nerve signals in Kody's spinal cord. And that had left him paralyzed. He was paralyzed. My dog, the focus of years of research and the careful execution of a detailed nutrition and exercise program, a supposed paragon of bodily fitness, the physical embodiment of all that Varsity Pets stood for, was paralyzed. It didn't seem possible. Didn't seem *fair*. I wanted to explain this all to the vet but couldn't muster the effort to try.

"We don't know that much yet," he said. "Might be temporary, might not. We should keep him overnight and you two should go home and get some rest. We'll give him a big dose of steroids and watch him carefully, see what happens. Sometimes a blast of steroids does a lot of good in cases like these. Call us in the morning—we do a shift change at seven. If he's showing signs of improvement by that point, well, then we'll have good reason to be optimistic."

Stacy drove us home. Most of our friends were still there. They had done the dishes and cleaned up the barbecue. We thanked them and tried to talk down the problem some more. Then they went home. I swallowed some NyQuil and drank some wine. I got into bed. Stacy rubbed my back and I tried to fall asleep.

***

At some point I drifted off. I woke in a drowsy haze early the next morning, before the sun and without an alarm. I lay there in the dark in the first few moments of wakefulness, blissfully un-remembering. Then the memories of the previous day came crashing in and I spent the rest of the morning in a fevered panic. I called the clinic at 7:01. A receptionist answered.

"Hi, I'm Daniel Schulof," I said. I was hunched over on the edge of our bed, my elbows making posts on my thighs, one hand propping up my chin and the other pressing the phone to my ear, a foot tapping spastically. Stacy was standing in the bedroom doorway, listening. "My dog Kody came in last night," I explained. "The doctor told us to call at seven to check on him. This is me calling."

"Okay, one moment." She put me on hold.

A different woman's voice, energetic and assertive, spoke next. "Mister Schulof?"

"Yes."

"Hi," she said. She introduced herself as the doctor who "will be taking care of Kody today." Not "this morning," but "today."

As she spoke I clenched my hand into a fist and pushed my chin into it. I chewed my lower lip. Once she had finished her introduction, my words came rushing out in squished-together sentences. "So how's he doing? They told me that they were going to give him some steroids. We were hoping that he'd be doing better by the morning. Is he?"

She drew a big breath. "Unfortunately, no." I mashed my eyelids closed and pursed my lips. I kicked the wall. "The steroids didn't have the effect that we had hoped for."

"He's not better?" I asked. Stacy flinched in the doorway and crossed her arms.

"No. He's not. He's worse."

***

We returned to the clinic later that day. We were ushered back into the guts of the building, back beyond the offices and the exam rooms, into a big space filled with cages and machines and operating tables. And there he was, in a little enclosure on the edge of the room. They had laid out a bedding of blankets and he was lying on his side looking up at the ceiling, the same resigned self that he had been when we last saw him, when they were rolling him away. The pose diminished him. Usually he liked to lie on one hip with his chest directly under his head, propped up on his forelimbs so that he could monitor his surroundings. He was now only a shadow of that proud, attentive former self. A rectangle had been shaved into one of his forelimbs and a cord was taped there. It was connected to a hanging bag half-filled with a clear fluid.

I tried to put on a good face. "Hi bud!" I exclaimed. It wasn't hard to conjure up my high-pitched baby voice—all I wanted was to cheer him up, to rouse him from this ridiculous funk, and the baby voice never failed. But he didn't move his head or try to gather his legs up under himself. He didn't even wag his stump, this being perhaps the first time that a gleeful burst of baby voice had failed to elicit that particular response. But he did roll his eyes and look toward the sound of my voice. I clutched at that.

An orderly opened the gate to the enclosure and we sat down on the blankets next to him. We stroked him for a while. He even felt diminished. He was still panting, his tongue a big, pink slug half-emerged from his mouth. We stroked him some more.

In time an orderly took us away and brought us to an exam room where we met with the clinic's chief surgeon, a man named Paul Morgan. Dr. Morgan was a big, powerfully built man with a kind face. Veins spiderwebbed down his tanned forearms and his feet were clad in the kind of flat-bottomed neon shoes popular with CrossFitters and powerlifters. He sat with his big shoulders squared to us and spoke gently but frankly.

"Your dog is paralyzed." He let the word hang in the little room for a moment. "He has no control whatsoever over three of his four limbs, and only minimal control over the fourth. In two of the four limbs he has no pain sensation either. The other two, a little bit."

"So he's not in pain?" I asked.

"Right. None whatsoever."

Stacy and I exchanged a glance.

Dr. Morgan went on. "So, conceptually, what we're dealing with is something disrupting the transmission of nerve signals through the spinal cord. For one reason or another, the signals—the ones that register pain and produce movement—they aren't making it through. The disruption is in the cervical vertebrae," he pointed to his own neck, "maybe C3, C4. High enough where function in all four limbs is jeopardized.

"As far as I can see, there are three possible causes. We don't currently know which one it is and without additional testing we aren't going to know for sure. But we can make a pretty good guess. A diagnosis by elimination.

"The first possibility," he began ticking them off on his fingers, "is cancer." I must have gasped because Dr. Morgan reached out and placed a steadying hand on my knee. "Look, it's part of the conversation but it's unlikely. The onset was too quick. With cancer the symptoms tend to progress over time. As the tumor grows it interferes more and more with nerve transmission and the symptoms get worse and worse. That's not what you saw, right?"

We shook our heads.

"Okay. So we'll call cancer 'unlikely' for now. Next possibility," he raised a second finger, "is a traumatic injury, something like a slipped disc or a broken vertebra. Also part of the conversation but also somewhat unlikely, because—"

"Because there wasn't any kind of trauma," I interrupted. "He's a muscle-head. It would take a hell of a lot of force to traumatize his body. And it's not like he got hit by a car or something. He was just lying there, and then..." I trailed off, making vague gestures with my hands.

Dr. Morgan nodded. "Right," he said. "He didn't cry out, didn't fall over, wasn't hit by anything. So we'll call that one 'unlikely' too. More likely than cancer but still not likely.

"The last possibility," he said, extending a third finger, "is what I'd say is the most likely culprit, given what we know at this point. A fibrocartilaginous embolism."

"A what?"

He said it again, slower this time, drawing out each of the eight syllables in the word fibrocartilaginous. "Quite a mouthful, right? We usually just say FCE. Are you familiar?"

We shook our heads again.

"Most folks aren't. They're rare. They occur when the soft disc tissue that separates one vertebrae from another bursts and the material inside leaks out, gets into the vasculature and blocks blood flow to an area of the spine. It's sort of like a stroke, but in the spine, not in the brain. For one reason or another, and, frankly, it's really not well-understood *why* or even *how* this happens, the cartilaginous disc tissue finds its way into the vasculature surrounding the spinal cord. The embolism blocks blood flow to the spine and, boom, there's your disruption."

This was not something we had considered. I had never even heard of an FCE. And, more surprisingly, Stacy hadn't either. In all her years working in ICUs she had never seen a single case, and hadn't learned about them in nursing school either. Dr. Morgan nodded patiently and explained that FCEs almost never occur in humans. They were much more common in large dogs, like Rottweilers.

"Now, if it is an FCE then the good news is it's not going to get any worse. What you see now is as bad as it's going to get. But the bad news is that in many cases it doesn't get any better either. Sometimes you see a full recovery, sometimes partial—regain a little movement in two of the legs, walk with a limp, something like that—and sometimes no recovery at all. We've got about a one-month window. Wherever he's at then, that's probably where he's gonna stay."

"So what happens if he doesn't recover?" I asked.

Dr. Morgan shrugged his big shoulders. "That'll be up to you. The reality is that you'll have a hundred-pound dog who can't really eat on his own, can't urinate or defecate on his own, and can no longer do any of the things that he used to enjoy. Is that a life worth living for the dog? Is it one you can handle as an owner? I can't answer those questions. But, in my experience, when dogs don't recover most owners choose to euthanize."

***

We took him home that day. I carried the potato sack back out to the Jeep and laid him down on the third row of seats. He didn't lift his head, just rested it there and pointed his sad eyes straight ahead, his new signature pose. I'm sure the whole situation must have struck him as profoundly bizarre, being such a sudden and dramatic change to everything he had come to know about life. It would be an exercise in speculation to comment on whether he felt nostalgic or wistful or even worried, but surely the whole thing must have been confusing and unpleasant.

It most certainly was for me. I left the clinic feeling lost, unsure of what the future held in store for us. Would he recover? Would I be able to care for him if he didn't? Would he even want to go on living? And how would this all impact my work—could I keep beating my chest about exercise and fitness without my muse? Would anyone even listen to what I had to say knowing that this had happened to my own dog?

But those were questions that could only be answered in time. So I steeled myself against the uncertainty and gave up looking for answers. I reached instead for a different kind of comfort, the comfort that comes from finding solutions. I was scared and I was lost and I wanted nothing more than something that would just make it better. So I drove to a place where solutions to pet-related problems are plentiful. Where the antidote to whatever ails your dog is just an aisle or two away. A place where legions of polite, well-dressed folks wait eagerly, ready to tell you precisely what you need to buy in order to improve your dog's life. I went to PetCo.

We left Kody in the car and spent the better part of an hour in the store. When we emerged I was pushing a buggy full of new wares. The strangest and most promising item was one that a clerk and I had settled upon after some discussion about the challenges posed by helping a 100-pound dog urinate when he couldn't even stand up on his own. It was a canine life preserver, neon yellow and designed to strap around a dog's chest, with a handle on top. The handle was for pulling dogs out of the water from above, like you'd do if you were floating beside a swimming dog in a low boat. But in our case the handle would be used, in theory, to help me hold Kody up while he did his outdoor business. It would minimize the amount of time that I'd need to spend bent over with my arms under his ribs, a pose which I felt was sure to give me a serious spinal injury of my own soon enough.

There were other items too. Waterproof tarps, purchased to limit the damage that any indoor accidents might cause. Blankets and bedding for building the new den in which he would be spending most of his time for the foreseeable future. And a half-dozen or so new toys, tugs and squeakers and fuzzies, bought just because we hoped they might cheer him up a little.

We brought it all home and I made a little den in my office. The bottom layer was a dog bed, one rimmed with arms that he could prop his chin on. On top of that were several layers of blankets. Then there were the tarps. And then, when it was all made-up and ready for him, the dog himself. I carried him in, kicked open the door to my office and laid him down on the bed in his pitiful new signature pose, like a perverse caricature of a groom carrying his new wife across the threshold of their first home. The dog looked up at me, his expression confused and pitiful and helpless. I looked down at him, feeling mostly the same.

I stroked him and told him he was a good boy. Then I sat down at my desk, fired up PubMed, and got to work learning everything that the veterinary medical community knows about canine FCEs. I wanted to know why these scary events happened. I wanted to know how they worked. And, more than anything, I wanted to know how to fix them—how to maximize my dog's chances of making a successful recovery.

I learned a lot that afternoon. As with many medical issues involving small animals, there is a woeful lack of high-quality, published research about FCEs. What studies do exist include statements like "controversies exist about the pathophysiology of the process, and the exact mechanism is still poorly understood." So I just resigned myself to doing the best that I could to understand everything the veterinary medical community actually *does* know about FCEs and how to fix them.

The first thing I looked into was the recovery rate. What studies there were weren't all that encouraging. They suggested that somewhere between 16% and 42% of all canine FCE victims simply don't recover. A wide range, but one that didn't exactly fill me with confidence. My paralyzed dog had a serious chance of never recovering his limb function. I didn't want to think too deeply about what that could mean for us. About how it would look to carry a 100-pound dog outside and hold his heavy body up day after day for the rest of his life. It seemed a bridge too far—if not for me then certainly for Stacy, who was probably incapable of carrying him outside even once. I didn't want to admit it, but I could understand why the owners of many paralyzed dogs decide to euthanize their best friends.

But another study offered some hope. It was published in 2003 in the *Journal of Small Animal Practice* and it was focused on recovery from FCEs— how recovery worked, what helped it along, what didn't. Its most basic conclusion was that a rigorous physical therapy program, begun as soon as possible after the event and carried out as swiftly and regularly as could be managed, helped to improve the chances of recovery dramatically. Apparently, regular activities like limb massage, stretching, joint rotation, and simple bodily movements could teach a dog to "remember" what his limbs felt like. The use of sophisticated rehabilitation technologies like hydrotherapy could speed the process up even more. Ultimately, over time, some canine FCE victims could "re-learn" what it felt like to stand on their own. To walk, even run.

It was while reading this study that I noticed Kody beginning to fret. He lifted his head a bit and looked up at me. He strained his neck against the arms of the bed and made what looked like attempts to prop himself up on the crown of his head. He seemed to be trying to use the one body part that was still within his physical control to push himself back to his feet. He didn't make much progress and soon gave up, flopped his head back down, and began panting, his rib cage rising and falling with rapid, shallow breaths. Dr. Morgan had warned us about this. This was Kody telling me that he needed to do his outdoor business.

I got up, bent over the dog, and gathered him up in my arms. I tried to lift with my legs and not with my back. He was more resistant to my touch than he had been back at the clinic, panting and struggling in what mild ways he could. When I had him up in my arms I reached out a foot to hook the doorknob. We'd need to pass through two doorways—doors which, dammit, I hadn't thought to open before I'd actually gathered him up—and down a steep flight of stairs before reaching the back yard. It was going to be a challenge. I tried to psyche myself up: *I can do this, we can do this.*

That's when I felt warmth beginning to spread across my shirt. It was liquid and it was copious and for one horrible moment I thought that it was blood. That the fragile dog had been ripped open by my effort to gather him up and that he was now spilling his inner self out onto his master. But then I smelled the stink of ammonia. It seemed that Kody's urge to urinate had passed from pressing to uncontrollable. The big potato sack was soaking me with pee.

I hooked the doorknob with an outstretched foot and flung it inward toward us. Urine poured down my shirt and rained onto the floor of the office. I scampered out into the hall, nearly slipping on the wet tiles. A domestic obstacle course separated us from the backyard and Kody would surely be done with his business by the time we navigated it. So instead I turned right and barged through the bathroom door.

I used a toe to flick open the toilet seat and then managed a clumsy step over the pot. I squatted down over it and lowered the two of us down towards the rim. Somehow I managed not to drop the poor dog as I repositioned him in my arms, the steady stream of urine splashing all about the tiny room. We jostled and tinkered and adjusted, trying to aim the arc of the delicate stream directly into the pot. Eventually we managed to get it right and I heard the flow begin to splash into the toilet water somewhere below. I looked at the strange image in the bathroom mirror. It showed a man awkwardly straddling a toilet bowl, soaked in piss and straining to hold up a big black dog, one panting and laboring and wearing a look of complete and utter shame.

***

That was how the tarps failed in their very first opportunity to help my dog. So that evening, when his need to relieve himself arose again, we tried the life preserver instead. I strapped the vest around his belly, rolling his body one way and then the other in order to make room for the straps. Then I buckled it, cinched it up tight, gathered him up in my arms, and struggled out toward the yard. We slowly navigated the doorways and the steep flight of stairs and finally made it out into the cool night air.

We found a suitable patch of grass and I bent down over him, cradling his bulk in the crotch of one elbow while delicately placing each of his four legs into what looked like a normal standing position with my free hand. Then, before releasing him from the grip of the supporting arm, I took hold of the handle. With the vest strapped around his body the strap was positioned squarely above his spine, right in his center of gravity. I took a deep breath then released him from the arm-cradle and let his weight sag against the vest, quickly getting my other hand around the handle too. I stood up and straightened my back. The contraption held. Kody dangled in the harness, his limp and lifeless paws hovering in the grass but bearing none of his considerable bulk. For my part, it was a pose I could hold without too much discomfort, my back straight and flat and my arms pulled downwards into the shape of a V, bearing the load somewhat like a weightlifter with a barbell hanging in his grip. The vest was probably too small and it certainly looked ridiculous—suspended in the vest, the dog called to mind the ribbon-trussed sheep in the Brooks Brothers logo—but I was starting to feel like it just might do the trick anyways.

"Go on. Go pee, buddy," I urged gently.

He seemed to be looking around and considering this idea. I grew optimistic, standing there in the dark, not just that urination was imminent but that this McGyver-style contraption might actually do the trick. That I might have purchased the solution to our problem. That the pet products industry might have helped me fix a real and serious issue for my dog. And then the handle broke.

It snapped at one of the two contact points where it was stitched to the spine of webbing that ran down the center of the vest. It broke cleanly and suddenly, making a popping sound. With nothing to support his weight, Kody immediately crashed to the ground, expelling what air had been in his lungs in a groan as he collapsed into the grass. He lay there motionless, limbs bent under his body in strange angles, chin resting in the deep grass, a bag of bones clad in a ridiculous yellow vest.

The soft grass probably saved him from orthopedic injuries. He was shamed, again, but otherwise didn't seem to be any worse for the wear. And after stripping the vest off and throwing it away I even managed to coax another urination out of him. But it wasn't easy. I had to bend down over him, straining my back muscles and supporting his full weight in my arms as we moved around the yard awkwardly. Afterwards I carried him back to his bed and fed him from a dish that was low enough so that he could just manage to angle his snout down into it. He licked the bowl and burped. Then we rested, he in his feeble new signature pose and me seated at my desk, my back aching.

Before turning in, I looked back through the FCE papers I'd collected that day. The last thing I read before heading off to bed was one of the closing lines of the 2003 *Journal of Small Animal Practice* study:

> Active nursing and intensive and early physiotherapy should be applied in as many cases of suspected fibrocartilaginous embolism as possible, as the authors are convinced that this plays a crucial role in the positive outcome of the disease.

The lines were still in my head when we began his therapy program the next morning. Unlike sufferers of orthopedic injuries, FCE victims don't have to wait out lengthy healing processes before beginning rehabilitation. There's no fractured bone that needs time to fuse, no pain that needs to subside. Patients can get started right away. Indeed, in cases where physical therapy is used to rehabilitate FCE victims, that is usually exactly what happens. The dogs that recovered so well on intensive therapy programs in the *Journal of Small Animal Practice* study all got started 24 to 48 hours after their injuries.

Kody's first session of physical therapy took place about 40 hours after his own FCE. We worked in my office and we kept it light—ten minutes of stretching, ten cycles of forward joint rotation, ten backwards, and maybe five minutes of massage. There was no real program to speak of, just my general intention of subjecting him to four sessions of movement a day. We'd do as much or as little as he was able, but we'd always aim for a little bit more than we had done the last time. And that was it.

The first day's sessions, conducted on my office floor during work breaks, were uneventful. He was still nothing but a shade of his former self— his rapidly atrophying muscles seemed almost hollow to my touch and I powered all the movement. Still, movement there was. And by the start of the second day there was even some joy. For though Kody's legs were limp and lifeless, his strong jaws still worked just fine and his play drive still burned brightly. So we added five minutes of prone-position tug games to the end of our sessions. And he may not have been as forceful as he once was, but he was still every bit as fierce—growling at the toy and gnashing his teeth, huffing and puffing and having an altogether great time. He dropped the tug when I cued him to "drop it" and grabbed it up again when I cued him to "take it." When I walked away with the toy at the end of the session, his wide, focused eyes rolled to follow me, practically begging his body to come along with them.

By day three we had moved beyond his pitiful signature pose. I'd set him up like the Sphinx, with his forelimbs stretched out in front of him. Then we'd play our tug games that way, so he could work on stabilizing himself. Sometimes he'd lose his balance and roll over onto his side again. But no problem, I'd just roll him back up again and we'd carry on. He tugged so enthusiastically that by the time it was over he was panting.

His enthusiastic play drive also allowed us to work scaled-down fetch games into our routine. I'd prop him in the Sphinx pose, place a tennis ball a distance in front of his snout, prompt him to "take it," and then let him do his best. Sometimes it was further away then he could manage. In those cases he'd struggle for a while then come to a stop, looking up to me for some kind of assistance. But most of the time he'd make it, and I'd choke back tears as he belly-crawled to the ball and gathered it up in his mouth, proud as ever.

By day four we had taken it outside and he was rolling up and righting himself without my assistance. By day five he was standing unsupported. And by day six, just the first weekend after a life-threatening fibrocartilaginous embolism had crippled him, Kody was standing up, stumbling 30 feet across our yard, and moving his bowels, all on his own. Stacy and I literally wept with joy as we watched.

***

The dog's recovery continued apace over the next few weeks, aided by a few sessions of exercise every day and even some day trips to a fancy canine rehabilitation center. By the time it was complete he was, functionally speaking, as good as new. He was running again, chasing tennis balls to exhaustion and accompanying me on hikes up in the Wastach Range. He was even doing jumping exercises and pouring himself eagerly into some of the other muscle-building activities that he had enjoyed so much before his FCE. Some of his musculature had atrophied during his period of inactivity but otherwise the terrifying event had been reduced to nothing more than a minor limp, one that remains with him to this day but usually goes unnoticed unless you're looking for it. It's really nothing more than a minor cosmetic blemish anyway. A beauty mark, if you will. It might ensure that he doesn't win any ribbons in the conformation ring, but it does nothing to diminish him as a pet or as a happy, healthy representative of his species. In both of those regards, he's right as rain again.

I took him out to see Dr. Morgan exactly one month after the FCE occurred, on the day that marked the supposed closing of the recovery window. We rode to the clinic in the Jeep, just as we had on the night of the accident. Only this time Kody wasn't lying in his prone and diminished pose. He was standing with his head out the window, scenting the breeze and smiling. When we reached the clinic he bounded down out of the Jeep all on his own. He even pulled on his leash a little as we made our way across the parking lot.

When Dr. Morgan came out to see us his eyes lit up and a big, goofy grin spread across his face. Kody ran to him, his body wiggling with enthusiasm and his stump wagging excitedly. "Oh wow! Look at you!" the big veterinarian declared as he bent down to greet the dog. Some of the others who had cared for him during his first visit to the clinic came out to see him too. They gathered around, taking turns petting him and making baby voices. All of us, dogs and humans alike, were overjoyed.

Chatting with me later, Dr. Morgan described Kody's recovery from his FCE as "off-the-charts" and "as good as anyone could ever have expected." If he didn't exactly beat the odds—a majority of canine FCE victims recover at least some limb function—he certainly stared some truly life-or-death consequences in the eye and then vanquished them. His recovery was an unqualified success story.

So why did it go so well? Every outcome is the product of a multiplicity of causes, so you reduce it to a simple cause-and-effect story at your own peril. And you could spin this particular story any number of ways. You could say that Kody was lucky to live with a human who worked from home and was physically strong enough to carry him outside (or hold him over a toilet bowl). You could say that it was a good thing that he had so much innate play drive, because it made him an ideal therapy patient, one easily motivated and always eager for physical activity. Or you could say that it was a good thing that he was young and healthy and muscular and fit going into the freak event.

They're all true to some degree but none of them is the version I like the most. Corny or not, the version of the story I like best is the one where science is the hero. And not the popular notion of science either—not eggheads with fancy gadgets having opaque, jargon-laced conversations. Science as a process. One that, in its capacity to shed light on hard-to-see truth, is both more mundane and infinitely more valuable than whatever the characters on *The Big Bang Theory* are going on about.

It's that deceptively simple process that revealed the importance of immediate and intensive physical therapy to recovery from FCE-induced paralysis. It's what allowed me, a guy with no previous experience with the subject, to come to understand and appreciate that importance. It's what led Kody and I to start our physical therapy work so soon after his FCE. And it very well might be the thing that saved his life. (Whether it was or not, I can state with categorical certainty that it wasn't all the junk I bought at PetCo that did the trick.)

And, of course, science isn't just the hero of Kody's little story. It's the hero of this book too. Because it is science that taught us that being fat is a lot like having an FCE—both are horrible for a dog's health, both can shorten lives that are too short in the first instance. But unlike an embolism that reduces a stout Rottweiler to a bag of bones in a matter of seconds, the effects of adiposity develop insidiously. They operate under the surface, they're hard to appreciate, and they're easy to overlook—just ask the 40 million Americans whose beloved fur babies are effectively smoking a pack a day. Still, because of science—the best method ever devised for revealing hard-to-see truths—we know that those effects are out there. And through science we can be smart about trying to avoid them.

This book has been my attempt to summarize what I believe science has taught us about the health dangers faced by fat dogs. Our understanding of this phenomenon remains imperfect, riddled with holes that will only be filled by future experimentation. And as our understanding changes, as smart folks push back against the conclusions reached here and as other books like this one are written, we'll gradually get better and better at making good decisions for our dogs. Better at rising above the torrent of emotional advertisements and misinformation that flows out of the business side of pet ownership.

Still, it's unlikely that our understanding of adiposity will ever be able to provide us with anything resembling a guarantee. No matter how careful we are, some lean, healthy dogs are still going to die young. I know because mine almost did. But the better our understanding gets, the better we will all become at stacking the odds in favor of our short-lived canine companions. The better we'll all get at making the best decisions we can on their behalf. And, if he could reflect on the matter for a minute and articulate his thoughts in a way that I could comprehend, that is about all that I think my dog would ask out of his big-brained human companion.

ACKNOWLEDGEMENTS

--

TO MY KNOWLEDGE, James Baldwin never published his own work. But he aptly summarized an important aspect of the self-publishing experience when he wrote "beyond talent lie all the usual words: discipline, love, luck, but most of all, endurance."

Writing a book is a laborious enterprise. All the more so when you're striving for a high level of intellectual rigor. And even more so when you're doing most of the work—research, writing, fact-checking, illustrations, marketing—all by yourself. Working on this book was, in one way or another, my full-time job for several years. It was hard work but the work was often enjoyable; it wouldn't really be fair to call it an exercise in endurance.

At least not for me.

But I was only able to write the thing because of the immense sacrifices that others made on my behalf. If writing the book was invigorating and exciting for me, it was a grueling test of endurance for many of the people I share my life with. Because, while I was working on it, I was a truly lousy husband, son, brother, friend, and CEO.

So, to Mike D'Amico, Nate Mostow, Steve Mize, Carrie, Mom, Ginny, Bill, Mike, and, far more than anyone else, Stacy: thank you. Thank you for your patience, for your support, for your faith in me. I love you all and I hope I can someday repay you for allowing me to write this book. And I hope the book makes you proud.

I'm also grateful for the phenomenal Rebecca Wilson and Caroline Ailanthus, whose careful and creative editorial work would be a bargain at ten times their going rates. For Linda Konner, who knew a first-time author like me wouldn't be able to sell a first-time book concept like this one, and who was willing to pour her heart into it nonetheless. For Jess Downer, Dan Gallery, Pete Hannon, Will Becker, Dainna Stelmach, Melissa Tucker, Aaron Jeffries, Gerard Kiernan, and Nils Parker, for taking the time to read and review early drafts of the book. For Pat and Peggy Paulus, Bobby Corliss, Terry Stemple, Richard Maudsley, and everyone else at Varsity Pets, for patiently holding down the fort while I followed the rabbit hole. And for Dan Stahler, Abby Nelson, Rick McIntyre, Mike Jimenez, Gary Taubes, Chris Kresser, Patrick Vlaskovitz, Rolf Peterson, Melissa Tucker, Steve Beckerman, Julie Churchill, Dorothy Laflamme, Alexander German, Victoria Stilwell, Kyra Sundance, Crystal McClaran, and everyone else who lent their time and expertise to helping me understand why America's dogs are dying from an epidemic of obesity.

Last but not least, there are a few dogs that deserve some special recognition. I hope by this point I've already made clear how grateful I am for Kody and Lucy. But I'd also like to thank all the dogs whose owners donated to this book's IndieGoGo fundraising campaign, once upon a time. The book simply wouldn't have been possible without generous contributions from the following adorable benefactors:

Chato, Max, Bronx, and Haley.
© 2016 Everett Alvarez.

Button.
© 2016 Allie Stone.

Winter and Angel.
© 2016 Cindy Ahn.

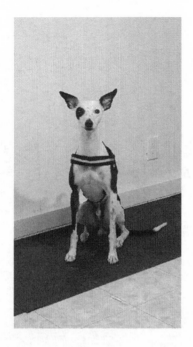

Squint.
© 2016 Tatum Love.

Ollie.
© 2016 Samantha Stewart.

Wendy.
© 2016 Sandi Means.

Bear and Molly.
© 2016 Alison Elter.

Waffles.
© 2016 Christina Mastor.

© 2016 Amelia Hastings.

Elvis.
© 2016 Fawna Bough.

Rooney and Brooklyn.
© 2016 Jennifer Parks.

Bubba and Georgia Belle.
© 2016 Marie Moy.

Gabriel.
© 2016 Kris Springer.

Shadow.
© 2016 Kris Springer.

Jake.
© 2016 Allison DeFer

Otis.
© 2016 Heather Rayburn

Petey.
© 2016 Corine Brosseau.

ACKNOWLEDGEMENTS

Sophia.
© *2016 Ramona Watras.*

SELECTED BIBLIOGRAPHY

--

Adams, V.J., Evans, K.M., Sampson, J., and Wood, J.L. 2010. "Methods and Mortality Results of a Health Survey of Purebred Dogs in the U.K." *Journal of Small Animal Practice*. 51(10):512–24.

Allan, S. 2012. "Leading the Charge in Leptin Research: An Interview with Jeffrey Friedman." *Disease Models & Mechanisms*. 5(5):576–79.

Allison, D.B., et al. 1997. "Hypothesis Concerning the U-Shaped Relation Between Body Mass Index and Mortality." *American Journal of Epidemiology*. 146(4):339–49.

Allison, D.B., et al. 2002. "Differential Associations of Body Mass Index and Adiposity with All-Cause Mortality Among Men in the First and Second National Health and Nutrition Examination Surveys (NHANES I and NHANES II) Follow-Up Studies." *International Journal of Obesity and Related Metabolic Disorders*. 26(3):410–16.

Altmann, J., Schoeller, D., Altmann, S.A., Muruthi, P., and Sapolsky, R. 1993. "Body Size and Fatness of Free-Living Baboons Reflect Food Availability and Activity Levels." *American Journal of Primatology*. 30(2):149–61.

Anker, S.D., et al. 1997. "Wasting as Independent Risk Factor for Mortality in Chronic Heart Failure." *Lancet*. 349(9058):1050–53.

Apple, S. "Why Are We So Fat? The Multimillion-Dollar Scientific Quest to Find Out." *Wired*. Aug. 19, 2014.

Archer, J. 1997. "Why Do People Love Their Pets?" *Evolution and Human Behavior*. 18(4):237–59.

Argenzio, R.A. 1989. "Secretory Functions of the Gastrointestinal Tract." In *Dukes' Physiology of Domestic Animals* (10th ed.). Swenson, M.J., ed. Ithaca, NY: Cornell University Press.

Artero, E.G., et al. 2011. "A Prospective Study of Muscular Strength and Mortality in Men With Hypertension." *Journal of the American College of Cardiology*. 57(18):1831–37.

Association of American Feed Control Officials Incorporated. 2016. *2016 Official Publication*. Champaign, IL: FASS Inc.

Astwood, E.B. 1962. "A Heritage of Corpulence." *Endocrinology*. 71:337–41.

Atkinson, F.S., et al. 2008. "International Table of Glycemic Index and Glycemic Load Values: 2008." *Diabetes Care*. 31(12):2281–83.

Axelsson, E., Ratnakumar, A., Arendt, M., Maqbool, K. Webster, M.T., Perloski, M., Liberg, O., Arnmeo, J.M., Hedhammer, A., Lindblad-Toh, K. 2013. "The Genomic Signature of Dog Domestication Reveals Adaptation to a Starch-Rich Diet." *Nature*. 495:360–64.

Ayres, B.D. "Families Learning of 39 Cultists Who Died Willingly." *New York Times*. Mar. 29, 1997.

Bach, J.F., et al. 2007. "Association of Expiratory Airway Dysfunction with Marked Obesity in Healthy Adult Dogs." *American Journal of Veterinary Research*. 68(6):670–75.

Baez, J.L., et al. 2007. "A Prospective Investigation of the Prevalence and Prognostic Significance of Weight Loss and Changes in Body Condition in Feline Cancer Patients." *Journal of Feline Medical Surgery*. 9(5):411–17.

Bailor, J. 2013. *The Calorie Myth: How to Eat More, Exercise Less, Lose Weight, and Live Better*. New York, NY: Harper Collins.

Bankhead, C. 1999. "Debate Swirls Around the Science of Epidemiology." *Journal of the National Cancer Institute*. 91(22): 1914–16.

Banks, W.A., Altmann, J., Sapolsky, R.M., Philips-Conroy, J.E., and Morley, J.E. 2003. "Serum Leptin Levels as a Marker for a Syndrome X-Like Condition in Wild Baboons." *Journal of Clinical Endocrinology & Metabolism*. 88(3):1234–40.

Banting, W. 2005. *Letter on Corpulence, Addressed to the Public* (4th ed.). London, U.K.: Harrison (republished, New York, NY: Cosimo Publishing) (originally published 1864).

Barrett, D. 2007. *Waistland: The (R)evolutionary Science Behind Our Weight and Fitness Craze.* New York, NY: W.W. Norton & Co.

Barrett, P.M. "Dog Food Fight! Purina Says Blue Buffalo 'Built on Lies.'" *Bloomberg Businessweek.* July 25, 2014.

Barrett, P.M. "In Court Fight Over Dog Food, Poultry By-Product Plays the Role of Smoking Gun." *Bloomberg Businessweek.* Nov. 24, 2014.

Barzilai, N. and Gupta, G. 1999. "Revisiting the Role of Fat Mass in the Life Extension Induced by Caloric Restriction." *Journals of Gerontology, Series A: Biological Sciences and Medical Sciences.* 54(3):B89–96.

Barzilai, N. and Gabriely, I. 2001. "The Role of Fat Depletion in the Biological Benefits of Caloric Restriction." *Journal of Nutrition.* 131(3):903S–906S.

Baumgartner, R.N., et al. 1998. "Epidemiology of Sarcopenia Among the Elderly in New Mexico." *American Journal of Epidemiology.* 147(8):755–63.

Bayliss, L.E., et al. 1933. "The Excretion of Protein by the Mammalian Kidney." *Journal of Physiology.* 77(4):386–98.

Bazzano, L.A., Hu, T., Reynolds, K., Yao, L., Bunol, C., Liu, Y., Chen, C-S., Klag, M.J., Whelton, P.K., and He, J. 2014. "Effects of Low-Carbohydrate and Low-Fat Diets: A Randomized Trial." *Annals of Internal Medicine.* 161(5):309–18.

Belo, P.S., Rosmos, D.R., and Leveille, G.A. 1976. "Influence of Diet on Glucose Tolerance, on the Rate of Glucose Utilization, and Gluconeogenic Enzyme Activities in the Dog." *Journal of Nutrition.* 106(10):1465–74.

Benthem, L., Mundinger, T.O., and Taborksy, G.J. 2000. "Meal-Induced Insulin Secretion in Dogs is Mediated by Both Branches of the Autonomic Nervous System." *American Journal of Physiology – Endocrinology and Metabolism.* 278(4):E603–E610.

Berridge, K.C. and Kringlebach, M.L. 2008. "Affective Neuroscience of Pleasure: Reward in Humans and Animals." *Psychopharmacology.* 199(3):457–80.

Berry, W. "The Melancholy of Anatomy." *Harper's Magazine.* Feb. 2015.

Berson, S.A. and Yalow, R.S. 1965. "Some Current Controversies in Diabetes Research." *Diabetes.* 14:549–72.

Bierer, T.L. and Bui, L.M. 2004. "High Protein Low-Carbohydrate Diets Enhance Weight Loss in Dogs." *Journal of Nutrition.* 134(8):2087S–89S.

Bigaard, J., et al. 2004. "Body Fat and Fat-Free Mass and All-Cause Mortality." *Obesity Research.* 12(7):1042–49.

Biolo, G. et al. 2002. "Inverse Regulation of Protein Turnover and Amino Acid Transport in Skeletal Muscle of Hypercatabolic Patients." *Journal of Clinical Endocrinology & Metabolism.* 87(7):3378–84.

Black, D., Vora, J., Hayward, M., and Marks, R. 1988. "Measurement of Subcutaneous Fat Thickness with High Frequency Pulsed Ultrasound: Comparisons with a Caliper and a Radiographic Technique." *Clinical Physics and Physiological Measurement.* 9(1):57-64.

Blackburn, H. and Jacobs, D. 2014. "Origins and Evolution of Body Mass Index (BMI): Continuing Saga." *International Journal of Epidemiology.* 43(3):665–69.

Blanchard, G., et al. 2004. "Rapid Weight Loss With a High-Protein Low-Energy Diet Allows the Recovery of Ideal Body Composition and Insulin Sensitivity in Obese Dogs." *Journal of Nutrition.* 134(8):2148S-2150S.

Bodey, A.R. and Mitchell, A.R. 1996. "Epidemiological Study of Blood Pressure in Domestic Dogs." *Journal of Small Animal Practice.* 37:116–25.

Boitani, L. "Wolf Conservation and Recovery." In *Wolves: Behavior, Ecology, and Conservation.* Mech, L.D. and Boitani, L., eds. 2003. Chicago, IL: University of Chicago Press.

Bortz II, W.M. 1982. "Disuse and Aging." *Journal of the American Medical Association.* 248(10):1203–08.

Bovée, K.C. 1991. "Influence of Dietary Protein on Renal Function in Dogs." *Journal of Nutrition.* 121 (11S):128–39.

Bovée, K.C. 1999. "Mythology of Protein Restriction for Dogs with Reduced Renal Function." Supplement to *Compendium on Continuing Education for the Practicing Veterinarian.* 21(11-K):15–20.

Braith, R.W. and Stewart, K.J. 2006. "Resistance Exercise Training – Its Role in the Prevention of Cardiovascular Disease." *Circulation.* 113:2642–50.

Brandt, A. 2009. *The Cigarette Century: The Rise, Fall, and Deadly Persistence of the Product That Defined America.* New York, NY: Basic Books.

Breslow, L. 2006. "Public Health Aspects of Weight Control." Reprinted in *International Journal of Epidemiology.* 35(1):10–12. Originally presented at the Annual Meeting of the Western Branch, American Public Health Association. Denver, CO. June 6, 1952.

Brobeck, J.R. 1946. "Mechanisms of the Development of Obesity in Animals with Hypothalamic Lesions." *Physiological Reviews.* 26(4):541-59.

Brown, P.J. and Konner, M. 1987. "An Anthropological Perspective on Obesity." *Annals of the New York Academy of Sciences.* 499:29–46.

Brownell, K.D. "Get Slim With Higher Taxes." *The New York Times.* Dec. 15, 1994.

Budiansky, S. "The Truth About Dogs." *The Atlantic.* July 1999.

Burns, K. "Calories to Appear on Pet Food Labels." *JAVMA News.* August 1, 2013.

Caballero, B. 2005. "A Nutrition Paradox – Underweight and Obesity in Developing Countries." *New England Journal of Medicine.* 352(15):1514–16.

Carciofi, A.C., Takaskura, F.S., de-Oliveira, L.D., Teshima, E., Jeremias, J.T., Brunette, M.A., and Prada, F. 2008. "Effects of Six Carbohydrate Sources on Dog Diet Digestibility and Post-Prandial Glucose and Insulin Response." *Journal of Animal Physiology and Animal Nutrition.* 92(3):326–336.

Case, L.P., Hayek, M.G., Daristotle, L., and Raasch, M.F. 2011. *Canine and Feline Nutrition – A Resource for Companion Animal Professionals,* Third Edition. Maryland Heights, MO: Mosby, Inc.

Centers for Disease Control and Prevention. 2015. "Current Cigarette Smoking Among Adults – United States, 2005–2014." *Morbidity and Mortality Weekly Report.* 64(44):1233–40.

Chen, P.W. "Getting Good Value in Health Care." *The New York Times.* July 23, 2009.

Cheuvront, S.N. 2003. "The Zone Diet Phenomenon: A Closer Look at the Science Behind the Claims." *Journal of the American College of Nutrition.* 22(1):9–17.

Chieri, R.A., Farina, J.M., Halperin, J., and Basabe, J.C. 1975. "Effect of Cephalic Glucose Infusion on Insulin Secretion." *Diabetologia.* 11(3):175–80.

Chikamune, T., et al. 1995. "Serum Lipid and Lipoprotein Concentrations in Obese Dogs." *Journal of Veterinary Medical Science.* 57(4):595–98.

Chowdhury, R., Warnakula, S., Kunutsor, S., Crowe, F., Ward, H.A., Johnson, L., Franco, O.H., Butterworth, A.S., Forouhi, N.G., Thompson, S.G., Khaw, K.T., Mozaffarian, D., Di Angelantonio, E. 2014. "Association of Dietary, Circulating, and Supplemental Fatty Acids With Coronary Risk: A Systematic Review And Meta-Analysis." *Annals of Internal Medicine.* 160(6):398–406.

Clausen, J.E., ed. 1916. *The Dog's Book of Verse.* Boston, MA: Small, Maynard, and Co.

Cohen, D.A. 2014. *A Big Fat Crisis: The Hidden Forces Behind the Obesity Epidemic—and How We Can End It*. New York, NY: Nation Books.

Conrad, J. 2010. *Heart of Darkness*. London, U.K.: Bibliolis Books, Ltd. (originally published 1902).

Coppinger, R. and Schneider, R. "Evolution of Working Dogs." In *The Domestic Dog: Its Evolution, Behavior, and Interactions With People*. Serpell, J., ed. 1995. Cambridge, UK: Cambridge University Press.

Cordain, L. 1999. "Cereal Grains: Humanity's Double-Edged Sword." *World Review of Nutrition and Dietetics*. 84:19–73.

Cordain, L. 2002. *The Paleo Diet: Lose Weight and Get Healthy by Eating the Food You Were Designed to Eat*. New York, NY: John Wiley & Sons, Inc.

Cordain, L., Miller, J.B., Eaton, S.B., Mann, N., Holt S., and Speth, J.D. 2000. "Plant-Animal Subsistence Ratios and Macronutrient Estimations in Worldwide Hunter-Gatherer Diets." *American Journal of Clinical Nutrition*. 71:682–92.

Coughlin, S.S. 1990. "Recall Bias in Epidemiological Studies." *Journal of Clinical Epidemiology*. 43(1):87–91.

Coussens, L.M. and Werb, Z. 2002. "Inflammation and Cancer." *Nature*. 420(6917):860–67.

Cubaynes, S., MacNulty, D.R., Stahler, D.R., Quimby, K.A., Smith, D.W., and Coulson, T. 2014. "Density-Dependent Intraspecific Aggression Regulates Survival in Northern Yellowstone Wolves (*Canis Lupis*)." *Journal of Animal Ecology*. 83(6):1344–56.

Cupp, C.J., et al. 2008. "The Role of Nutritional Interventions in the Longevity and Maintenance of Long-Term Health in Aging Cats." *International Journal of Applied Research in Veterinary Medicine*. 6(2):69–81.

Cupp, C.J., et al. 2010. "Effect of Diet and Body Composition on Life Span in Aging Cats." In *Proceedings of Nestle Purina Companion Animal Nutrition Summit, Focus on Gerontology*. Clearwater Beach, FL.

Dansinger, M.L., Tatsioni, A., Wong, W.B., Chung, M., and Balk, E.M. 2007. "Meta-Analysis: The Effect of Dietary Counseling for Weight Loss." *The Archives of Internal Medicine.* 147(1):41–50.

Darwin, C. 1869. *The Origin of Species By Means of Natural Selection or the Preservation of Favorable Races in the Struggle for Life* (Fifth British Edition). London, U.K.: John Murray.

Datz, T. "Harvard Serves Up Its Own 'Plate.'" *Harvard Gazette.* Sep. 14, 2011.

Davis, W. 2011. *Wheat Belly.* New York, NY: Rodale, Inc.

de Gonzalez, A.B., et al. 2010. "Body-Mass Index and Mortality Among 1.46 Million White Adults." *New England Journal of Medicine.* 363(23):2211–19.

de-Oliveira, L.D., Carciofi, A.C., Oliveira, M.C.C., Vasconcellos, R.S., Bazolli, R.S., Pereira, G.T., and Prada, F. 2014. "Effects of Six Carbohydrate Sources on Diet Digestibility and Postprandial Glucose and Insulin Responses in Cats." *Journal of Animal Science.* 86(9):2237–46.

de Risio, L., et al. 2010. "Fibrocartilaginous Embolic Myelopathy in Small Animals." *Veterinary Clinics: Small Animal Practice.* 40:859–69.

de Schutter, A., et al. 2014. "Body Composition and Mortality in a Large Cohort with Preserved Ejection Fraction: Untangling the Obesity Paradox." *Mayo Clinic Proceedings.* 89(8):1072–79.

DeJong, C., et al. 2016. "Pharmaceutical Industry-Sponsored Meals and Physician Prescribing Patterns for Medicare Beneficiaries." *JAMA Internal Medicine.* Published online: June 20, 2016. doi:10.1001/jamainternmed.2016.2765.

Denizet-Lewis, B. "Can the Bulldog Be Saved?" *The New York Times Magazine.* Nov. 22, 2011.

Dennett, D.C. 1995. *Darwin's Dangerous Idea: Evolution and the Meanings of Life.* New York, NY: Touchstone.

Dennis, B. "FDA's Anti-Smoking Campaign to Target Teens." *The Washington Post.* Dec. 9, 2013.

Dent, M. "Tim Noakes on Trial." *Runner's World.* April 5, 2016.

Derrell, C.J., Rager, D.R., Crowell-Davis, S., and Evans, D.L. 1997.
"Housing and Exercise of Dogs: Effects on Behavior, Immune
Function, and Cortisol Concentration." *Comparative Medicine.*
47(5):100–10.

des Courtis, X., Wei, A., Kass, P.H., Fascetti, A.J., Graham, J.L., Havel, P.J.,
and Ramsey, J.J. 2015. "Influence of Dietary Protein Levels on
Body Composition and Energy Expenditure in Calorically Restricted
Overweight Cats." *Journal of Animal Physiology and Animal Nutrition.*
99(3):474–82.

Deurenberg, P., et al. 1991. "Body Mass Index as a Measure of Body
Fatness: Age- and Sex-Specific Prediction Formulas." *British
Journal of Nutrition.* 65(2):105–14.

Diamond, J. "The Worst Mistake in the History of the Human Race."
Discover Magazine. May, 1987.

Diamond, J. 2002. "Evolution, Consequences and Future of Plant and
Animal Domestication." *Nature.* 418:700–07.

Diamond, P., and LeBlanc, J. 1988. "A Role for Insulin in Cephalic Phase
of Postprandial Thermogenesis in Dogs." *American Journal of
Physiology -- Endocrinology and Metabolism.* 254(5):E625–E632.

Diez, M., Nguyen, P., Jeusette, I., Devois, C., Istasse, L., and Biourge, V.
2002. "Weight Loss in Obese Dogs: Evaluation of a High-Protein,
Low-Carbohydrate Diet." *Journal of Nutrition.* 132(6):16855–75.

Dillitzer, N., et al. 2011. "Intake of Minerals, Trace Elements and Vitamins in
Bone and Raw Food Rations in Adult Dogs." *British Journal of
Nutrition.* 106(S1):S53–S56.

Dixon, J.B., et al. 2015. "'Obesity Paradox' Misunderstands the Biology of
Optimal Weight Throughout the Life Cycle." *International Journal of
Obesity.* 39:82–84.

Doig, P.A. 1975. "Specialization in Veterinary Medicine---Viewpoint of a
General Practitioner." *Canadian Veterinary Journal.* 16(10):297–
301.

Doll, R. and Hill, A.B. 1950. "Smoking and Carcinoma of the Lung." *British Medical Journal*. 2(4682):739–48.

Drewnowski, A. 1995. "Energy Intake and Sensory Properties of Food." *American Journal of Clinical Nutrition*. 62(5):1081S-85S.

Du Fort, G.G., Newman, S.C., and Bland, R.C. 1993. "Psychiatric Comorbidity and Treatment Seeking: Sources of Selection Bias in the Study of Clinical Populations." *Journal of Nervous & Mental Disease*. 181(8): 467.

Dwan, K., Gamble, C., Williamson, P.R., and Kirkham, J.J. 2013. "Systematic Review of the Empirical Evidence of Study Publication Bias and Outcome Reporting Bias—An Updated Review." *PLoS One*. 8(7):e66844.

Eaton, S.B. and Konner, M. 1985. "Paleolithic Nutrition—A Consideration of its Nature and Current Implications." *New England Journal of Medicine*. 312:283–89.

Eaton, S.B., Eaton III, S.B., and Konner, M. 1997. "Paleolithic Nutrition Revisited: A Twelve-Year Retrospective on its Nature and Implications." *European Journal of Clinical Nutrition*. 51:207–16.

Ebberling, C.B., Swain, J.F., Feldman, H.A., Wong, W.W., Hachey, D.L., Garcia-Lago, E., and Ludwig, D.S. 2012. "Effects of Dietary Composition on Energy Expenditure During Weight-Loss Maintenance." *Journal of the American Medical Association*. 307(24):2627–34.

Eirmann, L.A., et al. 2009. "Comparison of Adipokine Concentrations and Markers of Inflammation in Obese Versus Lean Dogs." *International Journal of Applied Research in Veterinary Medicine*. 7(4):196–205.

Eknoyan, G. 2006. "A History of Obesity, or How What Was Good Became Ugly and Then Bad." *Advances in Chronic Kidney Disease*. 13(4):421–27.

Eknoyan, G. 2008. "Adolphe Quetelet (1796–1874) – the Average Man and Indices of Obesity." *Nephrology Dialysis Transplantation*. 23(1):47–51.

Eldredge, D.M., Carlson, L.D., Carlson, D.G., and Griffin, J.M. 2007. *Dog Owner's Veterinary Handbook*. Hoboken, NJ: Howell Book House.

Ettinger, S.J. and Feldman, E.C, eds. 2010. *Textbook of Veterinary Internal Medicine (Seventh Edition)*. St. Louis, MO: Saunders-Elsevier.

Euromonitor International. 2014. *Passport: Dog Food in the U.S.*

Evans, W.J. and Campbell, W.W. 1993. "Sarcopenia and Age-Related Changes in Body Composition and Functional Capacity." *Journal of Nutrition*. 132(2):465S–68S.

Falecka-Wieczorek, I. and Kaciuba-Uscilko, H. 1984. "Metabolic and Hormonal Responses to Prolonged Physical Exercise in Dogs After a Single Fat-Enriched Meal." *European Journal of Applied Physiology and Occupational Physiology*. 53(3):267–73.

Fascetti, A.J. and Delaney, S.J., eds. 2012. *Applied Veterinary Clinical Nutrition*, First Edition. Ames, IA: John Wiley & Sons, Inc.

Fauber, J. "Drug Research Routinely Suppressed, Study Authors Find." *Milwaukee, Wisconsin Journal Sentinel*. Jan. 3, 2012.

Field, A.E., et al. 2001. "Impact of Overweight on the Risk of Developing Common Chronic Diseases During a 10-Year Period." *Archives of Internal Medicine*. 161(13):1581–86.

Finco, D.R., et al. 1994. "Effects of Aging and Dietary Protein Intake on Uninephrectomized Geriatric Dogs." *American Journal of Veterinary Research*. 55(9):1282–90.

Finn, E., et al. 2010. "The Relationship Between Body Weight, Body Condition, and Survival in Cats with Heart Failure." *Journal of Veterinary Internal Medicine*. 24(6):1369–74.

Finnerman, R.J., ed. 2002. *The Yeats Reader: A Portable Compendium of Poetry, Drama, and Prose*. New York, NY: Scribner Poetry.

Fitzgerland, M. 2012. *Racing Weight: How to Get Lean for Peak Performance*. Boulder, CO: VeloPress.

Fitzgerald, M. 2014. *Diet Cults: The Surprising Fallacy at the Core of Nutrition Fads and a Guide to Healthy Eating for the Rest of Us.* New York, NY: Pegasus Books.

Flegal, K.M., Carroll, M.D., Kuczmarski, R.J., and Johnson, C.L. 1998. "Overweight and Obesity in the United States: Prevalence and Trends, 1960–1994." *International Journal of Obesity.* 22(1):39–47.

Flegal, K.M., Carroll, MD., Ogden, C.L., and Johnson, C.L. 2002. "Prevalence and Trends in Obesity Among Adults, 1999–2000." *Journal of the American Medical Association.* 288(14):1723–27.

Flegal, K.M., Graubard, B.I., Williamson, D.F., Gail, M.H. 2005. "Excess Deaths Associated With Underweight, Overweight, and Obesity." *Journal of the American Medical Association.* 293(15):1861–67.

Flegal, K.M., Carroll, M.D., Ogden, C.L., and Curtin, L.R. 2010. "Prevalence and Trends in Obesity Among US Adults, 1999-2008." *Journal of the American Medical Association.* 303(3):235–41.

Flegal, K.M., Carroll, M.D., Kit, B.K., and Ogden, C.L. 2012. "Prevalence of Obesity and Trends in the Distribution of Body Mass Index Among US Adults, 1999–2010." *Journal of the American Medical Association.* 307(5):491–97.

Flegal, K.M. and Kalantar-Zadeh, K. 2013. "Overweight, Mortality and Survival." *Obesity.* 21(9):1744–45.

Fleming, J.M., Creevy, K.E., and Promislow, D.E.L. 2011. "Mortality in North American Dogs From 1984 to 2004: An Investigation into Age-, Size-, and Breed-Related Causes of Death." *Journal of Veterinary Internal Medicine.* 25:187–98.

Flier, J.S. and Maratos-Flier, E. 2007. "What Fuels Fat?" *Scientific American.* 297:72–81.

Fogel, R.W. 2004. *The Escape From Hunger and Premature Death, 1700-2100.* Cambridge, U.K.: Cambridge University Press.

Fogelholm, M. and Kukkonen-Harjula, K. 2000. "Does Physical Activity Prevent Weight Gain? – A Systematic Review." *Obesity Reviews.* 1(2):95–111.

Food and Agriculture Organization of the United Nations/World Food Programme. 2010. *The State of Food Insecurity in the World – Addressing Food Insecurity in Protracted Crises.* Rome, IT: FAO.

Foster-Powell, K., Holt, S.H.A., and Brand-Miller, J.C. 2002. "International Table of Glycemic Index and Glycemic Load Values." *American Journal of Clinical Nutrition.* 76(1):5–56.

Fox, M.W., Hodgkins, E., and Smart, M.E. 2009. *Not Fit For a Dog! – The Truth About Manufactured Cat and Dog Food.* Fresno, CA: Quill Driver Books.

Freedman, A.H., Gronau, I., Schweizer, R.M., Ortega-Del Vecchyo, D., Han., E., Silva, P.M., et al. 2014. "Genome Sequencing Highlights the Dynamic Early History of Dogs." *PLoS Genetics.* 10(1):e1004016.

Freeman, L.M. 2011. "Cachexia and Sarcopenia: Emerging Syndromes of Importance in Dos and Cats." *Journal of Veterinary Internal Medicine.* 26(1):3–17.

Freeman, L.M., et al. 2013. "Current Knowledge About the Risks and Benefits of Raw Meat-Based Diets for Dogs and Cats." *Journal of the American Veterinary Medical Association.* 243(11):1549–58.

Friedl, K.E., et al. 1994. "Lower Limit of Body Fat in Healthy Active Men." *Journal of Applied Physiology.* 77(2):933–40.

Frisch, R.E. and McArthur, J.W. 1974. "Menstrual Cycles: Fatness as a Determinant of Minimum Weight for Height Necessary for their Maintenance of Onset." *Science.* 185(4155):949–51.

Fritts, S.H., Stephenson, R.O., Hayes, R.D., and Boitani, L. "Wolves and Humans." In *Wolves: Behavior, Ecology, and Conservation.* Mech, L.D. and Boitani, L., eds. 2003. Chicago, IL: University of Chicago Press.

Gabriely, I., et al. 2002. "Removal of Visceral Fat Prevents Insulin Resistance and Glucose Resistance and Glucose Intolerance of Aging – An Adipokine-Mediated Process?" *Diabetes.* 51(10):2951–58.

Gallagher, D., Visser, M., et al. 1996. "How Useful is Body Mass Index for Comparison of Body Fatness Across Age, Sex, and Ethnic Groups?" *American Journal of Epidemiology.* 143(3):228–39.

Gandini, G., et al. 2003. "Fibrocartilaginous Embolism in 75 Dogs: Clinical Findings and Factors Influencing the Recovery Rate." *Journal of Small Animal Practice.* 44:76-80.

Gans, K. 2013. "Google's Most Popular Diet: 2013 Edition." *U.S. News and World Report.* Dec. 26, 2013.

Gardner, C.D., Kiazand, A., Alhassan, S., Kim, S., Stafford, R.S., Balise, R.R., Kraemer, H.C., and King, A.C. 2007. "Comparison of the Atkins, Zone, Ornish, and LEARN Diets for Change in Weight and Related Risk Factors Among Overweight Premenopausal Women." *Journal of the American Medical Association.* 297(9):969–77.

Garrow, J.S. and Summerbell, C.D. 1995. "Meta-Analysis: Effect of Exercise, With or Without Dieting, on the Body Composition of Overweight Subjects." *European Journal of Clinical Nutrition.* 49(1):1–10.

Gately, I. 2001. *Tobacco: A Cultural History of How an Exotic Plant Seduced Civilization.* New York, NY: Grove Press.

Gentry, T.R. and Wade, G.N. 1976. "Androgenic Control of Food Intake and Body Weight in Male Rats." *Journal of Comparative and Physiological Psychology.* 90(1):18–25.

German, A.J. 2006. "The Growing Problem of Obesity in Dogs and Cats." *Journal of Nutrition.* 136(7): 1940S–46S.

German, A.J., Holden, S.L., Moxham, G.L., Holmes, K.L., Hackett, R.M., Rawlings, J.M. 2006. "A Simple, Reliable Tool for Owners to Assess the Body Condition of Their Dog or Cat." *Journal of Nutrition.* 136:2031S–33S.

German, A.J., Ryan, V.H., German, A.C., Wood, I.S., Trayhurn, P. 2010. "Obesity, Its Associated Disorders and the Role of Inflammatory Adipokines in Companion Animals." *Veterinary Journal.* 185:4–9.

Gilmore, C.P. "Taking Exercise to Heart." *New York Times.* Oct. 27, 1977.

Giovino, G.A. 2001. "Epidemiology of Tobacco Use in the United States." *Oncogene.* 21(48):7326–40.

Glickman, L.T., Schofer, F.S., McKee, L.J., Reif, J.S., and Goldschmidt, M.H. 1989. "Epidemiologic Study of Insecticide Exposure, Obesity, Risk of Bladder Cancer in Household Dogs." *Journal of Toxicology and Environmental Health.* 28:407–14.

Goff, S.L., Foody, J.M., Inzucchi, S., Katz, D., Mayne, S.T., and Krumholz, H.M. 2006. "Nutrition and Weight Loss Information in a Popular Diet Book: Is It Fact, Fiction, or Something in Between?" *Journal of General Internal Medicine.* 21(7):769–74.

Goldberg, J. "Westminster Eugenics Show." *National Review.* Feb. 13, 2002.

Goldblatt, P.B., Moore, M.E., and Stunkard, A.J. 1965. "Social Factors in Obesity." *Journal of the American Medical Association.* 192:1039–44.

Grace, F.M., Buchan, D., Kilgore, L., and Baker, J.S. 2013. "The Obesity Paradox? Some Methodological Considerations and Potential Physiological Mechanisms." *Journal of Sports Medicine & Doping Studies.* 3:e133. doi: 10.4172/2161-0673.1000e133.

Graham, P.A., Maskell, I.E., and Nash, A.S. 1994. "Canned High Fiber Diet and Postprandial Glycemia in Dogs With Naturally Occurring Diabetes Mellitus. *Journal of Nutrition.* 124(12):2712S–15S.

Gray, J. 2007. *Straw Dogs: Thoughts on Humans and Other Animals.* New York, NY: Farrar, Straus and Giroux.

Gruberg, L., et al. 2002. "The Impact of Obesity on the Short-Term and Long-Term Outcomes After Percutaneous Coronary Intervention: An Obesity Paradox?" *Journal of the American College of Cardiology.* 39(4):578–84.

Hackmann, T.J. and Spain, J.N. 2010. "Ruminant Ecology and Evolution: Perspectives Useful to Ruminant Livestock Research and Production." *Journal of Dairy Science.* 93(4):1320–34.

Hamilton, D. and Johnson, S., prods. 2002. "Modern Meat." *Frontline.* PBS. WGBH Boston. Berkley, CA. Television.

Hancock, J.E. 2004. *Plant Evolution and the Origin of Crop Species (2nd Edition)*. Cambridge, MA: CABI Publishing.

Hand, M.S., et al., eds. 2000. *Small Animal Clinical Nutrition (4th Edition)*. Topeka, KS: Mark Morris Institute.

Hannah, S.S. 1999. "Role of Dietary Protein in Weight Management." Supplement to *Compendium on Continuing Education for the Practicing Veterinarian*. 21(11-K):32–33.

Harding, P. 2009. *Tinkers*. New York, NY: Bellevue Literary Press.

Harding, W. and Bode, C., eds. 1958. *The Correspondence of Henry David Thoreau*. New York, NY: New York University Press.

Harper, M., O'Connor, R.E., and O'Carroll, R.C. 2011. "Increased Mortality in Parents Bereaved in the First Year of Their Child's Life." *BMJ Supportive & Palliative Care*. 1(3): 306–09.

Harrison, J., prod. 2008. *Pedigree Dogs Exposed*. BBC One. London, UK: Passionate Productions. Television.

Hartroft, W.S. 1960. "The Pathology of Obesity." *Bulletin of the New York Academy of Medicine*. 36(5):313–22.

Haskell, W.L., Lee, I-M., Pate, R.R., Powell, K.E., and Blair, S.N. 2007. "Updated Recommendation for Adults From the American College of Sports Medicine and the American Heart Association." *Circulation*. 116(9):1081–93.

Haspel, T. "Farm Bill: Why Don't Taxpayers Subsidize the Foods that are Better for Us?" *Washington Post*. Feb. 18, 2014.

Heilbronn, L.K. and Ravussin, E. 2003. "Calorie Restriction and Aging: Review of the Literature and Implications for Studies in Humans." *American Journal of Clinical Nutrition*. 78(3):361–69.

Heitmann, B.L., et al. 2000. "Mortality Associated with Body Fat, Fat-Free Mass and Body Mass Index Among 60-Year-Old Swedish Men -- A 22-Year Follow-Up." *International Journal of Obesity and Related Metabolic Disorders*. 24(1):33–37.

Heitmann, B.L., et al. 2012. "Obesity, Leanness, and Mortality: Effect Modification by Physical Activity in Men and Women." *Obesity*. 17(1):136–42.

Hendrickson, M. and Heffernan, W. 2007. "Concentration in Agricultural Markets." Columbia, MO, Department of Rural Sociology, University of Missouri.

Henegar, J.R., et al. 2001. "Functional and Structural Changes in the Kidney in the Early Stages of Obesity." *Journal of the American Society of Nephrology*. 12(6):1211–17.

Hess, R.S. 1999. "Evaluation of Risk Factors for Fatal Acute Pancreatitis in Dogs." *Journal of the American Veterinary Medical Association*. 214(1):46–51.

Hetherington, A.W. and Ranson, S.W. 1942. "The Spontaneous Activity and Food Intake of Rats with Hypothalamic Lesions." *American Journal of Physiology*. 136(4):609–17.

Hewson-Hughes, A.K., Hewson-Hughes, V.L., et al. 2013. "Geometric Analysis of Macronutrient Selection in Breeds of the Domestic Dog, *Canis Lupus Familiaris*." *Behavioral Ecology*. 24(1): 293–304.

Hidaka, B.H. 2012. "Depression as a Disease of Modernity: Explanations for Increasing Prevalence." *Journal of Affective Disorders*. 140(3):205–14.

Hilderbrand, G.V. and Golden, H.N. 2013. "Body Composition of Free-Ranging Wolves." *Canadian Journal of Zoology*. 91(1):1–6.

Hill, R.C. 2006. "Challenges in Measuring Energy Expenditure in Companion Animals: A Clinician's Perspective." *Journal of Nutrition*. 136:1967S–1972S.

Hinchcliff, K.W., Reinhart, G.A., Burr, J.R., et al. 1997. "Metabolizable Energy Intake and Sustained Energy Expenditure of Alaskan Sled Dogs During Heavy Exertion in the Cold." *American Journal of Veterinary Research*. 58:1457–62.

Hoenig, M., Thomaseth, K., Waldron, M., and Ferguson, D.C. 2007. "Insulin Sensitivity, Fat Distribution, and Adipocytokine Response to Different Diets in Lean and Obese Cats Before and After Weight Loss." *American Journal of Physiology – Regulatory, Integrative, and Comparative Physiology.* 292(1):R227–R234.

Hong, N.S., et al. 2012. "The Association Between Obesity and Mortality in the Elderly Differs by Serum Concentrations of Persistent Organic Pollutants: A Possible Explanation for the Obesity Paradox." *International Journal of Obesity.* 36(9):1170–75.

Horgan, J. "Thin Body of Evidence: Why I Have Doubts About Gary Taubes's *Why We Get Fat.*" *Scientific American.* May 16, 2011.

Horowitz, A. 2009. *Inside of a Dog: What Dogs See, Smell, and Know.* New York, NY: Scribner.

Howard, B.V., Manson, J.E., Stefanick, M.L., et al. 2006. "Low-Fat Dietary Pattern and Weight Change Over 7 Years: The Women's Health Initiative Dietary Modification Trial." *Journal of the American Medical Association.* 295(1):39–49.

Hubbell, J.G. and Smith, R.W. 1992. "Neptune in America: Negotiating a Discovery." *Journal of the History of Astronomy.* 23(4):261–91.

Hubert, H.B., Feinleib, M., McNamara, P.M., and Castelli, W.P. 1983. "Obesity as an Independent Risk Factor for Cardiovascular Disease: A 26-Year Follow-Up of Participants in the Farmingham Heart Study." *Circulation.* 67(5):968–77.

Hughes, V. "News Feature: The Big Fat Truth." *Nature.* May 22, 2013.

Ioannidis, J.P.A. July 2005. "Contradicted and Initially Stronger Effects in Highly Cited Clinical Research." *Journal of the American Medical Association.* 294(2):218–28.

Ioannidis, J.P.A. August 2005. "Why Most Published Research Findings are False." *PLoS Medicine.* 2(8):e124.

Ishioka, K., et al. 2007. "Plasma Leptin Concentration in Dogs: Effects of Body Condition Score, Age, Gender, and Breeds." *Research in Veterinary Science.* 82(1):11–15.

Ivy, J.L., Zderic, T.W., and Fogt, D.L. 1999. "Prevention and Treatment of Non-Insulin Dependent Diabetes Mellitus." *Exercise and Sport Sciences Reviews.* 27:1–35.

Jamal, A., et al. 2015. "Current Cigarette Smoking Among Adults – United States, 2005–2014." *Morbidity and Mortality Weekly Report.* 64(44):1233–40.

James, S. "Between the Dog and the Wolf." *Harper's Magazine.* Feb. 2015.

Janssen, I., et al. 2005. "Body Mass Index is Inversely Related to Mortality in Older People After Adjustment for Waist Circumference." *Journal of the American Geriatrics Society.* 53(12):2112–18.

Japan Society for the Study of Obesity, Examination Committee of Criteria for 'Obesity Disease' in Japan. 2002. "New Criteria for 'Obesity Disease' in Japan." *Circulation Journal.* 66(11):987–92.

Jenkins, D.J., Wolvener, T.M., Taylor, R.H., Barker, H., Fielden, H., Baldwin, J.M., Bowling, A.C., Newman, H.C., Jenkins, A.L., and Goff, D.V. 1981. "Glycemic Index of Foods: A Physiological Basis For Carbohydrate Exchange." *American Journal of Clinical Nutrition.* 34(3):362–66.

Jeusette, I.C., et al. 2005. "Effects of Chronic Obesity and Weight Loss on Plasma Ghrelin and Leptin Concentrations in Dogs." *Research in Veterinary Science.* 79(2):169–75.

Johnstone, A.M., et al. 2005. "Factors Influencing Variation in Basal Metabolic Rate Include Fat-Free Mass, Fat Mass, Age, and Circulating Thyroxine But Not Sex, Circulating Leptin, or Triiodothyronine." *American Journal of Clinical Nutrition.* 82(5):941–48.

Kalantar-Zadeh, K., Rhee, C.M., and Amin, A.P. 2014. "To Legitimize the Contentious Obesity Paradox." *Mayo Clinic Proceedings.* 89(8):1033–35.

Kannel, W.B., D'Agostino, R.B., and Cobb, J.L. 1996. "Effect of Weight on Cardiovascular Disease." *American Journal of Clinical Nutrition.* 63(3):419S–422S.

Katch, V.L., et al. 1980. "Contribution of Breast Volume and Weight to Body Fat Distribution in Females." *American Journal of Physical Anthropology*. 53:93–100.

Katzmarzyk, P.T. and Craig, C.L. 2002. "Musculoskeletal Fitness and Risk of Mortality." *Medicine & Science in Sports & Exercise*. 34(5):740–44.

Kealy, R.D., Olsson, S.E., Monti, K.L., et al. 1992. "Effects of Limited Food Consumption on the Incidence of Hip Dysplasia in Growing Dogs." *Journal of the American Veterinary Medical Association*. 201: 857–63.

Kealy, R.D., Lawler, D.F., Ballam, J.M., Mantz, S.L., Biery, D.N., Greeley, E.H., Lust, G., Segre, M., Smith, G.K., and Stowe, H.D. 1997. "Five-Year Longitudinal Study on Limited Food Consumption and Development of Osteoarthritis in Coxofemoral Joints of Dogs." *Journal of the American Veterinary Medical Association*. 210: 222–25.

Kealy, R.D., Lawler, D.F., Ballam, J.M., Mantz, S.L., Biery, D.N., Greeley, E.H., Lust, G., Segre, M., Smith, G.K., and Stowe, H.D. 2000. "Evaluation of the Effect of Limited Food Consumption on Radiographic Evidence of Osteoarthritis in Dogs." *Journal of the American Veterinary Medical Association*. 217: 1678–80.

Kealy, R.D., Lawler, D.F., Ballam, J.M., Mantz, S.L., Biery, D.N., Greeley, E.H., Lust, G., Segre, M., Smith, G.K., and Stowe, H.D. 2002. "Effects of Diet Restriction on Life Span and Age-Related Changes in Dogs." *Journal of the American Veterinary Medical Association*. 220(9):1315–20.

Kessler, D. A. 2009. *The End of Overeating: Taking Control of the Insatiable American Appetite*. New York, NY: Rodale.

Keys, A, Brozek J., Henschel, A., Mickelsen, O., and Taylor, H.L. 1950. *The Biology of Human Starvation*. Oxford, U.K.: University of Minnesota Press.

Keys, A., Karvonen, N., Kimura, N., and Taylor, H.L. 1972. "Indices of Relative Weight and Obesity." *Journal of Chronic Diseases*. 25(6):329–43.

Keys, A., Toshima, H., Koga, Y., and Blackburn, H., eds. 1994. *Lessons for Science From the Seven Countries Study – A 35-Year Collaborative Experience in Cardiovascular Disease Epidemiology.* Tokyo, JP: Springer-Verlag.

Klimentidis, Y.C., Beasley, T.M., Lin, H.Y., Murati, G., Glass, G.E., Guyton, M., Newton, W., Jorgensen, M., Heymsfield, S.B., Kemnitz, J., Fairbanks, L., and Allison, D.B. 2011. "Canaries in the Coal Mine: A Cross-Species Analysis of the Plurality of Obesity Epidemics." *Proceedings of the Royal Society B – Biological Sciences.* 278(1712):1626–32.

Kodama, S. et al. 2009. "Cardiorespiratory Fitness as a Quantitative Predictor of All-Cause Mortality and Cardiovascular Events in Healthy Men and Women – A Meta-Analysis." *Journal of the American Medical Association.* 301(19):2024–35.

Kolata, G. "Carbophobia." *The New York Times.* Oct. 7, 2007.

Koppel, K. 2014. "Sensory Analysis of Pet Foods." *Journal of the Science of Food and Agriculture.* 94(11):2148–53.

Kreeger, T.J. "The Internal Wolf: Physiology, Pathology, and Pharmacology." In *Wolves: Behavior, Ecology, and Conservation.* Mech, L.D. and Boitani, L., eds. 2003. Chicago, IL: University of Chicago Press.

Kreeger, T.J., DelGiudice, G.D., and Mech, L.D. 1997. "Effects of Fasting and Refeeding on Body Composition of Captive Gray Wolves." *Canadian Journal of Zoology.* 75:1549–52.

Kremen, N.A., et al. 2013. "Body Composition and Amino Acid Concentrations of Select Birds and Mammals Consumed by Cats in Northern and Central California." *Journal of Animal Science.* 91(3):1270–76.

Kronfeld, D.S. 1973. "Diet and the Performance of Racing Sled Dogs." *Journal of the American Veterinary Medical Association.* 162:470–73.

Laflamme, D.P. 1997. "Development and Validation of a Body Condition Score System for Dogs." *Canine Practice.* 22(4):10–15.

Laflamme, D.P. 2006. "Understanding and Managing Obesity in Dogs and Cats." *Veterinary Clinics – Small Animal Practice.* 36:1283–95.

Laflamme, D.P. and Hannah, S.S. 2005. "Increased Dietary Protein Promotes Fat Loss and Reduces Loss of Lean Body Mass During Weight Loss in Cats." *International Journal of Applied Research in Veterinary Medicine.* 3(2):62–68.

Lane, C.H. 1902. *Dog Shows and Doggy People.* London, U.K.: Hutchinson & Co.

Larson, B.T., et al. 2003. "Improved Glucose Tolerance with Lifetime Diet Restriction Favorably Affects Disease and Survival in Dogs." *Journal of Nutrition.* 133:2887–92.

Larson, G., et al. 2014. "Current Perspectives and the Future of Domestication Studies." *Proceedings of the National Academy of Sciences of the United States of America.* 111(17):6139–46.

Laurence, W.L. "Obesity is Called Drag on Life Span." *The New York Times.* Oct. 23, 1952.

Lavizzo-Mourey, R. "We Must Focus on Preventing Disease if we Want Our Nation to Thrive." *The Atlantic.* May 30, 2012.

Lawler, D.F., Larson, B.T., Ballam, J.M., et al. 2008. "Diet Restriction and Ageing in the Dog: Major Observations Over Two Decades." *British Journal of Nutrition.* 99:793–805.

Lean, M.E.J. 2000. "Pathophysiology of Obesity." *Proceedings of the Nutrition Society.* 59(3):331–36.

Lecker, S.H., et al. 1999. "Muscle Protein Breakdown and the Role of the Ubiquitin-Proteasome Pathway in Normal and Disease States." *Journal of Nutrition.* 129(1):227S-237S.

Lee. H. "The Making of the Obesity Epidemic: How Food Activism Led Public Health Astray." *The Breakthrough.* Spring 2013.

Lehman, R. and Loder, E. 2012. "Missing Clinical Trial Data—A Threat to the Integrity of Evidence Based Medicine." *BMJ.* 344:d8158.

Leibel, R.I., Hirsch, J., Appel, B.E., and Checani, G.C. 1992. "Energy Intake Required to Maintain Body Weight is Not Affected by Wide Variation in Diet Composition." *American Journal of Clinical Nutrition.* 55(2):350–55.

Lenz, J., et al. 2009. "Perceptions, Practices, and Consequences Associated with Foodborne Pathogens and the Feeding of Raw Meat to Dogs." *Canadian Veterinary Journal.* 50(6):637–43.

Leonard, E.K., et al. 2011. "Evaluation of Pet-Related Management Factors and the Risk of *Salmonella* spp. Carriage in Pet Dogs from Volunteer Households in Ontario (2005-2006)." *Zoonoses and Public Health.* 58(2):140-49.

Li, Y., von Holdt, B.M., Reynolds, A. Boyko, A.R., Wayne, R.K., Wu, D.D., Zhang, Y.P. 2013. "Artificial Selection on Brain-Expressed Genes During the Domestication of Dog." *Molecular Biology and Evolution.* 30(8):1867–76.

Libby, P. and Theroux, P. 2005. "Pathophysiology of Coronary Heart Disease." *Circulation.* 111:3481–88.

Locke, J. 1996. *An Essay Concerning Human Understanding.* Cambridge, UK: Hackett Publishing Co., Inc. (originally published 1689).

Loftus, J.P., Yazwinski, M., Milizio, J.G., and Wakshlag, J.J. 2014. "Energy Requirements for Racing Endurance Sled Dogs." *Journal of Nutritional Science.* 3(e34):1–5.

Loucks, A.B. and Horvath, S.M. 1985. "Athletic Amenorrhea: A Review." *Medicine and Science in Sports and Exercise.* 17(1):56–72.

Loucks, A.B., Verdun, M., and Heath, E.M. 1998. "Low Energy Availability, Not Stress of Exercise, Alters LH Pulsatility in Exercising Women." *Journal of Applied Physiology.* 84(1):37–46.

Lucas, F., Bellisle, F., and Di Maio, A. 1987. "Spontaneous Insulin Fluctuations and the Preabsorptive Insulin Response to Food Ingestion in Humans." *Physiology & Behavior.* 40(5):631–36.

Ludwig, D. 2016. *Always Hungry?: Conquer Cravings, Retrain Your Fat Cells, and Lose Weight Permanently.* New York, NY: Grand Central Life & Style.

Lund, E.M., Armstrong, P.J., Kirk, C.A., Klausner, J.S. 2006. "Prevalence and Risk Factors for Obesity in Adult Dogs From Private US Veterinary Practices." *International Journal of Applied Research in Veterinary Medicine.* 4(2):177–86.

Lutz, T.A. and Woods, S.C. 2012. "Overview of Animal Models of Obesity." In *Current Protocols in Pharmacology.* Enna, S.J., et. al., eds. 2003. Ames, IA: John Wiley & Sons, Inc.

Macdonald, I.A. and Atkinson, R. 2011. "Public Health Initiatives in Obesity Prevention: The Need for Evidence-Based Policy." *International Journal of Obesity.* 35:483.

Manson, J.E., et al. 1987. "Body Weight and Longevity – A Reassessment." *Journal of the American Medical Association.* 257(3):353–58.

Manson, J.E., et al. 1990. "A Prospective Study of Obesity and Risk of Coronary Heart Disease in Women." *New England Journal of Medicine.* 322:882–89.

Manson, J.E., et al. 1995. "Body Weight and Mortality Among Women." *New England Journal of Medicine.* 333:677–85.

Markley, W.M. 1956. *Builders of Topeka, 1956: Who's Who in the Kansas Capital.* Topeka, KS: Capper Print Co.

Marshall, W.G., et al. 2010. "The Effect of Weight Loss on Lameness in Obese Dogs with Osteoarthritis." *Veterinary Research Communications.* 34(3):241–53.

Martin, A.N. 2008. *Food Pets Die For: Shocking Facts About Pet Food.* Troutdale, OR: NewSage Press.

Mattera, P. 2004. *USDA Inc.: How Agribusiness Has Hijacked Regulatory Policy at the U.S. Department of Agriculture.* Washington, D.C.: Corporate Research Project of Good Jobs First.

McAlister, A.R. and Cornwell, T.B. 2010. "Children's Brand Symbolism Understanding: Links to Theory of Mind and Executive Functioning." *Psychology & Marketing.* 27(3):203–28.

McGonigal, K. 2012. *The Willpower Instinct: How Self-Control Works, Why It Matters, and how to Get More of It.* New York, NY: Avery.

McGreevy, P.D., et al. 2005. "Prevalence of Obesity in Dogs Examined by Australian Veterinary Practices and the Risk Factors Involved." *Veterinary Record.* 156(22):695–702.

McLester, J.S. 1924. "The Principles Involved in the Treatment of Obesity." *Journal of the American Medical Association.* 82(26)2103–05.

Mech, L.D. and Boitani, L., eds. 2003. *Wolves: Behavior, Ecology, and Conservation.* Chicago, IL: University of Chicago Press.

Melmed, S., Polonsky, K.S., Larsen, P.R., and Kronenberg, H.M., eds. 2016. *Williams Textbook of Endocrinology, 13th Edition.* Philadelphia, PA: Elsevier, Inc.

Menand, L. 2002. *The Metaphysical Club – A Story of Ideas in America.* New York, NY: Farrar, Straus and Giroux.

Meyer, J., and Stadtfeld, G. "Investigation on the Body and Organ Structure of Dogs." In *Nutrition of the Dog and Cat*, ed. Anderson, R.S. 1980. Oxford, UK: Pergamon Press.

Michel, K.E. 2012. "Nutritional Management of Body Weight." In *Applied Veterinary Clinical Nutrition*, First Edition, eds. Fascetti, A.J. and Delaney, S.J. 2012. Ames, IA: John Wiley & Sons, Inc.

Michel, K.E. et al. 2004. "Evaluation of Body Condition and Weight Loss in Dogs Presented to a Veterinary Oncology Service." *Journal of Veterinary Internal Medicine.* 18(5):692–95.

Milliard, T. "Bodybuilding Changing, But It's Still Hard Work." *Las Vegas Review-Journal.* Sep. 6, 2011.

Moisse, K. "Going for the Gaunt: How Low Can an Athlete's Body Fat Go?" *Scientific American.* Feb. 19, 2010.

Mrosovsky, N. 1971. *Hibernation and the Hypothalamus.* New York, NY: Appleton-Century-Crofts.

Mrosovsky, N. 1976. "Lipid Programmes and Life Strategies in Hibernators." *American Zoologist.* 16(4): 685–97.

Mucci, L.A., et al. 2016. "Familial Risk and Heritability of Cancer Among Twins in Nordic Countries." *Journal of the American Medical Association.* 315(1): 68–76.

Nagel, T. 1974. "What Is It Like to Be a Bat?" *The Philosophical Review.* 83(4):435–50.

National Potato Council. 2015. *2015 Potato Statistical Yearbook.* Washington, D.C.: National Potato Council.

National Research Council (U.S.) – Agricultural Board, Division of Biology and Agriculture. 1968. *Body Composition in Animals and Man.* Washington, D.C.: National Academy of Sciences.

National Research Council (U.S.) – Committee on the National Needs for Research in Veterinary Science. 2005. *Critical Needs for Research in Veterinary Science.* Washington, D.C.: The National Academies Press.

National Research Council (U.S.) – Ad Hoc Committee on Dog and Cat Nutrition. 2006. *Nutrient Requirements of Dogs and Cats.* Washington, D.C.: The National Academies Press.

Neel, J.V. 1962. "Diabetes Mellitus: A 'Thrift' Genotype Rendered Detrimental by 'Progress'?" *American Journal of Human Genetics.* 14(4):353–62.

Nelson, C. "Skip the Nachos: An Interview with Brian M. Delaney on Caloric Restriction and Longevity." *SAGE: Science of Aging.* Nov. 18, 2014.

Nestle, M. 2008. *Pet Food Politics: The Chihuahua in the Coal Mine.* Berkeley and Los Angeles, CA: University of California Press.

Neyraud, E. 2014. "Role of Saliva in Oral Food Perception." *Monographs in Oral Science (Vol. 24) -- Saliva: Secretion and Functions.* Ligtenberg, A.J.M. and Veerman, E.C.I., eds. 2014. Basel, Switzerland: Karger.

Nguyen, P., Dumon, H., Buttin, P., Martin, L., and Gouro, A.S. 1994. "Composition of Meal Influences Changes in Postprandial Incremental Glucose and Insulin in Healthy Dogs." *Journal of Nutrition.* 124(12):2707S–2711S.

Nguyen, P., Dumon, H., Biourge, V., Pouteau, E. 1998. "Glycemic and Insulinemic Responses After Ingestion of Commercial Foods in Healthy Dogs: Influence of Food Composition" and "Measurement of Postprandial Incremental Glucose and Insulin Changes in Healthy Dogs: Influence of Food Adaptation and Length of Time of Blood Sampling." *Journal of Nutrition.* 128(12):2654S–62S.

Nindl, B.C., et al. 2007. "Physiological Consequences of U.S. Army Ranger Training." *Medicine and Science in Sports and Exercise.* 39(8):1380–87.

Noakes, T. 1985. *Lore of Running.* Cape Town, South Africa: Oxford University Press South Africa.

Nolen, R.S. "AVMA Enters Into Multimillion-Dollar Partnership With Companies." *JAVMANews.* July 15, 2008.

Norgan, N.G. 1997. "The Beneficial Effects of Body Fat and Adipose Tissue in Humans." *International Journal of Obesity.* 21:738–46.

Novak, N.L. and Brownell, K.D. 2012. "Role of Policy and Government in the Obesity Epidemic." *Circulation.* 126: 2345–52.

Ohlson, L.O., et al. 1985. "The Influence of Body Fat Distribution on the Incidence of Diabetes Mellitus – 13.5 Years of Follow-Up of the Participants in the Study of Men Born in 1913." *Diabetes.* 34:1055–58.

Olson, E.G. "Pet Food Wars: David v. Goliath Edition." *Fortune.* May 28, 2014.

Orphanidou, C., McCargar, L., et al. 1994. "Accuracy of Subcutaneous Fat Measurement: Comparison of Skinfold Calipers, Ultrasound, and Computed Tomography." *Journal of the Academy of Nutrition and Dietetics.* 94(8):855–58.

Owerkowicz, T. and Baudinette, R.V. 2008. "Exercise Training Enhances Aerobic Capacity in Juvenile Estuarine Crocodiles (*Crocodylus Porosus*)." *Comparative Biochemistry and Physiology.* 150(2):211– 16.

Pai, M.P. and Paloucek, F.P. 2000. "The Origins of the 'Ideal' Body Weight Equations." *Annals of Pharmacotherapy.* 34(9):1066–69.

Parker, V.J. and Freeman, L.M. 2011. "Association Between Body Condition and Survival in Dogs With Acquired Chronic Kidney Disease." *Journal of Veterinary Internal Medicine.* 25(6):1306–11.

Parker-Pope, T. "Colgate Gives Doctors Treats for Plugging its Food Brands." *The Wall Street Journal.* Nov. 3, 1997.

Pavlov, I.P. 1927. *Conditioned Reflexes: An Investigation of the Physiological Activity of the Cerebral Cortex.* London, U.K.: Oxford University Press.

Perez Alenza, D., et al. 1998. "Relation Between Habitual Diet and Canine Mammary Tumors in a Case-Control Study." *Journal of Veterinary Internal Medicine.* 12(3):132–39.

Perez-Camargo, G. 2004. "Cat Nutrition: What Is New in the Old?" *Supplement to Compendium on Continuing Education for the Practicing Veterinarian.* 26(2a):5–10.

Peterson, R.O. and Ciucci, P. "The Wolf as a Carnivore." In *Wolves: Behavior, Ecology, and Conservation.* Mech, L.D. and Boitani, L., eds. 2003. Chicago, IL: University of Chicago Press.

Picker, L. "Blue Buffalo Jumps in Debut After Raising $677 Million in IPO." *Bloomberg Businessweek.* July 21, 2015.

Pitts, G.C. and Bullard, T.R. "Some Interspecific Aspects of Body Composition in Mammals." In *Body Composition in Animals and Man.* National Research Council (U.S.) – Agricultural Board, Division of Biology and Agriculture. 1968. Washington, D.C.: National Academy of Sciences.

Pollack, A. "A.M.A. Recognizes Obesity as a Disease." *New York Times.* June 18, 2013.

Pollan, M. 2006. *The Omnivore's Dilemma: A Natural History of Four Meals.* New York, NY: The Penguin Press.

Pollock, M.L. et al. 2000. "Resistance Exercise in Individuals With and Without Cardiovascular Disease – Benefits, Rationale, Safety and Prescription From the Committee on Exercise, Rehabilitation, and Prevention, Council on Clinical Cardiology, American Heart Association." *Circulation.* 101:828–33.

Pontzer, H., Raichlen, D.A., Wood, B.M., Mabulla, A.Z.P., Racette, S.B., and Marlowe, F.W. 2012. "Hunter-Gatherer Energetics and Human Obesity." *PLoS One.* 7(7):e40503.

Popper, K. 1963. *Conjectures and Refutations: The Growth of Scientific Knowledge.* New York, NY: Routledge & Kegan Paul.

Popper, K. 1992. *The Logic of Scientific Discovery.* New York, NY: Routledge.

Proctor, R.N. 2001. "Commentary: Schairer and Schoniger's Forgotten Tobacco Epidemiology and the Nazi Quest for Racial Purity." *International Journal of Epidemiology.* 30(1):31–34.

Proctor, R.N. 2012. *Golden Holocaust: Origins of the Cigarette Catastrophe and the Case for Abolition.* Berkeley and Los Angeles, CA: University of California Press.

Prospective Studies Collaboration. 2009. "Body-Mass Index and Cause-Specific Mortality in 900,000 Adults: Collaborative Analyses of 57 Prospective Studies." *Lancet.* 373(9669):1083–96.

Ramsey, J.J. 2012. "Determining Energy Requirements." In *Applied Veterinary Clinical Nutrition,* First Edition, eds. Fascetti, A.J. and Delaney, S.J. Ames, IA: John Wiley & Sons, Inc.

Rand, J.S., Farrow, H.A., Fleeman, L.M., and Appleton, D.J. 2003. "Diet in the Prevention of Diabetes and Obesity in Companion Animals." *Proceedings of the Nutrition Society of Australia.* 27:S6.

Raniken, T. and Bouchard, C. 2002. "Dose-Response Issues Concerning the Relations Between Regular Physical Activity and Health." *President's Council on Physical Fitness & Sports – Research Digest.* 3(18):1–8.

Ratey, J.J. and Hagerman, E. 2008. *Spark: The Revolutionary New Science of Exercise and the Brain.* New York, NY: Hachette Book Group.

Raup, D.M. 1986. "Biological Extinction in Earth History." *Science.* 231:1528–33.

Redinger, R.N. 2007. "The Pathophysiology of Obesity and Its Clinical Manifestations." *Gastroenterology & Hepatology.* 3(11):856–63.

Reece, W.O. 2009. *Functional Anatomy and Physiology of Domestic Animals (Fourth Edition)*. Ames, IA: Wiley-Blackwell.

Remillard, R.L. "Obesity: A Disease to be Recognized and Managed." In *Textbook of Veterinary Internal Medicine (Seventh Edition)*, eds. Ettinger, S.J. and Feldman, E.C. 2010. St. Louis, MO: Saunders-Elsevier.

Renold, A.E., Crofford, O.B., Stauffacher, W., and Jeanreaud, B. 1965. "Hormonal Control of Adipose Tissue Metabolism: With Special Reference to the Effects of Insulin." *Diabetologia*. 1(1):4–12.

Richards, M.P. 2002. "A Brief Review of the Archaeological Evidence for Paleolithic and Neolithic Subsistence." *European Journal of Clinical Nutrition*. 56(12):1270–78.

Robertson, J.L., et al. 1986. "Long-Term Renal Responses to High Dietary Protein in Dogs With 75% Nephrectomy." *Kidney International*. 29(2):511–19.

Rogers, C.H., Floyd, F.J., Seltzer, M.M., Greenberg, J., and Hong, J. 2008. "Long-Term Effects of the Death of a Child on Parents' Adjustment in Midlife." *Journal of Family Psychology*. 22(2): 203–11.

Rosenbaum, L. 2015. "Understanding Bias—The Case For Careful Study." *New England Journal of Medicine*. 372:1959–63.

Roy, E.J. and Wade, G.N. 1977. "Role of Food Intake in Estradiol-Induced Body Weight Changes in Female Rats." *Hormones and Behavior*. 8(3):265–74.

Ruiz, J.R., et al. 2011. "Strenuous Endurance Exercise Improves Life Expectancy: It's In Our Genes." *British Journal of Sports Medicine*. 45:159–61.

Sahakian, B.J., Lean, M.E.J., Robbins, T.W., and James, W.P.T. 1981. "Salivation and Insulin Secretion in Response to Food in Non-Obese Men and Women." *Appetite*. 2(3):209–16.

Sakuma, K. and Yamaguchi, A. 2012. "Sarcopenia and Age-Related Endocrine Function." *International Journal of Endocrinology*. 2012:127362.

Sanchis-Gomar, F., et al. 2011. "Increased Average Longevity Among the 'Tour de France' Cyclists." *International Journal of Sports Medicine.* 32(8):644–47.

Sanderson, S. L. 2012. "The Epidemic of Canine Obesity and its Role in Osteoarthritis." *Israel Journal of Veterinary Medicine.* 67(4):195–202.

Saris, W.H.M. et al. 2003. "How Much Physical Activity is Enough to Prevent Unhealthy Weight Gain? Outcome of the IASO 1st Stock Conference and Consensus Statement." *Obesity Reviews.* 4(2):101–14.

Schaffer, M. 2009. *One Nation Under Dog: Adventures in the New World of Prozac-Popping Puppies, Dog-Park Politics, and Organic Pet Food.* New York, NY: Henry Holt & Co.

Schapira, D.V., et al. 1994. "Visceral Obesity and Breast Cancer Risk." *Cancer.* 74(2):632–39.

Schenkeveld, L., et al. 2012. "The Influence of Optimal Medical Treatment on the 'Obesity Paradox,' Body Mass Index and Long-Term Mortality in Patients Treated with Percutaneous Coronary Intervention: A Prospective Cohort Study." *BMJ Open.* 2:e000535 doi:10.1136/bmjopen-2011-000535.

Schlesinger, D.P. and Joffe, D.J. 2011. "Raw Food Diets in Companion Animals: A Critical Review." *Canadian Veterinary Journal.* 52(1):50–54.

Schlosser, E. 2001. *Fast Food Nation: The Dark Side of the All-American Meal.* New York, NY: Houghton Mifflin Harcourt Publishing Company.

Schlosser, E. "The Cow Jumped Over the U.S.D.A." *New York Times.* Jan. 2, 2004.

Schultz, W. 2006. "Behavioral Theories and the Neurophysiology of Reward." *Annual Review of Psychology.* 57:87–115.

Schwartz, H. 1983. *Never Satisfied: A Cultural History of Diets, Fantasies, and Fat.* New York, NY: Free Press.

Selmi, M., et al. 2011. "Contaminated Commercial Dehydrated Food as Source of Multiple *Salmonella* Serotypes Outbreak in a Municipal Kennel in Tuscany." *Veterinaria Italiana.* 47(2):183–90.

Serna-Saldivar, S.O. 2010. *Cereal Grains: Properties, Processing, and Nutritional Attributes.* Boca Raton, FL: CRC Press.

Serpell, J., ed. 1995. *The Domestic Dog: Its Evolution, Behaviour and Interactions with People.* New York, NY: Cambridge University Press.

Sessa, W.C., Pritchard, K., Seyedi, N., Wang, J., and Hintze, T.H. 1994. "Chronic Exercise in Dogs Increases Vascular Nitric Oxide Production and Endothelial Cell Nitric Oxide Synthase Gene Expression." *Circulation Research.* 74:349–53.

Shearer, P. "Literature Review: Canine, Feline, and Human Overweight and Obesity." *Banfield Applied Research and Knowledge Team.* Aug. 2010.

Shy, C.M. 1997. "The Failure of Academic Epidemiology: Witness for the Prosecution." *American Journal of Epidemiology.* 145(6):479–84.

Sifferlin, A. "The Obesity Paradox: Can Body Fat Ever Be Good For You?" *Time.* May 6, 2015.

Slupe, J.L, Freeman, L.M., and Rush, J.E. 2008. "Association of Body Weight and Body Condition Score With Survival in Dogs With Heart Failure." *Journal of Veterinary Internal Medicine.* 22(3):561–65.

Smith, G.K., et al. 2001. "Evaluation of Risk Factors for Degenerative Joint Disease Associated with Hip Dysplasia in German Shepherd Dogs, Golden Retrievers, Labrador Retrievers, and Rottweilers." *Journal of the American Veterinary Medical Association.* 219(12):1719–24.

Sonnenschein, E.G., Glickman, L.T., Goldschmidt, M.H., and McKee, L.J. 1991. "Body Conformation, Diet, and Risk of Breast Cancer in Pet Dogs: A Case-Control Study." *Journal of Epidemiology.* 133:694–703.

Sontag, S. 1978. *Illness as Metaphor and AIDS and Its Metaphors.* New York, NY: Picador.

Soule, A. "Wilton Premium Pet Food Co. Settles Class Actions." *Stamford Advocate.* Dec. 10, 2015.

Speakman, J., et al. 2008. "The Contribution of Animal Models to the Study of Obesity." *Laboratory Animals.* 42(4):413–32.

Stahler, D.R., Smith, D.W., and Guernsey, D.S. 2006. "Foraging and Feeding Ecology of the Gray Wolf (*Canis Lupis*): Lessons From Yellowstone National Park, Wyoming, USA." *Journal of Nutrition.* 136(7):1923S–26S.

Stearns, P.N. 1997. *Fat History: Bodies and Beauty in the Modern West.* New York, NY: New York University Press.

Stephens, J.R. 1992. *The Dog Lover's Literary Companion.* Rocklin, CA: Prima Publishing.

Stiver, S.L., et al. 2003. "Septicemic Salmonellosis in Two Cats Fed a Raw-Meat Diet." *Journal of the American Animal Hospital Association.* 39(6):538–42.

Stokes, A. 2014. "Using Maximum Weight to Redefine Body Mass Index Categories in Studies of the Mortality Risks of Obesity." *Population Health Metrics.* 12(1):6.

Stokes, A. and Preston, S.H. 2016. "Revealing the Burden of Obesity Using Weight Histories." *Proceedings of the National Academy of Sciences of the United States of America.* 113(3):572–77.

Stunkard, A. and McClaren-Hume, M. 1959. "The Results of Treatment for Obesity: A Review of the Literature and a Report of a Series." *Archives of Internal Medicine.* 103(1):79–85.

Such, Z.R. and German, A.J. 2015. "Best in Show But Not Best in Shape: A Photographic Assessment of Show Dog Body Condition." *Veterinary Record.* 177(5):125.

Swain, D.P. and Franklin, B.A. 2006. "Comparison of Cardioprotective Benefits of Vigorous Versus Moderate Intensity Aerobic Exercise." *American Journal of Cardiology.* 97(1):141–47.

Taubes, G. 1993. *Bad Science: The Short Life and Weird Times of Cold Fusion.* New York, NY: Random House.

Taubes, G. "What if It's All Been a Big, Fat Lie?" *The New York Times Magazine.* July 7, 2002.

Taubes, G. 2007. *Good Calories, Bad Calories.* New York, NY: Alfred A. Knopf.

Taubes, G. 2010. *Why We Get Fat—And What to Do About It.* New York, NY: Anchor Books.

Taylor, D.H., Hasselblad, V., Henley, S.J., Thun, M.J., and Sloan, F.A. 2002. "Benefits of Smoking Cessation for Longevity." *American Journal of Public Health.* 92(6):990–96.

Taylor, P, Funk, C., and Craighill, P. 2006. "Gauging Family Intimacy: Dogs Edge Cats (Dads Trail Both)." Pew Research Center, A Social Trends Report.

Tisdale, M.J. 1997. "Review – Biology of Cachexia." *Journal of the National Cancer Institute.* 89(23):1763–73.

Toriano, R.P., et al. 1996. "The Relationship Between Body Weight and Mortality: A Quantitative Analysis of Combined Information from Existing Studies." *International Journal of Obesity and Related Metabolic Disorders.* 20(1):63–75.

Torres, C.L., et al. 2003. "Palatability Affects the Percentage of Metabolizable Energy as Protein Selected by Adult Beagles." *Journal of Nutrition.* 133(11):3516–22.

Tsugane, S., et al. 2002. "Under- and Overweight Impact on Mortality Among Middle-Aged Japanese Men and Women: a 10-y Follow-Up of JPHC Study Cohort I." *International Journal of Obesity.* 26:529–37.

Tucker, T. 2006. *The Great Starvation Experiment: The Heroic Men Who Starved So That Millions Could Live.* New York, NY: Free Press.

Turner, C. "The Calorie Restriction Dieters." *The Telegraph.* July 25, 2010.

U.S. Department of Agriculture. 1992. "The Food Guide Pyramid." *Home and Garden Bulletin.* No. 252. Washington, D.C.: U.S. Government Printing Office.

U.S. Department of Agriculture – Center for Nutrition Policy and Prevention. 2001. "Nutrient Content of the U.S. Food Supply, 1909-97." *Home Economics Research Report.* No. 54. Washington, D.C.: U.S. Government Printing Office.

U.S. Department of Agriculture & U.S. Department of Health and Human Services. 2010. "Dietary Guidelines for Americans, 2010." Washington, D.C.: U.S. Government Printing Office.

U.S. Department of Health, Education, and Welfare – Surgeon General's Advisory Committee on Smoking and Health. 1964. "Smoking and Health." Washington, D.C.: U.S. Government Printing Office.

Vasconcellos, R.S., Borges, N.C., Goncalves, K.N.V., Canola, J.C., de Paula, F.J.A., Malheiros, E.B., Brunetto, M.A., and Carciofi, A.C. 2009. "Protein Intake During Weight Loss Influences the Energy Required for Weight Loss and Maintenance in Cats." *Journal of Nutrition.* 139(5):855–60.

Vendramini-Costa, D.B. and Carvalho, J.E. 2012. "Molecular Link Mechanisms Between Inflammation and Cancer." *Current Pharmaceutical Design.* 18(26):3831–52.

Venn, O., Turner, I., Mathieson, I., de Groot, N., Bontrop, R., McVean, G. 2014. "Strong Male Bias Drives Germline Mutation in Chimpanzees." *Science.* 344(6189):1272–75.

Wadd, W. 1829. *Comments on Corpulency.* London, U.K.: John Ebers.

Wade, G.N. and Schneider, J.E. 1992. "Metabolic Fuels and Reproduction in Female Mammals." *Neuroscience & Biobehavioral Reviews.* 16(2):235–72.

Wakshlag, J.J., Struble, A.M., Levine, C.B., Bushey, J.J., Laflamme, D.P., and Long, G.M. 2011. "The Effects of Weight Loss on Adipokines and Markers of Inflammation in Dogs." *British Journal of Nutrition.* 106:S11–S14.

Walsh, Bryan. "Ending the War on Fat." Jun. 12, 2014. *Time.*

Ward, E. 2010. *Chow Hounds: Why Our Dogs Are Getting Fatter – A Vet's Plan to Save Their Lives.* Deerfield Beach, FL.: Health Communications, Inc.

Wareham, N.J., van Sluijs, E.M.F., and Ekelund, U. 2005. "Physical Activity and Obesity Prevention: A Review of the Current Evidence." *Proceedings of the Nutrition Society.* 64(2):229–47.

Warren, M.P. 1983. "Effects of Undernutrition on Reproductive Function in the Human." *Endocrine Reviews.* 4(4):363–77.

Wartella, E.A., et al., eds. 2010. *Institute of Medicine (U.S.) Committee on Examination of Front-of-Package Nutrition Rating Systems and Symbols: Phase I Report.* Washington, D.C.: National Academies Press.

Wayne, R.K. 1993. "Molecular Evolution of the Dog Family." *Trends in Genetics.* 9(6):218–24.

Wayne, R.K. and Vila, Carles. "Molecular Genetic Studies of Wolves." In *Wolves: Behavior, Ecology, and Conservation.* Mech, L.D. and Boitani, L., eds. 2003. Chicago, IL: University of Chicago Press.

Webb-Johnson, C. 1923. *Why Be Fat?* London, U.K.: Mills and Boon.

Weeth, L.P., Fascetti, A.J., Kass, P.H., Suter, S.E., Santos, A.M., and Delaney, S.J. 2007. "Prevalence of Obese Dogs in a Population of Dogs With Cancer." *American Journal of Veterinary Research.* 68:389–98.

Wells, J.C.K. 2010. *The Evolutionary Biology of Human Body Fatness – Thrift and Control.* Cambridge, U.K.: Cambridge University Press.

White, R.A.S. and Williams, J.M. 1994. "Tracheal Collapse in the Dog: Is There Really a Role For Surgery?" *Journal of Small Animal Practice.* 35:191–96.

Whitford, D. and Burke, D. "Cargill: Inside the Quiet Giant that Rules the Food Business." *Fortune.* Oct. 27, 2011.

Willcox, B.J., et al. 2006. "Siblings of Okinawan Centenarians Share Lifelong Mortality Advantages." *Journal of Gerontology: BIOLOGICAL SCIENCES.* 61A(4):345–54.

Willcox, B.J., et al. 2007. "Caloric Restriction, the Traditional Okinawan Diet, and Healthy Aging – The Diet of the World's Longest-Lived People and Its Potential Impact on Morbidity and Life Span." *Annals of the New York Academy of Sciences.* 1114:434–55.

Willcox, D.C., et al. 2007. "Aging Gracefully: A Retrospective Analysis of Functional Status in Okinawan Centenarians." *American Journal of Geriatric Psychiatry*. 15:252–56.

Wing, R.R. 1999. "Physical Activity in the Treatment of Adult Overweight and Obesity: Current Evidence and Research Issues." *Medicine and Science in Sports and Exercise*. 31(11):S547–52.

Winslow, C.E.A. 1920. "The Untilled Field of Public Health." *Science*. 51(1306): 23–33.

Witherington, B.E., Martin, R.E., and Trindell, R.N. 2014. "Understanding, Assessing, and Resolving Light-Pollution Problems on Sea Turtle Nesting Beaches, Revised." *Florida Fish and Wildlife Research Institute Technical Report Tr-2*. vii + 83 p.

Wolfe, R.R. 2006. "The Underappreciated Role of Muscle in Health and Disease." *American Journal of Clinical Nutrition*. 84:475–82.

World Cancer Research Fund/American Institute for Cancer Research. 2007. *Food, Nutrition, Physical Activity, and the Prevention of Cancer: A Global Perspective*. Washington, D.C.: American Institute for Cancer Research.

World Health Organization. 2000. *Technical Report Series 894 – Obesity: Preventing and Managing the Global Epidemic: Report of a WHO Consultation*. Geneva, CH: WHO Press.

World Health Organization. 2015. *Fact Sheet No. 311: Obesity and Overweight*. Geneva, CH: WHO Press.

World Health Organization/International Association for the Study of Obesity/International Obesity Task Force. 2000. *The Asia-Pacific Perspective: Redefining Obesity and Its Treatment*. Melbourne, AU: Health Communications Australia Pty.

World Health Organization/World Heart Federation. 2005. *The SuRF Report 2 -- Surveillance of Chronic Disease Risk Factors: Country-Level Data and Comparable Estimates*. Geneva, CH: WHO Press.

Wright, R. 2004. *A Short History of Progress*. New York, NY: Carroll & Graf Publishers.

Wynder, E.L. and Graham, E.A. 1950. "Tobacco Smoking as a Possible Etiologic Factor in Bronchiogenic Carcinoma." *Journal of the American Medical Association*. 143(4):329–36.

Yancy, W.S., Olsen, M.K., Guyton, J.R., Bakst, R.P., Westman, E.C. 2004. "A Low-Carbohydrate, Ketogenic Diet Versus a Low-Fat Diet to Treat Obesity and Hyperlipidemia: A Randomized, Controlled Trial." *Annals of Internal Medicine*. 140(10):769–77.

Young, D.R., Iacovino, A., Erve, P., Mosher, R., and Spector, H. 1959. "Effect of Time After Feeding and Carbohydrate or Water Supplement on Work in Dogs." *Journal of Applied Physiology*. 14(6):1013–17.

Zhang, Y., Proenca, R., Maffei, M., Barone, M., Leopold, L., and Friedman, J.M. 1994. "Positional Cloning of the Mouse Obese Gene and Its Human Homologue." *Nature*. 372(6505):425–32.

Zhang, X.J., et al. 2006. "The Flow Phase of Wound Metabolism Is Characterized by Stimulated Protein Synthesis Rather Than Cell Proliferation." *Journal of Surgical Research*. 135(1):61–67.

Zhao, T., et al. 2002. "Occurrence of Salmonella Enterica Serotype Typhimurium DT104A in Retail Ground Beef." *Journal of Food Protection*. 65(2):403–07.

Zink, M.C. 1997. *Peak Performance: Coaching the Canine Athlete*. Ellicott City, MD: Canine Sports Productions.

Zink, M.C. 2001. *Dog Health and Nutrition for Dummies*. New York, NY: Hungry Minds, Inc.

Zolotukhin, S. 2013. "Metabolic Hormones in Saliva: Origin and Function." *Oral Disorders*. 19(3):219–29.

Zuk, M. 2013. *Paleofantasy: What Evolution Really Tells Us About Sex, Diet, and How We Live*. New York, NY: W.W. Norton & Co.

NOTES AND SOURCES

--

Chapter One: Dogs, Children, and Loss

". . . 'He doesn't seem like a little dog' . . .": Clausen 1916.

"There is a theory . . .": Archer 1997.

". . . 85% of Americans today . . .": Taylor et al. 2006.

"A photograph on his website . . ." and all other references to the website for the Association for Pet Obesity Prevention: http://www.petobesityprevention.org/ (last visited Feb. 1, 2016).

". . . one of Dr. Ward's diagnostic tools . . .": Ward 2010.

"Every peer-reviewed study I could find . . .": German 2006; Lund et al. 2006; Weeth et al. 2007; Wakshlag et al. 2011.

". . . 'a major concern' . . .": German et al. 2010.

". . . 'the most common' . . .": German 2006.

". . . 'the number one' . . .": Wakshlag et al. 2011.

"But most troubling of all . . .": Kealy et al. 2002.

". . . the average life expectancy difference between lifelong human smokers . . .": Taylor et al. 2002.

". . . 'Why do I love my dogs so much?' . . ." and all other references to Schulof: interviews, Patricia Schulof, 2014.

"According to the American Kennel Club . . .": www.akc.org/press-center/most-popular-dog-breeds-in-america/ (last visited Feb. 2, 2016).

"A 2008 study published in the *Journal of Family Psychology* . . .": Rogers et al. 2008.

"Mortality rates among bereaved mothers . . .": Harper et al. 2011.

"Most of us wait at least 20 years . . ." and other data on the age of first-time parents: www.cia.gov/library/publications/the-world-factbook/ (last visited Feb. 2, 2016).

"But with our canine children . . .": life expectancy data for Americans from Centers for Disease Control and Prevention report "Deaths: Final Data For 2013" (available at www.cdc.gov/nchs/fastats/life-expectancy.htm) (last visited Feb. 2, 2016); life expectancy data for American dogs from Fleming et al. 2011.

"In fact, about half of all . . .": ibid.

". . . cancer is the single most . . .": ibid. Additional facts about canine cancer prevalence rates available at National Canine Cancer Foundation website, www.wearethecure.org/ (last visited Feb. 2, 2016).

"Recent research has indisputably shown that one's genetic makeup . . .": Mucci et al. 2016.

"Studies have shown that dogs with a lot of fat in their bodies . . .": Glickman, et al. 1989; Sonnenschein et al. 1991; White et al. 1994; Bodey et al. 1996; Kealy et al. 1997; Kealy et al. 2000; Kealy et al. 2002; German 2006.

"Even in the Internet Age . . .": Goff et al. 2006.

". . . at least 1.9 billion people are overweight or obese . . .": World Health Organization, 2015. "Fact Sheet No. 311: Obesity and Overweight" (available at www.who.int/mediacentre/factsheets/fs311/en/) (last visited Feb. 2, 2016).

"In *Dog Health and Nutrition for Dummies* . . .": Zink 2001.

". . . the *Dog Owner's Home Veterinary Handbook* . . .": Eldredge et al. 2007.

". . . dietary fats, for instance, are . . ." and subsequent discussions of caloric content of macronutrients: National Research Council 2006; Case et al. 2011; Ramsey 2012. Each of these also provides a detailed explanation of the calories-in, calories-out theory of obesity, as it pertains to dogs and cats.

". . . 'the fundamental underlying cause of obesity' . . .": Case et al. 2011.

". . . 'animals become overweight as a consequence of' . . .": Fascetti et al. 2012.

". . . according to a 2006 paper published in the *Journal of General Internal Medicine* . . .": Goff et al. 2006.

". . . a 2003 study published in the *Journal of the American College of Nutrition* . . .": Cheuvront 2003.

"In a particularly infamous recent paper . . .": Ioannidis July 2005.

"Research teams from . . . Harvard . . .": Ebberling et al. 2012.

"Research teams from . . . Stanford . . .": Gardner et al. 2007.

"Research teams from . . . Duke . . .": Yancy et al. 2004.

"In an immensely popular YouTube video . . .": the video, "Sugar: the Bitter Truth," is available at www.youtube.com/watch?v=dBnniua6-oM (last visited Feb. 3, 2016).

"Sometimes our biases arise innocently . . ." and subsequent discussion of biases in research science: Coughlin 1990; Du Fort et al. 1993; Iaonnidis Aug. 2005; Dwan et al. 2013.

". . . most academic journals and research institutions . . .": for instance, the *New England Journal of Medicine*'s Editorial Policies include a "Financial Associations/Conflict of Interest" policy, providing in relevant part as follows: "NEJM is committed to publishing the highest quality research and reliable, authoritative review articles that are free from commercial influence. For all research articles we publish, NEJM lists study sponsorship and relevant financial information as disclosed by the authors." (available at www.nejm.org/page/about-nejm/editorial-policies/) (last visited Feb. 3, 2016).

". . . numerous cases have recently been reported . . ." and subsequent discussion of financial conflicts-of-interest in research science: Lehman et al. 2012; Fauber 2012.

". . . onto the vaunted pages of the *New England Journal of Medicine* . . .": Rosenbaum 2015.

"The U.S. market for pet food products exceeds $20 billion a year . . .": American Pet Products Association: "Pet Industry Market Size and Ownership Statistics." (available at www.americanpetproducts.org/press_industrytrends.asp/) (last visited Feb. 3, 2016).

". . . when it comes to veterinary nutrition, many of the field's . . .": detailed bibliographic information and source notes on the subject of financial conflicts-of-interest in veterinary research science can be found in *Chapter Four* and *Chapter Five* of this notes index.

". . . 'the single best idea anyone ever had' . . .": Dennett 1995.

Chapter Two: The Hour Between Dog and Wolf

"I decided to try to find my father in the woods.": Harding 2009.

"At least according to the . . .": Pollack 2013.

". . . it is beyond legitimate dispute that neither people nor dogs were particularly fat until rather recently, historically speaking.": a thorough discussion of human obesity rates in the Twentieth Century can be found in Flegal et al. 2002. Adiposity and diabetes in pre-modern humans is discussed in Neel 1962; Eaton et al. 1985; Brown et al. 1987; Pontzer et al. 2012.

". . . 'kids these days' societal gripes . . .": For instance, the following quote is often attributed to Socrates (although attempts to authenticate it have apparently been unsuccessful): "The children now love luxury; they have bad manners, contempt for authority; they show disrespect for elders and love chatter in place of exercise."

"Epidemics of deadly, non-communicable diseases don't really make evolutionary sense . . ." and subsequent discussion of genetics and chronic diseases: Neel 1962 (in this, his famous "Thrifty Gene" paper, Neel explains why the diabetes epidemic is a genetic "enigma"). There are, of course, other cases in which maladaptive traits can become widespread in specific populations, such as when the advantages conferred by some combination of genes outweigh their associated disadvantages.

". . . consider the sad case of beachfront lighting and its impact on the behavior of hatchling sea turtles . . ." and subsequent discussion of hatchling sea turtle behavior: Witherington et al. 2014.

"Rigorous attempts to use . . .": Neel 1962.

". . . two unlikely individuals published a short paper . . .": Eaton et al. 1985.

". . . there are at least two reasons why the Paleolithic . . ." and subsequent discussion of Paleolithic era: ibid; Cordain et al. 2000.

"It has its own professional society . . ." and subsequent discussion of the Ancestral Health Society: www.ancestralhealth.org (last visited Feb. 3, 2016).

"A 2012 paper published in the *Journal of Affective Disorders* summarized the evidence . . .": Hidaka 2012.

". . . the so-called 'Paleo diet' . . .": the term 'Paleo diet" dates at least to Cordain 2002. Professor Cordain holds the U.S. trademark for the term "Paleo Diet" and his books are largely responsible for popularizing the concept.

". . . an immensely popular dietary philosophy . . .": Gans 2013.

"The Paleo diet and the broader ancestral health movement have their critics.": Zuk 2013; Fitzgerald 2014.

"Wolves are indigenous . . ." and subsequent discussion of the history of the gray wolf in North America: Boitani 2003; Fritts et al. 2003; interview, Mike Jimenez, 2014; interviews, Abigail Nelson, 2014; interviews, Richard McIntyre, 2014 & 2015; interviews, Daniel Stahler, 2014 & 2015.

". . . it has been estimated that more than 99.9% of all species . . .": Raup 1986.

". . . 'extreme fecundity' . . .": interview, Abigail Nelson, 2014.

". . . study published in 2014 in the journal *PLoS Genetics* . . .": Freedman et al. 2014. There is considerable debate over when exactly dogs were domesticated. The major theories are outlined in Wayne et al. 2003.

". . . probably occurred some 13 *million* years ago . . .": Venn et al. 2014.

". . . the 60 million years or so that have transpired . . .": Wayne 1993.

". . . they share some 98% or more of their mitochondrial DNA . . .": Budiansky 1999; Wayne et al. 2003; Freedman et al. 2014.

"The overlap is so significant . . ." and subsequent discussion of wolf-dog hybrids: James 2015.

"And it turns out that most of the differences . . ." and subsequent discussion of genetic differences between dogs and wolves: Axelsson et al. 2013; Li et al. 2013.

". . . 'I'd say there is no evidence of obese wolves in the wild' . . .": interview, Rolf Peterson, 2013.

". . . 'I have never observed a wild wolf even approaching obesity' . . .": interview, Abigail Nelson, 2014.

". . . they carry it in most of the same places . . ." and subsequent discussion of wolf physiology: Kreeger 2003; Peterson et al. 2003.

". . . most definitive scientific analysis of the body composition of wild wolves . . .": Hilderbrand et al. 2013.

". . . recent study shows that even captive wolves . . .": Kreeger et al. 1997.

"The body compositions of other wild canine species have been studied too.": These papers are discussed in Hilderbrand et al. 2013.

". . . more than half of the dogs in the United States today have a BFP higher than 30% . . .": The methodology underpinning this statement and the bibliographical sources upon which it is based are discussed in *Chapter Seven* of this notes index.

". . . just about as fat as a garden-variety blue whale . . .": Pitts et al. 1968.

"Yellowstone presently is . . ." and subsequent discussion of wolves in Yellowstone: interview, Mike Jimenez, 2014; interviews, Abigail Nelson, 2014; interviews, Richard McIntyre, 2014 & 2015; interviews, Daniel Stahler, 2014 & 2015.

"Enter Dr. Daniel Stahler . . ." and subsequent discussion of Dr. Stahler's career studying wolves in Yellowstone: interviews, Daniel Stahler, 2014 & 2015.

". . . wolves in captivity often live as long as 15 years . . .": interview, Trent Redfield, 2015.

"Wild wolves, on the other hand, rarely do so well." and subsequent discussion of lifespan and causes of death among wolves in Yellowstone: interview, Daniel Stahler, 2014.

"A recent ten-year survey of more than 70,000 . . ." Fleming et al. 2011.

"Isolated cases of . . .": Kreeger 2003; Cubaynes et al. 2014.

". . . '[s]everal such reports . . .'": Kreeger 2003.

". . . only about 3% of Yellowstone's wolves die from starvation . . .": Cubaynes et al. 2014.

"In Yellowstone, elk are the primary . . . " and subsequent discussion of the dietary habits of Yellowstone's wolves: Stahler et al. 2006; interview, Daniel Stahler, 2015.

"In other parts of the world . . .": Peterson et al. 2003.

"When consuming a carcass . . .": ibid.; interview, Richard McIntyre, 2014; interviews, Daniel Stahler, 2014.

"They get every last calorie . . .": interview, Trent Redfield, 2015.

". . . a group of Yellowstone wolves nearly doubled . . .": Stahler et al. 2006.

"Others have reported similar . . .": Peterson et al. 2003.

". . . wolf-killed prey carcasses are a 'food bonanza' . . .": ibid.

". . . somewhere in the neighborhood of 0.10 kilograms . . .": ibid (including an analysis of at least 18 other food availability studies).

". . . typically go two or three days between elk kills . . .": interview, Daniel Stahler, 2014.

"... fasts commonly go on for *weeks*.": Peterson et al. 2003.

"... 'At a fresh kill' ..." and subsequent discussion of wolf eating habits: ibid.

"... 'wolves spend their lives doing one of five things' ...": interview, Daniel Stahler, 2014.

" ... 'Wolves sleep a tremendous amount' ...": interview, Trent Redfield, 2015.

"... wolves do tend to do a great deal of walking and other low-level physical activity ..." and subsequent discussion of physical activity in wolves: Peterson et al. 2003; interview, Mike Jimenez, 2014; interview, Daniel Stahler, 2015.

Chapter Three: Rethinking the Science of Obesity

"... 'Bold ideas, unjustified anticipations, and speculative thought' .. .": Popper 1992.

"As scientifically minded public intellectuals go, Gary Taubes occupies something of a unique place in the world ..." and subsequent discussion of Taubes's background and career: Taubes 2007; Taubes 2010; Apple 2014; interviews, Gary Taubes, 2016.

"But in another sense ...": At least the skeptical empiricist philosopher (and author of *The Black Swan*) Nassim Nicholas Taleb views Taubes in this light, having written that Taubes is a "true scientist" and a "true empiricist." (http://www.amazon.com/review/R3MW66SBINF0R7) (last visited Feb. 15, 2016).

"... John Horgan wrote in *Scientific American* in 2011 ...": Horgan 2011.

"... 'calling Gary critical' ...": ibid.

"... 'It begins with the obvious question' ...": Taubes 2007.

"... 'he would deserve and receive the Nobel Prize in Medicine' ...": ibid (the quote from Rhodes is featured prominently on the back cover of the hard cover edition).

". . . he had reported on a fiasco concerning . . .": Taubes 1993.

". . . 'Some of my physicist friends' . . .": interview, Gary Taubes, 2016.

"Public health is a field . . .": Winslow 1920.

"The field's recent accomplishments . . ." and subsequent discussion of public health topics: a broad historical overview of recent public health initiatives can be found on the website for the World Health Organization (www.who.int/topics/en/) (last visited Feb. 12, 2016).

". . . '[i]t is clear that' . . .": Breslow 2006.

". . . 'America's No. 1 Health Problem.'": Laurence 1952; Lee 2013.

"For the next 60 years . . ." and subsequent discussion of public health measures aimed at fighting obesity: Macdonald et al. 2011; Novak et al. 2012; Lee 2013.

"Many millions of dollars . . .": budgetary figures for the National Institutes of Health are available at https://report.nih.gov/categorical_spending.aspx (last visited Feb. 15, 2016).

"As of 1960, the rate of obesity among adults in the United States . . .": Flegal et al. 1998.

"But over the next 50 years . . ." and subsequent discussion of current American obesity rates: ibid.; Flegal et al. 2002; Flegal et al. 2010; Flegal et al. 2012.

"It has blossomed into . . .": Brownell 1994.

"One of the most common criticisms of public health work . . ." and subsequent discussion of debate over epidemiology and public health: Shy 1997; Bankhead 1999.

" . . . 'basic science of public health' . . .": Shy 1997.

". . . 'When I started looking at influential epidemiological studies . . .'": interview, Gary Taubes, 2016.

". . . 'The guy was clearly one of the worst . . .'": ibid.

". . . 'Bad scientists never get the right answer . . .'": ibid.

"Importantly, the idea isn't that calories have . . ." and subsequent discussion of the relevance of calories to obesity: Taubes 2007; Taubes 2010.

". . . 'toxic food environment' . . .": Brownell 1994.

". . . 'theories that diseases are caused' . . .": Sontag 1978.

". . . 'In science' . . .": interview, Gary Taubes, 2016.

". . . extremely poor populations experience high levels of *both* obesity and malnutrition . . .": Goldblatt et al. 1965; Caballero 2005; Taubes 2007; Taubes 2010.

". . . 'exercise explosion' . . .": Gilmore 1977

". . . the greatest period of fattening in . . .": Taubes 2007; Taubes 2010; Flegal et al. 2010; Flegal et al. 2012.

". . . extremely poor people tend to be . . .": Goldblatt et al. 1965; Caballero 2005; Taubes 2007; Taubes 2010.

". . . calorie-restricted diets have such a poor experimental track record . . .": Stunkard et al. 1959; Howard et al. 2006; Dansinger et al. 2007; Taubes 2007; Taubes 2010.

". . . using a simple example to drive the point home . . .": Taubes 2010.

". . . 'An animal whose food is suddenly restricted' . . .": Flier et al. 2007.

". . . 'undisputed heavyweight champ' . . .": interview, Richard McIntyre, 2015.

"In an effort to reconcile these misgivings . . ." and subsequent discussion of history of calories-in, calories-out model of obesity: Taubes 2007; Taubes 2010, interview, Gary Taubes, 2016.

"The Carbohydrate-Insulin Model of Obesity" and subsequent discussion of Gary Taubes's theory of obesity: ibid (all original sources are cited and discussed in the body and footnotes of Taubes 2007 and Taubes 2010).

"... 'we don't get fat because we overeat; we overeat because we're getting fat.'": Taubes 2010.

"... think of the children.": Another example of this phenomenon, from David Ludwig's *Always Hungry?* (Ludwig 2016): "consider what happens in pregnancy. The fetus doesn't grow because the mother eats more; she eats more because the fetus is growing."

"On average, they quadruple in size ..." and subsequent discussion of growth rates of children and adolescents: "Clinical Growth Charts" for American children and adolescents are available on the website for the CDC (http://www.cdc.gov/growthcharts/clinical_charts.htm) (last visited Feb. 22, 2016).

"A pair of experiments ...": Wade et al. 1992; Taubes 2007; Taubes 2010.

"He has castrated male rats ...": Gentry et al. 1976.

"He has shown that mating behavior by female rats ...": Wade et al. 1992.

"He has even sought to identify ...": ibid.

"... 'changes in food intake are neither' ...": Roy et al. 1977.

"... demonstrated that lesions in a brain region called the ventromedial hypothalamus (VMH) ...": Hetherington et al. 1942.

"... experimental manipulation of the hypothalamus has been used to induce sudden and extreme obesity ...": Brobeck 1946.

"... 'not responsive to diet and exercise' ...": Lustig, R.H. "Hypothalamic Obesity." Available at: https://pituitary.org/medical-resources/pavilions/pediatric-health/pediatric-health-archive/hypothalamic-obesity (last visited Feb. 24, 2016).

"... even when food is plentiful ...": Mrosovsky 1976.

"... 'the importance of this way of getting fat' ...": ibid.

"The prevailing theory, articulated by Mrosovsky and others ...": Mrosovsky 1971.

"... 'principal regulator of fat metabolism' ...": Berson et al. 1965; Taubes 2010.

"Insulin's role in the body ..." and subsequent discussion of glucose and insulin: Astwood 1962; Berson et al. 1965; Renold et al. 1965; National Research Council 2006; Taubes 2007; Taubes 2010; Case et al. 2011; Melmed et al. 2016.

"The starchy carbohydrate amylopectin A ...": Foster-Powell et al. 2002; Davis 2011.

"The GI scale was invented ...": Jenkins et al. 1981.

"In the 30 years or so ...": ibid; Foster-Powell et al. 2002.

"... 'the same factors account for the postprandial' ...": Nguyen et al. 1994.

"... 'the amount of starch consumed is the major determinant' ...": Nguyen et al. 1998 (emphasis mine).

"... 'it is accepted that carbohydrates, primarily starches, are the principal' ...": de-Oliveira et al. 2014.

"... researchers have quantified to a limited degree the impact that specific carbohydrate sources ...": and subsequent discussion of postprandial glucose and insulin responses in dogs: Graham et al. 1994; Nguyen et al. 1994; Nguyen et al. 1998; Carciofi et al. 2008.

"Indeed, by 1965 ...": Berson et al. 1965.

"... 'An anti-fat diet is based on the commonest and most active' ..." and other historical quotations on starches and obesity: all reported in Taubes 2010.

"... 'the cause of obesity as a primary disorder' ...": Remillard 2010. Neither the carbohydrate-insulin hypothesis nor the molecular biochemistry of adiposity is discussed in any of the other major veterinary nutrition textbooks either: Hand et al. 2000; Case et al. 2011; Fascetti et al. 2012.

"In a recent 'Literature Review' on 'Canine, Feline, and Human Overweight and Obesity' ...": Shearer 2010.

"Probably the best example of the efficacy of . . .": Gardner et al. 2007.

". . . 'a bitter pill to swallow' . . .": Taubes 2010.

"Perhaps an even more compelling piece of evidence . . .": Bazzano et al. 2014.

". . . a recent meta-analysis published in the *Annals of Internal Medicine* . . .": Chowdhury et al. 2014.

". . . a *Time* magazine cover story . . .": Walsh 2014.

". . . some very public back-tracking by . . .": Apple 2014.

". . . recently published a diet book . . .": Ludwig 2016.

". . . 'overeating doesn't make us fat' . . . " and other Ludwig quotations: ibid.

"His book has drawn praise from . . .": all endorsements from the hardcover edition of ibid.

"Dr. Timothy Noakes, one of the world's foremost . . ." and subsequent discussion of Dr. Noakes and his work: Noakes 1985; Dent 2016.

". . . in 2002, a group of veterinary researchers from institutions across Europe . . .": Diez et al. 2002.

"A study published in the *International Journal of Applied Research in Veterinary Medicine* . . .": Laflamme et al. 2005.

"In 2004, another group of veterinarians . . .": Bierer et al. 2004.

"It doesn't get much clearer than that.": These data are not cherry-picked. Cats fed low-carbohydrate, high-protein diets have consistently been shown to lose more body fat and less lean body mass than cats fed the same number of calories worth of a high-carbohydrate, low-protein food. See Hoenig et al. 2007; Vasconcellos et al. 2009; des Courtis et al. 2015.

"According to Daniel Stahler, Abby Nelson, and the rest of Yellowstone's wolf experts . . .": detailed bibliographic information and source notes on the subject of wolf ecology can be found in *Chapter Two* of this notes index.

". . . 'Let us take the case of the wolf' . . .": Darwin 1869.

"Let's take a moment and catalogue some of the wolf's . . ." and subsequent discussion of wolf physiology and psychology: Peterson et al. 2003.

"The constituent parts of plant matter . . .": detailed bibliographic information and source notes on the subject of ruminant digestive physiology can be found in *Chapter Four* of this notes index.

"Recent studies comparing the genomes of dogs and wolves have revealed . . ." and subsequent discussion of starch digestion by domestic dogs: Axelsson et al. 2013; Freedman et al. 2014.

". . . at the moment, carbohydrates are the most commonly consumed . . .": detailed bibliographic information and source notes on the subject of worldwide carbohydrate consumption can be found in *Chapter Four* of this notes index.

"According to the research summarized by the National Research Council . . .": National Research Council 2006.

". . . 'as in humans, there is probably an obligatory' . . .": ibid.

"Much like human beings, dogs do an admirable job . . ." and subsequent discussion of gluconeogenesis: Belo et al. 1976; National Research Council 2006.

"In a 1976 experiment, a group of young Beagles . . ." Belo et al. 1976.

"Other studies have looked at the effect of dietary composition . . .": Young et al. 1959; Falecka-Wieczorek et al. 1984.

"The fact that sled dogs are often, if not *usually*, fed zero-carbohydrate diets . . ." and subsequent discussion of diets of sled dogs: Kronfeld 1973; Hinchcliff et al. 1997; Loftus et al. 2014.

"The third and final line of evidence . . .": detailed bibliographic information and source notes on the subject of wolf behavior can be found in *Chapter Two* of this notes index.

"Probably the best-known example of strong predictive power in action . . ." and subsequent discussion of Leverrier's predictions: Hubbell et al. 1992.

"We also know that wolves never get fat . . .": By the way, there is an exception to the general rule that free-ranging animals don't become obese, and that is when they have free access to human garbage dumps. In those instances, the animals often *do* become obese. Not just big or functionally fat, but truly obese. In one recent study (Banks et al. 2003), wild baboons with access to human garbage dumps not only became significantly heavier and fatter than a control group, but they also developed a host of metabolic problems totally absent from control populations, including elevated levels of serum leptin, insulin, and glucose, as well as insulin resistance. In another (Altmann et al. 1993), baboons with access to garbage dumps averaged about 23% body fat, while those that didn't averaged *less than 2%*. And a recent meta-analysis (Klimentidis et al. 2011) of more than 20,000 representatives of a variety of different mammalian species living with or near humans picked up a broader trend, concluding that "over the past several decades, average mid-life body weights have risen among primates and rodents living in research colonies, as well as among feral rodents and domestic dogs and cats." In short, free-ranging wild animals don't become obese, but captive ones, as well as pets and those living near or among carbohydrate-crazed human beings do. Just like the carbohydrate-insulin model of obesity would predict.

Chapter Four: Big Kibble and the Carbohydrate Lobby

"There is an always-significant difference . . .": Berry 2015.

"Idaho's potatoes are . . ." and subsequent discussion of Idaho potato farming: all facts and figures come from the Idaho Potato Commission (https://idahopotato.com/)(last visited Feb. 29, 2016).

". . . 'warm days and cool nights' . . .": ibid.

"At the moment, Americans are 'asking for more' . . .": ibid.

". . . more than 40% of U.S. potatoes . . .": National Potato Council 2015.

". . . about 50 calories of chips and 50 calories of fries . . .": U.S. Department of Agriculture & U.S. Department of Health and Human Services 2010.

"For one, you've begun to drool." and subsequent discussion of pre-prandial salivation response in human beings: Zolotukhin 2013; Neyraud 2014.

"Dogs drool too, of course." and subsequent discussion of pre-prandial salivation response in dogs: National Research Council 2006.

". . . they've been shown to secrete up to ten times more . . .": Argenzio 1989.

". . . as Ivan Pavlov famously showed . . .": Pavlov 1927.

" . . . by initiating a second autonomic response . . ." and subsequent discussion of pre-prandial insulin response in human beings: Sahakian et al. 1981; Lucas et al. 1987; Taubes 2007; Taubes 2010.

". . . it's something dogs do too . . ." and subsequent discussion of insulin response in dogs: detailed bibliographic information and source notes on the subject of insulin can be found in *Chapter Three* of this notes index. See also Chieri et al. 1975; Diamond et al. 1988; Benthem et al. 2000.

". . . 'the principal nutrient' . . .": de-Oliveira et al. 2014.

"According to the United Nations . . .": statistical data on global food sources is available on the website for the Food and Agriculture Organization of the United Nations (www.faostat3.org) (last visited Mar. 8, 2016).

"Starches and sweets are the primary ingredients . . .": U.S. Department of Agriculture & U.S. Department of Health and Human Services 2010.

". . . more than 70% of the world's farmland . . .": Serna-Saldivar 2010.

". . . starchy crops weren't just uncommon . . ." and subsequent discussion of the availability of cereal grains and starchy carbohydrates to pre-agricultural humans: Eaton et al. 1985; Eaton et al. 1997; Cordain 1999.

"The cluster of technological innovations . . ." and subsequent discussion of Neolithic Revolution: Diamond 1987; Cordain 1999; Diamond 2002; Richards 2002; Hancock 2004; Wright 2004; Larson et al. 2014.

"Cereal grains are grasses . . ." and subsequent discussion of cereal grains: Cordain 1999; Serna-Saldivar 2010.

DOGS, DOG FOOD, AND DOGMA

". . . livestock could be selected for . . .": There was one group of animals that fit this bill particularly well: ruminants. This class of large, herbivorous mammals includes livestock animals such as cattle, goats, and sheep, as well as wild species like bison, moose, and deer. They are grazers who subsist entirely on plant matter. The word "ruminant" is a nod to an organ called the rumen, the defining component of the uniquely complex digestive infrastructure that these animals have evolved in order to turn prodigious quantities of plants into bodily tissues and energy. Their sophisticated digestive systems feature four-compartment stomachs (the rumen being just the first compartment), multiple rounds of chewing, swallowing, and regurgitating, and even a resident population of bacteria that live in the rumen and help to ferment ingested plant matter. This advanced process makes ruminants really good at turning cereal grains and other grasses into useful energy and bodily tissues. And that, combined with the fact that adult ruminants could each provide farmers with hundreds of pounds of nourishing meat and even grew large enough to do things like tow plows, made them ideal fits for early forays into animal husbandry. For more on ruminant physiology see Reece 2009; Hackmann et al. 2010. For more on the domestication of ruminants see ibid; Diamond 2002.

". . . 'the worst mistake in the history of the human race' . . .": Diamond 1987.

". . . carbs are everywhere . . ." and subsequent discussion of prevalence of carbohydrates in the food supply: for an introduction to the methods of production behind our modern-day food supply, no one does it better than U.C. Berkeley professor Michael Pollan. See particularly Pollan 2006. The nutritional content of packaged food products can be discerned from the "Nutrition Facts" labeling found on each item's packaging. Additional nutritional information about specific food products easily can be found on any number of online databases.

". . . its infamous Food Guide Pyramid . . ." and subsequent discussion of Food Guide Pyramid and its dietary recommendations: U.S. Department of Agriculture 1992; Taubes 2007; Taubes 2010.

". . . 'mix science with the influence of powerful agricultural interests' . . .": Datz 2011.

". . . four or fewer firms typically dominate . . ." and subsequent discussion of consolidation in food processing industries: Mattera 2004; Hendrickson et al. 2007.

"Cargill is no less than . . ." and subsequent discussion of Cargill, Inc.: all financial figures from Cargill Inc.'s 2015 Annual Report (available online at http://www.cargill.com/annual-report/) (last visited Mar. 12, 2016). Comparison of Cargill's annual revenues with other American businesses is based on the 2015 editions of *Forbes*'s "List of America's Largest Private Companies" and "The World's Biggest Public Companies" (available online at http://www.forbes.com/) (last visited Mar. 12, 2016).

"ADM is only slightly smaller . . .": financial figures and rankings from 2015 edition of the *Fortune* 500 list (available online at http://www.fortune.com/fortune500/) (last visited Mar. 12, 2016).

"One of the core business functions . . ." and subsequent discussion of food processing: Cargill Inc.'s 2015 Annual Report; Archer Daniels Midland Company's 2014 Annual Report; Mattera 2004; Pollan 2006; Hendrickson et al. 2007.

". . . 'You will not find the "Cargill" brand' . . .": from the Cargill website (http://www.cargill.com/products/brands-advertising/) (last visited Mar. 12, 2016).

". . . 'whatever you ate or drank today' . . .": Whitford et al. 2011.

"They include Coca-Cola . . ." all references to the *Fortune* 500 list come from the 2015 online edition.

"According to the Center for Responsive Politics . . .": all facts and figures from the public website for the Center for Responsive Politics (http://www.opensecrets.org) (last visited Mar. 13, 2016).

". . . the former Chief of Staff for the USDA . . .": Schlosser 2004.

". . . 'right now you'd have a hard time' . . .": ibid.

"Corn and wheat are the two most heavily subsidized crops in the country . . .": data from the public website for the Environmental Working Group (http://www.ewg.org) (last visited Mar. 13, 2016).

". . . of the 300 million or so acres . . ." and subsequent discussion of crop acreage totals: Haspel 2014.

"Just slightly more than 10% of . . ." and subsequent discussion of domestic corn use: 2015 data from the U.S.D.A., Economic Research Service (available online at http://www.ers.usda.gov/media/866543/cornusetable.html) (last visited Mar. 13, 2016).

". . . 'when scientists say a food is palatable' . . .": Kessler 2009.

"One of the most well-established facts in all of the nutritional science literature . . ." and subsequent discussion of human taste preferences: Drewnowski 1995.

". . . 'we once thought that in the absence of hunger' . . .": Kessler 2009.

"If you ask a neuroscientist . . ." and subsequent discussion of the neuroscience of pleasure: Schultz 2006; Berridge et al. 2008; Kessler 2009. At least a dozen other academic papers documenting these phenomena are discussed in Kessler 2009.

". . . Kessler claims that the simple carbohydrate sucrose . . .": ibid.

". . . 'the brain's big lie' . . .": McGonigal 2012.

"According to *Ad Age* . . .": "Meet America's 25 Biggest Advertisers: Most-Advertised Brands By 2012 U.S. Measured-Media Spending." *Ad Age.* July 8, 2013. (Available online at http://adage.com/article/news/meet-america-s-25-biggest-advertisers/242969/) (last visited Mar. 15, 2016).

"And according to Yale's Rudd Center . . .": "Sugary Drinks FACTS – Advertising Spending," Rudd Center for Food Policy & Obesity (available online at http://sugarydrinkfacts.org/marketing_rankings.aspx) (last visited Mar. 16, 2016).

". . . the technical sophistication with which they do so . . ." and subsequent discussion of sensory stimulation marketing and other high-tech marketing practices: Cohen 2014.

"Children as young as three years old . . .": McAlister et al. 2010.

"McDonald's restaurants are home to . . .": Schlosser 2001.

". . . a British High Court Justice affirmatively ruled that . . .": Barrett 2007.

". . . 'one of the most successful promotions in the history of American advertising' . . .": Schlosser 2001 (emphasis mine).

". . . 'Advertising efforts have shifted from persuasion to manipulation' . . .": Cohen 2014.

"In 2015, Americans spent upwards of $60 billion . . .": data from the publicly-available website for the American Pet Products Association (http://www.americanpetproducts.org/press_industrytrends.asp) (last visited Mar. 16, 2016).

"Together, this sector makes up more than a third . . ." and subsequent discussion of U.S. dog food market: ibid; Euromonitor International 2014.

". . . the eighth largest one in the country. . .": Schaffer 2009.

". . . Swiss corporation Nestlé, S.A. . . ." and subsequent discussion of Nestlé, S.A.: all facts and figures from the 2015 edition of *Fortune*'s Global 500 (http://fortune.com/global500/nestle-70/) (last visited Mar. 16, 2016).

"Second is Mars, Inc. . . ." and subsequent discussion of Mars, Inc. and Del Monte Foods: data from the 2015 edition of *Forbes*'s list of "America's Largest Private Companies" (available at http://www.forbes.com/largest-private-companies/) (last visited Mar. 16, 2016).

"The so-called "specialty' brands . . ." and subsequent discussion of specialty dog food market and market concentration in pet foods: Euromonitor International 2014.

". . . the businesses that actually print their names . . ." and subsequent discussion of the role of suppliers in pet food industry: Nestle 2008.

" . . . 'Pet food recipes may differ in proportions of ingredients' . . .": ibid.

"Nestle made this claim . . ." and subsequent discussion of melamine scandal: ibid.

". . . 'supplies all or a meaningful portion of the private-label wet food products' . . .": from the website for Simmons Pet Food (http://simmonspetfood.simmonsglobal.com/customers/) (last visited Mar. 22, 2014).

". . . as a series of experiments conducted in the United Kingdom recently demonstrated . . .": Hewson-Hughes et al. 2013.

". . . 'remarkable consistency' . . .": ibid.

"According to an *ad hoc* committee convened by the National Research Council . . .": National Research Council 2006.

"The story is said to have begun . . ." and subsequent discussion of the history of dog food: Lane 1902; Schaffer 2009.

". . . the company is probably employing some variant of the very same process . . ." and subsequent discussion of extrusion processing: Hand et al. 2000; National Research Council 2006; Fox et al. 2009; Schaffer 2009; Case et al. 2011. Extrusion processing is also described on the publicly-available website for the Pet Food Institute, a major pet food industry lobbying organization (http://petfoodinstitute.org/?page=DryPetFood) (last visited Mar. 21, 2016).

"I contacted Purina . . ." and subsequent discussion of Purina factory tour requests: personal e-mails, Oct. 2014.

"Historically, Blue Buffalo's advertisements . . ." and subsequent discussion of Blue Buffalo marketing practices: Olson 2014; Barrett July 2014; Barrett Nov. 2014.

". . . 'Love Them Like Family' . . ." and other Blue Buffalo marketing slogans: from Blue Buffalo's website (http://bluebuffalo.com) (last visited Mar. 21, 2016).

". . . 'Hi Daniel, Thank you for taking' . . .": personal e-mails, Oct. 2014.
". . . more marketing ploy than reality . . ." and subsequent discussion of Blue Buffalo's financial performance: Barrett July 2014; Barrett Nov. 2014; Olson 2014; Picker 2015.

"In 2014, Purina filed a multimillion-dollar . . ." and subsequent discussion of *Nestle-Purina PetCare Co. v. Blue Buffalo Co. Ltd.* (E.D. Mo. No. 4:14-cv-00859-RWS) and other Blue Buffalo lawsuits: Barrett July 2014; Barrett Nov. 2014; Soule 2015.

"It certainly didn't as of 2007 . . . ": Nestle 2008.

"They all denied my requests.": personal e-mails, Oct. 2014.

". . . 'We are the home for custom contract manufacturing' . . .": from the website for CJ Foods, Inc. (http://www.extrudedpetfood.com/) (last visited Mar. 22, 2014).

". . . 'The biggest brands in pet food partner with' . . .": from the website for American Nutrition (http://www.animanufacturing.com/) (last visited Mar. 22, 2014).

". . . 'We are one of the largest pet treat manufacturers' . . .": from the website for Mountain Country Foods (http://www.mcfoods.com/) (last visited May. 22, 2014).

"In exchange, you will receive about 540 calories . . .": from the website for McDonald's (http://www.mcdonalds.com) (last visited Mar. 22, 2014).

"If you buy from the online retailer Chewy.com . . .": from http://www.chewy.com (last visited Mar. 22, 2014).

"As much as 50% of beef . . ." and subsequent discussion of rendering industry: Fox et al. 2009.

"Human beings have been smoking tobacco since ancient times . . ." and subsequent discussion of the history of smoking: Gately 2001; Giovino 2001; Brandt 2009; Proctor 2012.

"But it wasn't until 1929 . . .": Proctor 2001.

"And the first major studies definitively linking lung cancer to smoking . . .": Doll et al. 1950; Wynder et al. 1950.

"In 1964, the Surgeon General . . .": U.S. Department of Health, Education, and Welfare 1964.

". . . it wasn't until about 1970 . . .": Giovino 2001.

"Even today there are more than 40 million . . ." and subsequent discussion of current smoking trends: Centers for Disease Control and Prevention 2015.

"I put together a short message.": and subsequent discussion of communications with Tiffany Bierer and Mars PetCare: personal e-mails, 2015-2016.

Chapter Five: Truth, Fiction, and Veterinary Nutritional Dogma

"'I believe that nicotine is not addictive' . . .": Hearing on the Regulation of Tobacco Products, House Committee on Energy and Commerce, Subcommittee on Health and the Environment, April 14, 1994 (transcript available online at http://senate.ucsf.edu/tobacco/executives1994congress.html) (last visited Feb. 29, 2016). On that day, Mr. Campbell was one of seven tobacco CEOs to testify under oath that nicotine is not addictive.

"There are only 30 AVMA-accredited veterinary schools . . ." and subsequent discussion of selectivity of veterinary school admissions processes: from the website for the Association of American Veterinary Medical Colleges (http://aavmc.org/) and the website for the American Veterinary Medical Association (https://www.avma.org/) (both visited May 20, 2016).

". . . not only must aspiring veterinarians demonstrate . . ." and subsequent discussion of licensure requirements: from the website for the AVMA (https://www.avma.org/) (visited May 20, 2016) (including links to individual state licensure boards) and the website for the National Board of Medical Examiners (www.nbvme.org/) (visited May 20, 2016).

"Melissa Tucker knew all this . . ." and subsequent discussion of Melissa Tucker's experiences with veterinary school and veterinary practice: interviews, Melissa Tucker, 2015-2016.

". . . 'Folks get most of their clothes' . . ." and other quotations: ibid.

". . . one of the most selective and prestigious veterinary schools in the country . . .": at the time of writing, the school was ranked in the top three in the country by *U.S. News & World Report*.

"Graduate programs in veterinary medicine are overseen by . . ." and subsequent discussion of AVMA's accreditation policies: from the website for the AVMA (https://www.avma.org/) (visited May 20, 2016).

". . . curricula tend to look pretty similar . . ." and subsequent discussion of DVM curricula: recent curricula for all 30 AVMA-accredited veterinary schools are available online, with the exception of Tuskegee University. In May of 2016, I personally reviewed the curriculum for each AVMA-accredited school, with the exception of Tuskegee. I also contacted the majority of the veterinary schools in the country and requested to interview a representative in order to glean additional information about course offerings and instruction. Of the schools I contacted, all but one—the University of Minnesota—either denied my requests or failed to respond to me.

". . . 'Veterinary Anatomy I' . . ." and other course names: all from the course catalog for the Midwestern University College of Veterinary Medicine (available online at https://www.midwestern.edu/course_catalog_home/glendale_az_campus_/college_of_veterinary_medicine/curriculum.html) (last visited May 20, 2016).

". . . for every dollar spent on human health care . . .": Chen 2009; Lavizzo-Mourey 2012.

". . . 'I'd say that precisely zero' . . .": interview, Jordan Scherk, 2016.

". . . 'the number one chronic health concern' . . .": Wakshlag et al. 2011.

". . . 'Ornamental Fish Medicine' and 'Equine Dentistry' . . .": both course names from the course catalog for the Oregon State University College of Veterinary Medicine (http://vetmed.oregonstate.edu/students/current/curriculum/year-4-curriculum) (last visited May 23, 2016).

" . . . 'In veterinary school, I'd been taught how to treat diseases' . . .": Ward 2010.

". . . has been coming around to since at least the 1970s . . .": Doig 1975.

". . . 'the practice of veterinary medicine is increasingly becoming' . . .": interview, Willem Becker, 2015.

"The American College of Veterinary Nutrition is the organization that provides . . ." and subsequent discussion of the ACVN: the Constitution and Bylaws of the ACVN (available online at http://www.acvn.org/constitution-and-bylaws/) (last visited May 24, 2016); the website for the ACVN (http://www.acvn.org/) (last visited May 24, 2016); personal e-mails, David Dzanis (ACVN Secretary), 2014.

". . . fewer than 80 of the more than 100,000 vets . . .": according to the
Diplomate Directory for the ACVN, as of May 24, 2016, there were only 78
ACVN diplomates living in the United States. According to the AVMA, as of
2015, there were 105,358 veterinarians in the United States
(https://www.avma.org/KB/Resources/Statistics/Pages/Market-research-
statistics-US-veterinarians.aspx) (last visited May 24, 2016).

"Many of the board-certified veterinary nutritionists in America . . ."
and subsequent discussion of employment of ACVN diplomates: personal e-
mails, David Dzanis (ACVN Secretary), 2014.

"The strategy of marketing dog food through . . ." and subsequent
discussion of marketing to veterinarians: Parker-Pope 1997; Martin 2008; Fox
et al. 2009; interviews, Melissa Tucker, 2015-2016 (Dr. Tucker is one of more
than a dozen veterinarians that I interviewed).

". . . rendering animal byproducts and packing meat . . .": Markley 1956.

". . . 'It's just like taking drugs' . . .": Parker-Pope 1997.

"The average tuition approaches $50,000 . . ." and subsequent discussion
of the financial costs of veterinary school: from the publicly-available website
for the Association of American Veterinary Medical Colleges
(http://aavmc.org/Media-FAQs.aspx) (last visited May 26, 2016).

". . . 'the bulk of our expenditure goes to' . . .": Parker-Pope 1997
(emphasis mine).

". . . 'brainwashed into thinking they have to' . . .": Martin 2008.

**". . . 'when the full extent of it is realized the reputation of the
veterinary community' . . ."**: Fox et al. 2009.

". . . 'share of mind' . . .": this same phrasing was used by a Purina-
employed veterinarian to describe the benefits of veterinarian-based
marketing strategies: Parker-Pope 1997. This perspective is also consistent
with a study published this year in *JAMA Internal Medicine*. Researchers
examined the drug-prescribing behavior of physicians who had received free
meals from drug manufacturers. They found that physicians who received
free meals were more likely to prescribe whatever brand-name drug was being
promoted. See DeJong 2016.

"The AVMA . . . received a $1.5 million donation from Hill's . . .": Nolen 2008.

". . . 'advancing the science and practice' . . .": from the publicly-available website for the AVMA (https://www.avma.org/) (last visited May 26, 2016).

". . . the World Small Animal Veterinary Association . . .": from the publicly-available website for the WSAVA (http://www.wsava.org/educational/global-nutrition-committee) (last visited May 26, 2016).

"Funding for companion animal research is notoriously hard to come by . . ." and subsequent discussion of small animal research: Parker-Pope 1997; National Research Council 2005; Koppel 2014; *AVMA Policy: Concept for the Institute for Companion Animal and Equine Research (ICAER)* (available online at https://www.avma.org/KB/Policies/Pages/Concept-for-the-ICAER.aspx) (last visited May 26, 2016).

". . . 'funding for health-related research dedicated to' . . .": ibid.

". . . the National Cancer Institute alone . . .": *National Cancer Institute Budget Fact Book Fiscal Year 2014* (available online at http://www.cancer.gov/about-nci/budget/fact-book) (last visited May 26, 2016).

". . . private donors and corporations provided more than $55 million . . .": National Research Council 2005.

"Since 2013, Hill's, Blue Buffalo, and PETCO have all donated . . ." and subsequent discussion of financial performance of the Morris Animal Foundation and the AKC Canine Health Foundation: all facts and figures from the annual reports for the organizations (available online at http://www.morrisanimalfoundation.org/about-maf/publications/annual-reports.html and http://www.akcchf.org/about-us/Financials/) (both visited on May 26, 2016).

". . . 'considerable research on companion animals is conducted' . . .": National Research Council 2005.

"A paper recently published in the *Journal of the Science of Food and Agriculture* . . .": Koppel 2014.

"Three of the four editors of *Canine and Feline Nutrition: A Resource for Companion Animal Professionals . . .*": Case et al. 2011.

"In the case of *Small Animal Clinical Nutrition . . .*": Hand et al. 2000.

" . . . at the federal level, the process is regulated primarily . . ." and subsequent discussion of the regulatory framework governing the sale of pet food in the United States: ibid; National Research Council 2006; Ward 2010; Case et al. 2011.

". . . 'arguably one of the most important animal food organizations' . . .": Ward 2010.

"AAFCO's stated goal is to ensure that . . .": and subsequent discussion of AAFCO requirements: Association of American Feed Control Officials Incorporated 2016. Summaries of the relevant terms of AAFCO's *Official Publication* can be found in Hand et al. 2000 and Case et al. 2011.

". . . the veterinary community has long been highly critical . . .": Fox et al. 2009; Ward 2010.

". . . until recently, AAFCO didn't require many producers to include . . ." and subsequent discussion of calorie labeling requirements in pet foods: Ward 2010; Association of American Feed Control Officials Incorporated 2016. The evolution of AAFCO's regulations is documented in the minutes of the semi-annual meetings of the organization's Pet Food Committee. Copies of meeting minutes dating back to 2005 are available online at http://www.aafco.org/Regulatory/Committees/Pet-Food (last visited May 30, 2016).

". . . representatives from Cargill, ADM, Purina . . .": Association of American Feed Control Officials Incorporated 2016.

". . . progressive, commonsensical pet food labeling requirements have . . .": from the meeting minutes of the semi-annual meetings of AAFCO's Pet Food Committee.

"Calorie labeling has been required on . . .": Wartella et al. 2010.

"A 2001 study revealed that 80% of pet owners . . .": Burns 2013.

" . . . 'regulators appear to be in favor of the proposal, industry opposes it' . . .": from the 2010 midyear meeting of AAFCO's Pet Food Committee.

"... 'dependent on the philosophy and marketing strategies of the individual manufacturer' . . .": from the publicly-available website for the ACVN (http://www.acvn.org/frequently-asked-questions/) (last visited May 31, 2016).

"Perhaps the best example of this common practice is the use of terms like . . ." and subsequent discussion of the perceived healthfulness of whole grains: Taubes 2007; Davis 2010; Taubes 2010.

"... 'Carbohydrates in nutritionally complete and balanced' . . .": from the publicly-available website for Purina Pro Plan Veterinary Diets (https://www.proplanveterinarydiets.com/pet-food-myths-and-facts/#cats-and-carbs) (last visited May 31, 2016).

"... 'Wheat is a valuable pet food ingredient' . . .": from the publicly-available website for Purina Pro Plan Veterinary Diets (https://www.proplanveterinarydiets.com/pet-food-myths-and-facts/#wheat) (last visited May 31, 2016).

"... 'Carbohydrates are a key source of energy for dogs and cats' . . .": from the publicly-available website for Blue Buffalo (http://bluebuffalo.com/why-choose-blue/nutrition-philosophy/) (last visited May 31, 2016).

"... 'Corn is an excellent ingredient because of' . . .": from a publicly-available website for Hill's pet products (http://www.hillspet.com.au/en-au/faq-ingredients-and-myths.html) (last visited May 31, 2016).

"... 'Starch is abundant in the seeds of cereal grains' . . .": from a publicly-available website for Eukanuba products (http://www.eukanuba.co.uk/professionals/articles/carbohydrates-for-dogs) (last visited May 31, 2016).

"... 'Cats and dogs can live without carbohydrates in their food' . . .": from a publicly-available website for Royal Canin products (http://www.royalcanin.com.au/health-nutrition/nutrients/carbohydrates/carbohydrates) (last visited May 31, 2016).

"... 'the veterinarian's nurse, laboratory technician' . . .": from the website for the National Association of Veterinary Technicians in America (http://www.navta.net/) (last visited May 31, 2016).

"... 'we do everything except' ...": from the publicly-available website for *U.S. News & World Report* (http://money.usnews.com/careers/best-jobs/veterinary-technologist-and-technician) (last visited May 31, 2016).

"... according to the Bureau of Labor Statistics ...": ibid.

"... 'This is a meeting for veterinary clinic employees' ...": personal e-mails, February 2015.

"... 'Pet Parents are Raving About' ..." and all other quotations (oral and written) from the event at the Doubletree were made or otherwise provided to me on March 4, 2015, at an event called "Veterinary Technical Nutrition Counselor – One Full Day of Interactive Veterinary Nutrition Education."

Chapter Six: The Magic of Exercise

"... 'Do what you love' ...": Harding et al. 1958.

"In 2013, at only two years of age ..." and other background information about Crystal McClaran and her dog Bo: interviews, Crystal McClaran, 2013.

"... the largest and most influential of which is ..." and subsequent discussion of DockDogs, Inc.: ibid.; publicly-available website for DockDogs, Inc. (http://www.dockdogs.com/) (last visited Mar. 26, 2016).

"... 'Effective weight reduction' ...": Shearer 2010.

"... 'If you're reading this book' ...": Ward 2010.

"In 2000, two public health researchers from Finland's University of Helsinki ...": Fogelholm et al. 2000.

"... 'The current physical activity guideline for adults' ...": Saris et al. 2003.

"... meta-analyses ... by a Brown University professor...": Wing 1999.

"... meta-analyses... by ... two doctors from the Medical College of St. Bartholomew's Hospital ...": Garrow et al. 1995.

" ... the largest academic society for the study of nutrition ...": from the publicly-available website for the Nutrition Society (http://www.nutritionsociety.org/) (last visited Mar. 24, 2016).

"... 'The majority of studies suggest that low levels of activity are only weakly associated' ...": Wareham et al. 2005.

" ... 'It seems reasonable that persons with' ...": Haskell et al. 2007 (emphasis mine).

" ... is a former boxer and college football player ...": Apple 2014.

"... he probably burns around 1,350 calories per day ...": National Research Council 2006.

"... he'll probably burn about 70 additional calories ...": ibid.

"... roughly one-fifth of one cup ...": calorie information from Blue Buffalo's publicly-available website (http://www.bluebuffalo.com/) (last visited Mar. 24, 2016).

"... or about a third of an Extra-Large Milkbone ...": calorie information from the publicly-available website from the Association for Pet Obesity Prevention (http://www.petobesityprevention.org/) (last visited Mar. 24, 2016).

"Perhaps the only peer-reviewed study to systematically examine ...": Derrell et al. 1997.

"... 'believe that "a tired dog is a happy dog"' ...": from the publicly-available website for the Tufts Animal Behavior Clinic (http://www. http://vet.tufts.edu/behavior-clinic/resources-behavior/canine-behavior-issues/) (last visited Mar. 26, 2016).

"... has famously described a bout of daily exercise as the single most important strategy ...": Milan is fond of expressing his behavior-modification strategy as three simple steps, "exercise, discipline, and affection, in that order." (From http://www.cesarsway.com/) (last visited Mar. 26, 2016).

"... Ernie Ward ... [has] written of the therapeutic effects of the daily walk ...": Ward 2010.

"... psychologist Alexandra Horowitz ... [has] written of the therapeutic effects of the daily walk ...": Horowitz 2009.

"... 'an inherent desire to protect home and family' ...": breed standard for the Rottweiler available online at http://www.akc.org/dog-breeds/rottweiler/) (last visited Mar. 26, 2016).

"It's just not that easy to know what's going on between the ears of a non-verbal animal ...": For an introduction to the various challenges inherent to thinking about the consciousness of non-human animals, see Nagel 1974.

"... 'happiness is novelty' ...": Horowitz 2009.

"... studies have consistently shown aerobic exercise to be an easy, natural, and highly effective fix ..." and subsequent discussion of the psychic benefits of exercise: Ratey et al. 2008 (and sources discussed therein).

"... 'the single most powerful tool' ...": ibid.

"... hundreds and hundreds of research papers' ...": ibid.

" Kyra Sundance ... once told me that she advises clients ...": interview, Kyra Sundance, 2014.

"Speaking at a medical conference in the fall of 1976 ..." and subsequent discussion of exercise trends in the 1970s: Gilmore 1977.

"... 'until just a few years ago' ...": ibid.

"... 'The new conventional wisdom' ...": ibid (emphasis mine).

"In 2009, for instance, a meta-analysis examining the link between cardiorespiratory fitness ...": Kodama et al. 2009.

"... only one way to improve cardiorespiratory fitness ...": this common-sense phenomenon has been documented in all manner of species, including crocodiles: Owerkowicz et al. 2008.

"As a team of researchers recently wrote in the *American Journal of Cardiology* ...": Swain et al. 2006.

"By 2007, the American Heart Association and the American College of Sports Medicine had made it official ...": Haskell et al. 2007.

"The epidemiological evidence shows that 'vigorous exercise' is more . . .": ibid.

". . . 'unclear at present' . . .": ibid.

"According to the CDC, heart disease is the number one . . .": according to the CDC's publicly-available website (http://www.cdc.gov/nchs/fastats/leading-causes-of-death.htm) (last visited Mar. 30, 2016), heart disease killed 611,105 Americans in 2014.

". . . only about one out of every ten adult dogs . . .": Fleming et al. 2011.

". . . a group of doctors from the Medical College of New York and Yale University has found that . . .": Sessa et al. 1994.

"It's a fact of life that as we (both human beings and dogs) age . . ." and subsequent discussion of sarcopenia: Meyer et al. 1980; Lawler et al. 2008; Freeman 2011.

"In human beings, sarcopenia has been shown to . . .": Sakuma et al. 2012.

". . . skeletal muscles are a 'sink' into which . . .": Braith et al. 2006.

"Studies have consistently shown that both muscular strength and resistance training itself . . .": Ivy et al. 1999; Katzmarzyk et al. 2002; Haskell et al. 2007.

" . . . the evidence suggests what's called a 'dose-response relationship' . . .": Raniken et al. 2002.

" . . . in the case of muscular fitness, the evidence seems to show what's called a 'threshold effect' . . .": Anker et al. 1997; Pollock et al. 2000; Artero et al. 2011.

"To become strong enough to enjoy these benefits . . ." and subsequent discussion of resistance training routines for human beings: Haskell et al. 2007.

"Several different technologies and methods . . .": Meyer et al. 1980; Lawler et al. 2009; Freeman 2011.

"Researchers have also found positive correlations between . . .": Slupe et al. 2008; Parker et al. 2011.

". . . 'emerging syndrome of importance in dogs and cats' . . .": Freeman 2011.

". . .'Bo has incredible drive' . . ." and other statements about Bo's behavior: interview, Crystal McClaran, 2013.

". . . 'When we think of dogs' . . .": Coppinger et al. 1995.

"In a 2011 cover story . . ." and subsequent discussion of English Bulldog breed standard: Denizet-Lewis 2011.

"A 2010 study published in the *Journal of Small Animal Practice* . . .": Adams et al. 2010.

Chapter Seven: How Fat is Too Fat?

". . . 'The history of science, like the history of all human ideas' . . .": Popper 1963.

"Steven Beckerman's first sighthound was . . ." and subsequent discussion of Beckerman's experiences with sighthounds: interviews, Steven Beckerman, 2014.

"Greyhounds are the fastest dogs in the world . . ." and subsequent discussion of greyhound speed: from the publicly-available websites for World's Fastest Dogs (http://www.worldsfastestdogs.com/) (last visited Mar. 31, 2016) and the Greyhound Hall of Fame (http://www.greyhoundhalloffame.com/) (last visited Mar. 31 2016).

"According to polling conducted by Dr. Ernie Ward . . .": according to APOP, 42% of dog and cat owners will admit that they have no idea how much their dogs should weigh (http://www.petobesityprevention.org/pet-obesity-remains-at-epidemic-levels-according-to-new-research/) (last visited Mar. 31, 2016).

". . . most of those that think they do . . .": according to APOP, 93% of obese dogs belong to owners who believe their dogs are in a "healthy" or "normal" weight range (http://www.petobesityprevention.org/pet-obesity-remains-at-epidemic-levels-according-to-new-research/) (last visited Mar. 31, 2016).

". . . 'The Fat Gap is rampant' . . .": ibid.

"Dr. Alexander German is one of the . . .": according to his profile on the academic research website ResearchGate, Dr. German's 141 academic publications have been cited more than 2,000 times. (https://www.researchgate.net/profile/Alexander_German) (last visited Apr. 7, 2016).

"Writing in 2006, Dr. German . . ." : German 2006 (emphasis mine).

"Once our ancestors recognized . . ." and subsequent discussion of the evolutionary descent of the domestic dog: Serpell 1995; Budiansky 1999.

". . . observe the domestic dog in Victorian England . . ." and subsequent discussion of both the history and modern practice of conformation dog shows: Lane 1902; Budiansky 1999; Goldberg 2002; Schaffer 2009; Denizet-Lewis 2011. Additional information from the publicly-available website for the American Kennel Club (http://www.akc.org) (last visited Apr. 12, 2016).

". . . the breed standard used by the American Kennel Club to evaluate Golden Retrievers is . . .": from the publicly-available website for the Golden Retriever Club of America (https://www.grca.org/about-the-breed/akc-breed-standard/) (last visited Apr. 12, 2016).

" . . . scandalous BBC One production . . .": Harrison 2008.

". . . 'protect and advance the interests of the breed' . . .": this statement is commonly found in the mission statements for individual breed organizations. See, for example, the publicly-available websites for the Pembroke Welsh Corgi Club of America (http://pwcca.org/about-the-pwcca/mission-statement/), the Kuvasz Club of America (http://kuvaszclubofamerica.org/about/constitution), and the American Lhasa Apso Club (https://www.lhasaapso.org/club/mission.html) (all visited on Apr. 12, 2016).

". . . 'curled as tightly as possible' . . .": from the publicly-available website for the Pug Dog Club of America (http://pugs.org/pug-standard/) (last visited Apr. 12, 2016).

". . . 'don't win in the conformation ring unless they are fat' . . .": Zink 1997.

DOGS, DOG FOOD, AND DOGMA

". . . 'if your dog is winning in the conformation ring' . . .": ibid.

". . . a recent study conducted by Dr. German and one of his University of Liverpool colleagues . . .": Such et al. 2015.

". . . in the case of the Newfoundland, the AKC's official breed standard recommends . . .": breed standard downloaded from the publicly-available website for the American Kennel Club on April 12, 2016.

" . . . 'proportionately tall' . . .": from the breed standard for the St. Bernard, downloaded from the publicly-available website for the American Kennel Club on April 12, 2016.

". . . 'solid and big for his inches' . . .": from the breed standard for the Beagle, downloaded from the publicly-available website for the American Kennel Club on April 12, 2016.

"Several such protocols . . . have been created and scientifically validated . . .": Laflamme 1997; German et al. 2006.

"The first scientifically validated canine . . ." and subsequent discussion of 9-category BCS protocol: Laflamme 1997.

". . . 'the correlation between BCS and percent body fat' . . .": ibid.

"This system was developed in 2006 by Alexander German . . ." and subsequent discussion of 7-category BCS protocol: German et al. 2006.

". . . 'The scores of the owners' . . .": ibid.

". . . 'More structured epidemiological studies are required' . . .": ibid.

"According to the W.H.O., more than 1.9 billion . . ." and subsequent discussion of human obesity epidemic: World Health Organization 2015.

". . . 'abnormal or excessive fat accumulation' . . .": ibid. Similar definitions have been used in the scientific literature on canine obesity too. See Laflamme 1997; German 2006; German et al. 2010.

". . . specific body condition norms have evolved . . ." and subsequent discussion of the evolution of body condition norms: Schwartz 1983; Stearns 1997; Fogel 2004; Eknoyan 2006; Barrett 2007; Taubes 2007; Taubes 2010; Wells 2010.

"... 'persons who are naturally very fat' ..." and quotations from Celsus of Alexandria and Ben Franklin were all gathered by Dr. Barrett and reported (with original source information) in Barrett 2007.

"... William Banting's *Letter on Corpulence* ...": Banting 2005.

"... William Wadd's *Comments on Corpulency* ...": Wadd 1829.

"... Cecil Webb-Johnson's *Why Be Fat?* ...": Webb-Johnson 1923.

"... 'to be thin is fashionable' ...": McLester 1924.

"In 1943, executives working on behalf of the Metropolitan Life Insurance Company ..." and subsequent discussion of MetLife's height-weight tables: Keys et al. 1972; Pai et al. 2000; Eknoyan 2006; Barrett 2007; Eknoyan 2008.

"The most obvious shortcoming ...": the height-weight tables attempted to address this issue by altering weight recommendations depending on an individual's "frame size." This imprecise criterion has been criticized by Dr. Barrett and others.

"Quetelet was, by all accounts ..." and subsequent discussion of Adolphe Quetelet and his creation of what came to be known as the Quetelet Index and, later, the Body Mass Index: Menand 2002; Eknoyan 2006; Eknoyan 2008.

"... with the publication of a well-known paper by the American scientist Ancel Keys ...": Keys et al. 1972.

"Keys was one of the leading . . ." and subsequent discussion of Ancel Keys: Keys et al. 1994; Taubes 2007; Blackburn et al. 2014. Keys's early work on emergency rations and starvation heavily influenced the way that the U.S. military fed its soldiers during World War II. But it was his later work on diet and cardiovascular disease that made him into a true science superstar and landed him on the cover of *Time* magazine. Keys was a vigorous proponent of the idea that diets high in total fat content and, more particularly, saturated fat, contribute to the development of heart disease. Most famously, intrigued by the relatively high concentration of centenarians in lipo-phobic cultures like those found in coastal Japan and Italy, he produced research showing a strong correlation between total fat consumption and heart disease (among other prominent associations) in seven different nations from far-flung corners of the world. Although his "Seven Countries Study" has been criticized for methodological shortcomings (particularly by Gary Taubes and his intellectual progeny), it nevertheless played a leading role in shaping the discourse over diet and heart disease during the second half of the Twentieth Century and beyond. And, whatever one thinks of the quality of the science underlying Keys's positions on diet and disease, it is worth observing that the man himself lived to the ripe old age of 101. His BMI paper was published more than ten years after his Seven Countries Study began. Though less well known, it is arguably even more enduring in its relevance.

". . . BMI is widely used by public health . . .": BMI-based overweight and obesity guidelines can be found on the publicly-available websites for each of the W.H.O. (http://www.who.int/topics/obesity/en/), the National Institutes of Health (http://www.nhlbi.nih.gov/health/health-topics/topics/obe/diagnosis), and the Centers for Disease Control and Prevention (http://www.cdc.gov/healthyweight/assessing/bmi/adult_bmi/index.html) (all last visited on Apr. 6, 2016).

". . . more than a few foreign public health bodies . . .": see, for example, Japan Society for the Study of Obesity 2002.

". . . 'simple, inexpensive, safe, and practical' . . .": Gallagher et al. 1996.

"Is it subject to errors . . .": For the most part, these shortcomings are only relevant in individual cases. When BMI is used to analyze large populations, individual deviations tend to come out in the wash. Which explains why large-scale epidemiological studies and public health organizations like the WHO so often gravitate towards BMI-based body fat analyses. In those contexts, BMI is particularly useful.

". . . Jay Cutler, the four-time IFBB . . ." and subsequent discussion about Jay Cutler and other bodybuilders: Milliard 2011.

"In 2000 the group published an extensive . . .": World Health Organization 2000.

". . . enormous body of evidence . . ." and subsequent discussion of evidence linking adiposity with specific diseases: ibid; Hubert et al. 1983; Ohlson et al. 1985; Manson et al. 1990; Schapira et al. 1994; Kannel et al. 1996; Field et al. 2001; World Cancer Research Fund/American Institute for Cancer Research 2007; Prospective Studies Collaboration 2009.

". . . a 500-page analysis of the links between cancer and obesity . . .": World Cancer Research Fund/American Institute for Cancer Research 2007.

"In his 1960 paper *The Pathology of Obesity* . . .": Hartroft 1960.

". . . 'Perhaps with the advent of more precise tools' . . .": ibid.

". . . by a young scientist named Jeffrey Freidman . . ." and subsequent discussion of Jeffrey Friedman's life and work: Allan 2012.

"In 1994, Friedman and his team published their findings . . .": Zhang et al. 1994.

". . . since the publication of Friedman's 1994 *Nature* paper, dozens of other body fat secretions . . ." and subsequent discussion of the pathophysiology of adiposity in humans: Lean 2000; Coussens et al. 2002; Libby et al. 2005; Redinger 2007. And in dogs: Eirmann et al. 2009; German et al. 2010; Wakshlag et al. 2011.

". . . 'an attractive environment for tumor growth' . . .": Coussens et al. 2002.

"Recent epidemiological data suggest that as many as 25% of all cancers . . .": Vendramini-Costa et al. 2012.

". . . all-cause mortality risk is higher than that of their somewhat fatter peers . . ." and subsequent discussion of relationship between adiposity and all-cause mortality: Toriano et al. 1996; World Health Organization 2000; Flegal et al. 2005; de Golzalez et al. 2010.

". . . the 'Obesity Paradox' . . .": the term "Obesity Paradox" seems to have originated in 2002: Gruberg et al. 2002.

"It is a topic that tends to provoke something resembling tribal warfare . . ." and subsequent discussion of disputes over the validity and existence of the Obesity Paradox: Flegal et al. 2013; Grace et al. 2013; Hughes 2013; Sifferlin 2015.

". . . no overwhelming consensus as to *how* adiposity is supposed to reduce mortality risk . . ." and subsequent discussion of the potential physiological causes of the Obesity Paradox: Hong et al. 2012; Schenkeveld et al. 2012; Flegal et al. 2013; Grace et al. 2013; Kalantar-Zadeh et al. 2014; Dixon et al. 2015; Sifferlin 2015.

". . . 'Metaphorically, we can liken such cardiovascular risk factors as obesity' . . .": Kalantar-Zadeh et al. 2014.

". . . perpetual process of degradation . . ." and subsequent discussion of protein turnover: Lecker et al. 1999; Biolo et al. 2002; Wolfe 2006; Zhang et al. 2006.

". . . 'Muscle plays a central role in whole-body protein metabolism' . . .": Wolfe 2006.

". . . 'essential to survival' . . .": ibid.

". . . in cases of fasting and starvation . . ." and subsequent discussion of muscle wasting attendant to starvation and fasting: Keys et al. 1950; Tucker 2006.

". . . sarcopenia, the muscle wasting . . ." and subsequent discussion of sarcopenia: Bortz II, 1982; Evans et al. 1993; Baumgartner et al. 1998.

". . . cachexia, a well-documented medical phenomenon . . ." and subsequent discussion of cachexia: Tisdale 1997; Biolo et al. 2002; Wolfe 2006; Zhang et al. 2006.

". . . 'has a relatively poor capacity' . . .": Wells 2010.

". . . measured the body fat mass and fat-free mass of individuals directly . . ." and subsequent discussion of experiments comparing the relationships between fat mass, fat-free mass, and mortality: Allison et al. 1997; Heitmann, et al. 2000; Allison et al. 2002; Bigaard et al. 2004; Janssen, et al. 2005; de Schutter et al. 2014.

". . . 'our findings suggest that BMI represents joint but opposite' . . .": Bigaard et al. 2004.

". . . 'these results support the hypothesis that the apparently deleterious' . . .": Allison et al. 2002.

". . . 'the apparent U-shaped association between BMI and total mortality' . . .": Heitmann et al. 2000.

". . . the evidence suggesting that many low BMI scores are caused by deadly diseases . . .": Manson et al. 1987; Manson et al. 1995; Stokes 2014; Stokes et al. 2016.

". . . 'No fear can stand up to hunger' . . .": Conrad 2010.

". . . a single, impressively detailed study. . ." and subsequent discussion of Ancel Keys's Minnesota Starvation Study: Keys et al. 1950; Tucker 2006.

". . . 'Most had gaunt pinched faces and the peculiar sallow color' . . .": ibid.

"According to Matt Fitzgerald . . ." and subsequent discussion of body fat levels among professional athletes: Fitzgerald 2012.

". . . according to an article published in *Scientific American* . . .": Moisse 2010.

"A study published in the *International Journal of Sports Medicine* . . .": Sanchis-Gomar et al. 2011.

"And that study isn't an outlier . . .": for a review of the published literature on the longevity benefit of endurance exercise, see Ruiz et al. 2011.

". . . the leanest population on the planet . . ." and subsequent discussion of Okinawans and longevity: Willcox et al. 2006; B.J. Willcox et al. 2007; D.C. Willcox et al. 2007.

". . . as current citizens of the famine-plagued Democratic Republic of Congo . . .": World Health Organization/World Heart Federation 2005; Food and Agriculture Organization of the United Nations/World Food Programme 2010.

". . . has been shown to extend average lifespans in all manner of species . . .": Heilbronn et al. 2003.

". . . 'is the most robust and reproducible' . . .": B.J. Willcox et al. 2007 (discussing "short-lived" animals).

". . . 'marked reduction in fat mass is' . . .": Barzilai et al. 2001.

". . . 'All of the benefits of' . . .": Barzilai et al. 1999.

". . . improved longevity through calorie restriction has garnered its share of believers . . ." and subsequent discussion of the popularity of calorie restriction: from the website for the Calorie Restriction Society (www.crsociety.org) (last visited Apr. 27, 2016) and Turner 2010.

". . . 'I don't recognize what I see in the mirror' . . .": Nelson 2014.

". . . 'we live like we're about' . . .": Turner 2010.

". . . the lipids composing adipose tissue are also used . . ." and subsequent discussion of functional uses of adipose tissue: an excellent overview of the published literature on the functional uses of adipose tissue can be found in Wells 2010 (chapter six). See also Norgan 1997.

". . . giving you a BMI that is likely to be well below . . .": Deurenberg et al. 1991.

"It is likely that your body uses about 1500 calories' worth of energy . . .": Johnstone et al. 2005.

"In human men, the lower limit looks to be about . . . " and subsequent discussion of essential fat stores in human men: Keys et al. 1950; Friedl et al. 1994; Norgan 1997; Nindl et al. 2007; Wells 2010.

"In women, a similar amount of fat . . ." and subsequent discussion of essential fat stores in human women: Katch et al. 1980; Norgan 1997; Wells 2010.

"Because reproduction is such a metabolically taxing enterprise . . ."
and subsequent discussion of relationship between adiposity and
fertility/reproduction: Frisch et al. 1974; Warren 1983; Loucks et al. 1985;
Norgan 1997; Loucks et al. 1998.

**"While rodents are by far the most common animal model of obesity . .
."** and subsequent discussion of animal models of obesity: Speakman et al.
2008; Lutz et al. 2012.

". . . 'have clear potential as a study model' . . .": Speakman et al. 2008.

". . . 'potential for the use of dogs to inform us' . . .": ibid.

". . . 'much that is written about "obesity" may have only' . . .": Wells
2010.

"The seminal study on the impact of obesity on dogs . . .": Kealy et al.
2002; Lawler et al. 2008.

**"According to a study recently published in the *British Journal of
Nutrition* . . ."**: Deurenberg et al. 1991.

"A recent study of species typically consumed by feral cats . . .":
Kremen et al. 2013.

"Similarly, in a paper presented at the 1967 research symposium . . .":
Pitts et al. 1968.

**". . . the difference in life expectancy between lifelong smokers and . .
."**: Taylor et al. 2002.

". . . between citizens of the United States and . . ." and other data on
life expectancy by nationality: www.cia.gov/library/publications/the-world-
factbook/ (last visited May 2, 2016).

"This conclusion has been confirmed time and again . . ." and
subsequent discussion of disease prevalence among fat dogs and relatively
lean dogs: Glickman et al. 1989; Sonnenschein et al. 1991; Chikamune et al.
1995; Perez Alenza et al. 1998; Hess et al. 1999; Henegar et al. 2001; Smith et
al. 2001; Bach et al. 2007; Marshall et al. 2010.

"The primary mechanism by which fat makes dogs sick . . ." and subsequent discussion of the pathophysiology of canine obesity: Jeusette et al. 2005; Ishioka et al. 2007; Eirmann et al. 2009; German et al. 2010; Wakshlag et al. 2011; Sanderson 2012.

". . . 'Advances in obesity research suggest that' . . .": Wakshlag et al. 2011.

". . . some 30% to 50% of dogs today . . ." and subsequent discussion of prevalence of canine obesity and overweight: McGreevy et al. 2005; German 2006; Lund et al. 2006; Weeth et al. 2007; Wakshlag et al. 2011.

". . . 'the leading cause of preventable disease and death' . . .": Jamal et al. 2015.

"It is considered such a serious and pervasive public health problem . . ." and subsequent discussion of smoking in the United States: Dennis 2013; Jamal et al. 2015.

". . . a dog counts as overweight if he has a BCS of 6/9 or above . . .": In many cases, researchers use a simpler five-category BCS framework, whereby any score above a 3/5 is considered "overweight." Because there are no published studies validating any five-category BCS protocol, it's not covered in depth in this book. But it's the same idea as all the others. A 3/5 on the five-category scale is more-or-less equivalent to a 5/9 on the nine-category scale.

"One such study was published in 2007 . . .": Weeth et al. 2007.
Surprisingly, the "overweight" and "obese" dogs in this study were found to
be slightly *less* likely to be diagnosed with cancer than the "ideal" dogs. The
researchers could only speculate as to why they didn't observe a positive
correlation between cancer and obesity, as so many others had in the past.
But they seemed to gravitate towards one explanation in particular: being
relatively lean wasn't causing the dogs to develop cancer, *having cancer was
causing them to become lean*, and that was skewing the numbers. Cancer-caused
cachexia is a well-documented medical phenomenon, both in humans and in
dogs (Michel et al. 2004 suggests that nearly a quarter of dogs lose 10% or
more of their total body weight between preliminary cancer diagnosis and the
next follow-up visit). The study's authors reasoned that dogs who were so
sick that a trip to the vet for a cancer screening was deemed necessary would
have already experienced significant weight-loss by the time their body
conditions were evaluated. Of course, this explanation makes their data
about the relative infrequency of cancer among the very leanest dogs even
more persuasive.

"Similar findings were documented in another recent study . . .":
Sonnenschein et al. 1991.

". . . 'a thin body conformation at' . . .": ibid.

"According to Dr. Alexander German's seven-category . . ." and
subsequent discussion of Dr. German's BCS protocol: German et al. 2006.

"The same idea can be seen in Dr. Dottie Laflamme's . . ." and
subsequent discussion of Dr. Laflamme's BCS protocol: Laflamme 1997.

"Surgical removal of fat tissue from mice . . .": Gabriely et al. 2002.

". . . 'the most robust and reproducible means' . . .": B.J. Willcox et al.
2007.

"Dr. Laflamme continued to defend the U-shaped model . . .": personal
e-mails, Sep. 2014.

"The handful of studies she cited . . .": Tsugane et al. 2002; Flegal et al.
2005; Prospective Studies Collaboration 2009.

". . . 'Much of the association' . . .": personal e-mail, Sep. 2014.

". . . some interesting studies involving elderly cats . . .": Perez-Camargo 2004; Cupp et al. 2008; Cupp et al. 2010. In a set of related studies (Dr. Laflamme didn't cite these ones as influencing her thinking, I just dug them up myself), a similar phenomenon has also been documented: small animals with relatively high BCS scores tend to live longer after being diagnosed with life-threatening diseases than do lower-BCS animals. See Baez et al. 2007 (cancer); Slupe et al. 2008 (congestive heart failure); Parker et al. 2011 (chronic kidney disease). But in all these cases the culprit seems to be scrawniness, not leanness. Just like humans with high BMI scores, animals with high BCS scores tend to have both more adipose tissue *and more lean tissue* (notably, more skeletal musculature) in their bodies. And most experts seem to believe that it's the extra lean tissue that's helping them battle deadly diseases, not the extra adipose tissue. They know this because they understand, to at least some degree, how these deadly chronic diseases work. And they know that one of the things that happens to small animals when they fall victim to cancer, congestive heart failure, or kidney disease, is their bodies begin to rapidly catabolize their protein-rich lean body tissues (the process known as cachexia). Here's how Dr. Lisa Freeman, one of the world's leading experts on cachexia in small animals and a researcher involved with more than one of the aforementioned studies recently put it: "The weight loss that occurs in cachexia is unlike that seen in a healthy animal that loses weight. In a healthy animal that is receiving insufficient calories to meet requirements, metabolic adaptations allow fat to be used as the primary fuel source, thus preserving lean body mass. In animals with chronic disease, the primary energy source continues to be amino acids from muscle so that these animals quickly catabolize muscle and lean body mass, causing cachexia." Freeman 2011. Thus, as Dr. Freeman and colleagues have also explained, when it comes to chronic diseases, the benefit of a high BCS score "is likely due more to a *lack* of cachexia, rather than to the obesity per se, given the adverse effects associated with cachexia." Finn et al. 2010.

". . . 'likely reflects the onset of chronic disease and more rapid' . . .": Cupp et al. 2010.

". . . an article that she had written herself . . .": Laflamme 2006.

Chapter Eight: The Optimal Dog

". . . 'I've always thought' . . .": Locke 1996.

". . . 'Kibble Crack' . . .": Ward 2010.

"Dogs have been shown to prefer foods spiked with . . .": Torres et al. 2003.

". . . plenty of other mammalian species have been shown to prefer . . .": for discussions of the evidence supporting this assertion see Ward 2010 and Kessler 2009.

"Take Snausages Snaw Somes! . . .": all nutritional information from the website for Big Heart Pet Brands (http://snausages.com/products/beef-and-cheese-snawsomes/) (last visited May 10, 2016).

"Or consider Pedigree's large Jumbone . . .": all nutritional information from the website for Mars, Inc. (http://www.pedigree.com/really-good-food/jumbone-treats-large.aspx) (last visited May 10, 2016).

"Under AAFCO rules, commercially prepared pet foods must fulfill *all* of a dog's . . ." and subsequent discussion of AAFCO regulations: Association of American Feed Control Officials Incorporated 2016.

" . . . 'one of the foremost experts in pet healthcare' . . .": from the blog of Dr. Jean Dodd (http://drjeandoddspethealthresource.tumblr.com/post/34362052572/raw-dog-food-versus-cooked#.VHSyvYdOxbs) (last visited May 10, 2016).

"The AVMA, the ACVN, and the American Animal Hospital Association . . .": policy statements for the AVMA (https://www.avma.org/KB/Policies/Pages/Raw-or-Undercooked-Animal-Source-Protein-in-Cat-and-Dog-Diets.aspx), the ACVN (http://www.acvn.org/frequently-asked-questions/), and the AAHA (https://www.aaha.org/professional/resources/raw_protein_diet.aspx#gsc.tab=0) (all visited May 10, 2016) can all be found online.

" . . . 'There are many anecdotal reports' . . .": from the website for the AVMA (https://www.avma.org/KB/Resources/FAQs/Pages/Raw-Pet-Foods-and-the-AVMA-Policy-FAQ.aspx) (last visited May 10, 2016).

" . . . 'Advocates of raw diets claim' . . .": from the website for the ACVN (http://www.acvn.org/frequently-asked-questions/) (last visited May 10, 2016).

". . .raw animal meat is prone to contamination . . ." and subsequent discussion of raw meat contamination issues: Hamilton et al. 2002 (much of the information from the PBS *Frontline* production "Modern Meat" is also available online at http://www.pbs.org/wgbh/pages/frontline/shows/meat/ (last visited May 10, 2016)); Zhao et al. 2002.

". . . approximately one million cases of *Salmonella* . . .": from the publicly-available website for the CDC (http://www.cdc.gov/foodborneburden/PDFs/pathogens-complete-list-01-12.pdf) (last visited May 10, 2016).

"While dogs are susceptible to infection by common food-borne pathogens . . ." and subsequent discussion of safety/contamination issues associated with raw dog food products: Stiver et al. 2003 (including documentation of clinical symptoms associated with *Salmonella* infection in cats); Lenz et al. 2009; Leonard et al. 2011; Schlesinger et al. 2011; Selmi et al. 2011; Freeman et al. 2013.

". . . 'there have been no studies conclusively documenting' . . .": Schlesinger et al. 2011.

"According to both AAFCO and the National Research Council's . . ." and subsequent discussion of canine micronutrient requirements: National Research Council 2007; Association of American Feed Control Officials Incorporated 2016.

". . . according to a study published in the *British Journal of Nutrition* in 2011 . . .": Dillitzer et al. 2011.

". . . a critical review of the evidence both in favor of and against raw diets . . .": Schlesinger et al. 2011.

"This is the process used to create almost all of the 'light,' 'lite,' 'weight-loss,' and 'low calorie' . . ." and subsequent discussion of low-calorie dog foods: National Research Council 2007; Nestle 2008; Fox et al. 2009; Ward 2010; Association of American Feed Control Officials Incorporated 2016.

". . . its Orijen product was named the Glycemic Research Institute's . . .": from the publicly-available website for Champion Petfoods (http://www.championpetfoods.com/home-usa/) (last visited May 11, 2016).

"... 'Carbohydrates are an empty calorie' ...": from a publicly-available website for Champion Petfoods (http://www.orijen.ca/faq/) (last visited May 11, 2016).

"... only about 30% of the calories in Orijen's ..." and subsequent discussion of nutritional and ingredient content of Orijen dry dog foods: all information from Champion's website (last visited May 11, 2016).

"Legumes register far lower ..." and subsequent discussion of Glycemic Index scores: Atkinson et al. 2008.

"... of all the manufacturers I contacted ...": personal e-mails, 2014-2015.

"... the veterinary community has yet to come up with a formula that definitively ..." and subsequent discussion of formulas linking nutritional requirements and other measurable variables (including specific equations): Bayliss et al. 1933; Hand et al. 2000; Hill 2006; National Research Council 2007 (featuring a helpful index of other relevant studies).

"... 'are only an educated guess' ...": Hill 2006.

"... 'At present, the energy requirements of an individual dog' ...": National Research Council 2007.

"It has been 200 years since French physiologist Francois Magendie ...": ibid.

"This myth has been roundly debunked ..." and subsequent discussion of effects of protein consumption on renal function: Robertson et al. 1986; Bovée 1991; Finco et al. 1994; Bovée 1999.

"Of particular interest, a 1986 study published in the journal *Kidney International* ...": Robertson et al. 1986.

"In a 1991 review paper published in the *Journal of Nutrition* ...": Bovée 1991.

"... delivered a paper at the Purina Nutrition Forum ...": Bovée 1999.

"... 'may be more optimal' ...": Freeman 2011.

"In a 2005 paper, Dr. Dottie Laflamme and a colleague reported . . .": Laflamme et al. 2005.

"Dr. Laflamme has also used the same rate . . .": as described in Hannah 1999.

"In his book *Chow Hounds*, Dr. Ernie Ward . . .": Ward 2010.

"A rate of 1% to 2% of total body weight per week . . . in 2002 . . .": Diez et al. 2002.

"A rate of 1% to 2% of total body weight per week . . . in 2004 . . .": Bierer et al. 2004.

"In a 2004 study entitled 'Rapid Weight Loss with . . .'": Blanchard et al. 2004.

Epilogue

"'Philosophers have always tried to' . . .": Gray 2007.

". . . 'controversies exist about the pathophysiology of the problem' . . .": Gandini et al. 2003.

"The first thing I looked into was . . ." and subsequent discussion of FCE recovery rates: ibid; de Risio et al. 2010.

"But another study offered some . . .": Gandini et al. 2003.

". . . 'Active nursing and intensive and early physiotherapy should be' . . .": ibid.

ILLUSTRATION CREDITS AND SOURCES

--

Figure 1(a). Source: www.caloriecount.com.

Figure 1(b). Image © 2016 Online Labels, Inc. Source: www.caloriecount.com

Figure 2(a). Image courtesy of the Nestle-Purina PetCare Co.

Figure 2(b). Image courtesy of Mars Petcare.

Figure 3(a). Source: Laflamme 1997.

Figure 3(b). Source: German et al. 2006.

Figures 4(a) & 4(b). Sources: Keys et al. 1972; Pai et al. 2000; Eknoyan 2006; Barrett 2007; Eknoyan 2008.

Figure 5. Source: www.who.int/topics/obesity/en/

Figure 6. Source: Laflamme 2006.

Figures 7(a) & 7(b). Sources: Hand et al. 2000; Hill 2006; National Research Council 2007.

Figure 8. Source: National Research Council 2007.

Made in the USA
Middletown, DE
15 November 2016